A FIELD G

BIRDS

OF SOUTHERN AFRICA

HarperCollins Publishers Ltd.
77–85 Fulham Palace Road
Hammersmith
London W6 8JB

The Collins website address is:
www.collins.co.uk

Collins is a registered trademark of
HarperCollins Publishers Ltd.

To my brave daughter Susan Wambui

First published 1999
This edition published in 2009

Text © Ber van Perlo, 1999, 2009
Illustrations © Ber van Perlo, 1999, 2009

11 10 09 08 07
10 9 8 7 6 5 4 3 2 1

A catalogue record for this book is available from the British Library.

ISBN 978 0 00 728514 3

Collins uses papers that are natural, renewable and recyclable products made from wood
grown in sustainable forests. The manufacturing processes conform to the environmental
regulations of the country of origin.

Printed and bound in Hong Kong by Printing Express Ltd.

A FIELD GUIDE TO THE
BIRDS
OF SOUTHERN AFRICA

Ber van Perlo

Collins

ACKNOWLEDGEMENTS

Writing and illustrating a book is a lonely business and I would not have succeeded without the encouragement and support of my friends and family.

My special thanks go to my brother, Cees van Perlo in Mozambique, for the marvellous job he did again with the distribution maps and for other important contributions to the book, to my old friend, Bori Goldschmidt, for all her generous help, and to Andre van Loon who checked and commented upon the text and plates.

I express my gratitude also to Mrs Elna Kotze from South Africa, and to Sr Gonçales Elias from Portugal who supplied, respectively, the Afrikaans and the Portuguese names in the appendix of this book. Finally, I am very grateful to Myles Archibald for his encouragement and understanding and to Claire Daniel for her editing work and kind cooperation.

Ber van Perlo
Wijchen
The Netherlands

CONTENTS

INTRODUCTION

AREA AND SPECIES COVERED

This book lists all the bird species in Angola (including Cabinda), Botswana, Lesotho, Malawi, Mozambique, Namibia, South Africa, Swaziland, Zambia and Zimbabwe. It gives illustrations, key notes for identification, basic information about habitat and a distribution map for all species and vocalisations for most. Only a few birds, such as a recently discovered lark and a pipit species, could not be depicted but are described in the text. This list is based on *A Contribution to the Distribution and Taxonomy of Afrotropical and Malagasy Birds* (1993) edited by R.J. Dowsett & F. Dowsett-Lemaire, supplemented by data from the published volumes of the handbook series *Birds of Africa* and other sources (see Bibliography).

NOMENCLATURE

Birding has become something with an international allure which makes it desirable that birds have the same names wherever you go. There is an established international system for scientific names, although names change constantly – for instance, when scientists lump species together or split one. There is not, however, such a generally accepted system for English names, so that names in South Africa in many cases differ from those used in other parts of Africa. To avoid this problem this book normally uses the English and scientific names as in the first five published volumes of *Birds of Africa* and those in the work of R.J. Dowsett & F. Dowsett-Lemaire (see under 'Area and species covered') for the birds in the last two (out of seven) unpublished volumes. Even then it seemed impossible to compose a consistent list of names for all birds so that in a few cases I had to use my own judgment. The English names are written for each species in bold capitals. So as not to disappoint readers who are used to the traditional South African names, and to avoid confusion, you will find these traditional names as alternatives written in lower case type in brackets.

The scientific name of a species is composed of two parts; the first part refers to the genus in which similar species are placed together, and the second part defines the specific species.

For example, there are similar looking sparrows which belong to the genus *Passer*. By adding *domesticus* we know that we are talking about the House Sparrow. This species has different subspecies (or 'races', the term used in this book for its shortness). After Linnaeus described the House Sparrow, and gave it its scientific name, *Passer domesticus*, other races of this sparrow were discovered outside Europe, which differed, for example, in size or colouring. The first race, as described by Linnaeus, was then given a name composed of three parts, *Passer domesticus domesticus*, shortened to nominate, which term is also used in this book. Another race is the Asian *Passer domesticus indicus*, which was introduced in South Africa (see caption, Plate 77).

IDENTIFICATION

Identification of a bird is based upon how it looks (jizz, appearance) together with what it does (habits), where we see it (habitat), the chance or probability that we see it there (occurrence) and the sounds it makes (voice).

What birders call jizz is a difficult to define combination of size, relative proportions and body carriage of a bird. Part of a bird's jizz can be its stance, or the angle of its body to the flat earth or a horizontal perch.

Appearance

Each species is illustrated as an adult male in breeding plumage. Other plumages are added when different, in which case the female is normally shown behind the male in a more horizontal position. The symbols and abbreviations used in the text and on the plates are as follows:

SYMBOL	EXPLANATION
♂	male
♀	female
imm	immature
br	breeding plumage
n-br	non-breeding (or winter) plumage

Many species have a breeding and a non-breeding plumage. Most of these are shown but in a few cases (some sunbirds, weavers, indigobirds) they are omitted because the non-breeding plumage of the male closely resembles the normal femal plumage.

Every bird that has not attained full adult plumage is called an immature in this book. In a few cases, however, it was necessary to differentiate further as follows:

ABBREVIATION	EXPLANATION
juv	an immature in its first plumage following the natal down
1stW or (1stS)	an immature in its plumage in the first winter or summer after hatching
2ndW or (2ndS)	an immature in its plumage in the second winter or summer after hatching
sub-adult	an immature in its last plumage before moulting to full adult plumage

Different RACES are illustrated in many cases when they are recognisable as such. Some species have similar looking races, as well as one or more that is more distinct. Only the distinct races are marked (as a, b, c etc) on the plates, mentioned in the text and indicated on the maps.

A COLOUR FORM is a variation of the normal plumage. These forms are represented on the plates where there is a chance of seeing them, for instance where at least 5–15% of the total population of a species is coloured differently in some way.

The text opposite the plates gives information about size, main characteristics and differences between similar species.

The SIZE is given in centimetres.

● For most species, size is the total length between the tip of the bill and end of tail (L); the extra length for tail streamers is given in brackets e.g. L 12 (+5) cm.
● For seabirds the size is given as wingspan (W).
● For a few tall birds the size is height (H).

Because measuring birds is difficult, size data in literature are not uniform. For this reason sizes above 25 cm are given in multiples of 5 cm. This enables the user to compare the size of a bird he/she wants to identify with the size of other birds.

Full descriptions of feathering and bare parts are not given because the plates contain sufficient information on these features. Only when these are the most essential features or when they are not visible on the plate are they mentioned.

Habits

Information about habits – though an important identification tool – has been given sparingly in order to keep the book to an optimal size.

Habitat

CLIMATE

The fact that the Tropic of Capricorn runs right across Southern Africa, from Walvis Bay in Namibia to Inhambane in Mozambique, has far-reaching consequences for the local climate and thus dominates the migration movements of the birds. It is doubtful whether people from Europe, North-America and Asia realize fully how cold it can be in Johannesburg when it is summer in the northern hemisphere. South of the Tropic the weather is governed by a summer-winter rhythm, which merges into a seasonal rain system north of it. In the southern summer half year (October–March) Southern Africa hosts two types of migrants, namely palaearctic visitors (mainly from Europe) in winter plumage, and intra-African migrants, many of which come to breed and thus are seen in breeding plumage.

The following maps give some information about the differences in rainfall in the area and the temperatures in the main cities in the summer and winter periods.

Note the arid and dry areas in the south-western parts where several endemic species, adapted to this type of climate, occur.

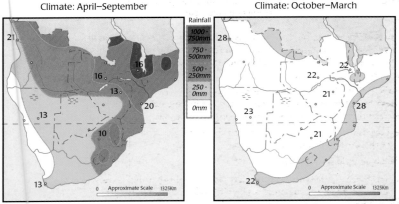

Climate: April–September

Climate: October–March

Rainfall
1000 - 750mm
750 - 500mm
500 - 250mm
250 - 0mm
0mm

Numbers on the map indicate June temperatures

Numbers on the map indicate December temperatures

ALTITUDE AND EARTH SURFACE FORM

The main characteristic of the altitudinal structure of Southern Africa seems to be its saucer form (see map below). In the middle there is an extensive, almost drainless depression with the famous Okavanga Swamp and, further westwards, the Etosha Pan; at the edges this depression rises on all sides to form rather high mountain ranges, which, on the outside, descend via steep escarpments to the hot, coastal lowlands, particularly wide in Mozambique.

The pattern of long narrow lakes and mountain ridges in the north-east is the fading end of the East African Rift Valley system.

Escarpments are the tall, steep faces of a plateau and are very interesting for birders because they guide migration streams and, within a short range, offer a large diversity of habitats, each with its own bird species. In addition, they are favourite places for large raptors which benefit from the strong, uprising winds.

Highveld and lowveld, terms often used in South African literature, are the areas above 1500 metres west of the eastern mountain ranges, and below the 650 metre contour on their

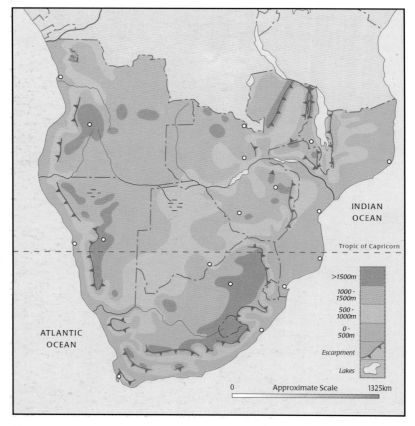

INDIAN OCEAN

Tropic of Capricorn

>1500m

1000 - 1500m

500 - 1000m

0 - 500m

Escarpment

Lakes

ATLANTIC OCEAN

0   Approximate Scale   1325km

eastern flanks. The South African highveld consists mainly of grassland, a unique African habitat with several endemics.

VEGETATION

The map with natural habitats (below) shows the landscape as it would be without human intervention. Depending on the fertility of the soil, the availability of water and other factors, much of the vegetation, locally more than 95%, is transformed into farmland, exotic plantations and urban settlement.

Further details about the different types of habitats shown on the map below, are given on pp.12–13.

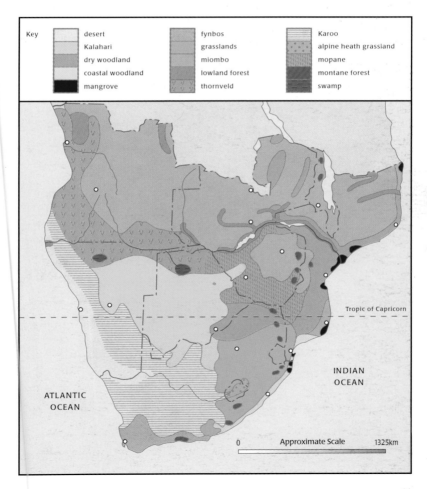

Key

- desert
- Kalahari
- dry woodland
- coastal woodland
- mangrove
- fynbos
- grasslands
- miombo
- lowland forest
- thornveld
- Karoo
- alpine heath grassland
- mopane
- montane forest
- swamp

Tropic of Capricorn

INDIAN OCEAN

ATLANTIC OCEAN

0   Approximate Scale   1325km

DRY HABITATS

desert

Karoo: semi-desert or stony plains with some grass, shrub and low-growing succulents

Kalahari: bushveld, more or less wooded with thorny acacias (Fig. 3) and/or tufty grasses

dry woodland: habitat with low rainfall where mid-high trees dominate without forming a continuous, completely closed canopy

thornveld, where acacia (Fig. 3) species dominate

mopane, where the tree species *Colophospernum mopane* (Fig. 1) dominates

COASTAL HABITATS

coastal woodland, bush and scrub

mangrove

fynbos (or macchia): small-leafed, evergreen scrub with protea (Fig. 2), erica (heath) and other scrub species

MONTANE HABITATS

grasslands of the highveld

heath grassland with alpine character

montane forest

WETLANDS

Okivanga swamp and Etosha pan. (Other wetlands are too small for mapping on this scale)

FORESTS

miombo: a type of woodland in areas with higher rainfall where trees of the genus *Brachystegia* (Fig. 4) dominate

lowland forest: habitat in which the canopy of tall trees is continuous and completely closed. Only in NW Angola is there an area with lowland forest resembling true rainforest. Elsewhere forest is found in narrow 'galleries' along rivers.

OTHER HABITATS MENTIONED IN THIS BOOK

Vlei: a small, drainless depression where a marshy habitat is formed in the rainy season.
Riverine belt: any area alongside a river or stream that is richer in trees, bush or other vegetation than its surroundings. The most luxurious form is tropical, gallery forest which resembles rainforest.
Wooded area: a place with some trees, but where bush, scrub or grass tend to be more dominant.
Cultivation: in this book, an area of small-holder plots.
Baobab: a woodland tree of hotter areas with a typically swollen stem (Fig. 5).

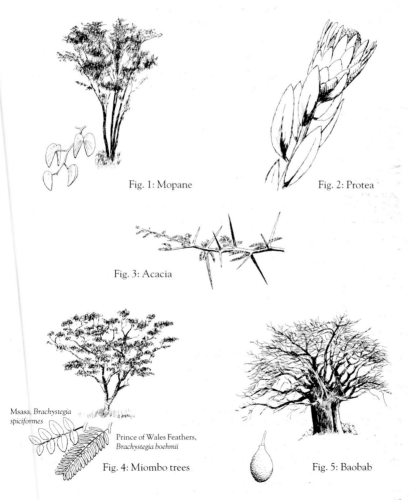

Fig. 1: Mopane

Fig. 2: Protea

Fig. 3: Acacia

Msasa, *Brachystegia spiciformes*

Prince of Wales Feathers, *Brachystegia boehmii*

Fig. 4: Miombo trees

Fig. 5: Baobab

Occurrence

Range, season and status determine the possibility of seeing a species in a certain area. This information can be found on the DISTRIBUTION maps (after the plates).

The shaded areas are an indication of the RANGE of a species.

The presence of most MIGRANTS depends on the northern or tropical seasons, but be aware that individual birds may stay behind when all other members of that species return for instance to their breeding grounds in Europe or Asia.

STATUS	CHANCE OF SEEING SPECIES	MAPS	INDICATION IN THE TEXT
Common	60–100%	Dark shading	
Frequent	10–60%	Mid-grey shading	
Uncommon	Very small	Pale grey shading	U
Rare or vagrant	Negligible	Small cross	R
Uncertain	?	?	(?)

See also the introduction to the maps directly following Plate 84.

The status of a species can be described as in the key above. The chance of seeing a particular bird refers to the likelihood of its being seen in its habitat and range. A species is rare when its range is very restricted or its total population very small. A vagrant lives in other parts of the world, reaches the region only by accident and hence has been seen less than approximately five times. The south-west coast of South Africa and Namibia is an area to look out for vagrants, mainly from America.

Always look at the map to see if your identification of an unknown bird is supported by the given range. In the text only uncommon and rare (or vagrant) species are indicated by, respectively, U and R.

(?) in the text means that occurrence of the species in Southern Africa is insufficiently substantiated.

MIGRATION KEY					
S	Summer visitor only	W	Winter visitor only	SW	All-year visitor*
S(W)	Summer visitor mainly, some stay in winter	W(S)	Winter visitor mainly, some stay in summer		
(S)	Breeding resident mainly with some n-br visitors	(W)	Resident mainly with some winter visitors	(SW)	Mainly resident, partly all-year visitor
brS	Breeding summer visitor				

brS(W)	Breeding summer visitor, some stay winter	brW(S)	Breeding winter visitor, some stay in summer
(br)S	Partly breeding, partly non-breeding summer-visitor		
(brS)	Breeding resident mainly with some breeding visitors		

* (All-year visitor means that there are records of the visitor from different times of the year, independent of season).

A question mark, as in S?W, SW? or br?S, reflects on the symbol directly preceding it and means that there are doubtful records in summer (S?W), winter (SW?) or about breeding (br?S).

In the text the symbols U and R and those for migrants are combined. US(W) for instance means that the species is an uncommon, non-breeding, summer visitor with rare records also in winter.

Voice

Information about song and call is given for many birds, especially for those with a hidden way of living (those that live in forests and swamps and those that are active at night), those that are difficult to identify from appearance only (nightjars, swifts, larks, pipits and cisticolas) and those that are well known for their vocal abilities (thrushes and warblers). Note, however, that it has not been possible to give the whole vocabulary, or to give voice examples for every species. In the vocalisations, distinction between calls and song is only made in a few cases. The most striking sound has been given as a transcription in italics between quotation marks. This is a hazardous endeavour because these transcriptions may well look confusing and even funny. However, if the reader is able to overcome his embarrassment and tries to pronounce the transcriptions in the given speed and pitch, he may have found another tool to confirm an identification, which is the main reason for their inclusion.

Attention has been paid to pitch, loudness, sound quality, length and structure. General pitch has been given on a rough, subjective scale:

DESCRIPTION	EXPLANATION
Extreme low	As low as you can imagine (e.g. Eurasian Bittern)
Very low	(e.g. Feral Dove)
Low	Pitch of an average man's voice (e.g. Corncrake)
Mid-high	Pitch of an average woman's voice (e.g. Blue-eared Starling)
High	(e.g. Common Bulbul)
Very high	(e.g. Mousebird)
Extreme high	So high that the sound is just within human hearing range (ear-reach) (e.g. Yellow-bellied Sunbird)

LOUDNESS is generally indicated by general terms such as soft, loud and crescendo. Louder parts of the calls are put in capitals.

SOUND QUALITY has been described in terms such as shrieking, magpie-like, liquid etc. Often songs and calls are compared to those of other birds like reed warblers (for example the well-known Eurasian Reed Warbler, *Acrocephalus scirpaceus*, 68.7) or to the miauling of a domestic cat.

LENGTH: if a transcription ends on '-' the call or song continues with at least three similar notes, syllables or phrases.

STRUCTURE: changes in pitch are often indicated by á, é, í, ó or ú for parts of the song that are higher and *a̱, e̱, i̱, o̱* or *u̱* for parts that are lower. The way in which notes follow each other is described in terms such as accelerated, staccato and unstructured, and indicated by the way the parts of a transcription are connected. For instance, in '*treet treet treet*' each syllable is well separated, '*treet-treet-treet*' sounds as one 'word' and '*treettreettreet*' as almost a trill.

A strophe is a recognisable, complete part of a bird's repertoire that can be dissected successively into phrases, syllables and notes. Strophes can, however, be as short as one note.

A special feature of the song and/or call of many bird species is that it is given in duet. This means that two birds (normally a female and a male) produce sounds that might follow each other so closely or are interwoven so harmoniously that the resulting song or call sounds as if it is from a single bird.

Endemism

This is a fascinating phenomenon. An endemic is a species that occurs only in an area with well-defined boundaries like a continent, a country, an island or a habitat.

There are several habitats in Southern Africa which have their own endemics (e.g. fynbos, Karoo semi-desert, Kalahari bushveld, montane grasslands) but in this book only the endemic birds of the countries are marked E at the end of the relevant text entry, followed by the name of the country to which they belong (in brackets). This inventory is as accurate as possible so that birds that occur both in South Africa and in Lesotho have not been given the E-status.

In this way there are 10 endemic bird species in Angola, 2 in Namibia, 14 in South Africa and 1 in Zambia.

PARTS OF A BIRD

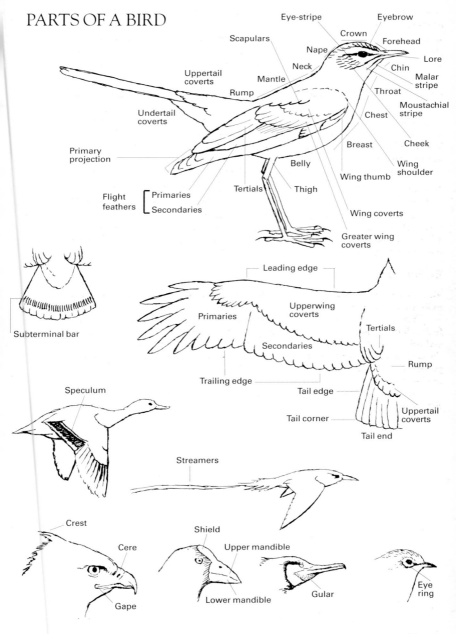

Eye-stripe
Eyebrow
Crown
Forehead
Scapulars
Nape
Lore
Neck
Chin
Uppertail coverts
Mantle
Malar stripe
Rump
Throat
Moustachial stripe
Undertail coverts
Chest
Breast
Cheek
Primary projection
Wing shoulder
Wing thumb
Belly
Flight feathers [Primaries / Secondaries]
Tertials
Thigh
Wing coverts
Greater wing coverts

Subterminal bar

Leading edge
Upperwing coverts
Primaries
Tertials
Secondaries
Rump
Trailing edge
Tail edge
Uppertail coverts
Speculum
Tail corner
Tail end

Streamers

Crest
Shield
Cere
Upper mandible
Eye ring
Gape
Lower mandible
Gular

The Plates

Rheidae Casuariidae Dromaiidae Apterygidae Tinamidae b

♂

♀

ostrich
struthio camelus

OSTRICH *Struthio camelus* (previous page)   H 210 cm. Most ostriches in the region are from feral stock, a mixture of different African races. Genuine wild ostriches occur only in North Namibia, the Kalahari and (maybe) in South-west Angola. Note blue sheen and buff-orange tail. Habitat: dry, open plains and semi-desert. Voice: very low, lion-like, well separated '*who who whooooi*' gliding down at the end (heard in early morning and in the evening). (No map.)

Plate 1

1   **WANDERING ALBATROSS** *Diomedea exulans*   W 330 cm. Note all-white back of adult. Goes through 7 stages from juv to adult plumage, each time with more white on body and wings. Note black tips to tail feathers of all imm stages (5th stage **(a)** shown). Habitat: open sea. W

2   **ROYAL ALBATROSS** *Diomedea epomophora*   W 330 cm. All races and stages with diagnostic, black cutting edge to bill and with black eyelids (only visible at close range). Goes through less imm stages than 1, but most of these do not have any black in tail. Nominate **(a**, not yet seen near southern Africa) and race *sanfordi* **(b)** shown, latter with diagnostic, unconnected black on upperwings of adult (unlike any other albatross in the area) and some dark mottling on crown of juv. Habitat: open sea. W

3   **SHY ALBATROSS** *Diomedea cauta*   W 250 cm. Underwing with narrow, black leading edge culminating in diagnostic, black spot near body. Imm has black-tipped bill. Habitat: open sea. W(S)

4   **YELLOW-NOSED ALBATROSS** *Diomedea chlororhynchos*   W 205 cm. Nominate **(a)** with greyer head than race *bassi* **(b)**. Both races with yellow restricted to upper mandible. Black leading edge on underwing wider than trailing edge. Imm has all-black bill. Habitat: open sea. W

5   **BLACK-BROWED ALBATROSS** *Diomedea melanophrys*   W 225 cm. Note all-yellow, dark-tipped bill and wide, black leading edge to underwing. Imm as imm 8 but head less grey and bill with paler central area. Habitat: open sea. SW

6   **SOOTY ALBATROSS** *Phoebetria fusca*   W 205 cm. Imm from adult 7 by less extensive pale upperparts and without white primary shafts or stripe on lower mandible. Habitat: open sea. UW

7   **LIGHT-MANTLED SOOTY ALBATROSS** *Phoebetria palpebrata*   W 215 cm. Imm has rather scaly upperparts and lacks white on lower mandible and on primary shafts. Habitat: open sea. RW

8   **GREY-HEADED ALBATROSS** *Diomedea chrysostema*   W 220 cm. Adult from 4a by having yellow line also along underside of bill and more black on underwing, imm by all-black underwing. Habitat: open sea. RW

9   **LAYSAN ALBATROSS** *Diomedea immutabilis*   W 210 cm. Projecting yellow feet diagnostic. Note dark wedge from mantle pointing to tail. Imm (not shown) as adult but with darker bare parts. Habitat: open sea. R(W)

10   **SOUTHERN GIANT PETREL** *Macronectes giganteus*   W 195 cm. White **(a)** and dark **(b)** forms shown. From 11 by pale yellow bill with greenish tip. Imm not so dark as imm 11. Looks hump-backed in flight. Habitat: open sea, seashore, harbours. Often near seal colonies. SW

11   **NORTHERN GIANT PETREL** *Macronectes halli*   W 190 cm. No white form. Head hooded and less pale than 10. Bill pinkish with darker tip. Imm very dark, sooty black. Looks hump-backed in flight. Habitat: open sea, seashore, harbours. Often near seal colonies. SW

12   **BULLER'S ALBATROSS** *Diomedea bulleri*   W 210 cm. Head of adult very much like 8 but with whiter forehead and crown, strongly contrasting with rest of head, which is grey, and with more uniform yellow-orange rim around bill. Underwing of adult with parallel-running, black leading edge, wider than that of 4 but narrower and straighter than that of 8. Imm (photographed near Cape Town in 1995) as adult but with horn-coloured (not orange-yellow) bill rim, juv with all-black bill. (Not illustrated, no map). R

Plate 1

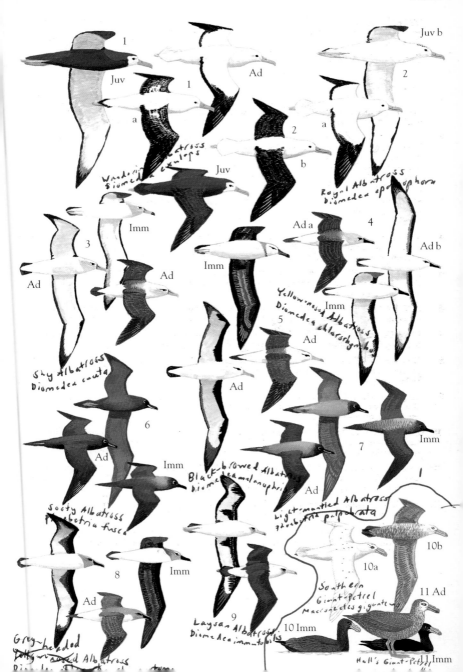

Wandering Albatross
Diomedea exulans 1

Royal Albatross
Diomedea epomophora 2

Shy Albatross
Diomedea cauta 3

Yellow-nosed Albatross
Diomedea chlororhynchos 4

Black-browed Albatross
Diomedea melanophris 5

Sooty Albatross
Phoebetria fusca 6

Light-mantled Albatross
Phoebetria palpebrata 7

Grey-headed Albatross
Yellow-nosed Albatross
Diomedea 8

Laysan Albatross
Diomedea immutabilis 9

Southern Giant-Petrel
Macronectes giganteus 10

Hall's Giant-Petrel 11

Plate 2

Note: genus *Procellaria* includes large seabirds with pale, strong bills and powerful, gliding flight with slow wing beats.

1   **WHITE-CHINNED PETREL** *Procellaria aequinoctialis*   W 140 cm. Nominate **(a)** with variable amount of white on chin, race *conspicillata* **(b)** with white extending to sides of face. Habitat: open sea. W(S)

2   **GREY PETREL** *Procellaria cinerea*   W 120 cm. Contrast between blackish underwings and pale belly diagnostic. Bill pale with dark spot near tip. Habitat: far out at open sea. US

Note: genus *Puffinus* includes seabirds of varying size, but generally with slender bills and rather straight wings. Often in flocks. In flight, alternates glides and series of rather flapping wing beats.

3   **FLESH-FOOTED SHEARWATER** *Puffinus carneipes*   W 105 cm. Uniform dark plumage with pink legs and flesh-coloured, dark-tipped bill. Tail is rounded, not pointed. Habitat: open sea. USW

4   **AUDUBON'S SHEARWATER** *Puffinus lherminieri*   W 70 cm. From 5 and 6 by more restricted white on underwing. Dark undertail coverts diagnostic. Brownish-black cap encloses eye. Habitat: open sea. R

5   **MANX SHEARWATER** *Puffinus puffinus*   W 80 cm. Combination of black cheeks and white undertail coverts diagnostic. Flight action (rapid flutters interspersed with short glides) as 4 and 6 but often with longer glides. Habitat: open sea, coastal areas. RS

6   **LITTLE SHEARWATER** *Puffinus assimilis*   W 60 cm. Underwing almost completely white. Rare nominate **(a)** with white cheeks, very rare race *elegans* **(b)** with dark cheeks. Habitat: open sea. US. Note: *Puffinus puffinus* (5), shown from above, should have the same white cheek as the bird shown from below, while *Puffinus assimilis* race *elegans*, shown from above (6b), should have a black (not white as shown) cheek.

7   **WEDGE-TAILED SHEARWATER** *Puffinus pacificus*   W 100 cm. Dark morph **(a)** and pale morph **(b**, which is not yet recorded from Southern Africa) shown. Note slender build, thin, grey-brown (not pink) bill and long, pointed tail. Habitat: open sea. R

8   **SOOTY SHEARWATER** *Puffinus griseus*   W 105 cm. Note complicated, black-and-white underwing pattern, which, from a distance, shows as a grey central area. Habitat: open sea. Also near coast. W(S)

9   **GREAT SHEARWATER** *Puffinus gravis*   W 110 cm. Note large body and small head with thin, black bill. From 10 and 11 by blacker cap, dark undertail coverts, dark smudge on belly, more striking, white collar and uppertail coverts. Habitat: open sea. S(W)

Note: genus *Calonectris* includes medium-sized seabirds with long bills and gliding flight.

10   **CORY'S SHEARWATER** *Calonectris diomedea*   W 115 cm. From 9 by clean white underwing, paler cap and lack of hind collar. Varying amount of white on lower rump. Yellowish, dark-ringed bill diagnostic. Habitat: open sea, often near coast. S

11   **WHITE-FACED SHEARWATER** *Calonectris leucomelas*   W 120 cm. Note long, slender bill, whitish face, blotched neck and wide, dark trailing edge to underwing. Habitat: open sea. R

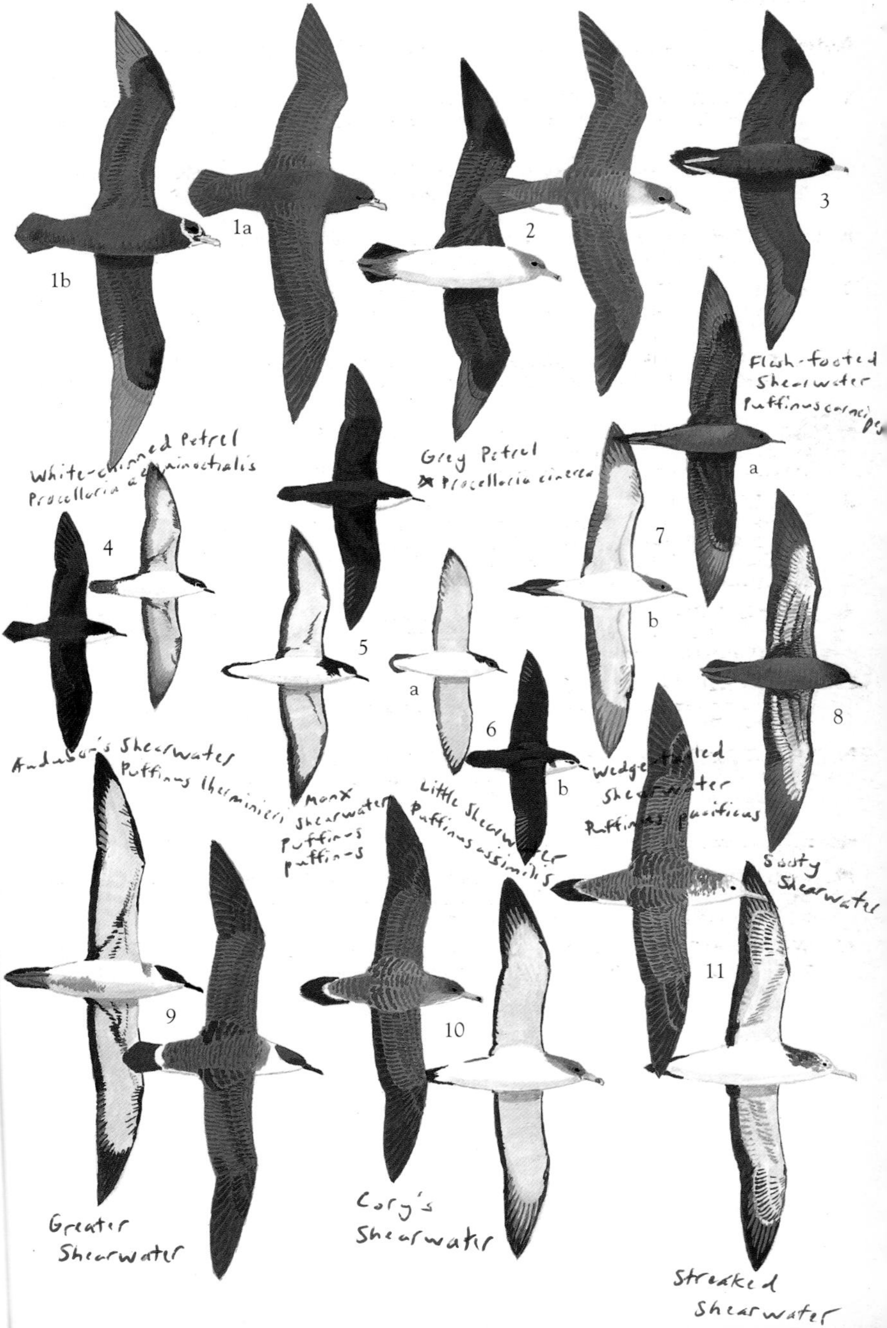

Plate 2

1a

1b

3

Flesh-footed
Shearwater
Puffinus carneipes

White-chinned Petrel
Procellaria aequinoctialis

Grey Petrel
Procellaria cinerea

a

4

7

b

5

a

8

6

b

Audubon's Shearwater
Puffinus lherminieri

Manx
Shearwater
*Puffinus
puffinus*

Little Shearwater
Puffinus assimilis

Wedge-tailed
Shearwater
Puffinus pacificus

Sooty
Shearwater

9

10

11

Greater
Shearwater

Cory's
Shearwater

Streaked
Shearwater

Plate 3

Note: genus *Pterodroma* includes mainly rare petrels. Strong but short, black bills are characteristic. Normally solitary. Wings often bowed and flexed at the wrist. Flight swift and powerful in wide arcs high above the sea.

1   **ATLANTIC PETREL** *Pterodroma incerta*   W 105 cm. Fresh plumage **(a)** is strongly and contrastingly patterned, in worn plumage **(b)** with much paler chin and throat. Habitat: open sea. RW

2   **GREAT-WINGED PETREL** *Pterodroma macroptera*   W 95 cm. From 2.1 by smaller size and different jizz (wings bent at wrists). Base of black (not pale) bill completely encircled with white. Habitat: open sea. SW

3   **KERGUELEN PETREL** *Pterodroma brevirostris*   W 80 cm. Strongly reflecting underwings. Overall dark, greyish-brown with black bill. Leading edge of wing whitish when seen head-on. Pale primary bases. Arches to great heights. Habitat: open sea. RW?

4   **WHITE-HEADED PETREL** *Pterodroma lessonii*   W 110 cm. Diagnostic contrast between mainly dark wings and rest of underbody, which is white. Note dark, M-shaped mark on back and wings. Larger-sized than 3.11 and 4.1–4. Habitat: open sea. RW

5   **SOFT-PLUMAGED PETREL** *Pterodroma mollis*   W 90 cm. Dark **(a)** and pale **(b)** forms shown. Intensity of upper- and underwing pattern depends on light conditions. Rare, dark form **(a)** from 3 by less pale primary bases. Habitat: open sea. W(S)

6   **PINTADO PETREL** (or Cape Pigeon) *Daption capense*   W 85 cm. Unmistakable. Singly-large flocks often near trawlers. Habitat: open sea but also near shore. S?W

7   **BULWER'S PETREL** *Bulweria bulwerii*   W 65 cm. Note long, pointed tail, small head, pale bar on upperwing. Erratic flight close to sea surface. Habitat: open sea. R

8   **JOUANIN'S PETREL** *Bulweria fallax*   W 80 cm. From 7 by proportionally larger head and short, less pointed tail. Wing bar absent or less conspicuous. Flight strong and sweeping. Habitat: open sea. (?)

9   **ANTARCTIC FULMAR** *Fulmarus glacialoides*   W 115 cm. White wing patches diagnostic. Solitary. Follows trawlers. Habitat: open sea. UW

10   **ANTARCTIC PETREL** *Thalassoica antarctica*   W 100 cm. From 6 by less complicated upperwing pattern. Habitat: open sea. R

11   **BLUE PETREL** *Halobaena caerulea*   W 60 cm. From 4.1–4 by white (not black) tail tip and darker cap and cheek. Habitat: open sea. RW

Plate 3

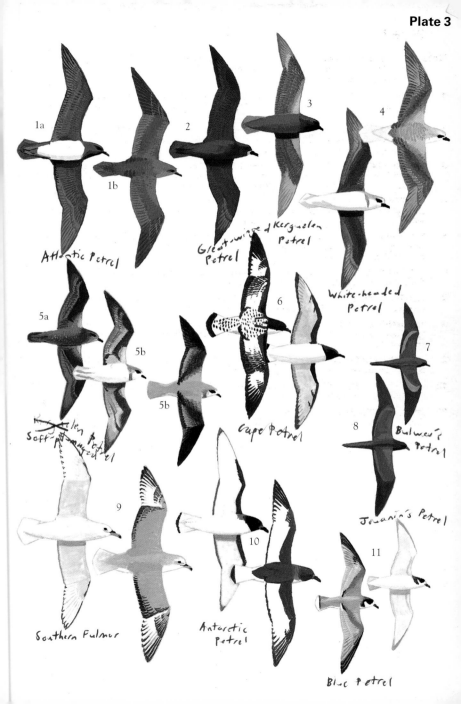

1a

1b

Atlantic Petrel

2

Great-winged & Kerguelen
Petrel

3

Kerguelen
Petrel

4

White-headed
Petrel

5a

5b

5b

Kerguelen Petrel
Soft-plumaged Petrel

6

Cape Petrel

7

8

Bulwer's
Petrel

Jouanin's Petrel

9

Southern Fulmar

10

Antarctic
Petrel

11

Blue Petrel

Plate 4

Note: genus *Pachyptila* includes small, blue-grey seabirds with characteristic 'M' mark on back and wings and with black tail tip. Often in flocks. Flight is fast and erratic with much twisting from side to side.

1   **BROAD-BILLED PRION** *Pachyptila vittata*   W 60 cm. Note prominent 'M' mark, large, dark head, large bill and restricted black tail bar. Habitat: open sea. W(S)

2   **SLENDER-BILLED PRION** *Pachyptila belcheri*   W 60 cm. Note rather pale 'M' mark, thin bill and grey collar, which is interrupted on throat. Habitat: open sea. RW

3   **ANTARCTIC** (or Dove) **PRION** *Pachyptila desolata*   W 60 cm. Note strong 'M' mark and rather extensive patches on sides of neck. Rather large bill appears bluish. Habitat: open sea. W

4   **FAIRY PRION** *Pachyptila turtur*   W 55 cm. Broad, black tail bar diagnostic. Generally rather pale including head, which has indistinct stripe through eye. Habitat: open sea. UW

Note: storm petrels are sparrow- to starling-sized seabirds, many with feet projecting in flight. Often paddle the water surface when feeding.

5   **BRITISH** (or European) **STORM PETREL** *Hydrobates pelagicus*   L 15 cm. White underwing stripe diagnostic. Feet do not project in flight. Often in large flocks. Habitat: open sea, occasionally inshore. S(W)

6   **WILSON'S STORM PETREL** *Oceanites oceanicus*   L 17 cm. As 7 but tail not, or hardly, forked. White on uppertail coverts extends further down to lower belly. When seen from nearby, yellow webs of feet diagnostic. Feet project in flight. Swallow-like, gliding flight, usually in flocks. Habitat: normally at open sea. SW

7   **LEACH'S STORM PETREL** *Oceanodroma leucorhoa*   L 20 cm. Wing bar more pronounced than in 6. Feet do not project. Does not patter on water surface. Flight erratic. Normally solitary. Habitat: open sea. U(br?)S

8   **MATSUDAIRA'S STORM PETREL** *Oceanodroma matsudairae*   L 24 cm. From 3.7 by smaller size and shorter wing. Pale patch formed by white primary shafts diagnostic. Forked tail normally held closed. Slow, erratic flight. Habitat: open sea. (?)

9   **BLACK-BELLIED STORM PETREL** *Fregetta tropica*   L 20 cm. Note black stripe over belly, broad, black leading edge to wing and dark wrist patch on underwing, which give bird darker appearance than 10. Dances and bounces over waves. Habitat: open sea. RW

10   **WHITE-BELLIED STORM PETREL** *Fregetta grallaria*   L 20 cm. From 9 by cleaner, white underwing and greyer upperparts. Habitat: open sea. RW

11   **WHITE-FACED STORM PETREL** *Pelagodroma marina*   L 20 cm. Note white eyebrow and grey rump. Gregarious. Habitat: open sea. (?)

Plate 4

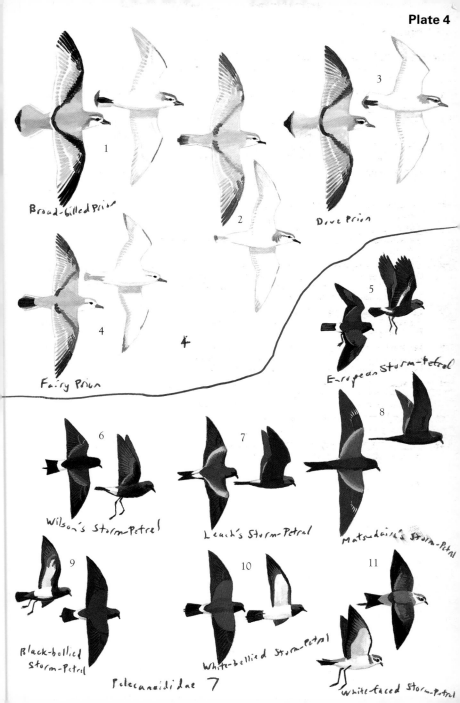

Broad-billed Prion

1

2

Dive Prion

3

Fairy Prion

4

4

European Storm-Petrel

5

Wilson's Storm-Petrel

6

Leach's Storm-Petrel

7

Matsudaira's Storm-Petrel

8

Black-bellied Storm-Petrel

9

White-bellied Storm-Petrel

10

White-faced Storm-Petrel

11

Pelecanoididae 7

Plate 5

Note: frigatebirds are spectacular fliers but extremely difficult to identify. This is because ♂♂ and ♀♀ both go through up to 6 different stages between juvenile and final adult plumage. Most important feature to establish (and write down for further diagnosis at home!) is distribution and form of white on underparts and in armpits. Note red gular pouch of ♂♂.

1   **ASCENCION FRIGATEBIRD** *Fregata aquila*   W 200 cm. Adult ♂ is completely black, including upperwing and legs. The ♀ has a white-bellied **(a)** and a dark **(b)** form, both with black legs but red toes and a complete, pale-brown collar, separating head from rest of body. Juv has all-white head, which, in following stages, becomes increasingly spotted and blotched black. Habitat: open sea. (?)

2   **GREATER FRIGATEBIRD** *Fregata minor*   W 220 cm. Adult ♂ is all black except for paler bar on upperwings and red legs. Note black cap of ♀, pale neck and restricted white in armpit. Juv shows almost complete breast band, which gradually recedes in following stages. Underwing only exceptionally with some white in armpit as shown. Habitat: open sea. R

3   **LESSER FRIGATEBIRD** *Fregata ariel*   W 185 cm. Adult ♂ is black except for white flank and underwing bar and dark, reddish feet. Note black head and white underwing bar of ♀. Juv (some with complete, black breast band) shows triangular, white armpits. Habitat: open sea. R

Note: gannets and boobies are large seabirds with straight, steady flight in which flapping and gliding alternate. Only Cape Gannet is frequent to common in the region; the other species are rare vagrants.

4   **CAPE GANNET** *Sula capensis*   W 165 cm. Black tail and long gular stripe diagnostic. Imm/2ndS (shown) as imm 5 but with longer gular stripe (very difficult to see). Habitat: open sea. Breeds on islands off south-west coast of South Africa and Namibia; disperses from there in winter.

5   **AUSTRALIAN GANNET** *Sula serrator*   W 170 cm. From 4 by short gular stripe and white tail feathers except black middle pair. Juv/1stS not safely separable from juv 4. R

6   **MASKED BOOBY** *Sula dactylatra*   W 150 cm. From 4 and 5 by green (not bluish) bill, red (not creamy) eyes and lack of yellow on head and nape. Note complete, black trailing edge of wings touching body. Imm has brown head, white collar and rather pale underwing. Habitat: open sea. R

7   **BROWN BOOBY** *Sula leucogaster*   W 140 cm. Adult is black above and has restricted white below. Note pale underwing area of juv, contrasting with darker flanks. Habitat: open sea. R

8   **RED-FOOTED BOOBY** *Sula sula*   W 150 cm. White form **(a)** and uncommon, dark form **(b)** with white rear body, shown . Red legs diagnostic. Note whitish underparts of juv, contrasting with mainly dark underwing. Habitat: open sea. R

Plate 5

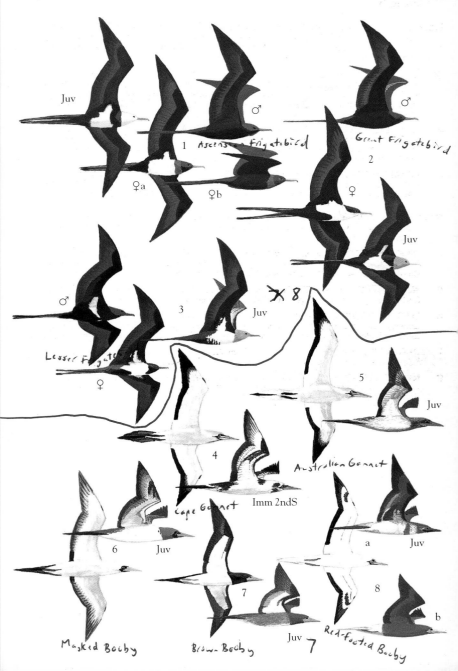

Juv

♀a

♀b

♂

1 Ascension Frigatebird

♂ Giant Frigatebird

2

♀

Juv

♂

3

Juv

Lesser Frigate

♀

X 8

5

Juv

4

Australian Gannet

Cape Gannet

Imm 2ndS

6 Juv

a Juv

7

8

Masked Booby

Brown Booby

Juv 7

Red-footed Booby

b

Plate 6

1   **AFRICAN FINFOOT** *Podica senegalensis*   L 65 cm. Red bill (and feet) diagnostic. Swims with 'pumping' head movements, not submerged as 7.9. Habitat: quiet rivers, streams, pools with fringing vegetation and overhanging trees. Voice: mid-high, dry, bouncing '*crut crut-crut crut crut*'. U

2   **GREAT CRESTED GREBE** *Podiceps cristatus*   L 50 cm. Unmistakable. In flight, white forewing connected via tertials with white secondaries. Habitat: larger, cool, inland water bodies. Voice: low and mid-high, raucous growls and grunts.

3   **BLACK-NECKED GREBE.** *Podiceps nigricollis*   L 30 cm. Note red eye. Habitat: lakes, dams, pans, swamp, ponds, even at sea. Voice: very high, chattering '*weet-weet-weeriet*'. U

4   **LITTLE GREBE** (or Dabchick) *Tachybaptus ruficollis*   L 20 cm. Bill shape with yellowish spot at corner diagnostic. Underparts pale brown, not white as 2 and 3. Faint wing bar in flight. Habitat: quiet rivers, lakes, dams, pans, ponds, pools. Voice: very high, fast, whinnying trill.

5   **GREATER SHEATHBILL** *Chionis alba*   L 40 cm. Reached South Africa once, probably ship-assisted. Breeds on sub-antarctic islands near South America. Similar Lesser Sheathbill, *Chionis minor* (with all-black bill), which breeds on sub-antarctic islands of Indian Ocean, not yet seen in South Africa. R

6   **JACKASS PENGUIN** *Spheniscus demersus*   L 60 cm. Single, encircling breast band **(a)** diagnostic. Many birds, however, show at least a small, extra breast spot **(b)**, rarely developed into a double collar **(c)**. This form resembles **(d)** Magellanic Penguin, *S. magellanicus*, with white line below bill base, which is not known from Africa. Habitat: breeds on offshore islands; sometimes seen near or on coast, especially near Namibia and south-west South Africa. Voice: very much like braying of donkey.

7   **KING PENGUIN** *Aptonodytes patagonicus*   L 95 cm. Long bill diagnostic. Greyer than similar, extra-limital Emperor Penguin. R

8   **ROCKHOPPER PENGUIN** *Eudyptes chrysocome*   L 60 cm. From 9 by shorter bill and black tail base. Note yellow crest plumes which are not connected on forehead. R

9   **MACARONI PENGUIN** *Eudyptes chrysolophus*   L 70 cm. From 8 by white tail base. Note that plumes are orange and connected on forehead. R

10   **GENTOO PENGUIN** *Pygoscelis papua*   L 80 cm. White patch over eye diagnostic. R

Plate 6

Rhynochetidae Eurypygidae Cariamidae 2b

♂ ♀ Imm

1

African Finfoot

2 N-br 1 2

Great crested Grebe
Podiceps cristatus

3 N-br 3

Black-necked Grebe
Podiceps nigricollis

4 N-br 4

Dabchick
Tachybaptus ruficollis

5

Snowy Sheathbill

33

d

a c

6

Imm b

Jackass Penguin
Spheniscus demersus

Gaviidae 6

7

King Penguin
Aptenodytes patagonicus

8 Rockhopper Penguin
Eudyptes chrysocome

9 Macaroni Penguin
Eudyptes chrysolophus

10 Gentoo Penguin
Pygoscelis papua

Plate 7

1 **RED-TAILED TROPICBIRD** *Phaethon rubricauda* W 105 cm. Some adults have rosy tinge. Imm has rather coarse barring on upperparts and black bill, while all primaries are striped lengthwise without forming a black patch as in 2 and 3. Habitat: open sea. U(S)

2 **RED-BILLED TROPICBIRD** *Phaethon aethereus* W 105 cm. Adult from 1 by black outerwings, from 1 and 3 by different mantle and rump pattern. Imm has large, black area on outerwing, buff-orange, dark-tipped bill and, on neck, connected eye stripes. Habitat: open sea. R

3 **WHITE-TAILED TROPICBIRD** *Phaethon lepturus* W 90 cm. Some adults have overall apricot wash. Imm from imms 1 and 2 by partly yellow bill, short eye stripe and from imm 1 by more black on outer primaries. R

4 **CAPE CORMORANT** *Phalacrocorax capensis* L 65 cm. Yellow gular (paler when n-br), short tail and absence of crest diagnostic. Imm is paler below than above. Large to very large flocks, which fly in long lines to fishing waters. Habitat: coastal waters. Feeds at sea but may enter estuaries.

5 **BANK CORMORANT** *Phalacrocorax neglectus* L 75 cm. Robust build. Pale eye in all-black face diagnostic. N-br adult (shown in flight) without white rump patch. Imm is uniformly dark with black eye. Feeds alone or in small groups. Habitat: only at sea.

6 **GREAT** (or White-breasted) **CORMORANT** *Phalacrocorax carbo* L 90 cm. N-br adult without white flank patches. Imm extensively white below. Habitat: large lakes and rivers with open banks and shores; also marshes, inundations, coastal lagoons, estuaries.

7 **CROWNED CORMORANT** *Phalacrocorax coronatus* L 50 cm. From 8 by blacker upperparts all year round and slightly shorter tail. Solitary or in small groups. Habitat: unlike 8, only at the sea coast. U

8 **LONG-TAILED** (or Reed) **CORMORANT** *Phalacrocorax africanus* L 55 cm. Br plumage as 7 but upperparts browner. N-br plumage lacks crest. Imm extensively pale below. Prefers perching in trees, not on the ground. Habitat: inland rivers, lakes, marshes, inundations with fringing vegetation and trees. Rarely near the coast.

9 **DARTER** *Anhinga melanogaster* L 80 cm. Slender, kinked neck diagnostic. Often swims submerged. Habitat: mainly along fresh water bodies with fringing vegetation and trees. Sometimes in coastal lagoons.

Plate 7

1 Imm

2 Imm

3 Imm

1

2

Red-tailed Tropicbird

3

Red-billed Tropicbird

White-tailed Tropicbird

8

4

4

Br

N-br

5

Cape Cormorant

Imm

5

Imm

6

Imm

7

Bank Cormorant

6
N-br

7

Imm

9 ♀

5

Crowned Cormorant

Common Cormorant

8

8

Br

N-br

Imm

African Darter

Reed Cormorant

9

9 ♂

Plate 8

1   **GREATER FLAMINGO** *Phoenicopterus ruber*   L 140 cm. Larger and paler than 2 with pink (not dark red) bill and, in flight, with more extensively pink upperwing. Habitat: shallow lakes, salt pans, estuaries, lagoons. (br)S

2   **LESSER FLAMINGO** *Phoenicopterus minor*   L 100 cm. Dark red bill diagnostic. In flight, with triangular, pink patch on upperwing. Habitat: larger, inland lakes. Also in estuaries, lagoons. (br)S

3   **GREY HERON** *Ardea cinerea*   L 100 cm. White crown, yellow bill and yellowish (or pinkish) legs diagnostic. Imm from imm 6 by white thighs and yellowish upperlegs. Note uniform grey underwing in flight. Habitat: open or reedy margins and nearby areas of lakes, rivers, marshes, estuaries.

4   **PURPLE HERON** *Ardea purpurea*   L 90 cm. Skulking behaviour and slender, streaked head and neck diagnostic. Imm is rufous and tawny. In flight from 5 by large 'V' mark over flanks and belly. Habitat: reed beds along rivers, lakes, dams, ponds; occasionally on coastal mud flats.

5   **GOLIATH HERON** *Ardea goliath*   L 140 cm H 150 cm. No black on flanks in flight. Imm (not shown) as adult but overall slightly more rufous (less so than imm 4). Habitat: shallow water of lakes, rivers, creeks, marshes, mangroves.

6   **BLACK-HEADED HERON** *Ardea melanocephala*   L 95 cm. Black crown and legs diagnostic. Imm from imm 3 by grey (not white) thighs, dark (not yellowish) legs and some rufous on neck. Habitat: open, grassy areas, farmlands, forest clearings near lakes, marshes, estuaries, coastal areas. Often away from water.

7   **SHOEBILL** *Balaeniceps rex*   L 150 cm. Unmistakable. Habitat: large swamps with tall papyrus or reeds. U

8   **GREAT** (or Eastern) **WHITE PELICAN** *Pelecanus onocrotalus*   L 155 cm W 315 cm. From 9 by whiter plumage and more colourful bare parts. Underwing black-and-white. Imm has dark bar on underwing coverts. Often seen fishing in a co-operating, synchronised group. Habitat: large, freshwater lakes, but also in estuaries.

9   **PINK-BACKED PELICAN** *Pelecanus rufescens*   L 125 cm. Smaller and less white than 8. On underwing flight feathers slightly darker than wing coverts. Fishes alone. Habitat: coastal estuaries but also on inland waters.

Plate 8

8

8 Imm

9

3

4

5

6

1

2

1

2

Greater Flamingo

Lesser Flamingo

Achinidae H.

Common Heron

3

Imm

Imm

4

Purple Heron

6

Imm

Blackheaded Heron

5

Goliath Heron

7

Shoebill

10

8

9

Great White Pelican

5 Pink-backed Pelican

Plate 9

1 **SQUACCO HERON** *Ardeola ralloides* L 40 cm. Skulking and very well camouflaged. Shows surprisingly white wings on take-off. Habitat: fringing vegetation of marshes, pans, lakes, slow streams. (S)

2 **MALAGASY POND HERON** *Ardeola idae* L 45 cm. In n-br plumage from 1 by much heavier streaking. Less skulking than 1. (Br plumage probably not seen outside Madagascar). Habitat: wooded marshes. W

3 **RUFOUS-BELLIED HERON** *Ardeola rufiventris* L 60 cm. Note white chin of ♀. Skulking. Habitat: swamps, inundations, reedy edges of lakes and swamps. Voice: rasping '*graak*' and other grunts. U

4 **WHITE-BACKED NIGHT HERON** *Gorsachius leuconotus* L 55 cm. Note exceptionally large eyes. Imm from imm 5 by grey head and dark eye. Nocturnal. Habitat: dense, waterside undergrowth near slow streams and lakes. Voice: low, crow-like '*cra cra cra cra*' or '*craak-craak-craak-craak*'. U

5 **BLACK-CROWNED NIGHT HERON** *Nycticorax nycticorax* L 55 cm. Not really secretive. Often gregarious. Nocturnal. Habitat: lake edges, rivers with bordering trees, bush, papyrus, reed beds. Voice: mid-high, pushed-out, short, barking '*wha wha*'. (S)

6 **LITTLE BITTERN** *Ixobrychus minutus* L 35 cm. Pale wing patches especially striking in flight. Imm (not shown) has even more buffy feather edges than ♀. Skulking. Habitat: marshes, wet grasslands. Voice: mid-high, dark, regular '*roa roa roa*'. U(S)

7 **GREEN-BACKED HERON** *Butorides striatus* L 40 cm. Well camouflaged but not necessarily secretive. Hunts by day. Habitat: bodies of water with dense, fringing vegetation, open, coastal mud flats. Voice: mid-high '*tsjah tsjah tsjah*' when flushed.

8 **DWARF BITTERN** *Ixobrychus sturmii* L 25 cm. Note small size, black eye, dark appearance. Largely nocturnal. Habitat: thick, reedy cover with some trees and shrub in or near marshes, lakes, streams, inundations, flooded woods. Voice: mid-high, dull '*roap-roap-roap*'. UbrS

9 **BITTERN** *Botaurus stellaris* L 65 cm. More often heard than seen. In flight, with rufous wings and far-protruding feet. Habitat: at edges of lakes and rivers with bordering trees, papyrus, reeds. Voice: extreme low, pushed-out, booming '*uhtHOOO uhtHOOO*'. U

10 **WHITE-CRESTED TIGER HERON** *Tigriornis leucolophus* L 65 cm. From all other herons by finely barred plumage. Erectile crest normally hidden. Evasive. Habitat: marshy woodland, undergrowth near forest streams. R

11 **BLACK EGRET** *Egretta ardesiaca* L 65 cm. Note black legs with yellow feet, characteristic head profile with long plumes and black eye. Unfolds wings repeatedly (like a fast-opening umbrella) to shut off glare when fishing **(a)**. Habitat: lake margins, river edges, marshes, inundations; occasionally at the seaside.

12 **SLATY EGRET** *Egretta vinaceigula* L 60 cm. Only black egret with all-yellow legs. Head plumes absent in n-br plumage. Habitat: flood plains, shallow water with tall grass. U

13 **GREAT** (White) **EGRET** *Egretta alba* L 95 cm. Note black gape line extending up behind eye. Habitat: margins of large bodies of water.

14 **CATTLE EGRET** *Bubulcus ibis* L 55 cm. Note short, robust bill. Bulky flight silhouette. Normally forages near cattle and game; also at grass fires. Flies to roost in low-flying, 'V' formations. Habitat: breeds in reed beds and trees near water edges.

15 **LITTLE BLUE HERON** *Egretta caerulea* L 65 cm. Vagrant from America. Adult from 11, 12 and 16a by all-black legs, from 11 by pale eye, from 12 and 16a by black-purplish chin. Imm from other white egrets by all-yellow legs. Habitat in America: all types of inland and coastal wetlands. R

16 **LITTLE EGRET** *Egretta garzetta* L 65 cm. Yellow feet (and eyes) diagnostic. Normal, white **(a)** and rare, black **(b)** forms shown. Note slender, mainly black bill. Habitat: shallow, fresh water, estuaries, seashore pools.

17 **YELLOW-BILLED EGRET** *Egretta intermedia* L 65 cm. From 13 by smaller size, shorter bill and yellow upperlegs. From 16 by heavier jizz, all-yellow bill, yellow upperlegs. Gape does not extend beyond eye. Habitat: swampy areas, inundations, flood plains, edges of inland waters; occasionally on mudflats in estuaries.

Plate 9

1 N-br
Squacco Heron

2 N-br
Madagascar Pond-Heron

1

2

9

9 Great Bittern

8

3 ♀
R-tarsi-bellied Heron

3

Imm

6

Little Bittern

8 Dwarf Bittern

Imm

4
White-backed Night-Heron

Imm

Imm

7 Striated B Heron

10 White-crested Bittern

5
N-br
Black-crowned Night-Heron

4

Imm

5 br

13 N-br

14

11

11a

12

Br

Common Egret

14 N-br

Black Heron

15

16

16

Ad

Imm

16a

b

16

N-br

17

8

Plate 10

1   **BLACK STORK** *Ciconia nigra*   L 95 cm. Red legs and black rump of adult diagnostic. Imm from 2 by absence of red, bare skin on head. Note that black leading edge on underwing widens outwards. Parties of up to 4. Habitat: tall grass, reeds and herbage near streams and other small water bodies, but also in open, dry grassland. U

2   **ABDIM'S STORK** *Ciconia abdimii*   L 75 cm. White rump diagnostic. Note narrow, even, black leading edge of underwing. Very gregarious. Habitat: open grassland, farmlands, often near settlement. S

3   **WHITE STORK** *Ciconia ciconia*   L 100 cm. Unmistakable. A small breeding colony exists in extreme southern Cape. Habitat: any open area with large insects, mice, frogs and other small prey. (br)S

4   **MARABOU STORK** *Leptoptilos crumeniferus*   L 150 cm. Unmistakable. Only stork with retracted head in flight. Mainly in or near wildlife sanctuaries, mixing with vultures. U

5   **WOOLLY-NECKED STORK** *Ciconia episcopus*   L 85 cm. Black breast band diagnostic. Long, white undertail coverts conceal black tail in flight. Gregarious but only at dusk. Habitat: open shores of all types of large and small water bodies; also in grassland. U

6   **AFRICAN OPEN-BILLED STORK** *Anastomus lamelligerus*   L 95 cm. Unmistakable, especially if 'open' bill can be seen. Gregarious, especially in breeding season. Habitat: feeds on molluscs with its specially adapted bill, at water edge often in wooded areas. US(W)

7   **YELLOW-BILLED STORK** *Mycteria ibis*   L 95 cm. Yellow bill diagnostic. In soaring flight outer wings do not spread as in 3, but are bent backwards; black tail in flight difficult to see. Habitat: any area with fish, especially at larger water bodies.

8   **SADDLE-BILLED STORK** *Ephippiorhynchus senegalensis*   L 145 cm. Note different eye colour of ♂ and ♀. Habitat: any shallow water and swampy area. U

9   **AFRICAN SPOONBILL** *Platalea alba*   L 90 cm. Flies with outstretched neck, unlike white egrets. Habitat: shallow parts of permanent and seasonal, inland water bodies and estuaries.

10   (Southern) **BALD IBIS** *Geronticus calvus*   L 80 cm. Bald, bi-coloured head and black plumage diagnostic. Habitat: breeds on cliffs but feeds in short, overgrazed or burnt, upland grassland. Voice: occasionally in flight, high, fluting 'whuuhuh whuuh'.

11   **HADADA** *Bostrychia hagedash*   L 75 cm. Note white cheek stripe and red ridge of bill. Very vocal in flight. Habitat: cultivated areas, lawns, moist grassland, marshes, wooded streams. Voice: mid-high, loud, raucous 'haaah hahah haoh hahah'.

12   **SPOT-BREASTED IBIS** *Bostrychia rara*   L 45 cm. Note crest and spotting. Habitat: in or close to forests. Voice: very noisy at dusk, 'hakhak kakkah'. R

13   **GLOSSY IBIS** *Plegadis falcinellus*   L 65 cm. Slim, long-legged and -necked appearance diagnostic. Habitat: swamps, flood plains, lake margins, vleis and dams. Voice: normally silent.

14   **SACRED IBIS** *Threskiornis aethiopica*   L 75 cm. Note red stripe and narrow, black trailing edge on underwing. Habitat: wetlands, farmland, sewage ponds, coastal beaches, offshore islands. Voice: occasionally in flight, mid-high 'kreh kreh'.

15   **HAMERKOP** *Scopus umbretta*   L 55 cm. Builds huge nests of sticks in trees or on cliffs, which, however, are often taken over by owls, kestrels, ducks, monitor lizards or snakes. Habitat: muddy margins and shallow parts of all types of inland water bodies.

Plate 10

Imm

1

1

2

2

3

3

4

5

5

6

6

7

7

Imm

8

♀

♂

10

8

9

10   Imm   11

Bald Ibis   Hadada   African Spoonbill

12   13   14   15

Spot-breasted Ibis   Glossy Ibis   Sacred Ibis

Plate 11

Note: Mute Swan, *Cygnus olor*, introduced in South Africa, not shown.

1   **SPUR-WINGED GOOSE** *Plectropterus gambensis*   L 100 cm (♂), 75 cm (♀). Southern race *niger* shown. Note irregular, white feathering on face, underparts and upper- and underwing coverts. Nominate (not shown) north of Zambezi has even more white on face and underparts. Rests by day at large water bodies or in wetlands. Grazes in grass- and floodlands early morning, late evening and often at night. Voice: very high, yelping '*juWéet juWéet*' or '*Pickwick*'.

2   **EGYPTIAN GOOSE** *Alopochen aegyptiacus*   L 70 cm. Always in pairs. Gregarious outside breeding season. The ♀♀ are smaller than ♂♂, otherwise similar. Habitat: rivers, streams, lakes, dams, ponds; normally not in saline waters. Voice: mallard-like, husky, scraped '*sruuuh sruuuh sruuuh*' of ♂ with '*kah-kah-kah-kah*' of ♀, uttered by both with extended neck.

3   **SOUTH-AFRICAN SHELDUCK** *Tadorna cana*   L 65 cm. From 2 by leg colour, less straight neck, black bill and thin, black line through white on forewing. Note that ♂ and ♀ differ (unlike 2). Habitat: freshwater and brackish water bodies of any type and size. May breed away from water. Voice: mid-high, rather timid '*raak raak raak -*' of ♂ together with '*roh roh roh -*' of ♀.

4   **KNOB-BILLED DUCK** *Sarkidiornis melanotos*   L 75 cm (♂), 50 cm (♀). Unmistakable. Habitat: wetlands near or surrounded by woodland. Voice: normally silent; mid-high, drawn-out '*wrroh wrruh-wrruh*'.

5   **WHITE-BACKED DUCK** *Thalassornis leuconotus*   L 40 cm. Note white spot at bill base. White back and rump only visible in flight. Habitat: secluded parts of lakes, dams, pools with some floating and fringing vegetation. Voice: extremely high '*witLéeet*' or drawn-out '*oooWóuw*'.

6   **AFRICAN PYGMY GOOSE** *Nettapus auritus*   L 30 cm. Note white secondaries in flight. Habitat: quiet, clear waters with some floating and emergent vegetation. Voice: very high, fluted, short '*feewée-feewée-tutukwéet*' or rapid, liquid '*ripripripripri-*'. U

7   **SOUTHERN POCHARD** *Netta erythrophthalma*   L 50 cm. The ♂ differs from ♂ 10 by dark belly and red eye, ♀ by pale crescent on face sides. Habitat: clear, deep lakes with reedy margins. Voice: high, soft, fluted '*rrrhew rrrhew rrrhew*' of ♂ and mid-high, raucous '*rrah rrah*' of ♀.

8   **MACCOA DUCK** *Oxyura maccoa*   L 50 cm. Note uniform dark brown wings and often stiff, erect tail. The ♀ has pale, horizontal lines below eye. N-br ♂ (not shown) as ♀. Habitat: quiet, shallow, freshwater lakes with emergent and fringing vegetation. Voice: very low, dry, drawn-out '*purrrrrr*' (like a very small engine).

9   **HARTLAUB'S DUCK** *Pteronetta hartlaubii*   L 50 cm. From most other ducks by habitat. Blue forewing diagnostic. From 8 by different range. Habitat: well-wooded streams, especially in forests. Voice: very low, soft, raucous, muttered '*rrarrarrar-ra—*'. R

10   **TUFTED DUCK** *Aythya fuligula*   L 45 cm. Mixed flocks of white-bellied ♂♂ and dark ♀♀ makes confusion with 7 improbable. Habitat: open water of deep lakes, dams, rivers. Voice: very short, compressed, melodious shiver, '*wfirr*'. R

11   **RINGED TEAL** *Callonetta leucophrys*   L 35 cm. Note: this species was seen in 1994 and 1995 at Norton, Lake Manyame, Zimbabwe. As this forest duck from central South America is not known as a long-distance migrant these records must be of escapees. Unlike any other duck in the area; small with dark brown stripe from bill over crown to mantle and plain, pale brown face sides (♂) or white face sides with dark, broad eye stripe and cheek patch (♀); black-and-white vent. In flight shows blackish wings with diagnostic, round, white spot on greater wing coverts. (Not illustrated, no map.) R

Plate 11

Plate 12

1   **WHITE-FACED WHISTLING DUCK** *Dendrocygna viduata*   L 50 cm. Erect stance combined with white face diagnostic. Highly gregarious. Habitat: large rivers, lakes, sewage ponds, dams with some floating vegetation. Also in swampy areas. Voice: extremely high, lashing, rapid, fluted '*weehweeh-weeh*'.

2   **FULVOUS WHISTLING DUCK** *Dendrocygna bicolor*   L 45 cm. Note erect stance and white uppertail coverts. Pairs or small flocks. Habitat: large rivers, lakes, dams, inundations, other water bodies with some floating vegetation. Voice: not very vocal; high '*tuwéee*' ('*tu-*' separated from, or as an undertone to '*-wéee*').

3   **YELLOW-BILLED DUCK** *Anas undulata*   L 55 cm. Only duck with yellow bill. Gregarious. Habitat: lakes, dams, rivers, estuaries, pools, sewage ponds. Voice: as 5 but slightly sharper.

4   **AFRICAN BLACK DUCK** *Anas sparsa*   L 55 cm. Evasive, swims between and under fringing vegetation. In pairs. Habitat: well-wooded streams with stony bottoms, especially in mountainous areas, but moves at night, often to large, open waters. Voice: mid-high, loud, mallard-like '*wrah-wrah-wrah*' by ♀.

5   **MALLARD** *Anas platyrhynchos*   L 60 cm. Occurs only as feral populations in some large cities. Voice: well-known duck-gaggling. U

6   **CAPE SHOVELER** *Anas smithii*   L 55 cm. The ♂ and ♀ differ from ♀ 7 by black bill and darker plumage. Habitat: sewage ponds, lagoons, estuaries. Avoids large, open water bodies. Voice: mid-high, mallard-like '*week-wekwekwek*' of ♀ and low '*rokrokrokrok*' of ♂. U

7   **NORTHERN** (or European) **SHOVELER** *Anas clypeata*   L 55 cm. Larger-billed than 6. N-br ♂ as ♀ but with yellow eyes. Habitat: shallow, fresh lakes, pools, inundations, marshes. Voice: mid-high, rattling '*raptaptap*' and low '*ko-kropkokkerop*'. RS

8   **GARGENEY** *Anas querquedula*   L 40 cm. Note small size and graceful profile. N-br ♂ as ♀ but with less well defined face pattern and different upperwing pattern. The ♀ has pale streak above and below eye. Habitat: mainly sheltered, shallow parts of freshwater lakes, dams, estuaries. Voice: low, dry, wooden, short, rattled '*crrrrruh*' of ♂ and mid-high, loud, hoarse cacklings of ♀. RS

9   **CAPE TEAL** *Anas capensis*   L 45 cm. Note pale head and red, black-based bill. Habitat: mainly brackish waters, sewage ponds, alkaline lakes. Voice: extremely high, smooth '*feeeweeet*' and mallard-like '*wèèk-wèèk-wèèk—*'.

10   **HOTTENTOT TEAL** *Anas hottentota*   L 35 cm. Note white cheek with dark smear. Rear end of body almost without dark blotching and spotting. Habitat: sewage ponds, shallow water with fringing, reedy vegetation. Also on large, open dams. Voice: very high, dry, chuckled '*kèhèhè-hèhèh*'.

11   **RED-BILLED TEAL** *Anas erythrorhyncha*   L 50 cm. Note dark cap and red bill. In flight, large, creamy speculum. Gregarious. Habitat: open, shallow fresh lakes, dams, inundations with submerged, floating and fringing vegetation. Voice: soft '*meeéh meeéh meeéh*' of ♂ and cacklings of ♀.

12   **NORTHERN PINTAIL** *Anas acuta*.   L 50 (+10) cm. Note slim, graceful profile. Rear end of ♀ and n-br ♂ is finely speckled, contrasting with scalloped flanks. N-br ♂ from ♀ by more contrastingly patterned bill and, in flight, by different upperwing colouring. Habitat: dams, ponds, estuaries, other fresh and brackish waters. Voice: very high, liquid, rattled '*krruh krruh-kruh*' and short, whistled '*fiu-fiu-fiu*'. RS

Plate 12

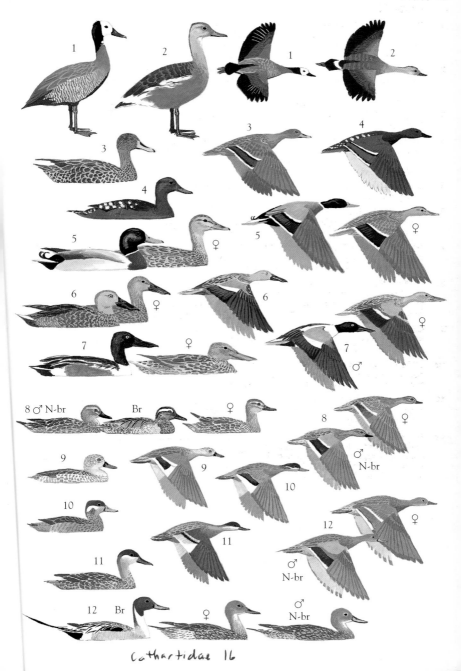

Cathartidae 16

Plate 13

1   **PALE CHANTING GOSHAWK** *Melierax canorus*   L 55 cm. Note erect stance on top of bush or post. From 2 by paler appearance, white rump and almost white secondaries in flight. Folded wing is rather contrastingly white and grey. Imm from imm 2 by blotched, rather than barred, underparts and by white panels on primaries. Habitat: open thornveld and woodland. Voice: mid-high, resounding, rapid '*wuut-whut-wuutwuutwuutwuut*' slightly rising in pitch and volume; also mid-high, descending, bouncing '*wooh-wikwikwikwirrrr*'.

2   **DARK CHANTING GOSHAWK** *Melierax metabates*   L 50 cm. Erect stance as 1, but is darker. Folded wings look even-coloured. Fine barring makes rump in flight look grey. Note finely barred underparts of imm. Habitat: as 1 but often in less dry areas.(Ranges hardly overlap). Voice: high, loud, fluted '*wiooh wiooh wiooh wiooh -*' (each '*wiooh*' sharply descending).

3   **GABAR GOSHAWK** *Micronisus gabar*   L 30 cm. Normal **(a)** and dark **(b)** forms shown. Note dark eye, pale grey breast, white rump and white edge to secondaries and tail sides. Dark form from dark 7 by absence of white streaks on tail shafts and by showing some barring in flight feathers. Imm (with pale eye) from imm 4 by white rump. Hunts from perch in cover. Habitat: woodland, open thornveld and scrubland, suburban gardens, villages.

4   **SHIKRA** (or Little Banded Goshawk) *Accipiter badius*   L 30 cm (♂), 35 cm (♀). Unbarred central tail feathers diagnostic. The ♂ is finely barred rufous. Imm has grey (not white) rump and rather broad streaks and bars on underparts. May perch exposed. Habitat: woodland and thornveld with tall-grassed parts.

5   **AFRICAN GOSHAWK** *Accipiter tachiro*   L 35 cm (♂), 45 cm (♀). Plumage, especially of ♀, more brown than grey. Cere grey, not yellow. Note white barring (brown in ♀) of tail. Imm is heavily blotched and barred below. Skulking. Habitat: in and near forests, dense thornveld and other woodland, riverine belts, suburban gardens. Voice: high, sharp '*whip*' in flight or from perch. Rather vocal.

6   **AFRICAN LITTLE SPARROWHAWK** *Accipiter minullus*   L 25 cm (♂), 30 cm (♀). Small size, white rump and tail spots diagnostic. Imm has tail spots too, but less white on rump. Habitat: woodland and thornveld; less in forests than 10.

7   **OVAMBO SPARROWHAWK** *Accipiter ovampensis*   L 30 cm (♂), 35 cm (♀). Note dark-eyed appearance. Throat indistinctly barred grey. Small, white streaks on tail shafts diagnostic even in rare, black form **(a)**. Dark **(b)** and pale **(c)** immature forms shown, both with brown, almost black eyes. Hunts from perch in cover or exposed. Habitat: open woodland, thornveld, eucalyptus and other exotic plantations.

8   **BLACK SPARROWHAWK** *Accipiter melanoleucus*   L 45 cm (♂), 55 cm (♀). Normal **(a)** and rare, dark **(b)** forms may be paired. From 16.7 (and 16.5) by dark eye, unfeathered lower legs and absence of crest. May soar but is rather secretive, though not shy. Habitat: forests, woodland, exotic plantations, suburbs.

9   **RUFOUS-CHESTED** (or Red-breasted) **SPARROWHAWK** *Accipiter rufiventris*   L 30 cm (♂), 35 cm (♀). Rufous underparts and brown upperparts diagnostic. Imm has irregularly streaked (not barred) underparts. Secretive. Habitat: mountainous forests, woodland, plantations including surrounding open country.

10   **RED-THIGHED SPARROWHAWK** *Accipiter erythropus*   L 25 cm (♂), 30 cm (♀). All-black above except for conspicuous, white rump. Note also the small, white spots on scapulars and on all but central tail feathers. Eye red (not yellow as 6). Yellow-eyed imm shows fine barring below. Habitat: dense forests. R

Note: see also 84.5, when in Cabinda.

Plate 13

Plate 14

1   **AFRICAN MARSH HARRIER** *Circus ranivorus*   L 45 cm. Adult from 2 by less pale head and barred flight feathers and tail. Note pale breast band of imm. Habitat: larger swamps; also in grass- and farmland.

2   **NORTHERN** (or European) **MARSH HARRIER** *Circus aeruginosus*   L 50 cm. Note unbarred tail and flight feathers. Pale heads of ♂, ♀ and imm rather sharply demarcated from rest of body. The ♂ has grey wings and tail, ♀ and imm show dark underwing. Imm from ♀ by dark eye and absence of pale breast band. Habitat: marshes, reed beds, tall grass. US

3   **BLACK HARRIER** *Circus maurus*   L 50 cm. Note yellow (not dark) eye of imm and dark breast band. Underside of ♂ and imm flight feathers unbarred, white. Habitat: dry, open country, grass- and farmland. U

4   **MONTAGU'S HARRIER** *Circus pygargus*   L 50 cm. Wing tip reaches tail tip when perched. From 5 by shorter legs, greyer plumage, more black in wings (including a wing bar), some chestnut streaking on underparts and underwings. The ♀ from ♀ 5 by paler facial disc, which is not separated by white line from streaks on sides of neck. The ♀ also has paler secondaries below than ♀ 5, while neatly arranged barring on underwing coverts is more chestnut. Habitat: dry, open, natural and cultivated plains, even at high altitudes. US

5   **PALLID HARRIER** *Circus macrourus*   L 40 cm. Wing tip falls short of tail tip when perched. Imm from imm 4 by more pronounced facial disc, separated by whitish line from more extensively dark-brown neck. Habitat: as 4 but occasionally in wetter areas. US

6   **BLACK-SHOULDERED KITE** *Elanus caeruleus*   L 35 cm. Note conspicuous, black shoulder patch. Hovers frequently, but also perches on posts, power lines and dead branches. Habitat: open, wooded and bushed areas, cultivations, plantations, suburbs. Voice: rather silent.

7   **GYMNOGENE** *Polyboroides typus*   L 60 cm. Raids weaver nests and extracts nestlings from tree holes with its specially adapted, flexible legs. Habitat: forest edges, moist, wooded areas, suburbs. Voice: very high, plaintive '*phyweeee*'.

8   **YELLOW-BILLED KITE** *Milvus migrans parasitus*   L 55 cm. From 9 by yellow bill (adult only) and darker head. Manoeuvres dexterously with strongly bent wings and constantly twisting tail. Habitat: roadsides, suburban gardens, refuse sites. Voice: very high, quavering '*pth-rrrrrrr*', slightly higher than 9. brS

9   **BLACK KITE** *Milvus migrans migrans*   L 55 cm. Black, yellow-based bill and pale head of adult diagnostic. Habitat: as 8. Voice: very high, quavering, slow, trilled '*pihurrrrrrr*' ('*pih-*' lashing, short). S

Plate 14

Plate 15

1   **AFRICAN CUCKOO HAWK** *Aviceda cuculoides*   L 40 cm. Note crest both of adult and imm. Perches conspicuously and flies from tree to tree in light, kite-like fashion. Habitat: forest edges, woodland, riverine belts, cultivations. Voice: very high, gliding-down '*píeuuh*' and staccato '*pi-pi-peh-*' with '*fíeuuh*' from a pair. U

2   **LIZARD BUZZARD** *Kaupifalco monogrammicus*   L 35 cm. Note black streak down throat centre and black tail with one **(a)** or rarely two **(b)** bars. Normally perches in exposed position. Habitat: forest edges, woodland, thornveld, cultivated areas, farmland. Voice: very high, liquid '*weeeweeeweeeweeeweee*' in display flight.

3   **HONEY BUZZARD** *Pernis apivorus*   L 55 cm. From most raptors by absence of dark eyebrow (or overshadowing ridge), which gives this species a rather pigeon-like expression. Many colour forms exist, of which pale **(a)** and dark **(b)** examples are shown. Note, in flight, smallish, protruding head and tail pattern where one bar appears to be missing (not so in imm). Imm (not shown perched) has yellow cere, dark eye and different tail pattern. Habitat: forest edges, open woodland. Voice: very high, sharp '*fíéeeeh*'. US

4   **AUGUR BUZZARD** *Buteo augur*   L 50 cm (♂), 55 cm (♀). From 6 by different underparts and by black-and-white, barred tertials and some mantle feathers (not only secondaries). Habitat: hilly, open areas, woodland, cultivations, suburbs. Voice: in flight, high '*kjow-kjow-kjow-kjow*'. S

5   **STEPPE BUZZARD** *Buteo buteo vulpinus*   L 45 cm (♂), 55 cm (♀). Normally has a pale, chestnut-brown tail with broad terminal bar (unlike 7). From 9 by less distinct, pale panel on upperwing. Note streaked (not barred) underparts of imm with narrowly barred tail (not with broad terminal bar). Habitat: open, natural and cultivated areas with at least a few look-out posts. Voice: in flight, very high, sharp, rapidly descending, whistled '*Níau*'. S

6   **JACKALL BUZZARD** *Buteo rufofuscus*   L 50 cm (♂), 55 cm (♀). Some individuals may lack the chestnut breast band but all have black (not white as 4) underwing coverts. Imm has unbarred tail. Habitat: mountainous, open areas. Voice: mid-high, jackal-like '*íauegh-íauegh-íahugh*' in flight.

7   **MOUNTAIN BUZZARD** *Buteo oreophilus*   L 40 cm (♂), 45 cm (♀). (Formerly known as Forest Buzzard, *Buteo tachardus*). Normally brown without any rufous. Underparts spotted (not streaked, striped or barred). Tail has indistinct terminal bar. Habitat: in and around mountain forests. Voice: in flight, high, short, slightly descending '*piuuh*'.

8   **RED-NECKED BUZZARD** *Buteo auguralis*   L 40 cm (♂), 45 cm (♀). Note characteristic reddish glow. Imm is mainly brown with only one broad terminal tail bar. Habitat: forest edges, heavily wooded areas.

9   **LONG-LEGGED BUZZARD** *Buteo rufinus*   L 50 cm (♂), 65 cm (♀). Pale **(a)** and very rare, dark **(b)** forms shown. Note bulky, pale-headed appearance of form **a** with unbarred, cinnamon tail and (in flight) dark wrist patches. Adult from imm 5 by unstreaked, normally more or less rufous underparts. Tail of imm has only narrow, evenly spaced bars. Very pale panel on upperwings diagnostic. Habitat: semi-desert and other open areas. Voice: rather silent; rarely loud, explosive, descending '*íau*'. RS

Plate 15

Plate 16

1   **AFRICAN FISH EAGLE** *Haliaeetus vocifer*   L 65 cm. Unmistakable. Habitat: large lakes, rivers, inundations, estuaries, seashore. Voice: free, triumphant, herring gull-like '*waaak waaa waaa kaa-ka-ka*', often in an unsynchronized duet of ♂ and ♀.

2   **OSPREY** *Pandion haliaetus*   L 55 cm. Note, in flight, wings bent at wrist. Adult from most other raptors by (long) eye stripe. Imm (not shown) from adult by paler eye stripe and more striped head and underparts, from imm 1 by pale eye and longer tail. US(W)

3   **LONG-CRESTED EAGLE** *Lophaetus occipitalis*   L 50 cm (♂), 55 cm (♀). Unmistakable. Habitat: forest edges, swampy, bushed grassland, cultivation, suburban gardens. Voice: high, drawn-out '*feeeeeh*'.

4   **AFRICAN HAWK EAGLE** *Hieraaetus spilogaster*   L 65 cm (♂), 80 cm (♀). Note large size, feathered legs, rounded wings (in flight). Perches in cover but can be seen soaring freely, especially in morning. Habitat: open woodland, thornveld with some large trees, often near streams and rocky hillsides. Voice: Fish eagle-like (1), slightly rising '*keekeekeek-*' (6–7 times). U

5   **AYRES'S HAWK EAGLE** *Hieraaetus ayresii*   L 45 cm (♂), 55 cm (♀). White forehead of adult diagnostic but small crest often hidden. Note heavily barred underwings and tail. Habitat: canopy of forest and woodland. Voice: very high, pushed-out '*fuweéh fuweéh -*'. US

6   **BOOTED EAGLE** *Hieraaetus pennatus*   L 45 cm (♂), 55 cm (♀). Pale **(a)** and rather uncommon, dark **(b)** forms shown. Note characteristic upperwing and mantle pattern of perched and flying bird. Shows white spots at base of wings in flight ('head lights'). Habitat: forest, dry woodland, open or slightly bushed and wooded, hilly country, desert. Normally at higher elevations. Voice: very high, staccato, sustained '*djip-djip-djip-djip—*'. US

7   **CASSIN'S HAWK EAGLE** *Spizaetus africanus*   L 55 cm (♂), 60 cm (♀). Note short-winged and long-tailed appearance. In flight shows clean, white underparts, contrasting with dark underwing coverts. Imm is spotted, not streaked below. Adult from 13.8 by feathered lower legs. Rarely seen except soaring low over forest. Habitat: forest canopy. R

Plate 16

Plate 17

1   **BATELEUR** *Terathopius ecaudatus*   L 55 cm. Note unique flight silhouette with very short tail. Habitat: common over and near the major game reserves, elsewhere becoming rare. U

2   **BROWN SNAKE EAGLE** *Circaetus cinereus*   L 70 cm. Note large size, broad face with large, yellow eyes and erect stance on top of tree or post. Habitat: dense thornveld and woodland with some large trees. Voice: very high, sharp, piercing yelps, '*tjark tjark tjark*'.

3   **SMALLER** (or Western) **BANDED SNAKE EAGLE** *Circaetus cinerascens*   L 55 cm. Tail pattern diagnostic. Barring on underparts not very pronounced. Cere and gape yellow. Normally perches in (not on) dead or sparsely-leaved trees. Habitat: riverine belts and forest patches in open country. Voice: mid-high, toy trumpet-like '*uRúh kkruruh*', high, descending '*ko-ko-ko-ko-ko-koh*'. U

4   **SOUTHERN BANDED SNAKE EAGLE** *Circaetus fasciolatus*   L 55 cm. Note difference between plain, brown breast and prominent barring on belly. Underwings more densely barred than 3. Imm as imm 3 but with different tail pattern. Habitat: coastal forests. Voice: mid-high, bouncing, rapid '*kokokokokoah*' and high '*kah-kah-kah-kah-kah-kah*'. U

5   **BLACK-BREASTED SNAKE EAGLE** *Circaetus gallicus pectoralis*   L 65 cm. Note grey cere and pale legs. Perches conspicuously. May hover. Habitat: dry, stony, lightly wooded plains and hillsides, often near water. Voice: high (or low), sometimes accelerated, whistled '*fiuu fiuu fiuu -*'. (SW)

6   **CONGO SERPENT EAGLE** *Dryotriorchis spectabilis*   L 60 cm. Note long tail, short wings, black throat, large eye. Habitat: mid- and ground strata of dense forest. U

Plate 17

1 Imm

1 ♂

♀

Imm

♂

♀

2

Ad

2

Imm

3

Imm

3

4

4

Imm

4

5

Imm

5

5

Imm

6

Imm

7

Imm

Plate 18

1   **VERREAUX'S EAGLE** *Aquila verreauxii*   L 75 cm (♂), 90 cm (♀). Note narrow-based, rounded wingform in flight silhouette. Imm reaches full adult plumage after 5 years, in first stage starting to turn black on face sides. Habitat: bushed and wooded mountain sides with cliffs and rocky ravines.

2   **STEPPE EAGLE** *Aquila nipalensis*   L 65 cm (♂), 80 cm (♀). Nominate **(a)** is darkest of all Steppe (2) and Tawny (3) Eagle forms with gape extending well beyond eye and with tawny nape. In flight, faint barring of flight feathers and tail visible. Bases of primaries form paler panel on upperwing than those of 3. Imm nominate (not shown) has pale, banded uppertail. Race *orientalis* (**b**, less dark than **a**) has gape extending just beyond middle of eye. Imm has diagnostic, broad, whitish edge to underwing coverts; this feature still more or less visible in sub-adult. Note shaggy trousers of Steppe Eagle and next species, but Steppe Eagle is normally darker and larger. Steppe Eagle perches more often on the ground than 3. Habitat: dry, open, bushed and wooded country. US

3   **TAWNY EAGLE** *Aquila rapax*   L 65 cm (♂), 80 cm (♀). Several colour forms; of these pale **(a)**, streaked **(b)** and dark **(c**, in flight.**)** forms shown. Gape stops just beneath middle of eye. Adult from 2 by diagnostic, oval (not round as 2) nostrils and by narrower, pale-edged secondaries and wing coverts (see perched birds), less obvious upperwing panel on soaring bird and absence of visible barring of flight feathers and tail. Habitat: as 2. U

4   **LESSER SPOTTED EAGLE** *Aquila pomarina*   L 60 cm (♂), 70 cm (♀). Note overall dark appearance of adult and imm and absence of tawny nape. Adult in flight shows contrasting, white, U-shaped patch on rump and white bases of flight feathers. Note diagnostic rows of white spots on upperwing coverts of imm. Generally upper- and underwing coverts of both adult and imm are paler than flight feathers. From 2 and 3 also by tight trousers. Habitat: open woodland. US

5   **WAHLBERG'S EAGLE** *Aquila wahlbergi*   L 55 cm (♂), 60 cm (♀). Many colour forms; of these **a** (most common), **b**, **c** (rarest) and **d** shown. From other eagles by more clearly visible barring of flight feathers and tail. Note large, black eyes and rather long tail. May show slight crest **(b)**. Flies with closed tail, giving cross-form to flight silhouette. Imm (not shown) as adult but feather edges are paler and head and neck more streaked. Habitat: no preferred habitat but not in forest. brS

6   **GREATER SPOTTED EAGLE** *Aquila clanga*   L 65 cm (♂), 75 cm (♀). Note: it is possible that this eagle, which has not yet been sighted in Southern Africa, turns up in the region, especially in Zambia. Adult and imm very much like 4 but (much) darker, heavier-bodied, larger-winged and normally with darker upper- and undercoverts than flight feathers (this feature reversed in 4). Imm from imm 4 by more (rows of) white wing spots. Adult from dark form of 3 by smaller size, purplish gloss on fresh plumage and, on ground, by longer, narrower-trousered legs. (?) (Not illustrated.)

Plate 18

Imm

1

1

Imm

2

Imm

Ad

Sub-adult

Imm

2

a

2

b

Imm

3

3

3 Imm

a

b

Imm

3

c

b

Imm

4

Imm

4

Imm

5a

b

c

d

c

5

a

Plate 19

1 **PALM-NUT VULTURE** *Gypohierax angolensis* L 60 cm. Note pink, bare skin around eye. Imm from imm 2 by rounded (not wedged) tail and pale band along wing coverts. Habitat: open forest and plantations with oil palms (the fruits of which it eats). Voice: very high, drawn-out, whistled '*feeeeeh*', often rising in pitch. U

2 **EGYPTIAN VULTURE** *Neophron percnopterus* L 60 cm. Note wedge-shaped tail (white in adult). Imm from imm 20.2 and 20.3 by longer feathers of crown and nape. Scavenger in and near game reserves, rare elsewhere. U

3 **LAMMERGEIER** (or Bearded Vulture) *Gypaetus barbatus* L 110 cm. Very large size with long, narrow wings and wedge-shaped tail. Habitat: mountainous cliffs, gorges and adjacent country. U

4 **MARTIAL EAGLE** *Polemaetus bellicosus* L 80 cm. Largest of all eagles. Adult shows fine, black spotting on underparts and has fully feathered legs. Imm is very pale below with narrow barring of flight feathers and tail. Habitat: semi-desert, more or less wooded and bushed areas. Voice: in display flight, very high '*fju-wírr*' and '*fwee-fwee-fwee–*'. U

5 **CROWNED EAGLE** *Stephanoaetus coronatus* L 80 cm. Note orange gape, large, yellow toes with enormous claws, short wings, long tail. Perched imm from imm 4 by spotted leggings. Habitat: in and near main game reserves. Elsewhere rare. Voice: very high, excited '*puwéepuwéepuwée–*', undulating in pitch and volume, synchronised with up-and-down display flight.

Plate 19

Plate 20

1 **LAPPET-FACED VULTURE** *Aegypius tracheliotus* L 100 cm. Note black feather garlands on breast. Large size and aggressive, dominant behaviour at carcasses make it unmistakable. Imm has dark trousers. Habitat: in and near main game reserves. Elsewhere rare. U

2 **WHITE-HEADED VULTURE** *Aegypius occipitalis* L 80 cm. From 1 by much smaller size and pink bill and legs. Habitat: rare outside main game reserves. U

3 **HOODED VULTURE** *Necrosyrtes monachus* L 70 cm. Note thin bill and dark underparts. Imm has dark down (no feathers) on head and neck. Habitat: rare outside main game reserves. U

4 **CAPE VULTURE** *Gyps coprotheres* L 115 cm. Note very large size and pale, brown appearance. Adult from 5 by pale eyes, pale blue, bare skin, dark centres of first row of upperwing coverts. Imm shows pink (not brownish), bare neck. See also imm 19.2. Habitat: only common in some areas of the Drakensberg and Transkei. U

5 **AFRICAN WHITE-BACKED VULTURE** *Gyps africanus* L 95 cm. From 4 by greyish-brown (not tawny-brown) colouring, blackish, bare skin. First row of upperwing coverts is only narrowly edged pale. White rump patch in flight diagnostic. Imm shows pale bars on underwing coverts. See also imm 19.2. Habitat: open, bushed and wooded habitats.

Plate 20

Plate 21

1   **BAT HAWK** *Macheiramphus alcinus*   L 45 cm. Note striking, large, yellow eyes. Hunts small bats and other prey at dusk in open spaces among trees or buildings or at cave mouths. In daytime perches quietly in well-foliaged trees. Habitat: forest edges, woodland, lake sides, seashores, towns. Voice: very high, sharp, fluted '*wiiiu-wiiiu-wiiiu-wiiiu*' slightly rising in pitch and volume. Also high '*wikkeh-wikkeh-wikkeh-wikke-wik-wik*'. U

2   **TAITA FALCON** *Falco fasciinucha*   L 30 cm. Small and compact appearance. Black above with grey rump and tail. Note large claws. Smaller and darker than 4. Chestnut nape patch diagnostic. Habitat: mountainous, dry, open country, normally near cliffs. U

3   **PEREGRINE FALCON** *Falco peregrinus*   L 35 cm. Race *minor* with black cheek and dense barring below shown. Race *calidus* (rare winter visitor, not shown) is larger, paler grey above and whiter below with less barring and spotting. Note compact build, short wings and tail when perched, pointed wings in flight. Flight with rather fluttering wing beats but extremely fast in attack and pursuit. Habitat: open country, sea coast, city centres. Often near cliffs or high buildings. U(S)

4   **LANNER FALCON** *Falco biarmicus*   L 40 cm. ♂♂ of the African races of the Lanner Falcon have almost plain underparts. Larger ♀♀ are browner above and more spotted below. Chestnut crown and nape of adult (whitish in imm) diagnostic. In flight rather pale. Habitat: open country, often near cliffs and buildings. May enter cities.

5   **RED-NECKED FALCON** *Falco chicquera*   L 30 cm. Note reddish head and pale grey, finely barred upperparts. Tail in perched bird much longer than wing tip. Flies (and hunts) in very swift flight without gliding. Habitat: open, tall-grassed or swampy areas. Prefers places with Borassus palms (a palm species with a characteristic swelling concentrated halfway up). U

6   **ELEONORA'S FALCON** *Falco eleonorae*   L 35 cm. Dark, blackish underwing diagnostic. Always appears dark (including pale **(a)** form) with long tail and exceptionally long and narrow wings. Easy, graceful flight with soft wing beats alternated with smooth gliding. Imm from imm 7 by thinner moustache and contrasting, pale flight feathers below. Habitat: migrates, probably at great heights, from Mediterranean breeding quarters to Madagascar. RS

7   (European) **HOBBY** *Falco subbuteo*   L 30 cm. Note slim build, rufous undertail coverts, streaked belly and underwing, short tail. Fast flier, may overtake swallows, but also catches flying termites. Habitat: forest edges, thornveld, more or less wooded, natural and cultivated areas. US

8   **AFRICAN HOBBY** *Falco cuvieri*   L 30 cm. More graceful, less compact than 2. Rump concolorous with rest of upperparts. Darker above than 7. Habitat: forest edges, open landscapes with scattered trees, densely populated, rural areas. U(brS)

Plate 21

Accipitridae 84

Plate 22

1   **DICKINSON'S KESTREL** *Falco dickinsoni*   L 30 cm. Barred tail and white rump diagnostic. Head paler than breast and mantle. Hunts from perch. Habitat: open woodland, plantations, edges of flood plains. Often near palms. U

2   **GREY KESTREL** *Falco ardosiaceus*   L 30 cm. From 3 by absence of moustachial stripe, faint barring of flight feathers below. Tail longer than wing tip when perched. Hunts at dusk from perch or in low flight over ground. Habitat: more or less wooded grassland, often near palms and water. U

3   **SOOTY FALCON** *Falco concolor*   L 30 cm. Rare, normal (**a**) and very rare, black (**b**) forms shown. Wing extends beyond tail tip. Note white chin, black moustache, absence of barring on underwing. Imm from all other immature falcons by lack of distinct eyebrow, except from 21.3, which is larger, shorter-tailed and with paler underwings. Normally hunts small birds from perch at dusk. Habitat: coastal areas near forests or tree stands. US

4   **EASTERN RED-FOOTED FALCON** *Falco amurensis*   L 30 cm. Perched ♂ is almost inseparable from ♂ 5 but is paler below, making black eye area more conspicuous. In flight, white underwing coverts diagnostic. The ♀ resembles several other falcons, but note red legs and eye ring. Imm from imm 5 by slightly whiter underparts. Habitat: open country. S

5   (Western) **RED-FOOTED FALCON** *Falco vespertinus*   L 30 cm. Black underwing of ♂ diagnostic. The ♀ resembles several other chestnut falcons but is much paler grey above and has red legs. Flight kestrel-like with much gliding but hardly any hovering. Hunts in flocks, catching mainly insects. Habitat: dry, open areas, cultivated lands. S

6   **GREATER KESTREL** *Falco rupicoloides*   L 35 cm. Pale eye of adult (visible at close range) diagnostic. From other kestrels by more uniform rufous colouring without cap or moustachial stripe and by relatively longer wings, which reach tail tip. Normally hunts from perch, taking small prey from ground. Habitat: dry, open country with scattered trees.

7   **LESSER KESTREL** *Falco naumanni*   L 30 cm. Normally in flocks. Often together with other falcons. From 8 (which is solitary) by less hovering and wing tip reaching tail tip. The ♀ from ♀ 8 by brown (not greyish) crown and uppertail. Habitat: open, bushed and wooded areas, short grass- and farmland. Flocks may roost in towns. S

8   **COMMON** (or Rock) **KESTREL** *Falco tinnunculus*   L 35 cm. The ♀ from ♂ by barred tail and subdued colouring. Imm from imm 6 by moustachial stripe and shorter wing. This is the common, hovering falcon seen at roadsides. Habitat: open or lightly wooded country, often near cliffs or tall buildings.

9   **PYGMY FALCON** *Polihierax semitorquatus*   L 18 cm. Perches shrike-like on top of tree or post. Roosts and breeds inside nests of Sociable Weavers (77.13). Habitat: more or less bushed areas and semi-desert where there are trees containing the large, communal nests of their host weavers. U

Plate 22

Megapodiidae Cracidae Meleagrididae Tetraonidae 23

Plate 23

Note: all ♂♂ francolins have 1 or 2 spurs (per leg), which are absent or reduced in ♀♀.

1   **RED-NECKED FRANCOLIN** *Francolinus afer*   L 35 cm. Races *castaneiventer* **(a)**, *swynnertoni* **(e)** and *cranchii* **(f)** shown. Forms *notatus* **(b)**, *lehmanni* **(c)** and *cunensis* **(d)** no longer recognised as races. Red legs and bare head parts diagnostic. Habitat: forest patches, other bushed and wooded, natural and cultivated areas with long grass. Voice: mid-high, indignant, hurried, descending '*kúkukruk-kúkukruk-kúkukruk*' or '*corrúpt-corrúpt-corrúpt*'.

2   **SWAINSON'S FRANCOLIN** *Francolinus swainsonii*   L 40 cm. Note black upper mandible and blackish legs. Habitat: extensively used grasslands, thornveld, open woodland. Voice: mid-high, loud, grating '*korrah korrah korrah-*'.

3   **RED-BILLED FRANCOLIN** *Francolinus adspersus*   L 35 cm. Note yellow eye ring, black lore, red bill and pink legs. Less shy than other francolins. Habitat: low scrub, riverine thickets, woodland edges. Voice: mid-high, loud, resounding, rising '*gukgukgukgukKírrik*'.

4   **NATAL FRANCOLIN** *Francolinus natalensis*   L 35 cm. Note pink bill and legs. Underparts paler than upperparts. Habitat: rocky, wooded hillsides, riverine thickets. Voice: very harsh, loud, excited '*kekkerrek kekkerrek kekkerrek*' or '*kurRúk kurRúk-*'.

5   **CAPE FRANCOLIN** *Francolinus capensis*   L 40 cm. Note large size, pink legs, pink, black-tipped upper mandible, white streaking on underparts, blackish tail in flight. Habitat: coastal fynbos, riverine scrub. Voice: high, cackled '*purwríut-purwríut-purpúpperwrans*'.

6   **ORANGE RIVER FRANCOLIN** *Francolinus levaillantoides*   L 35 cm. Forms nominate **(a)**, *langi* **(b)** and *pallidior* **(c)** are now placed together in one race (nominate). Note white chin, prominent, double necklaces, absence of black-and-white feathering on underparts. Habitat: dry, rocky, grassy, more or less wooded and bushed areas. Voice: very high, piercing '*turk-chéerup*'.

7   **REDWING FRANCOLIN** *Francolinus levaillantii*   L 40 cm. Note tawny-rufous throat surrounded by speckled necklace connected with speckled collar. Habitat: stony slopes, woodland with scrub, tall grass and reedy spots. Voice: very high, sharp '*tiktiktiktiktik-let's-GO-then*'.

8   **GREYWING FRANCOLIN** *Francolinus africanus*   L 35 cm. From 7 by 'reversed' neck and throat pattern. Belly finely spotted and barred black. Speckled throat diagnostic. Habitat: grassy slopes at all altitudes. Voice: very high, fluting '*weeweeh-weeweeh-*'.

9   **SHELLEY'S FRANCOLIN** *Francolinus shelleyi*   L 35 cm. Nominate **(a)** from 6 by black-and-white feathered belly and darker upperparts. Race *whytei* **(b)** from 7 by all-buff throat and greatly reduced mottling on upperparts. Habitat: stony, more or less wooded and bushed habitats, often with rocky outcrops. Voice: very high, sharp, fluting '*wukwuk-weekweek-wukwuk weekweek-*'.

10   **FINSCH'S FRANCOLIN** *Francolinus finschi*   L 35 cm. Note absence of black marking. Habitat: grassland near forest and woodland, at higher altitudes also on bare slopes. U E (Angola)

11   **CRESTED FRANCOLIN** *Francolinus sephaena*   L 35 cm. Nominate **(a)** and race *rovuma* **(b)** shown. Note prominent, white eyebrow, red legs and, in flight, black tail. Habitat: dry, bushed and shrubbed areas with some grass cover. Voice: mid-high, loud, scraping '*kurrk-KRí-kurrk-KRí*'.

12   **WHITE-THROATED FRANCOLIN** *Francolinus albogularis*   L 25 cm. Red wings, as 6, 7, 8, 9 and 10, but with different jizz and smaller bill. Note whitish chin. Habitat: dry, open areas with some grass cover, often near forest and water. R

13   **HARTLAUB'S FRANCOLIN** *Francolinus hartlaubi*   L 25 cm. Note small size, short eyebrow, large bill, black-streaked (♂) or rufous (♀) underparts. Habitat: slopes with large boulders. Voice: very high, excited, hurried '*near-here near-here near-here –*'. U

14   **COQUI FRANCOLIN** *Francolinus coqui*   L 30 cm. The ♀ from 6, 7, 8, 9 and 10 by smaller size, barred underparts and, in flight, absence of red in wings. Habitat: grassy, more or less wooded and bushed areas. Voice: very high, sharp: '*keh-kwee-keh-kwee-keh-kwee-*' or very high '*keh-kríh kehkerriiii*'.

15   **HILDEBRANDT'S FRANCOLIN** *Francolinus hildebrandti*   L 35 cm. Note scaly underparts of ♂, rufous underparts of ♀ and red legs of both. Habitat: rocky hillsides with rough grass. U

16   **GREY-STRIPED FRANCOLIN** *Francolinus griseostriatus*   L 35 cm. Note all-rufous colouring, red bill and legs. Habitat: dense undergrowth of forest and woodland. R E (Angola)

17   **SCALY FRANCOLIN** *Francolinus squamatus*   L 30 cm. From 3 by white chin and absence of yellow eye ring. Habitat: tall-grassed glades and forest edges. Voice: very high, hoarse, running-up '*skreetchuskreetchuskreetch–*'. R

▶

Plate 23

1 Red-necked Sp-fowl

2 Swainson's Sp-fowl

3 Red-billed Francolin

Crested Francolin

Hartlaub's Francolin

Coqui Francolin

Grey-striped Francolin

Phasianidae 25

Chukar

Plate 23 (çontinued)

18   **SWIERSTRA'S FRANCOLIN** *Francolinus swierstrai*   L 35 cm. Habitat: montane forest, grassy, rocky mountain slopes. R E (Angola)

19   **CHUKAR** *Alectoris chukar*   L 30 cm. Introduced on Robben Island (normal range Turkey–Korea). R

Plate 24

1   **AFRICAN WATER RAIL** *Rallus caerulescens*   L 30 cm. Secretive. Habitat: reed beds of marshes, lake margins, stream banks. Voice: very high, fluting, slowed down, slightly lowered, piping trill, ending in mid-high '- *piu piu piu*'.

2   **BLACK CRAKE** *Amaurornis flavirostris*   L 20 cm. Note yellow bill and red legs. Not secretive or shy. Habitat: edge of reed beds, papyrus, shrubbery at lake margins, dams, ponds, streams. Voice: high, excited chuckling, closely followed by a very low grunt '*retretretretret-growl*'.

3   **ALLEN'S** (or Lesser) **GALLINULE** *Porphyrio alleni*   L 25 cm. Note small size, blue shield and red legs. Shield in n-br plumage is almost brown. Imm from imm 4 by pale-orange (not greenish) legs and prominent, buffy scaling on upperparts. Habitat: marshes, inundations with tall grass and other vegetation. Voice: high, raucous '*kreeg-kreeg-kreeg*' or '*tuk tuk tuk*'. brS(W)

4   (American) **PURPLE GALLINULE** *Porphyrio martinica*   L 35 cm. Note pale blue shield, yellow legs and yellow-tipped bill. Imm (not shown) from imm 3 by almost yellow bill and far less buffy scaling above. Vagrant from America, normally arriving as brownish-buff sub-adult with blue feathering coming through on underparts. Voice: cackling '*tuk-tuk-tuk–*' (6 times or more). RW

5   **PURPLE SWAMPHEN** (or Gallinule) *Porphyrio porphyrio*   L 45 cm. Habitat: large swamps and shallow lakes with reeds, papyrus and floating vegetation. Voice: raucous, repeated, goose-like grunts, shrieks and cackles, like '*krieg-krieg-krieg-*' or '*tuk-tuk-tuk-*'.

6   **LESSER MOORHEN** *Gallinula angulata*   L 25 cm. Secretive. Habitat: dams, ponds, swamps, flood plains. Voice: very high, bouncing '*peek peek peek*' or hurried '*treektreektreek*'. brS.

7   **COMMON MOORHEN** *Gallinula chloropus*   L 30 cm. Habitat: fresh lakes, ponds, marshes with fringing vegetation. Voice: high, sharp, fast tinking: '*bekbekbek*' or '*wek wek wek -*'.

8   **RED-KNOBBED COOT** *Fulica cristata*   L 45 cm. Habitat: all types of quiet, fresh water bodies. Voice: mid-high, coughing '*uhurk uhurk*'.

9   **STRIPED CRAKE** *Aenigmatolimnas marginalis*   L 20 cm. Note rufous undertail and flanks. Habitat: dense vegetation in marshes, inundations and similar areas. Voice: mid-high, dry, fast, prolonged, mechanical trill, '*trrrrrrr-*'. UbrS

10   **SPOTTED CRAKE** *Porzana porzana*   L 20 cm. Note yellow bill with rosy base and extensive white spotting above and below. Secretive. Habitat: dense reeds and herbage in shallow parts of marshes, inundations, ponds. Voice: usually silent in Africa. Very high, lashing, '*wheet wheet wheet wheet -*'. US

11   **BAILLON'S CRAKE** *Porzana pusilla*   L 18 cm. From 12 by darker overall colouring, absence of rosy bill base, different leg colour. Note white-centred, black markings above. The ♂ and ♀ similar, but ♀ paler below. Habitat: reed beds and dense, tall vegetation in wet places. Voice: low, short, dry rattle, slackened just at the end. U

12   **LITTLE CRAKE** *Porzana parva*   L 20 cm. Note green legs and rosy-based bill. The ♂ and ♀ dissimilar. Habitat: swamps and other places with reeds and tall grass. Voice: e.g. high '*purrrr purrrr*' or nasal '*pweet pweet pweet pweet-pweet-pweetpweetpweet*'. R

13   **AFRICAN CRAKE** *Crex egregia*   L 25 cm. Note short bill, small, white eyebrow, bold flank barring, dark-centred feathers above. Secretive. Habitat: reed beds of marshes, lakes and streams. Voice: mid-high, loud, cackled '*kek-kek-krekkek-kek-kerrek kerrek -*'. UbrS

14   **CORNCRAKE** *Crex crex*   L 30 cm. Red wings in flight diagnostic. Habitat: prefers drier, grassy, cultivated and natural habitats. Sometimes near streams and vleis. Voice: silent in Africa. Low, dry double-rattle, '*crex-crex crex-crex*'. US

15   **CRESTED GUINEAFOWL** *Guttera pucherani*   L 50 cm. Habitat: dense undergrowth of forest and woodland. Voice: low, speeded-up cackles and rattles like '*tetrút-tetrút-trrrueh*'. U

16   **HELMETED GUINEAFOWL** *Numida meleagris*   L 55 cm. Habitat: dry, natural and cultivated areas with more or less tree cover, shrub and bush. Voice: high, fluted '*puWEEET puWEEET puWEEET*' ('*pu-*' barely audible).

Plate 24

Numididae 84

Plate 25

Note: Unlike flufftails, quails do not show dangling feet in flight and have faster wing beats than button-quails.

1   **AFRICAN BLUE QUAIL** *Coturnix adansonii*   L 15 cm. The ♂ from other quails by red wings, ♀ from other ♀♀ quails by barred (not streaked) underparts. Not gregarious. Habitat: moist, open grassland near swamps. Voice: mid-high, descending, hoarse '*wéhwehweh-wéhwehweh -*'. U

2   **HARLEQUIN QUAIL** *Coturnix delegorguei*   L 18 cm. The ♂ from 1 by white eyebrow. Note black streaks on back and head of ♀. Slightly gregarious. Habitat: slightly bushed grass- and farmland. Voice: very high, clicked, irregular '*witwit witwit-wit witwit witwit witwit-wit*'. U

3   **COMMON QUAIL** *Coturnix coturnix*   L 18 cm. The ♂ from ♀ 2 by white streaks along flanks, ♀ by paler and less buffy colouring. Flight, as all quails, with rapid wing beats interspersed with short glides. Habitat: dry areas with grass or crops of varied height. Voice: very high, liquid, staccato, rapid '*getmethen-getmethen*'. S

4   **BLACK-RUMPED BUTTON-QUAIL** *Turnix hottentotta*   L 14 cm. From quails by more rufous plumage and creamy eye. Long, buff streaks along scapulars diagnostic. In flight looks long-necked and shows pale upperwing coverts. Habitat: short, partly bare grassland and floodplains. Voice: strange, very low, pumping, regular '*wuh-wuh-wuh-wuh–*'. U(S)

5   **LITTLE** (or Kurrichane) **BUTTON-QUAIL** *Turnix sylvatica*   L 14 cm. From 4 by absence of black rump in flight. Habitat: tall grass- and farmland. Voice: strange, very low, hollow, slightly crescendoing '*woooooo woooooooooh*'.

6   **CHESTNUT-HEADED FLUFFTAIL** *Sarothrura lugens*   L 15 cm. Black-tailed ♂ from 7 and 8 by absence of rufous on breast, ♀ from other ♀♀ flufftails by streaked (not barred or blotched) plumage. Habitat: tall, wet grassland near marshes, woodland or forest. Voice: long sequence of slowly speeded-up '*oohoohooh–*' slightly rising in pitch and volume and trailing off at the end. Also mid-high '*ooeh ooeh ooeh -*' ('*ooeh*' repeated twice every 3 seconds). R

7   **BOEHM'S** (or Streaky-breasted) **FLUFFTAIL** *Sarothrura boehmi*   L 15 cm. The ♂ from 8 by whitish chin and belly and very short tail; ♂ and ♀ have pale lower mandible. Habitat: short, wet grassland, inundations and river margins. Voice: mid-high, level, rhythmic, hooted '*hooh hooh hooh -*', also with shorter intervals, and '*uhooh-uhooh-uhooh–*' ('*u-*' as very low undertone). RbrS

8   **RED-CHESTED FLUFFTAIL** *Sarothrura rufa*   L 16 cm. See 7. Habitat: marshy reed beds and papyrus swamp, thick herbage and tall grass near rivers and pools. Voice: mid-high, hooted '*hoo hoo hoo hoo-*' often in duet with very high contra-song, '*piu piu piu -*' ('*hoo*' and '*piu*' alternating). Also a call resembling alarm cry of Blacktailed Godwit (27.4).

9   **STRIPED FLUFFTAIL** *Sarothrura affinis*   L 15 cm. Nominate **(a)** from 6 by red tail (♂) or buff-orange, black-striped tail (♀). Race *antonii* **(b)** from all other red-tailed and -breasted flufftails by white throat and streaking below. Habitat: dry grassland (unlike 6). Voice: mid-high, thin, hollow '*hooo hooo hooo -*' (25 times per minute), each '*hooo*' crescendoing. Also a mid-high, sharp rattle, ending in prolonged '*wekwekwekwek*'.

10   **WHITE-SPOTTED FLUFFTAIL** *Sarothrura pulchra*   L 15 cm. Note pale eye of ♂ and ♀. Habitat: swampy forest and surrounding areas with tree cover. Voice: high, hurried, hooted '*poopoopoopoopoo*', mid-high, fluted, rapid, slightly speeded-up '*poo-poo-poo-poo-poo–*' and very fast, high '*tutitititi*'.

11   **BUFF-SPOTTED FLUFFTAIL** *Sarothrura elegans*   L 16 cm. From 10 by barred tail. The ♀ lacks clear diagnostic features. Habitat: forest, bamboo, dense bush, cultivation, gardens with dense undergrowth. Voice: low, hollow, level, crescendoing '*hooooo-*' (3 seconds) and extreme low, hollow, rolling '*rurururu–*'.

12   **WHITE-WINGED FLUFFTAIL** *Sarothrura ayresi*   L 15 cm. Habitat: marshes, reed beds, rough, wet grass. Voice: low '*oow-oow-oow-oow–*' (each '*oow*' lashed-up) and other rhythmic calls of pigeon-like quality. Rbr?S

13   **AFRICAN JACANA** *Actophilornis africana*   L 30 cm. Note white underparts of imm. Habitat: swamps, lakes, ponds, slow streams with floating vegetation. Voice: high, often descending, yelping '*wetwetwetwet-wetwet-wet-wet–*' or mid-high '*weh-weh-weh-weh–*'.

14   **LESSER JACANA** *Micromparra capensis*   L 15 cm. Adult from imm 13 by much smaller size, paler upperparts and chestnut (not black) nape. Habitat: as 13. Voice: very high, fast, angry '*diditititi–*' U

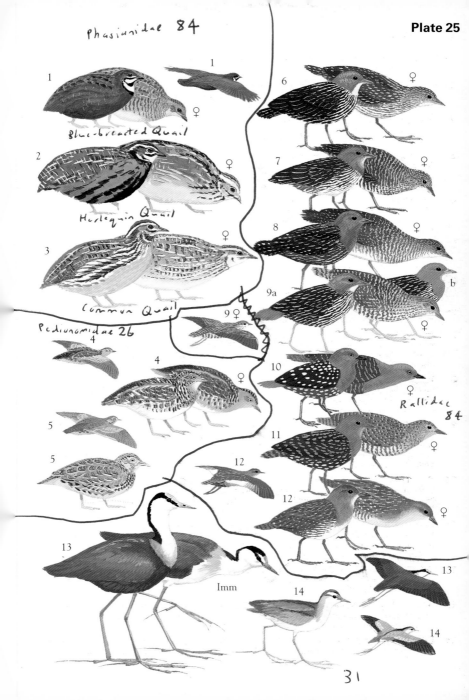

Plate 25

Phasianidae 84

1

1 ♀

Blue-breasted Quail

2 ♀

Harlequin Quail

3 ♀

Common Quail

Pedionomidae 26

4

4 ♀

5

5

13

Imm

6 ♀

7 ♀

8 ♀

9a

9 ♀

9 b ♀

10 ♀

Rallidae 84

11 ♀

12

12 ♀

13

14

14

31

Plate 26

1   **WATTLED CRANE** *Bugeranus carunculatus*   H 125 cm. Note black belly in flight. Habitat: shallow water of wet, wide-open areas. U

2   **BLUE CRANE** *Anthropoides paradisea*   H 105 cm. In flight, from 1 by grey belly. Habitat: natural and cultivated, open areas with or without low scrub.

3   **GREY** (or Southern) **CROWNED CRANE** *Balearica regulorum*   H 95 cm. Unmistakable. Habitat: roosts and nests in or near wet places but feeds in open or wooded grass- and farmland.

4   **SECRETARY BIRD** *Sagittarius serpentarius*   H 90 cm. Unmistakable. Habitat: dry, open, bushed and wooded, natural or cultivated areas.

5   **KORI BUSTARD** *Ardeotis kori*   H 85 cm. Note predominantly grey wings in flight. From other bustards by shaggy neck feathers. Habitat: dry, open plains with some trees and bush. U

6   **DENHAM'S** (or Stanley's) **BUSTARD** *Neotis denhami*   H 75 cm. Note facial pattern, large, black-and-white area on folded wing, tawny-rufous hindneck. From 7 by grey foreneck, mainly black upperprimary coverts. Habitat: slightly wooded, natural and cultivated areas. U

7   **LUDWIG'S BUSTARD** *Neotis ludwigii*   H 70 cm. Note darkish head, small, white spots on mantle and scapulars. Upperprimary coverts mainly white. Habitat: dry areas, especially in the Karoo and Namib desert. U

8   **RUEPPELL'S KORHAAN** *Eupodotis rueppellii*   H 50 cm. Note pale head and neck with streaks down neck and throat. From 11 by plain (not barred) upperparts and mainly cream upperwing in flight. Habitat: vast, dry plains with sparse grass or scrub.

9   **KAROO KORHAAN** *Eupodotis vigorsii*   H 50 cm. From 8 by small, black patches only on throat and nape (which can be puffed-up and -out in display). Also shows much more dark brown on wing in flight. Habitat: dry scrubland of the Karoo and Namib desert with adjacent, cultivated grass- and croplands.

10   **BLUE KORHAAN** *Eupodotis caerulescens*   H 50 cm. Note blue colouring of underparts and on upperwing. Habitat: open, short grasslands.

11   **WHITE-BELLIED BUSTARD** *Eupodotis senegalensis*   H 45 cm. Note blue (in front) and sandy-brown (backside) colouring of neck of ♂. From 8 and 9 by red-based bill. The ♀ from ♀ 12 by different jizz with much shorter neck and legs and paler underwing. Habitat: grassy, lightly bushed and wooded parts (often near streams) of natural and cultivated areas.

12   **BLACK-BELLIED BUSTARD** *Eupodotis melanogaster*   H 55 cm. Note striking, long, thin neck and legs, narrow, black stripe running up front of neck and extensively white upperwing. The ♀ from ♀♀ 8, 9 and 11 by blackish-brown, not (partly) creamy-buff, wings. Habitat: tall grassland with some trees and lightly wooded farmland.

13   (Red-) **CRESTED BUSTARD** *Eupodotis ruficrista*   H 50 cm. Reddish crest normally concealed. The ♂ and ♀ from ♀♀ 14 and 15 by different pattern on upperparts (chevrons instead of fine barring). Note the two conspicuous, white patches within the black area of the breast. Habitat: open woodland, locally in treeless grasslands.

14   **WHITE-WINGED BLACK KORHAAN** *Eupodotis afraoides*   H 45 cm. The ♂ from ♂ 15 by white area in wing and darker crown, ♀ by finer, regular barring of upperparts. Habitat: open, dry grassland locally mixed with shrub- and woodland.

15   **BLACK KORHAAN** *Eupodotis afra*   H 45 cm. See 14. Habitat: extensive, lightly wooded grassland. E (South Africa).

Aramidae Psophiidae 24

Plate 26

21

Stanley Bustard

Kori Bustard

25

Ludwig's Bustard

Rueppell's Bustard

Karoo Bustard

Blue Bustard

white-bellied Bustard

Black-bellied Bustard

Red-crested Bustard

Black Bustard

Plate 27

1 **EURASIAN AVOCET** *Recurvirostra avosetta* L 40 cm. Unmistakable. Habitat: feeds and rests knee-deep in water along lake edges, estuary streams, seashore. (S)

2 **BAR-TAILED GODWIT** *Limosa lapponica* L 40 cm. In n-br plumage (normally seen in Southern Africa) from 3 and 4 by finely striped upperparts and neck. Note slightly upturned bill, barred tail, absence of wing bar, non-protruding feet in flight. Habitat: rarely away from the sea coast. Voice: high '*witwit witwitwit*'. S

3 **HUDSONIAN GODWIT** *Limosa haemastica* L 40 cm. Jizz more like 2 than like 4. Thin bill slightly upturned. Note diagnostic, black underwing. Habitat: vagrant from America at the coast. RS

4 **BLACK-TAILED GODWIT** *Limosa limosa* L 40 cm. Note long legs and neck, absence of streaking on n-br plumage, white wing bar and underwing, black tail. Habitat: in this part of Africa seen more at inland waters. Voice: silent in Africa. US

5 **EURASIAN OYSTERCATCHER** *Haematopus ostralegus* L 45 cm. Unmistakable. Habitat: open, sandy and rocky shores (mainly) at sea. RS(W)

6 **AFRICAN BLACK OYSTERCATCHER** *Haematopus moquini* L 45 cm. Unmistakable. Habitat: at or very near the seashore.

7 **COMMON** (or Black-winged) **STILT** *Himantopus himantopus* L 40 cm. Note variable, not sex-related head markings (**a** and **b**), but ♀ with browner mantle and wings. Habitat: shallow lakes, estuaries, inundations. Rarely at the open sea coast.

8 **EGYPTIAN-PLOVER** *Pluvianus aegyptius* L 20 cm. Unmistakable. Habitat: sandy river banks, lake shores. U

9 **CRAB PLOVER** *Dromas ardeola* L 40 cm. Unmistakable. Habitat: sea coast, estuaries, lagoons. S(W)

10 **WHIMBREL** *Numenius phaeopus* L 45 cm. Note white streak over middle of crown, diagnostic, dark streaks on head above and below eyebrow. From 11 also by smaller size, darker upperparts and flight feathers. Habitat: mainly seashore and other coastal areas. Voice: diagnostic call sounds as high, rapid '*bibibibibibibi*' (7 times '*bi*'). S

11 **EURASIAN CURLEW** *Numenius arquata* L 55 cm. Larger and longer-billed than all other shorebirds. Habitat: sea and lake shores, estuaries, sand dunes, river banks, grassland. Voice: high, beautiful, liquid, mellow, slightly trilled '*fruuwfuuifuuui*'. S(W)

12 **SPOTTED THICK-KNEE** *Burhinus capensis* L 45 cm. From 13 by spotted upperparts. Note conspicuous, large eye, absence of grey wing bar, small, white spots on flight feathers. Habitat: open, dry, rocky river beds and other arid, more or less wooded, natural and cultivated areas. Voice: very high, slightly undulating, yelping '*wuuiwuuiwuui–*' at night.

13 **WATER THICK-KNEE** *Burhinus vermiculatus* L 40 cm. Note grey-and-white wing bar. Habitat: prefers wetter habitats than 12. River banks, lake shores, estuaries, lagoons. Voice: very high, sharp '*tjeetjuutju–*' (15–20 times), first half speeded-up and rising, second half slackened and falling off, heard at night.

14 **RUDDY TURNSTONE** *Arenaria interpres* L 23 cm. Note characteristic jizz (drawn-in head, hunched body, short legs). Black crescents on sides of breast (br and n-br) diagnostic. Habitat: normally at rocky seashore. SW

Plate 27

27

1

1

9

9

2 N-br
Br

2

10

10

Scolopacidae
29

3

Br

3

11

11

4 N-br

Br ♀

4

12

5

Br

12

N-br

5 N-br
Ibidorhynchidae
27

13

Burhinidae
84

6

6

13

7

a

b

Imm

7

27

8

N-br

14

14

Br

Glareolidae 32

Plate 28

1   **RINGED PLOVER** *Charadrius hiaticula*   L 16 cm. Note orange-pink bill base and legs. From 2 by obscure eye ring and white wing bar in flight. Imm has dark breast patches (almost forming a collar) and pinkish (not yellow) legs. Habitat: seashore, lake edges, river banks. Occasionally away from water. S(W)

2   **LITTLE RINGED PLOVER** *Charadrius dubius*   L 15 cm. From 1 by yellow legs and eye ring, absence of wing bar and all-black bill (except base of lower mandible in br plumage). Habitat: lake margins; avoids the seashore. R

3   **THREE-BANDED PLOVER** *Charadrius tricollaris*   L 18 cm. Note long eyebrows forming complete circle around cap, grey (not brown) face sides and narrow, white wing bar. Habitat: edges of ponds, streams, sewage ponds. Rarely at salt water.

4   **FORBES'S PLOVER** *Charadrius forbesi*   L 19 cm. Eyebrows only connected on nape, not on forehead. From 3 by brown face sides and absence of wing bar. Note long, tapered jizz. Habitat: open, more or less grassy places away from water, but occasionally on mud flats at lakes and river sides. U

5   **KITTLITZ'S PLOVER** *Charadrius pecuarius*   L 16 cm. From most other small plovers by absence of dark breast band or patches. Note dark, brown (not grey) upperparts, diagnostic, buff breast and isolated, white throat. Imm has unique, buff face. Habitat: dry, short grass near lakes and dams, sandy and muddy edges of lakes and streams.

6   **CHESTNUT-BANDED PLOVER** *Charadrius pallidus*   L 15 cm. Narrow, chestnut breast band diagnostic. The ♂ from ♀ by small, black frontal patch. Note grey colouring of upperparts. Flies with projecting feet. Imm has pale, almost white neck and necklace interrupted at front. Habitat: brackish lagoons, lakes, dams. Avoids fresh water or the actual sea coast. U

7   **KENTISH PLOVER** *Charadrius alexandrinus*   L 16 cm. Note interrupted, black necklace of ♂. In all plumages with striking, white hindneck and dark, brownish-grey upperparts. Imm from imm 8 by reduced buff feather edging and darker cheeks. Habitat: muddy beaches at the coast, lagoons. R

8   **WHITE-FRONTED PLOVER** *Charadrius marginatus*   L 18 cm. Very pale plumage lacking breast band and patches. Longer-tailed and shorter-legged than 7. Most ♂♂ less rufous than shown. Habitat: sandy and rocky seashores, lake sides, river banks.

9   **CASPIAN PLOVER** *Charadrius asiaticus*   L 22 cm. Note tall, slender profile, small head, thin bill, long legs. Prominent eyebrow, giving capped appearance. In flight shows faint wing bar, dusky underwing, little white at tail sides and protruding feet. Habitat: prefers dry places, even in coastal areas: short grass, burnt ground, sand dunes. S

10   **GREATER SAND PLOVER** *Charadrius leschenaultii*   L 22 cm. From 11 by larger size, taller stance, heavier bill, paler and longer legs, feet protruding in flight. The ♂ from ♂ 11 by more extensive rufous on nape, ♀ by less black marking on head. N-br plumage from n-br 11 by longer, black lores. Habitat: open seashore and other open, sandy and muddy coastal places. Occasionally at lakes. Voice: call more trilling than 11. S

11   **MONGOLIAN PLOVER** *Charadrius mongolus*   L 19 cm. Note reduced black on lore of n-br plumage. Smaller, darker-legged and finer-billed than 10. Habitat: as 10. S

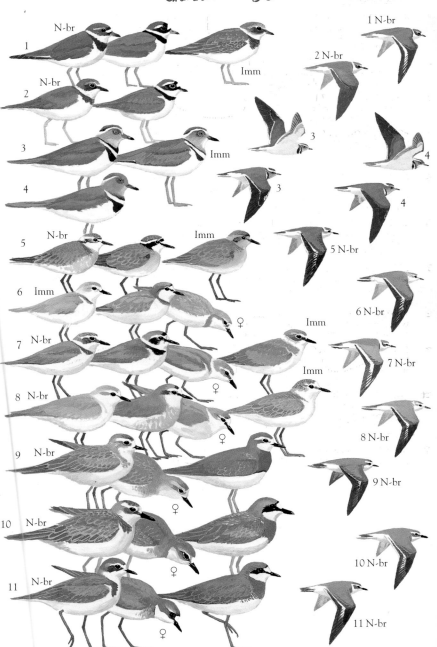

Plate 28

Charadriidae 30

Plate 29

1 **RED KNOT** *Calidris canutus* L 25 cm. Note large size, greenish legs and finely barred flanks of n-br plumage. In flight shows seemingly grey rump and unmarked tail. Habitat: seashore and other coastal habitats. S(W)

2 **CURLEW SANDPIPER** *Calidris ferruginea* L 19 cm. Note white rump in flight, long legs and gradually curved bill. N-br plumage with little or no streaking on breast. Habitat: prefers coastal areas, but occasionally found also at muddy, fresh water and alkaline lake sides, dams, pans, inundations. S(W)

3 **DUNLIN** *Calidris alpina* L 18 cm. From 2 by shorter bill, which is curved at tip, absence of eyebrow and shorter legs. Note black stripe through middle of rump in flight. Habitat: normally in coastal areas but is seen at inland dams. RS

4 **SANDERLING** *Calidris alba* L 19 cm. Winter plumage is very pale with darker shoulder. Br plumage (rarely seen in Africa) often less colourful than shown. Conspicuous, white wing bar in flight. Habitat: actual seashore. Runs up and down the beach with each advancing and retreating wave. S(W)

5 **PECTORAL SANDPIPER** *Calidris melanotos* L 19 cm. Note sharp demarcation between white underparts and grey breast. Bill has pale base and there is a faint wing bar in flight. Habitat: marsh, wet grassland, muddy water edges. Rarely at the coast. RS

6 **WHITE-RUMPED SANDPIPER** *Calidris fuscicollis* L 17 cm. Note long wings clearly projecting beyond tail, slightly decurved bill, unmarked upperparts of n-br plumage, flesh-coloured base of lower mandible. In flight, white rump diagnostic. Habitat: coastal mudflats, estuaries, inland pools, marshes. RS

7 **BAIRD'S SANDPIPER** *Calidris bairdii* L 17 cm. Note long, tapered jizz with wing tips clearly projecting beyond tail, brown-scaled (not grey-scaled) upperparts and streaked breast of n-br plumage. Habitat: inland and coastal areas, shallow pools, lagoons, edges of marshes. RS

8 **LITTLE STINT** *Calidris minuta* L 14 cm. In n-br plumage very difficult to separate from other small stints, especially from 9, which is less compact, slightly shorter-legged and prefers another habitat. Habitat: more at fresh water bodies than at the actual seashore. SW

9 **RUFOUS-** (or Red-) **NECKED STINT** *Calidris ruficollis* L 14 cm. Note black legs as 8 but is slightly longer-tapered. Habitat: normally at the seashore but could be seen together with 8 at inland waters. RS

10 **TEMMINCK'S STINT** *Calidris temminckii* L 14 cm. Note uniform grey breast and upperparts, greenish (not black) legs, narrow, black line from rump to tail tip. Habitat: marsh pools, muddy lake edges. Unlikely to be found at the seashore. RS

11 **LONG-TOED STINT** *Calidris subminuta* L 14 cm. From 8, 9 and 10 by longer neck when stretched in alarm. Note yellowish legs. Habitat: normally at muddy lake edges but in Southern Africa mainly seen near the sea. RS

12 **BROAD-BILLED SANDPIPER** *Limicola falcinellus* L 17 cm. Note striped head, kinked bill, greenish legs. Habitat: muddy and sandy sea and lake shores. RS

Plate 30

Note: lapwings are called plovers in most African field guides.

1 **BLACK-WINGED LAPWING** *Vanellus melanopterus* L 25 cm. Note white forehead and eyebrow gradually becoming grey on nape and cheeks. From 3 by red (not black) legs. See diagnostic, upper- and underwing pattern. Imm shows buff eyebrow and foreneck. Habitat: prefers grassland and burnt ground at higher altitudes. U

2 **CROWNED LAPWING** *Vanellus coronatus* L 30 cm. Imm from adult by yellow (not red) bare parts. Noisy. Habitat: drier areas with more or less short, grass cover and some shrub and trees. Often at airfields, golf courses. Voice: high, loud, grating '*kreeep*' or '*kreekreekreekreeip*', especially in flight.

3 **LESSER BLACK-WINGED LAPWING** *Vanellus lugubris* L 22 cm. Note sharp demarcation of white on forehead. Wing pattern diagnostic. Imm lacks distinct eyebrow. Habitat: dry, open, short grassland with some shrub at lower altitudes. U

4 **AFRICAN WATTLED LAPWING** *Vanellus senegallus* L 35 cm. Note large size. From 6 by more uniform colouring. Habitat: bare, muddy, sandy or short-grassed ground near marshes and lakes, pond and river shores.

5 **LONG-TOED LAPWING** *Vanellus crassirostris* L 30 cm. Unmistakable. Habitat: floating vegetation at lake shores and calm river banks, large swamps, inundations.

6 **WHITE-HEADED** (or -crowned) **LAPWING** *Vanellus albiceps* L 30 cm. From 4 by all-white underparts and different upperwing pattern. Habitat: sandy river banks in forested areas.

7 **BLACKSMITH LAPWING** *Vanellus armatus* L 30 cm. Unmistakable. Habitat: dry, muddy or marshy shores of lakes, dams, ponds, lagoons, swamps. Voice: extreme high, metallic '*tinktink -*' (hence the species' name).

8 **BROWN-CHESTED LAPWING** *Vanellus superciliosus* L 25 cm. Imm from imm 1 and 3 by bulkier build, darker crown, less fierce eye, less projecting primaries, different range. Habitat: dry, short grassland, bare fields, often near river and lake shores. R

9 **SPUR-WINGED LAPWING** *Vanellus spinosus* L 25 cm. Habitat: normally at bare, sandy or muddy and grassy lake shores and river banks. R

10 **BUFF-BREASTED SANDPIPER** *Tryngites subruficollis* L 18 cm. Imm (shown) as adult, which has narrower, pale feather edges. Note plump, small-headed, short-billed jizz. Pale ring as white 'lips' around bill base. Habitat: marshes and short grassland. RS

11 **RUFF** (♂), **REEVE** (♀) *Philomachus pugnax* L 30 cm (♂), 24 cm (♀). The ♂♂ attain spectacular br plumages, which are not, however, (fully) seen in Africa. From 10 by (much) larger size and diagnostic, white, oval patches at either side of rump. Habitat: river banks, lake edges, dams, inundations. S

12 **GREY PLOVER** *Pluvialis squatarola* L 30 cm. From 13 and 14 in n-br plumage by larger size and heavier bill. Note diagnostic, black armpit. Habitat: mainly seashore, lagoons; rarely at lakes and pools. S(W)

13 **AMERICAN** (or Lesser) **GOLDEN PLOVER** *Pluvialis dominica* L 25 cm. In br and n-br plumage with larger, dark centres to feathers of upperparts, making this species look darker, less bright than 14. Primary projection beyond tertials shows four primaries, while 14 shows three (but beware of wing moult). Feet of flying bird project more than 14. Habitat: in America, short grassland away from the coast, but for Southern Africa see map. RS

14 **PACIFIC GOLDEN PLOVER** *Pluvialis fulva* L 25 cm. See 13. Habitat: normally in freshwater habitats in coastal regions. R

Plate 30

27

Plate 31

1 **GREATER YELLOWLEGS** *Tringa melanoleuca* L 30 cm. Bill longer than head and slightly upturned. Less approachable than 2. Habitat: in America, from where it comes as a vagrant, normally at inland lakes, marshes, lagoons, mudflats in coastal areas. R

2 **LESSER YELLOWLEGS** *Tringa flavipes* L 25 cm. Bill same length as head and straight. Body looks more tapered and longer-winged than 1. Habitat: another vagrant from America where it is found in all types of coastal and inland wetlands. RS

3 **COMMON GREENSHANK** *Tringa nebularia* L 30 cm. Note large size, grey-and-white colouring, upturned, pale-based bill, green legs, long, white, rump wedge. From 8 by much larger size and heavier, upturned bill. Habitat: muddy shores, river banks, pools, lagoons. Voice: high, melodious 'tjuutjuutjuu-' ('tjuu' 3 times or more). SW

4 **SPOTTED REDSHANK** *Tringa erythropus* L 30 cm. Note large size, slender build, prominent, white eyebrow (n-br), long, red-based bill. Streaked rump and tail look grey in flight with only a small wedge into back. Pale, finely speckled secondaries look paler than rest of (opened) upperwing. From red-legged 7 by more slender jizz with longer bill and legs. Habitat: muddy and marshy pools and river banks. RS

5 **GREEN SANDPIPER** *Tringa ochropus* L 20 cm. Compact jizz with short neck and legs. Note white eye ring and narrow, black lore. In flight looks very dark above (also on underwing) with contrasting, square, white, rump patch. Habitat: sheltered pools, streams, creeks, sewage ponds. Voice: very loud 'weereet-weet-weet' when flushed. US

6 **WOOD SANDPIPER** *Tringa glareola* L 20 cm. Note slender profile, yellowish-green legs, long, diffuse eyebrow. From 5, in flight, by further protruding feet and paler overall colouring. Habitat: secluded parts of marshes, inundations, pools, creeks, sewage ponds. Voice: very high, staccato, slightly descending 'tritrititit'. S(W)

7 **COMMON REDSHANK** *Tringa totanus* L 30 cm. Note compact build, red legs, black-tipped bill. Broad, white trailing edge to upperwing and wedge on back are diagnostic. Habitat: short grass near and at edges of lakes, ponds, streams, seashore, creeks, estuaries. Voice: in flight, high 'Tjuu-wuh'. Alarm call 'tiutiutiu-'. US

8 **MARSH SANDPIPER** *Tringa stagnatilis* L 30 cm. Note fine, needle-like bill, very white underparts, dark wing shoulders in n-br plumage. From 3 by finer, more slender build and fine, needle-like bill. Habitat: muddy and marshy lake shores, river banks, streams, pools. Voice: very high, sharp 'tsjik tsjik tsjik-tsjik-' when flushed. S

9 **SOLITARY SANDPIPER** *Tringa solitaria* L 20 cm. Note dark rump and banded tail sides. Habitat: vagrant from America where it inhabits marshes, muddy shores of streams and ponds. R

10 **COMMON SANDPIPER** *Actitis hypoleucos* L 20 cm. Tail projects beyond wing tip. Note white patch in front of folded wing. Prominent, white wing bar in flight diagnostic. Habitat: short grass near and at edge of lakes, ponds, streams, seashore, creeks, estuaries. Voice: extreme high, sharp 'feetfeetfeet' when flushed. S(W)

11 **TEREK SANDPIPER** *Xenus cinereus* L 25 cm. Note yellow-based, upturned bill, yellow legs and black V-mark (faint in n-br plumage) on back. White trailing edge to upperwing as 7 but no white wedge into back. Habitat: seashore, muddy lake, creek and river edges. S(W)

12 **GREATER PAINTED-SNIPE** *Rostratula benghalensis* L 24 cm. Note the down-curving bill and the pale line, which makes the wings appear separate from the body. Normally skulking and crepuscular. When flushed flies away with dangling feet. Habitat: muddy places in fringing vegetation of lakes, dams, ponds, slow rivers. Voice: mid-high, rather pigeon-like 'wákkuh-wákkuh' or 'ukrúk ukrúk'. U

13 **JACK SNIPE** *Lymnocryptes minimus* L 19 cm. Note small size, double eyebrow, dark line through crown and absence of white or rufous in tail. Difficult to flush but if so it rises silently and flies straight away over only 50–100 m before dropping down into cover again. Habitat: swamps, short-grassed lake shores, inundations. R

14 **AFRICAN SNIPE** *Gallinago nigripennis* L 30 cm. Note long bill, short wings, dark upperparts, contrasting white belly. White outer tail feathers obscured by black barring. When flushed rises explosively and steeply, calling 'tsjuk', and zigzags (but less so than 16) away before dropping into cover within 100–200 m. Habitat: moorland, marshes, grassy lake shores and inundations at higher elevations. Voice: ♂ ♂ produce quivering roars with spread tail in display flight.

▶

Plate 31

Plate 31 (continued)

15 GREAT SNIPE *Gallinago media* L 30 cm. Note striking, white wing bar, faint, white trailing edge to secondaries, extensive, white outer tail feathers, barred belly, spotted (not barred) neck sides. When flushed at 5–10 m shoots away at shallow angle, silently or with soft *'itch-itch'*, flies in straight line and disappears abruptly into cover within 30–50 m. Habitat: swamp and lake edges, also in short, wet grass away from water. US(W)

16 COMMON SNIPE *Gallinago gallinago* L 25 cm. From 14 by less contrast between upper- and underparts, shorter bill and relatively longer wings. Tail predominantly rufous with narrow, white margins. When flushed at 10–15 m rises steeply and explosively, calls *'tweek'* 1–2 times while zigzagging away; sometimes circles around before dropping into cover within 200–300 m. Habitat: marshes, grassy lake shores, inundations. (Range differs from that of 14.) US

Plate 32

1 BLACK-WINGED PRATINCOLE *Glareola nordmanni* L 25 cm. Note absence of white trailing edge to wing in flight. From 2 also by darker appearance and black underwing. Wing projects beyond tail tip in perched bird. Habitat: open, sandy areas with some grass near lakes, rivers. Rarely at the sea coast. S

2 COLLARED (or Red-winged) PRATINCOLE *Glareola pratincola* L 25 cm. Note white trailing edge to wing. Underwing is dark reddish. Wings not longer than tail. Open areas near lakes, rivers, seashore. brW

3 ROCK PRATINCOLE *Glareola nuchalis* L 18 cm. Note white cheek and bar on underwing. Habitat: rocky, river and lake shores; also on sandy and muddy beaches. brS

4 MADAGASCAR PRATINCOLE *Glareola ocularis* L 24 cm. Note very short tail (perched and in flight) and partly rufous belly. From 2 also by brighter, rufous underwing. Habitat: open lake and seashores, muddy (not rocky) river banks. S

5 TEMMINCK'S COURSER *Cursorius temminckii* L 20 cm. Note orange (-rufous) crown, small, black breast patch, all-black flight feathers. Habitat: dry, more or less bushed habitats, bare fields, burnt ground. Voice: high, hooted, unhurried *'hak hak hak zunk'* (*'zunk'* slightly lower and inhaled).

6 BURCHELL'S COURSER *Cursorius rufus* L 21 cm. Note partly grey crown, grey band across belly, white secondaries. Habitat: arid areas with more or less grass cover. Voice: rather silent. U

7 DOUBLE-BANDED COURSER *Cursorius africanus* L 22 cm. Note two narrow, black bands across breast and (in flight) rufous in wings. Mainly active at night. Habitat: arid and dry areas with little grass and occasionally some scrub. Voice: mid-high, dry rattles, high, scolding, sharp *'sheet-sheet'* and very high, piercing *'fifififi–'* in several variations, all heard at night.

8 THREE-BANDED COURSER *Cursorius cinctus* L 25 cm. Note white underwing and complicated collar pattern. Nocturnal. Habitat: dry, open woodland and thornveld. Voice: high, excited, staccato yelps, *'wew wew wew -'*, heard after dark.

9 BRONZE-WINGED COURSER *Cursorius chalcopterus* L 25 cm. Note large, red-rimmed eye. Beautiful, purple tips of flight feathers not visible in folded wing. Nocturnal. Habitat: more or less wooded and bushed areas. Voice: strange, high, peacock-like, repeated *'miáu-gh'* at night.

10 WILSON'S PHALAROPE *Phalaropus tricolor* L 23 cm. Straggler from America. Swims less and forages more on land than 11 and 12, from which it differs also by all-white rump. Rather plump yet graceful. In n-br plumage shows long, thin bill, no black eye patch, yellow legs (black in br plumage), no wing bar, no stripe through middle of rump. Note: legs of br ♂ should be black, not pale yellowish as shown on plate. Habitat: in America, normally at inland waters, marshes. RS

11 RED-NECKED PHALAROPE *Phalaropus lobatus* L 18 cm. From 12 by short, needle-like bill. N-br plumage is darker above than 12 so white wing bar in flight is better defined and striking. Habitat: open sea, large lakes, occasionally at pools and sewage ponds. US

12 GREY PHALAROPE *Phalaropus fulicarius* L 20 cm. From 11 by less slender jizz and stubbier bill. Habitat: normally at open sea, rarely on inland waters. S

Plate 32

Plate 33

1   **SOUTH POLAR SKUA** *Catharacta maccormicki*   L 55 cm. Of several colour forms, pale **(a)**, dark **(b)** and intermediate **(c**, in flight) forms shown. Note cold-brown wings of all forms. Dark form has densely golden-striped neck. Imm (not shown) as **c** but without pale feather edging (which makes it look cleaner) and with bi-coloured bill (as e.g. imm 3). Habitat: open sea. RW

2   **BROWN** (or Subantarctic) **SKUA** *Catharacta lonnbergi*   L 65 cm. Note very heavy bill, uniform warm-brown colouring, fine, pale streaks on neck sides, variable amount of pale blotching on mantle feathers. Imm (not shown) as adult but normally slightly darker. Habitat: open sea, seashore. W(S)

3   **POMARINE SKUA** *Stercorarius pomarinus*   L 50 (+20) cm. Pale **(a)** and uncommon, dark **(b)** forms shown. Br ♀ has more barred flanks than br ♂. Br adult always with darker cap and more yellow neck than 4. N-br adult as br ♀ but yellow on neck replaced by pale, brownish barring and upper- and undertail coverts barred like imm. Note diagnostic, bi-coloured, heavy bill. Imm is highly variable but many have dark head, pale panel on underside of primaries and a smaller, second, concentric panel on underprimary coverts. S

4   **ARCTIC SKUA** *Stercorarius parasiticus*   L 45 (+10) cm. Highly variable; palest **(a)** and darkest **(b)** forms shown. All forms have dark cap. Form **a** from 3 by less bulky build, narrower wings, paler, rear underparts, rather thin bill and short, pointed (if not lost!) streamers. N-br plumage is with full, rather barred breast band, upperflanks and upper- and undertail coverts. S(W)

5   **LONG-TAILED SKUA** *Stercorarius longicaudus*   L 35 (+20) cm. Pale **(a)** and very rare, dark **(b)** forms shown. Note short bill, pale undertail coverts, pale upperparts, absence of panel on underwing. Imm is cold-greyish brown with pale nape and evenly barred upper- and undertail coverts. Habitat: open sea. US

6   **KELP GULL** *Larus dominicanus*   L 60 cm. Wing tip in flight no blacker than rest of wing. Note large, stocky build with short wings and colour of legs (paler than 7); two out of every three birds have dark eye as shown, rest have creamy eye as 7. Juv has all-black bill, 2ndW shows some white parts in and near armpit. Habitat: sea, beach and nearby areas, but is also increasingly seen inland. Voice: high, almost double-toned '*tjik-tjiktjiktjik-*'.

7   **LESSER BLACK-BACKED GULL** *Larus fuscus graellsii*   L 55 cm. Note black wing tips, sharply demarcated from dark grey of remainder of upperwing. Juv and imm from imm 6 by more grey than brown colouring. Note further development of 2ndW plumage than in similar-aged 6. Habitat: prefers inland waters, but is also seen at the seashore. Voice: call is less sharp than that of 6, '*aow aow aow - -*'. US(W)

8.   **HERRING GULL** *Larus argentatus*   L 60 cm. Pale wings with black tips diagnostic. Juv has dark bill with flesh-coloured base. Tertials in 2ndW plumage are 'adult'-grey. Habitat: seashore, rarely inland. Voice: high, single-toned '*pjauw pjauw-*' RS. Note: In flight **(a)** is depicted the common Herring Gull from Europe. However, it is highly unlikely that this species has been seen in Southern Africa. More probably, Heuglin's Gull, *Larus heuglini*, will wander to the region. This species has two possible races: *taimyrensis* **(b)**, which is larger, only slightly paler than 7 and shows extensive streaking on nape and crown in winter, or nominate (not shown), which is even darker than 7.

Plate 33

1
b
c
a
2

b
3
b
a
♀ Br
Imm
♂ Br
3
♀ Br

Imm
4
a
b
Imm
4
Br

Imm
5
N-br
a
b
5
Br

33

Juv
6
Juv
2nd W
6

Juv
7
Juv
N-br
2nd W
7

Juv
8a
Juv
N-br
2nd W
8
b
N-br

Plate 34

1 **SABINE'S GULL** *Larus sabini* L 35 cm. Yellow-tipped bill and striking wing pattern diagnostic. Note that imm, unlike several other immature gulls, lacks white hind collar. Habitat: open sea but also at inland waters not too far from the sea. S(W)

2 **BLACK-LEGGED KITTIWAKE** *Rissa tridactyla* L 40 cm. Yellow bill and short legs diagnostic. Note small, 'cut-off', triangled wing tips in flight. Imm from imm 6 by interruption of 'M' mark on back, pure white (not grey) crown, black stripe across neck (see perched birds). Habitat: open sea. RS

3 **HARTLAUB'S GULL** *Larus hartlaubii* L 40 cm. From 5 in br plumage by smaller size, black eye, only traces of a grey hood; in n-br plumage by all-white head and less dark outer wings; imm from imm 5 by only faint terminal tail bar, absence of 'ear-phones' and black (not rosy) bill. Habitat: at or very close to sea coast.

4 **BLACK-HEADED GULL** *Larus ridibundus* L 35 cm. Note white-rimmed eye in short hood of br plumage. Shows a characteristic, widening, white leading edge to upperwing. Imm as imm 5 but shows more white on primaries. Habitat: prefers coastal habitats but may also be found at inland waters, farmland, refuse dumps. RS

5 **GREY-HEADED GULL** *Larus cirrocephalus* L 40 cm. Note the diagnostic, creamy eyes of adult and bright red legs. Habitat: normally at the seashore and larger inland waters.

6 **LITTLE GULL** *Larus minutus* L 25 cm. Note black underwing and all-grey upperwing of adult; 2ndW plumage (not shown) may have some black at wing tip. Black-billed imm has 'M' mark on upperparts with legs of 'M' connected on back. Habitat: normally in coastal habitats. R

7 **FRANKLIN'S GULL** *Larus pipixcan* L 35 cm. Wing tips as 2 but black separated from grey by wider, white line. Note also that white parts at primary tips are larger. N-br adult and imm have partial black or grey hood. Upperwing of imm from imm 9 by greyer, less brownish colouring. Habitat: in America, from where it comes as a vagrant, normally in marshes, lakes with fringing vegetation, also at the sea coast. Often feeds away from water on grass- and farmland. RSW

8 **HEMPRICH'S GULL** *Larus hemprichii* L 45 cm. Adult and imm from 10 by large, deep bill (yellow-based in adults). Only upper eyelid white. Habitat: coastal areas. R

9 **LAUGHING GULL** *Larus atricilla* L 40 cm. From 7 by proportionally larger bill, less white on primaries, no white between black wing tip and grey rest of wings. In n-br plumage less clearly hooded than 7. Habitat: vagrant from America; there normally in coastal areas. R

10 **WHITE-EYED GULL** *Larus leucophthalmus* L 35 cm. From 8 by red, unusually long bill, white upper- and lower eyelids, black (not brown) hood. No white visible at primary tips in folded wing. Habitat: coastal areas. (?)

Plate 34

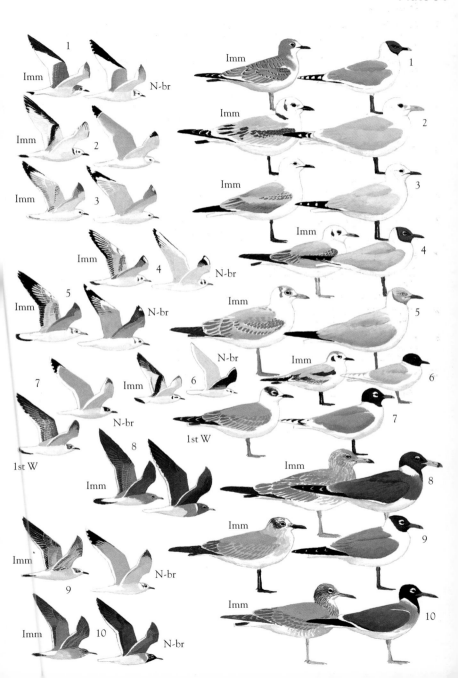

Plate 35

1   **SWIFT TERN** *Sterna bergii*   L 45 cm. Note chrome-yellow bill and white forehead. Slimmer than 2, larger than 3 and darker above than 2 and 3. Note dark secondaries of imm in flight. Habitat: seashore and nearby areas.

2   **ROYAL TERN** *Sterna maxima*   L 50 cm. From 11 by thinner, orange-red (not red, black-tipped) bill and paler upperwing. Heavier build, longer-legged and -billed and paler above than 3. Note dark forewing of imm. So far not seen in eastern coastal areas. Habitat: seashore and nearby areas. RW

3   **LESSER CRESTED TERN** *Sterna bengalensis*   L 40 cm. Note orange bill, grey rump and uppertail. In n-br plumage from 2 by wider eye ring and more black behind eye. Habitat: seashore. So far not seen in western coastal areas. S(W)

4   **SANDWICH TERN** *Sterna sandvicensis*   L 45 cm. Note slender, black, yellow-tipped bill and flat crown. In n-br plumage dark area on forewing is narrow and widens out. Imm has black bill and less dark secondaries than immature 1, 2 and 3. Habitat: offshore but also in coastal areas. Voice: raucous '*kirrewèk*'. S(W)

5   **GULL-BILLED TERN** *Gelochelidon nilotica*   L 40 cm. Note short, black bill, rounded head, long legs, all-grey upperparts. Imm and n-br adult show little black behind eye. Flight straight, less buoyant than other terns. Habitat: seashore, inland lakes, wetlands. Voice: high, rasping, pushed-out '*kuréet*' and mid-high, bleating chatters. RSW

6   **ARCTIC TERN** *Sterna paradisaea*   L 35 cm. Best compared with 7, 8 and 9 as 10 is too rare. Note short legs, short bill, long tail (reaching wing tip or just beyond), narrow, dark trailing edge to primaries, 'translucent' flight feathers. In br plumage with all-red bill and white cheek separated from greyer underparts. Imm has rather uniform grey upperparts in flight. Mostly on west coast, uncommon on south-east coast. Habitat: more offshore than inshore. However, may wander inland. Voice: mid-high '*eEEEhr*', lowered at the end. S

7   **COMMON TERN** *Sterna hirundo*   L 35 cm. From 6 by heavier build, longer bill, longer legs. N-br adult often shows reddish bill base and dark wedge between mid-grey outer and pale-grey inner primaries. Secondaries are not clearly white-edged. Br adult from 9 by absence of pink wash below and shorter streamers. Imm normally has bi-coloured bill. Habitat: all seashores. Rarely inland. Voice: '*KEE-er*' ('*KEE*' high and sharp). S(W)

8   **ANTARCTIC TERN** *Sterna vittata*   L 40 cm. From 6 by shorter tail, longer legs, more uniform grey upperwing without dark trailing edge. More likely to have a red or partly reddish bill in all plumages than 6, 7 and 9. Imm has darker bars on upperwing than other immatures. Habitat: open sea, inland waters near the coast. Voice: high '*puREEpuREEpuREE*'. W

9   **ROSEATE TERN** *Sterna dougallii*   L 40 cm. From 7 by longer tail and paler upperparts. In br plumage shows an all-red bill only during a few weeks. Note wedge-shaped, darker leading edge of wing. Wing of imm rather pale without much contrast. Only seen at south-east coast but uncommon there. Habitat: seashore. Voice: as 4, but different from 7, very high '*WéeWée*'. U

10   **WHITE-CHEEKED TERN** *Sterna repressa*   L 35 cm. Br plumage darkest of all terns (except 36.4 and 36.5) with conspicuous, narrow, white cheek. From 7 and 9 by smaller size, shorter legs and more compact flight silhouette. Note diagnostic, dark line around primaries above and below. N-br and imm with rather extensive, black cap. Tail and rump concolorous with rest of upperparts. Vagrant from north-east Africa and Arabia. Habitat: seashore. RS

11   **CASPIAN TERN** *Sterna caspia*   L 55 cm. From 2 by larger size, more (top-) heavy jizz, striking, red bill with subterminal, dark spot (most obvious in br plumage). N-br and imm normally with densely spotted forehead. Dark underprimaries diagnostic. Habitat: seashore. Voice: mid-high, pressed-out, raucous '*pfweeeet*'.

12   **AFRICAN SKIMMER** *Rhynchops flavirostris*   L 40 cm. Characterised by unique fishing method in which bill snaps shut when longer lower mandible (ploughing through water surface) touches fish **(a)**. Habitat: large rivers, lakes, lagoons with sandbars. brW(S)

Plate 35

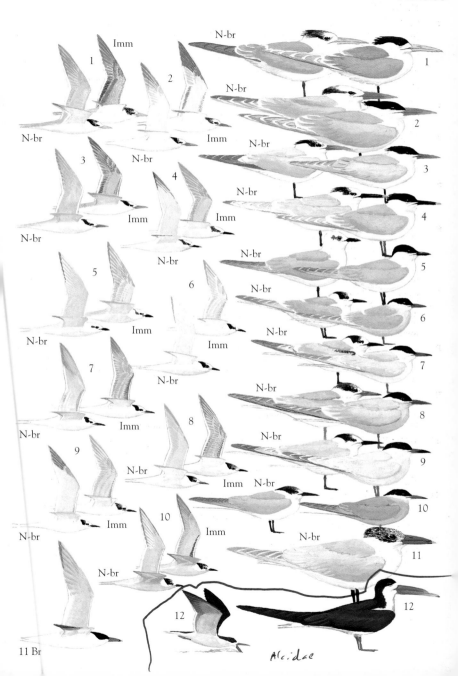

Alcidae

Plate 36

1   **LITTLE TERN** *Sterna albifrons* L 24 cm. Flies with fast wing beats. Note small size, white rump and tail and dark, first 3–4 primaries of adult. Black tip of bill in br plumage may be absent. Imm (especially juv) shows contrasting white secondaries. Habitat: seashore. Voice: very high *'peel peee peee'*. S

2   **DAMARA TERN** *Sterna balaeanarum* L 23 cm. Note long, slightly decurved bill, grey rump and tail, black cap (of br adult). Habitat: prefers inshore, coastal waters. Voice: very high, almost sparrow-like *'sree-sreeetiti'*. brS

3   **BLACK-NAPED TERN** *Sterna sumatrana* L 30 cm. Note narrow, black line through eye, widening towards nape. Very pale upperparts and black line on first primary diagnostic. Imm from all other immature terns by delicate, black patterning and narrow, black lore. Habitat: in Asia, from where it comes as a vagrant, normally at offshore islands, reefs and atolls. Voice: very high *'tjeeptjeep tjeerp-tjeerp'*. RS

4   **BRIDLED TERN** *Sterna anaethetus* L 35 cm. Note black cap in br plumage, contrasting with dark brown upperparts, and long tail, projecting beyond wing tip. White eyebrow extends behind eye. N-br adult has brown (not black) cap. Habitat: seashore. RS

5   **SOOTY TERN** *Sterna fuscata* L 45 cm. Cap and upperparts concolorous black, white eyebrow extends just up above eye. N-br adult shows some white spotting on crown. Note dark underparts of imm. Habitat: seashore. US

6   **BROWN NODDY** *Anous stolidus* L 40 cm. From 7 and 8 by larger size, pale-centred underwing, dark tail (darker than rump) and pale wing bar. Imm (not shown) with less white cap and pale edges to feathers of upperparts. Habitat: normally at offshore islands and atolls. RS

7   **LESSER NODDY** *Anous tenuirostris* L 30 cm. From 8 by gradual transition between white forehead and darker cheek and chin. All upperparts are uniform brown. Habitat: mainly at open sea. RW

8   **BLACK NODDY** *Anous minutus* L 35 cm. From 7 by sharply demarcated, white cap. Imm (not shown) as adult but with some pale edging to feathers of upperparts. Habitat: normally at offshore islands. (?)

9   **BLACK TERN** *Chlidonias niger* L 23 cm. Br adult has diagnostic, pale underwings and reddish-black legs. Note characteristic dark patch on breast sides of n-br adult and imm, grey rump and (in n-br plumage) extensive, black cap extending below eye. Habitat: inshore areas near the coast. S

10   **WHITE-WINGED BLACK TERN** *Chlidonias leucopterus* L 23 cm. N-br adult and imm show white rump, shorter bill and longer legs than 9 and 11. From 9 by absence of breast patches and less black on head and nape (in n-br plumage). Habitat: lakes, but can be seen feeding on insects away from water; does not plunge-dive but snatches food from water surface. S

11   **WHISKERED TERN** *Chlidonias hybridus* L 25 cm. Note grey rump. From very rare 35.10 by shorter, barely forked tail and different n-br upperwing pattern. Note dark saddle of imm (similar to white-rumped imm 10). From 10 in n-br plumage by lack of, or restricted, darker breast patches, longer wings and deeper wing beat. Habitat: open, inland waters, occasionally at seashore. Feeding behaviour as 10 but also plunge-dives. Voice: mid-high *'scratchscratch scratch'*.

Plate 36

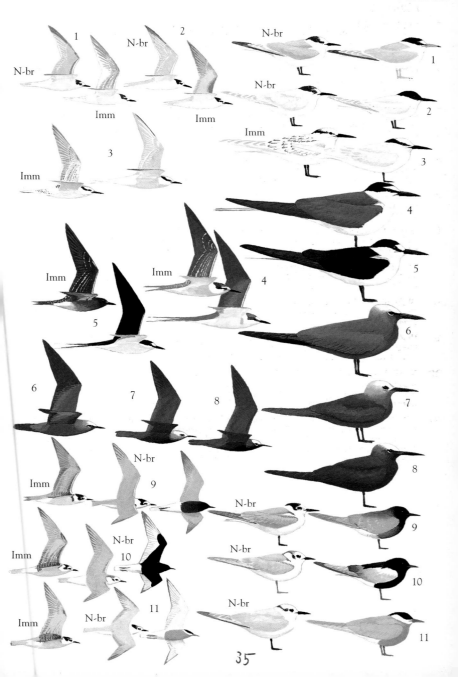

35

Plate 37

1 **SPECKLED** (or Rock) **PIGEON** *Columba guinea* L 40 cm. Shows striking, white rump in flight. Habitat: areas near cliffs and buildings including towns and villages. Voice: mid-high (or high), slightly rising 'coocoocoo–' (10–20 times 'coo') or 'R<u>o</u>oc<u>o</u>oc<u>o</u>o R<u>o</u>oc<u>o</u>oc<u>o</u>o -'.

2 **OLIVE** (or Rameron) **PIGEON** *Columba arquatrix* L 40 cm. Very dark with yellow bare parts. Habitat: canopy of forests and plantations. Voice: low, rattled, drawn-up 'kukururururúkukukururu' and scolding, shrieked 'kuRèèèt' ('ku-' very short and low).

3 **FERAL PIGEON** *Columba livia* L 35 cm. Shown on the plate is the original Rock Dove (found wild e.g. in North Africa), from which all feral pigeons descend; often they still show basic features such as black wing bars and purple-green neck patches. Habitat: large towns.

4 **EASTERN BRONZE-NAPED** (or Delegorgue's) **PIGEON** *Columba delegorguei* L 35 cm. Small, very dark pigeon. The ♂ with white neck patch, ♀ with bronze head resembling 7, but larger and living in the forest canopy. Habitat: forests. Voice: high, rising, accelerated then descending 'hoo-koo hoo kóo koo-koo-kookookoo'. U

5 **AFEP PIGEON** *Columba unicincta* L 35 cm. Large, forest pigeon with striking, pale tail bar in flight. Habitat: forest canopy. Voice: hurried, low 'oooh-oooh-oooh-oooh'. R

6 **AFRICAN GREEN PIGEON** *Treron calva* L 30 cm. Only green pigeon in the region. Habitat: forest edges, cultivation, suburbs (wherever it finds wild figs to eat). Voice: combination of mid-high, frog-like grunts, short, fast rattles and other sounds.

7 **LEMON** (or Cinnamon) **DOVE** *Aplopelia larvata* L 25 cm. Nominate **(a)** and race *jacksoni* **(b)** shown, differing in colouring of underparts. Rather plain and dark above. Habitat: undergrowth and ground of dense forests, parks and gardens. Voice: mid-high, hollow 'hoop hoop hoop -' ('hoop' twice every 3 seconds).

8 **NAMAQUA DOVE** *Oena capensis* L 25 cm. Normally in pairs, showing the white rump patch when flushed. Habitat: semi-desert, dry, more or less bushed and shrubbed areas. Voice: high, hollow 'uhwHOoo' or 'UH-rh<u>o</u>o-rh<u>o</u>o'.

9 **AFRICAN MOURNING DOVE** *Streptopelia decipiens* L 30 cm. Note pale-yellow, red-rimmed eye and black, white-edged neck patch. In flight shows grey wing bar and white uppertail margins. Dark tail base not visible when tail is folded. Habitat: dry, wooded areas with some grass, often near streams. Also in gardens. Voice: e.g. combination of high 'wóodurrr' and short 'woo' or low 'd<u>u</u>rrr'.

10 **RED-EYED DOVE** *Streptopelia semitorquata* L 30 cm. Red colour of eyes only visible at close range. Note small, greyish tail corners and dark tail feather bases, visible when tail is closed. Upperwing coverts area hardly, or not edged grey. Habitat: forest edges, woodland, suburbs. Voice: high, hurried 'kóo-kóo-kookookookoo' or 'frur kóokoo'.

11 **RING-NECKED** (or Cape Turtle) **DOVE** *Streptopelia capicola* L 25 cm. Note small, pale, black-eyed appearance and large, white tail corners. Habitat: forest edges, open woodland, suburbs. Voice: very high, sustained 'wikwirrik-w<u>u</u>k-'.

12 **DUSKY TURTLE DOVE** *Streptopelia lugens* L 30 cm. Note all-black neck patches without white, and absence of white in tail. Habitat: edges of montane forests, suburbs, woodland. Voice: low, raucous, repeated 'kkroarrr-kroarrr -'. R

13 **EUROPEAN TURTLE DOVE** *Streptopelia turtur* L 30 cm. Note striped neck patches and rufous wing coverts and tertials. In flight shows white, black-edged tail corners. Habitat: found in thornveld. Voice: mid-high, guttural, level 'gruurrr gruurr gruuurrr' or 'kruKrurrr-gruuuu'. R

14 **LAUGHING DOVE** *Streptopelia senegalensis* L 25 cm. Note buff-rufous, black-speckled band on upperbreast, pale, rufous colouring of upperparts, broad, grey wing bar in flight, large, white tail corners. Habitat: suburbs, cultivation near settlement, more or less bushed grassland. Voice: 'ooh-wuwuwu' ('ooh' very short).

15 **EMERALD-** (or Green-) **SPOTTED WOOD DOVE** *Turtur chalcospilos* L 20 cm. From 16 by black bill. Habitat: woodland. Voice: as 16 but with more double-notes, 'ookoo ookoo ookoo'.

16 **BLUE-SPOTTED WOOD DOVE** *Turtur afer* L 20 cm. From 15 by red, yellow-tipped bill. Habitat: rather moist forest. Voice: high, starting very slow, lazy, hesitating; slowly speeding up and descending with a bouncing finale, 'oo oo oo oo oo oo oo oo-oo-oo-ookookookookoo'. U

17 **TAMBOURINE DOVE** *Turtur tympanistria* L 25 cm. Habitat: forest, scrub- and woodland, plantations, suburbs. Voice: as 15 and 16 but whole sequence starts at a lower pitch.

Plate 37

Imm
Columbidae 84

Plate 38

1   **RED-FACED MOUSEBIRD** *Urocolius indicus*   L 35 cm. Note thin, long tail and red bare parts. Eye may be black (shown), pale blue or yellow. Habitat: wooded scrub- and bushland, gardens.

2   **SPECKLED MOUSEBIRD** *Colius striatus*   L 35 cm. Nominate **(a)** with blackish legs and race *rhodesia* **(b)** with red legs shown. Rump is concolorous with rest of upperparts. Habitat: open forest, wooded grassland, orchards, suburbs.

3   **WHITE-BACKED MOUSEBIRD** *Colius colius*   L 30 cm. Note pale, dark-tipped bill and white back. Habitat: dry, bushed and wooded areas.

4   **RED-BACKED MOUSEBIRD** *Colius castanotus*   L 35 cm. From 2 by chestnut rump and different range. Habitat: dry, wooded and bushed grasslands. E (Angola)

5   **DOUBLE-BANDED SANDGROUSE** *Pterocles bicinctus*   L 25 cm. Note diagnostic, black bar on forehead of ♂. The ♀ from ♀ 7 by square-cut (not pointed) tail and pale-edged tertials and scapulars. Comes to drink late after sunset. Habitat: dry areas at lower altitudes. Voice: high, explosive, liquid 'weeWéetitweeweeweeoh'.

6   **YELLOW-THROATED SANDGROUSE** *Pterocles gutturalis*   L 30 cm. Note pale eyebrow and black-bordered, creamy throat of ♂. The ♀ from other female sandgrouse by thin, dark lore. Comes to drink within 1–3 hours after sunrise. Habitat: sparsely wooded grass- and farmland at higher altitudes. Voice: flight call is high, rasping, frog-like 'chuwchuw' and 'chieriet'. U(S)brW

7   **NAMAQUA SANDGROUSE** *Pterocles namaqua*   L 25 cm. Note unmarked head and bi-coloured breast band of ♂. The ♀ as ♀ 5 but showing more rufous in barring. Drinks in the morning. Habitat: desert and semi-desert with little grass cover at lower altitudes. Voice: flight call is mid-high, nasal 'where is it now'.

8   **BURCHELL'S SANDGROUSE** *Pterocles burchelli*   L 25 cm. From other sandgrouse by longer legs. Drinks 2–4 hours after sunrise. Habitat: dry, grassy areas with some scrub. Voice: flight call is high, mellow 'tuweet tuweet tuweet'.

9   **ROSY-FACED LOVEBIRD** *Agapornis roseicollis*   L 16 cm. Note rosy cheeks, faint, pale eye ring, blue rump. Habitat: dry, wooded and open areas at higher altitudes.

10   **LILIAN'S LOVEBIRD** *Agapornis lilianae*   L 14 cm. Note yellow nape and neck and pale, green rump. Habitat: more or less wooded country.

11   **RED-HEADED LOVEBIRD** *Agapornis pullaria*   L 13 cm. Note yellow nape and neck and pale, blue rump. Habitat: moist, wooded areas at lower altitudes. R. Only lovebird with red visible in folded tail. For all other lovebirds normally the red is visible only when tail is spread (eg. in flight).

12   **BLACK-CHEEKED LOVEBIRD** *Agapornis nigrigenis*   L 14 cm. Note dark face and green rump. Habitat: thornveld, open woodland.

13   **BROWN-NECKED** (or Cape) **PARROT** *Poicephalus robustus*   L 35 cm. Note pale, olive head, red 'socks', red on shoulder. Not all ♀♀ have reddish forehead as shown. Imm without any red. Habitat: forest at mid-high altitudes and woodland. U

14   **MEYER'S PARROT** *Poicephalus meyeri*   L 22 cm. Note blue-green lower breast. From 15 and 16 by smaller, yellow area on underwing. Upperparts mainly brown with **(a)** or without **(b)** yellow forehead. Habitat: more or less wooded grassland.

15   **BROWN-HEADED PARROT** *Poicephalus cryptoxanthus*   L 25 cm. Predominantly green with brown head and yellow underwing coverts. Note bi-coloured bill. Habitat: more or less wooded grassland, thornveld, plantations.

16   **RUEPPELL'S PARROT** *Poicephalus rueppellii*   L 23 cm. Brown with yellow shoulder, yellow underwing coverts and blue belly without any green. Blue of ♀ deeper. Habitat: dry, grassy thornveld, woodland. U

17   **RED-FRONTED PARROT** *Poicephalus gulielmi*   L 30 cm. Note brilliant, green plumage with darker face and wings, yellowish-green rump. Habitat: forest canopy. R

18   **ROSE-RINGED PARAKEET** *Psittacula krameri*   L 40 cm. Unmistakable. Occurs only as feral populations in parks of large cities. R

19   **GREY PARROT** *Psittacus erithacus*   L 30 cm. Unmistakable. Habitat: forests. R

20   **HOOPOE** *Upupa epops*   L 30 cm. Habitat: normally forages in short grass in more or less bushed and wooded areas including suburbs. Voice: mid-high, regular, hurried 'oopoop oopoopoop-'.

Plate 38

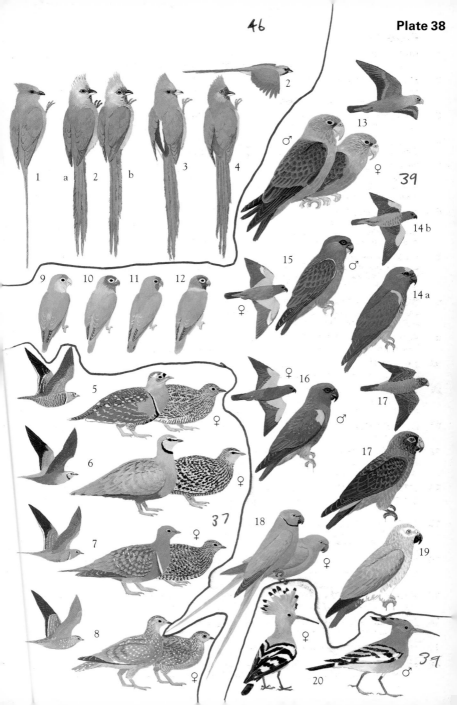

Plate 39

1 **GREEN TURACO** *Tauraco persa* L 45 cm. Note diagnostic, rosy-red bill. Races *livingstoni* (**a**, Livingstone's Lourie), *schalowi* (**b**, Schalow's Lourie) and *corythaix* (**c**, Knysna Lourie) shown. Habitat: mid-strata and canopy of rather dense forests and woodland. Voice: high, loud, barking '*wah-wah-Wraah-Wraah-WRaah-WRAah*'.

2 **RED-CRESTED TURACO** *Tauraco erythrolophus* L 45 cm. Unmistakable. Note yellow bill and red crest. Habitat: forest. E (Angola)

3 **PURPLE-CRESTED TURACO** (or Lourie) *Tauraco porphyreolophus* L 40 cm. Unmistakable. Habitat: well-wooded streams, forests, woodland, dense bushland, plantations, gardens. Voice: starting low and very rapid, then rising and slowing down and ending very loud, '*toktoktoktoktoktok-tok-Thok-Thok-Thok* THOK THOK THOK'.

4 **BLACK-BILLED TURACO** *Tauraco schuettii* L 40 cm. From 1 by black bill. Habitat: forest canopy. Voice: mid-high, sustained '*Wahweh-Wahweh-Wahweh-*' (like barking of small dogs). R

5 **GREY GO-AWAY BIRD** (or Lourie) *Corythaixoides concolor* L 50 cm. Unmistakable. Habitat: thornveld, dry, open woodland. Voice: mid-high, mewing, gliding-down '*mùèegh*'. Note: the name Go-away bird is derived from the call of the East African White-bellied Go-away Bird, '*g'wa*'.

6 **BARE-FACED GO-AWAY BIRD** *Corythaixoides personata* L 50 cm. Unmistakable. Habitat: more or less wooded, natural and cultivated areas. R

7 **GREAT BLUE TURACO** *Corythaeola cristata* L 75 cm. Unmistakable. Habitat: canopies of forests, riverine belts, forest remains. R

8 **ROSS'S TURACO** (or Lourie) *Musophaga rossae* L 50 cm. Habitat: canopy of forest remains, miombo, gardens. Often near streams. Voice: high, short, slowed-down, cackled '*rututut-Tut Tut*'.

9 **RUFOUS-CROWNED** (or Purple) **ROLLER** *Coracias naevia* L 35 cm. Note large and shaggy appearance. Habitat: dry areas with tall trees and bush.

10 **LILAC-BREASTED ROLLER** *Coracias caudata* L 30 (+10) cm. Imm is buff (not purple) and shows more overall white streaking. Habitat: dry, bushed and wooded, natural and cultivated areas including suburbs.

11 **RACKET-TAILED ROLLER** *Coracias spatulata* L 30 (+10) cm. Note that buffy-purple is confined to sides of breast. In flight shows rufous of tertials extended onto coverts. Habitat: open woodland. U

12 **EUROPEAN ROLLER** *Coracias garrulus* L 30 cm. Note absence of white eyebrow. All flight feathers black (not partly blue-black). Crown (especially of imm) often more green than blue. Habitat: forest edges, more or less wooded and bushed, natural and cultivated areas. S

13 **BROAD-BILLED ROLLER** *Eurystomus glaucurus* L 25 cm. Note short, yellow bill, shallow-forked tail and purple underparts. Habitat: forest glades and edges, wet woodland, grass- and farmland with scattered trees near streams and marshes. Voice: low, raucous, rather frog-like '*draaaf-draaaf-*'. brS

14 **BLUE-THROATED ROLLER** *Eurystomus gularis* L 25 cm. From 13 by blue chin, brown underparts and, in flight, paler-based flight feathers. Habitat: more or less extensively cultivated areas with forest patches. Voice: very high, slightly hoarse '*hew hew hew -*'. R

15 **VIOLET WOOD HOOPOE** *Phoeniculus damarensis* L 40 cm. From 16 by mainly purple (not green, purple and blue) iridescence. Note that bill base may be black (not shown); imm has all-black bill. Small parties. Habitat: dry bushland, thornveld, often near water. Voice: mid-high cackling, starting low and rising to excited climax, '*rgchararará...*' with characteristic '*ah*'-sound.

16 **GREEN** (or Red-billed) **WOOD HOOPOE** *Phoeniculus purpureus* L 40 cm. Note green iridescence on nape and mantle. Small parties. Habitat: open wood- and bushland, well-wooded streams, suburbs. Voice: mid-high to high, magpie-like, fast, excited chatters sounding as '*chachachacha —*'.

17 (Greater) **SCIMITARBILL** *Phoeniculus cyanomelas* L 30 cm. From 15 and 16 by strongly decurved bill and less noisy behaviour. Habitat: dry bushland, thornveld. Voice: very high, fluted '*pwuupwuu*', each '*pwuu-*' slightly lashed-up.

Plate 39

Musophagidae 8F

a

b

c

1

1

5

6

7

2

3

4

8

8

Brachypterociidae
Leptosomatidae
38

9

10

11

11

12

10

12

13

13

14

14

15

16

Imm

17

44

Plate 40

1 **DUSKY LONG-TAILED CUCKOO** *Cercococcyx mechowi* L 35 cm. Very difficult to separate from 2 and 3 (especially immatures). From 3 by preference for lowlands, from 2 and 3 by voice. Habitat: mainly lowland forest. Undergrowth near streams. Voice: very high, climbing, lashing '*pu wee Wir*' (reminiscent of 9), fluted, descending, rapid '*tijuwtijuwtijuw-tijuw-tijuw-*'. R

2 **OLIVE LONG-TAILED CUCKOO** *Cercococcyx olivinus* L 35 cm. Habitat: lowlands. Less restricted to dense forest than 1. Voice: mid-high, fluted, sustained '*fiuw-fiuw-fiuw–*' (each '*fiuw*' with slight, inbuilt tremolo), or high, very lazy '*it will rain*'. R

3 **BARRED LONG-TAILED CUCKOO** *Cercococcyx montanus* L 35 cm. From 1 and 2 by different range. Habitat: prefers montane forest edges. Voice: high, loud '*weet-wéet-weet-weh*' or long sequence of slowly rising '*fiuu-fiuu-fiuu-fijuu-fijuu—-*' (up to 20 times '*fijuu*'). U(brS)

4 **GREAT SPOTTED CUCKOO** *Clamator glandarius* L 40 cm. Habitat: dry, more or less wooded and bushed, natural and cultivated areas. Voice: high, slightly chattered '*rrrrriú*' or very high, loud, rattled, sharp '*ririrririririririri*'. S(W)

5 **JACOBIN CUCKOO** *Oxylophus jacobinus* L 35 cm. White-bellied (**a**) and black (**b**) forms shown (latter common in southern areas). Note wing bar across primary bases. Habitat: dry grassland with scattered trees and bush. Voice: very high, piped '*piu piu piu piu - -*' (each '*piu*' gliding down) or '*tjiu-tjiu-wéet*'. S

6 **AFRICAN STRIPED CUCKOO** *Oxylophus levaillantii* L 35 cm. Note relatively long tail. Habitat: forest edges, wooded swamps, dense bushland, gardens. Voice very high, piped '*piu piu piu - -*' (each '*piu*' gliding off) or high, chattered rattle, '*chachacha—*'. (brS).

7 **YELLOWBILL** (or Green Coucal) *Ceuthmochares aureus* L 35 cm. Note heavy, yellow bill. Solitary and skulking. Habitat: dense undergrowth at forest edges with connected riverine belts. Voice: song starts with extreme high, staccato '*tic's*, then changes to mid-high, scolding '*kah-kah-kah—*' which ends in a trill. Many variations of this series. Also very high '*fu Wéeeh*'.

8 **THICK-BILLED CUCKOO** *Pachycoccyx audeberti* L 35 cm. Note upright stance with drooping wings and short legs. Imm from 4 by whitish head and barred tail. Habitat: miombo, thornveld, riverine belts. Voice: extreme high, lashing '*weeehwit weeehwit*'. U

9 **RED-CHESTED CUCKOO** *Cuculus solitarius* L 30 cm. From 14b by pale upperparts, grey chin and throat; imm from adult 14b by lack of rufous. Often heard but seldom seen. Habitat: forest belts, cultivations, suburbs. Voice: very high, unhurried '*IT-will-rain IT-will-rain*'. brS

10 **COMMON** (or European) **CUCKOO** *Cuculus canorus* L 35 cm. From 11 by less barred undertail. Other than by size, not safely separable from 12 and 13. Rufous (**b**) form of ♀ rare. Imm as imm 11, but also rufous and grey forms known. Habitat: more or less wooded and bushed habitats. Voice: silent in Africa. S

11 **AFRICAN CUCKOO** *Cuculus gularis* L 35 cm. See 10. Bill base often rather extensively yellow, but variation of this feature means it cannot be relied on for diagnosis or separation from 10, 12 and 13. Habitat: hilly, dry, more or less wooded and bushed areas. Voice: mid-high, rather level '*ku-koo ku-koo ku-koo*'. brS(W)

12 **ASIAN LESSER CUCKOO** *Cuculus poliocephalus* L 25 cm. From 10 by smaller size. Differences in voice not helpful feature because 10, 12 and 13 are probably silent in Africa. Habitat: forest edges and undergrowth in wood- and bushland. Voice: yelping, rapid '*djipdjipdjipdjip*'. S

13 **MADAGASCAR LESSER CUCKOO** *Cuculus rochii* L 30 cm. Often shows less undertail barring than 12. Habitat: forest, woodland and bushed areas. Voice: high, liquid, yelping, rapid '*woopwoopwoop-wop*' (lower in pitch than 12). US

14 **BLACK CUCKOO** *Cuculus clamosus* L 30 cm. Nominate (**a**) and race *gabonensis* (**b**) shown. From 5b by absence of crest and wing bar. Habitat: canopy at forest edges, woodland, bush- and scrubland, gardens. Voice: mid-high, fluted, unhurried '*fiufiuu-fiúu*' of ♂ together with hurried, rising '*wowowowikkewikkewikkewikke*' of ♀. brS

15 **DIEDERIK CUCKOO** *Chrysococcyx caprius* L 20 cm. Note white spots, arranged in a wedge on closed wing. Normal imm form shown, not the uncommon, rufous form. Habitat: forests and other more or less wooded and bushed areas including cultivation and gardens. Voice: very high, fluted '*it is not good so*' or '*weet-weet-wéetrr*'. BrS

16 **KLAAS'S CUCKOO** *Chrysococcyx klaas* L 15 cm. The ♀ from ♀ 17 by white eye stripe. Habitat: forest patches, parks and gardens. Voice: very high, plaintive '*trúe dear*'. brS(W)

▶

Plate 40

1

Imm

8

Imm

9

♀

♂

Imm

2

10

♀a

♀b

10

3

11

Imm

4

Imm

12

10

♀

5

a

b

11

13

6

5b

12

14a

a

b

Imm

14

7

♀

Imm

♀

♀

15

16

17

Cuculidae
42

Plate 40 (continued)

17   **AFRICAN EMERALD CUCKOO** *Chrysococcyx cupreus*   L 25 cm. Note regular barring of ♀.
Habitat: forest glades and edges, wood- and bushland, cultivation, suburbs. Voice: very high,
mellow, liquid, affirmative '*hellọh judy*'. brS(W)

Plate 41

Note: nightjars are very difficult to identify by sight only (e.g. when flushed in daytime). So it is
    advisable to check the maps for their ranges and to compare the nocturnal songs with the written
    vocalisations below. There are two basic song types: either a short, liquid, melodious whistle (A),
    or a very long, sustained churr (B). Most nightjars are either whistlers or churrers. The white (or
    buff) markings on wing tips and tail are helpful features e.g. for identifying traffic victims.

1   **FIERY-NECKED NIGHTJAR** *Caprimulgus pectoralis*   L 24 cm. The ♂ from 2 by less pale neck
and collar, moister habitat and different voice; from 3 by smaller size, more patterning (not
uniform freckling) above, larger wing spots, moister habitat and different voice; from rather
dissimilar 9 by smaller size, more rufous colouring, no grey trailing edge to wing and crosswise (not
lengthwise) perching. The ♀ from ♀♀ 3 and 9 by white tail corners. Shares range with 2, 3 and 9
but hardly at all with similar, but uncommon 6. Habitat: wooded areas including gardens. Voice:
sings from tree perch, high '*tjuụú-tuwịrrrr*' (song type A, see introductory note above).

2   **RUFOUS-CHEEKED NIGHTJAR** *Caprimulgus rufigena*   L 24 cm. Tail pattern of ♂ as ♂♂ 1
(which see), 3 and 9. Habitat: dry woodland, thornveld, scrub desert. Voice: sings from ground
(occasionally from perch), low, sewing machine-like '*rrrrrr—*' (song type B) sustained for several
minutes, preceded by soft '*tjuw tjuw tjuw*'. brS

3   **FRECKLED NIGHTJAR** *Caprimulgus tristigma*   L 30 cm. Tail pattern of ♂ as ♂♂ 1 (which
see), 2 and 9. Note large size, dark, uniform freckling and characteristic habitat. Rests by day on
bare rock (never in trees). Probably nests also on flat roofs in cities. Habitat: bare (or sparsely
overgrown), rocky outcrops and ravines. Voice: sings from ground, very high, staccato '*whewwhew
whewwhew whewhew -*' (resembling very slow song type B) sustained for up to 30 seconds.

4   **SQUARE-TAILED** (or Mozambique) **NIGHTJAR** *Caprimulgus fossii*   L 24 cm. Note white
outer tail feathers. From uncommon 5 by less crude patterning above and drier habitat, from rare 7
and 8 by smaller wing spots, ♀ from ♀♀ 7 and 8 by buff (not finely barred) outer tail feathers.
Note that only outer pair of tail feathers is all-white and, from next pair, only the terminal half.
Habitat: grassy and sandy areas often at woodland edges near lakes and rivers. Voice: sings from
ground (and maybe from tree perch), mid-high, rapid, staccato rattle, irregular, alternating
between '*-ru-*' (10–20 times) and '*-ri-*' (20–30 times) as '*rururuririri—*' (song type B), sustained for
up to 2–3 minutes.

5   **SWAMP** (or Natal) **NIGHTJAR** *Caprimulgus natalensis*   L 24 cm. Note rather crude blotching
above. Range shared with 4 (except near Durban) and with 8 but not with 7. Note all-white
colouring of outer two pairs of tail feathers. Habitat: damp, grassy places near swamps and vleis.
Also in woodland. Often associated with palms. Voice: sings from ground, high, staccato
'*kukukuk—*' like small river boat (song type B), sustained for up to 30 seconds, and high, level
'*wuwirrrr*' (song type A) with '*wu*' as very short undertone at beginning. U

6   **MOUNTAIN NIGHTJAR** *Caprimulgus poliocephalus*   L 25 cm. Note dark appearance. The ♂
has less white in tail than most other nightjars; white even further reduced in ♀. Restricted range
in Angola and area of Malawi-Zambia border. Habitat: prefers higher altitudes. Open forests, moist
woodland. Voice: sings from dead tree branch or telephone line, very high, fluting '*péeuj pjurrr*'
(song type A). R

7   **SLENDER-TAILED NIGHTJAR** *Caprimulgus clarus*   L 30 cm. Occurrence in NE Mozambique
uncertain. From 8 by duskier, less rufous colouring, shorter tail and slower song tempo. Habitat:
dry, wooded and bushed areas. Voice: sings from ground, high, staccato, sustained '*ririri—*' (song
type B), like a rapid sewing machine. (?)

8   **LONG-TAILED NIGHTJAR** *Caprimulgus climacurus*   L 25 (+10) cm. White spots also on
outer primaries; 7 and 8 share the white trailing edge to wings, the pale, buff line along the coverts
and the whitish bar across the central area of the coverts. Habitat: semi-desert, bushed and wooded
grassland, extensive fields, open woodland. Voice: sings from ground, high (sometimes low), very
fast, rattled '*rrrrr—*' (song type B), faster than sewing machine. R

▶

Plate 41

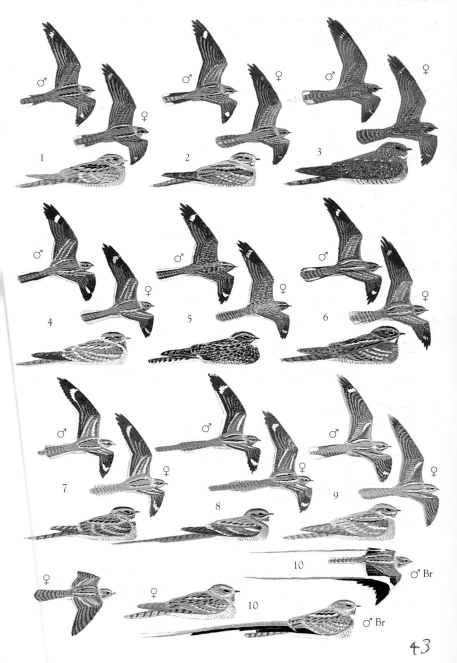

43

Plate 41 (continued)

9 EUROPEAN NIGHTJAR *Caprimulgus europaeus*   L 25 cm. Note grey trailing edge to wings. Compare with 1, 2 and 6. Perches lengthwise on tree branches. Habitat: bushed and wooded, natural and cultivated areas. Voice: rarely heard in Africa. Sings from branch of tree, mid-high 'rrri————' narrowed to 'rrru–' at irregular intervals (song type B), sustained for up to 5 minutes. S

10 PENNANT-WINGED NIGHTJAR *Macrodipteryx vexillarius*   L 30 cm. N-br plumage of ♂ (not shown) retains most of the black-and-white wing pattern but without pennants. Note absence of wing spots in ♀. Habitat: woodland, often in stony, hilly areas. Voice: sings in flight or from low perch, extreme high, insect-like, shivering phrases of irregular length, '*sisisisisi*—'. brS

Plate 42 (continued)

16   **SENEGAL COUCAL** *Centropus senegalensis*   L 40 cm. Note bright, rufous mantle and unbarred uppertail coverts (barred in not-shown imm). Habitat: rather dry bushveld, forest edges, swamps. Voice: as 15 but at mid-high pitch.

17   **WHITE-BROWED COUCAL** *Centropus superciliosus*   L 45 cm. From immature coucals by white, black-edged nape and neck feathers. Habitat: areas with tall grass, reeds and some trees, semi-desert. Voice: mid-high, hollow '*uhuhuhuhurrrrrruhuhuhuh*' with a lower trill in the middle.

18   **GABON COUCAL** *Centropus anselli*   L 50 cm. Note buff underparts. Habitat: dense undergrowth of swampy forest, old cultivations. Voice: mid-high, hooting, slightly descending '*foo-foo fooh fooh foo*' or very high '*fooh-fooh-fooh-fooh-wukwukwukwukwuk-wooh wooh wooh wooh*' ('*wukwuk*' part very high). R

19   **BURCHELL'S COUCAL** *Centropus burchelli*   L 45 cm. Only coucal in most of its range except black 14. Habitat: moist, grassy areas with some trees, gardens. Voice: as 15 but at mid-high pitch and speeded up, or as 17.

Plate 42

1 **AFRICAN WOOD OWL** *Strix woodfordii* L 35 cm. Plumage varies from pale brown via russet to dark brown; dark form shown. Note black eyes set in white face, and barring below. Habitat: forest, plantations, suburbs. Voice: high and mid-high, barking '*wóo-woo wóorrorrwoo*'.

2 **PEARL-SPOTTED OWLET** *Glaucidium perlatum* L 20 cm. Note streaking, not barring, below, long tail, pseudo-face at back of head. Often seen by day. Habitat: open woodland, bushveld with some trees. Voice: high '*puukpuukpuuk——*' sustained for 20–30 seconds and very high, piercing, descending '*piiiuuu*' (like fireworks).

3 **AFRICAN BARRED OWLET** *Glaucidium capense* L 25 cm. Note regular barring above and below. Habitat: more or less dense forest, often near water. Voice: very high, staccato '*pjuipjuipjuipjui*–' (each '*pjui*' descending) and very high '*wruhwruhwruh*—'.

4 **WHITE-FACED SCOPS OWL** *Otus leucotis* L 30 cm. Note orange eyes and pale, grey feathering. Habitat: large trees in woodland. Voice: mid-high, trilling, cooing '*bbbbb-woouow*' ('*bbbbb*' as slow trill).

5 **AFRICAN SCOPS OWL** *Otus senegalensis* L 20 cm. Grey (**a**) form seen more than rufous (**b**) and other forms. 'Ears' not always obvious. Variable in stance (thickset or slender). Habitat: more or less wooded habitats including gardens. Voice: very high '*prriur prriur*' with 4 second intervals.

6 **PEL'S FISHING OWL** *Scotopelia peli* L 70 cm. Unmistakable. Habitat: well-forested streams and lakes. Voice: extreme low, sinister '*hoop ho hoop ho -*'. U

7 **VERREAUX'S** (or Giant) **EAGLE OWL** *Bubo lacteus* L 65 cm. Unmistakable. Habitat: well-wooded streams, other areas with some large trees. Voice: extreme low '*prooh prooh prooh*' (each '*prooh*' very short.

8 **CAPE EAGLE OWL** *Bubo capensis* L 55 cm. From 9 by orange (not yellow) eyes, boldly blotched (not finely barred) upper- and underparts, coarse, lengthwise streaking on crown (no fine barring, concentric to facial disc). Habitat: rocky valleys and cliffs with some shrub and grass cover. Can be seen in daytime perched on rocks or ground in shade. Voice: low, hooted '*hooh hootooh*'. U

9 **SPOTTED EAGLE OWL** *Bubo africanus* L 50 cm. Note fine barring. May have orange (instead of normal yellow) eyes. Habitat: open forest, rocky desert, woodland, suburbs. Voice: '*hoooi hooooi*', lower and more drawn-out than 8.

10 **BARN OWL** *Tyto alba* L 35 cm. Note upright stance. Does not perch on the ground. Habitat: near caves, buildings, Hamerkop nests; not in true forest. Voice: very high, loud, shivering '*wrurururuu*' and drawn-up, shrieking '*frrrruuuui*'.

11 **AFRICAN GRASS OWL** *Tyto capensis* L 35 cm. From 12 by long-legged build and absence of dark wrist patches on underwing. Habitat: moist grass- and moorland. Voice: high shriek, '*frieeet*', and low, mallard-like '*kweh kweh kweh kweh*'. U

12 **MARSH OWL** *Asio capensis* L 35 cm. Note seemingly large eyes, buff window on upperwing, crouched stance. Active at sunrise and sunset. Will approach and circle intruder. Habitat: short grassland, marshes, swamps. Voice: mid-high, snipe-like '*krèèh*', mid-high, duck-like, barked '*ruururu*', loud, explosive shrieks.

Note: coucals (13–19) are members of the cuckoo family (Plate 40) but appear on this plate for reasons of layout of the book.

13 **BLUE-HEADED COUCAL** *Centropus monachus* L 45 cm. From 16 by larger size, heavier bill, less reddish-rufous upperparts; from 15, 18 and 19 by unbarred uppertail coverts. Note blue sheen on head and neck. Imm (not shown) has faintly streaked uppertail coverts and pale-streaked, brown crown. Habitat: reed beds, shrubbery, at riverbanks or in forest clearings. Voice: e.g. mid-high, hollow, piping '*poo-poo-poo-poopoo-poo*'. R

14 **BLACK COUCAL** *Centropus grillii* L 35 cm. Note absence of eyebrow in n-br plumage. Habitat: marshes, inundations with some bush and shrub. Voice: mid-high, mellow '*wukwuk wukwuk wukwuk*'. brS(W)

15 **COPPERY-TAILED COUCAL** *Centropus cupreicaudus* L 50 cm. Undertail coverts palest area of underparts (see 13, 16 and 19). From 18 by paler underparts, from 16 and 19 by darker mantle gradually merging into neck and crown. Habitat: reed beds, papyrus, tall grass, shrubbery. Voice: low, piping, rapid, slightly descending '*poopoopoopuppupuppup*', like water running out of a bottle. U

◄

Plate 42

Strigidae
84

Br   N-br   Imm

42

Plate 43

1   **ALPINE SWIFT** *Tachymarptis melba*   L 22 cm. Note white throat and belly. Habitat: breeds in rocky mountains and cliffs, but travels daily far afield. Voice: extreme high, very fast '*swiswiswiwititititi*', slowed-down at the end.

2   **MOTTLED SWIFT** *Tachymarptis aequatorialis*   L 22 cm. Note large size and mottling below. Mantle darker than head and rump. Habitat: as 1. Voice: extreme high, sweeping '*tcheeET tcheeET*'. U

3   **BRADFIELD'S SWIFT** *Apus bradfieldi*   L 17 cm. Slightly paler than 4, 5 and 7. Mottled below; primaries and tail darker than mantle and rump. Habitat: as 1. Voice: very high screams at slightly lower pitch than 4 and 5, '*sreeEEEeah*', with some emphasis on middle part.

4   **EUROPEAN SWIFT** *Apus apus*   L 15 cm. Note sooty black colouring with paler throat patch. Rather uniform upperparts. Habitat: any open area. Voice: extreme high, sharp, hurried screams, '*tsjeetsjee tsjee*' (each '*tsjee*' slightly falling off). S

5   **AFRICAN BLACK SWIFT** *Apus barbatus*   L 18 cm. Separation of pale throat patch from breast gradually scaled. Belly, rump and underwing feathers slightly pale-fringed. Inner secondaries (seen from above) paler than rest of upperparts. Habitat: as 1. Voice: extreme high, sharp screams, '*tsjieeeah tsjieeeeah -*' (each '*tsjieeeah*' longer than 4 seconds and falling off in '*-ah*').

6   **PALLID SWIFT** *Apus pallidus*   L 15 cm. In mixed flocks looks paler than other swifts. Note large throat patch extending up to forehead, giving very pale head-on view. Mantle darkest part above. Broader-winged and bulkier than other swifts. Habitat: normally prefers coastal areas but in Southern Africa only recorded inland. Voice: from 4 by less extreme high, shorter shrieks, '*sréeh sréeh*'. RS

7   **FERNANDO PO SWIFT** *Apus barbatus sladeniae*   L 18 cm. From 5 (of which it is a race) by very black plumage with very dark throat. Habitat: mountainous areas. Voice: very high, 2-noted, short shrieks, '*scréeh scréeh scréehscréeh*'. R

8   **LITTLE SWIFT** *Apus affinis*   L 12 cm. Note white rump and very short, square tail. Often seen as screaming, intertwining 'balls' of many birds high over towns. Habitat: breeds under eaves, bridges and rocks. Voice: extreme high, fast '*pirrrrrrpirrprr*' (each syllable bouncing down).

9   **HORUS SWIFT** *Apus horus*   L 15 cm. Looks stout, like a fork-tailed version of 8. White of rump extends to lower flanks. Habitat: prefers higher altitudes. Breeds in sandcliff tunnels excavated by bee-eaters, kingfishers or martins. Often seen over water. Voice: high, plover-like, fluted '*piu-purrr piu-purrr*'. U

10   **WHITE-RUMPED SWIFT** *Apus caffer*   L 15 cm. Note slender silhouette, deeply forked tail, narrow, white crescent across rump, which is connected to white rear edges of secondaries. Habitat: 'steals' nests from swallows under rocks, bridges, roofs. Voice: mid-high, short, rather sparrow-like chatter, '*prepprepprip-*', or very high, short shrieks.

11   **SCARCE SWIFT** *Schoutedenapus myoptilus*   L 17 cm. Note tightly closed tail, narrow wings, contrasting black eye patch. Best identified in mixed flocks by voice. Habitat: as 1, but feeds mainly over forests. Voice: combination of high, rapid, running-up '*wutwutwut*' with diagnostic '*tiktik tikkerik*', (reminiscent of Blacksmith Lapwing, 30.7). U

12   **AFRICAN PALM SWIFT** *Cypsiurus parvus*   L 17 cm. Note pale, very slim, long-tailed silhouette. Habitat: any area with palm trees. Voice: extreme high, twittered chatter, '*twirrr*', or '*srrrr*'.

13   **BAT-LIKE** (or Böhm's) **SPINETAIL** *Neafrapus boehmi*   L 10 cm. Note diagnostic, seemingly tail-less appearance, white underparts and rump, characteristic wing shape. Slow, erratic, bat-like flight around trees. Habitat: open woodland, especially near baobab trees. Voice: very high, twittered, fast trill, '*tsririririririritwgeh*'. U

14   **MOTTLED SPINETAIL** *Telacanthura ussheri*   L 14 cm. From 8 by indistinctly pale-mottled throat, narrow, white bar across belly, blacker upperparts, different wing shape, more fluttering flight. Habitat: forest edges, dry woodland, especially near baobab. Voice: high, dry, sparrow-like '*tsju tsjrrrsjrr*'. U

15   **BLACK SPINETAIL** *Telacanthura melanopygia*   L 16 cm. Note blackish appearance, square tail, narrow wing base. Flight fast at lower levels, often in flocks mixed with other swifts. Habitat: forest glades, plantations. Voice: mid-high, short, scratchy or hurried, muttered rattles. R

Plate 43

Hemiprocnidae Trochilidae 38

Plate 44

1 **BLUE-BREASTED BEE-EATER** *Merops variegatus* L 20 cm. As 2, but yellow throat looks paler due to more white below black ear coverts. Habitat: generally in moister habitats than 2. Humid, grassy areas at forest edges or lake sides.

2 **LITTLE BEE-EATER** *Merops pusillus* L 17 cm. See 1. Habitat: bushland and forest edges, often near water.

3 **WHITE-FRONTED BEE-EATER** *Merops bullockoides* L 24 cm. Note striking, white forehead, white chin, pink throat and blue rear underparts. Habitat: wooded and bushed areas, swamp edges, other open areas, not too far away from sand cliffs where it breeds.

4 **BLACK BEE-EATER** *Merops gularis* L 20 cm. From all other bee-eaters by habitat. Habitat: forest interiors. R

5 **EUROPEAN BEE-EATER** *Merops apiaster* L 30 cm. Often heard and seen passing overhead in loose, seemingly aimless flying flocks. Habitat: more or less wooded areas, suburbs. Voice: high, melodious, liquid, short fluted '*prjuur*' and '*iup*'. (br)S

6 **BLUE-CHEEKED BEE-EATER** *Merops persicus* L 25 (+6) cm. Note head pattern with blue cheeks, large size, overall bright green colouring. Habitat: open, wooded and bushed grassland, lake and swamp edges. Voice: high, short '*pjuur-pjuur*', sharper than 5. S

7 **MADAGASCAR** (or Olive) **BEE-EATER** *Merops superciliosus* L 25 (+6) cm. From 2 by rufous-brown throat and cheek, less brilliant green plumage, deep rufous underwings. Note dark-brown cap. Habitat: as 6. U(br)S

8 **WHITE-THROATED BEE-EATER** *Merops albicollis* L 20 (+10) cm. Unmistakable. Habitat: normally in wooded and bushed areas, also in forests, plantations, gardens. R

9 **CARMINE BEE-EATER** *Merops nubicoides* L 25 (+10) cm. Unmistakable. Habitat: wooded and bushed, natural and cultivated areas including roadsides. brS

10 **SWALLOW-TAILED BEE-EATER** *Merops hirundineus* L 22 cm. From 1 and 2 by long, blue, forked tail. Habitat: wooded and bushed grassland.

11 **BOEHM'S BEE-EATER** *Merops boehmi* L 21 cm. Note rich russet head. Unlike 6 and 7, not gregarious. Hawks insects in short sallies from perch. Habitat: forest edges near rivers and streams.

12 **AFRICAN GREY HORNBILL** *Tockus nasutus* L 50 cm. From 13 by white stripe through middle of rump, different bill pattern and generally more southern range. Habitat: dry, more or less wooded areas with some bush. Voice: high, unhurried, piping '*pipipipipiupiupléepléeplee*' (middle part extreme high) and high, fluted '*tuuutjuh-tuuutjeh*'.

13 **PALE-BILLED HORNBILL** *Tockus pallidirostris* L 45 cm. From 12 by yellow, orange-rimmed bill and plain, brown rump. Habitat: dry miombo.

14 **MONTEIRO'S HORNBILL** *Tockus monteiri* L 55 cm. From 16 and 17 by speckled, partly white wings and white outer tail feathers, from 18 and 19 by dark throat and breast. Feeds mainly on the ground. Habitat: desert and semi-desert with scarce scrub and trees. Voice: low, mumbled '*toktoktoktaktakkarrekarrekarrekarre*', rising in pitch, lowered at the end and starting afresh.

15 **AFRICAN PIED HORNBILL** *Tockus fasciatus* L 50 cm. Note tail pattern and bright-yellow, red-tipped bill. Arboreal. Habitat: forest and surrounding areas. Voice: very high, rather short phrases, '*fjuk-fjuk-fjuk-fjukfjuk-fjukfjukfjuk*'.

16 **CROWNED HORNBILL** *Tockus alboterminatus* L 50 cm. Note white streaks around cheek. Upperparts uniform dark brown. Habitat: forest patches, woodland. Voice: very high, staccato, rapid '*wutweetweetweet—*' (up to 15 seconds), slightly varying in pitch, lowered at the end.

17 **BRADFIELD'S HORNBILL** *Tockus bradfieldi* L 55 cm. From 16 by less dark upperparts and paler-edged feathers. Flight feathers and outer tail feathers darker than rest of plumage. Arboreal but feeds also on the ground. Habitat: open woodland, thornveld. Voice: very high, sharp, fluting '*wikwikwikwikwikwikwik*' (up to 10 seconds), rising in pitch at the beginning.

18 **SOUTHERN YELLOW-BILLED HORNBILL** *Tockus leucomelas* L 50 cm. From 19 by yellow bill and fewer white spots on primaries. Feeds on the ground. Habitat: dry, more or less wooded and bushed areas. Voice: mid-high, fast '*wokwokwok–*' (up to 30 seconds), ending in excited yelps.

19 **RED-BILLED HORNBILL** *Tockus erythrorhynchus* L 45 cm. From 14 by smaller size, pale head and breast; from 18 by red bill. Feeds on the ground. Habitat: as 18. Voice: high to mid-high, excited, rapid, hoarse, yelping '*wekwekwekwek–*' (up to 25 seconds), falling-off at the end.

Plate 45

Note: normally the crows (1–4) would have been treated in the second half of this book. For reasons of layout and their similarity in size and mainly black colouring, they are placed together here with the large hornbills.

1   **PIED CROW** *Corvus albus*   L 45 cm. Habitat: towns and villages, wooded grassland, areas near rivers, lakes, swamps.

2   **WHITE-NECKED RAVEN** *Corvus albicollis*   L 55 cm. Habitat: rocky, bushed and wooded mountainous areas.

3   **BLACK CROW** *Corvus capensis*   L 45 cm. Note long, slender bill. Usually in flocks. Habitat: grassland with some trees.

4   **HOUSE CROW** *Corvus splendens*   L 45 cm. Note hooded appearance and greyish-brown neck. Originally from Asia. Habitat: established in some towns at the coast. May spread inland from there. U

5   **WHITE-CRESTED HORNBILL** *Tockus albocristatus*   L 65 cm. Note very long tail. Habitat: dense forests and surrounding areas. Voice: very high, rising to extreme high '*eeeeoouWOW*'. R

6   **BLACK-CASQUED WATTLED HORNBILL** *Ceratogymna atrata*   L 80 cm. Note very large size, cobalt-blue bare parts of head, dark brown upperparts. Only white at outer tail tips. Habitat: moist, lowland forest, riverine belts, plantations. Voice: low, hoarse, chattered, fast '*rhoarhoarhoarhoa–*' (often partly breaking up two octaves) or '*tettetrhoaauh -*' or herring gull-like screams in flight. R

7   **SOUTHERN GROUND HORNBILL** *Bucorvus cafer*   L 105 cm. Note white outer wings, which are only visible in flight. Habitat: wooded and bushed areas. Voice: extreme low, booming '*ohooh ohooh ohooh ohooh*' often in duet of ♂ and ♀.

8   **TRUMPETER HORNBILL** *Ceratogymna bucinator*   L 65 cm. Note red orbital skin and all-blackish bill. Habitat: montane rivers and connected riverine belts. Voice: mid-high, loud, resounding, bleating, slightly lowered '*weeeeee*' and excited '*wèhwèhwèhwèh*'.

9   **SILVERY-CHEEKED HORNBILL** *Ceratogymna brevis*   L 75 cm. Note dark bill with all-pale casque and mainly black wings. Habitat: forests and riverine belts. Voice: loud '*uHUH uHUH*' in noisy flight. U

10   **BLACK-AND-WHITE-CASQUED HORNBILL** *Ceratogymna subcylindricus*   L 75 cm. From 8 by bi-coloured casque, purplish-black orbital skin, more white on wing, rump and tail. Habitat: moist forests and surrounding areas. Voice: low, mallard-like chattering, '*chaa-chaa-chaa—*', (up to 25 times).

11   **PIPING HORNBILL** *Ceratogymna fistulator*   L 60 cm. Note dark, central patch on small-casqued bill and all-white outer tail feathers. Habitat: moist forests. Voice: mid-high, rapid, fast, magpie-like chattering, '*pipitjitjaktjaktjak–*' (up to 5 seconds).

Note: the noisy, whizzing flight of large hornbills is brought about by the lack of greater primary coverts on underwing whereby the air is forced through the openings between the primary bases with each wing beat.

Plate 45

The End

Bucerotidae 84

Plate 46

1   **PIED KINGFISHER** *Ceryle rudis*   L 24 cm. The ♂ has a double, ♀ a single (interrupted) breast collar. Habitat: lakes, dams, rivers, creeks, estuaries, lagoons.

2   **AFRICAN GIANT KINGFISHER** *Megaceryle maxima*   L 40 cm. The ♀ from ♂ by much more extensive rufous colouring below. Habitat: streams, ponds, lagoons with overhanging trees and shrub. May be seen at garden pools. Voice: mid-high, loud, nasal shrieks, '*kaai-kaai-kaai–*'.

3   **MALACHITE KINGFISHER** *Corythornis cristata*   L 12 cm. From 6 and 8 by blue cap touching (not separated from) eye, lack of violet behind eye; from 6, 7 and 8 by different habitat. May show crest. Habitat: reed beds, papyrus, shrubbery along lakes, dams, ponds, rivers, streams, creeks. Voice: very high, sharp '*tsip tsip tsip–*' of ♂, short, trilled '*trwwwi*' of ♀.

4   **HALF-COLLARED KINGFISHER** *Alcedo semitorquata*   L 19 cm. Note black bill, pale but brilliant colouring. From 5 by all-white neck spots; from 3, 6, 7 and 8 by blue cheeks. Habitat: rivers, streams, lakes, lagoons, normally with overhanging trees. Voice: extreme high, staccato '*tseep tseep-tseep tseep*'. U

5   **SHINING-BLUE KINGFISHER** *Alcedo quadribrachys*   L 19 cm. From 4 by darker colouring and plain, less spotted wings. Habitat: ponds, streams in forests; also at wooded, reedy fringes of lakes, rivers. Voice: extreme high, irregular '*sweep sweep sweep-sweep-*' (just within ear reach). U

6   **WHITE-BELLIED KINGFISHER** *Corythornis leucogaster*   L 13 cm. Forest species, not seen at open water. White belly diagnostic. Habitat: dense, swampy forest. R

7   **AFRICAN DWARF KINGFISHER** *Ceyx lecontei*   L 10 cm. Note diagnostic, rufous crown and nape. Tiny forest species, normally away from water. Habitat: dense forest undergrowth. Voice: extreme high, irregular '*see see see*'. R

8   **AFRICAN PYGMY KINGFISHER** *Ceyx picta*   L 12 cm. From 3 by long, rufous-violet eyebrow. Habitat: ground strata of dry wood-, bush- and scrubland, tall-grassed forest glades, lake and river edges. Feeds on insects taken from ground, rarely catches fish in water. Voice: very high, mumbled, fast trill, '*trrrt-trut trrrtrrrrtrit-*', or extreme high '*tseet tseet*'. brS

9   **WOODLAND KINGFISHER** *Halcyon senegalensis*   L 21 cm. From 10 by bi-coloured bill, from 14 by paler plumage without blue breast band or black wrist patch on underwing. Habitat: dry, open wood- and bushland, often near streams. Voice: very high, fast trill, '*tiútrrrrrrrrrrúgh*'. brS

10   **MANGROVE KINGFISHER** *Halcyon senegaloides*   L 22 cm. Note all-red bill. Habitat: mangroves, forests, more or less wooded grassland, cultivation, lake margins, river banks. Voice: very high, descending, sharp '*treet treet treet-treetreet treetreetrrrrt*'. U

11   **STRIPED KINGFISHER** *Halcyon chelicuti*   L 17 cm. Unobtrusive but striking blue in flight. Underwing of ♀ plain grey without black bar or carpal patch. Habitat: open woodland, bushveld, often away from water. Voice: very high, short, fluted '*tee*', '*trrrrr*' or '*twee tweetwee*'. Also a duet of ♂ and ♀ sounding as one short phrase, '*téewuh*'.

12   **CHOCOLATE-BACKED KINGFISHER** *Halcyon badia*   L 20 cm. Habitat: undergrowth at well-wooded streams. Voice: mid-high, fluted, unhurried '*wéeh fufeefeeféefée tenk fju fjuh*' (middle part highest-pitched). R

13   **GREY-HEADED** (or -hooded) **KINGFISHER** *Halcyon leucocephala*   L 20 cm. Imm from adult 15 by duller bill and unstreaked, slightly scaled head. Habitat: woodland, bushveld. Voice: very high, up-and-down, warbled '*tsitsitsitjutjitjitjitju*' or '*tsjurrr-tsjurrrr*'. UbrS

14   **BLUE-BREASTED KINGFISHER** *Halcyon malimbica*   L 25 cm. From 9 by grey crown, blue breast band, black carpal patch on underwing. Habitat: forests, riverine belts. Voice: extreme high, loud, fluted, sharp '*tiu-titititititiutiutiu*'.

15   **BROWN-HOODED KINGFISHER** *Halcyon albiventris*   L 20 cm. Note streaked crown and underparts and buff underwing. The ♀ browner above than ♂. Habitat: open forests, wooded areas, suburbs. Voice: very high, short, sharp, fast chatter, '*wí-wuwuwu*'.

16   **BAR-TAILED TROGON** *Apaloderma vittatum*   L 30 cm. From 17 by darker head and more distinct wing barring. Barred undertail diagnostic. Habitat: mid-strata of montane forests. Voice: high, loud, crescendoing '*hoo-hoo-hoo-Hoo-Hoo-HOo-HOo-HOO-HOO-HOO*'. R

17   **NARINA'S TROGON** *Apaloderma narina*   L 30 cm. Note white outer tail feathers (especially striking in rapidly flapping flight). Sits motionless and hunched on perch from where it hawks insects in short sallies. Habitat: more or less open forests, large gardens, at all altitudes. Voice: loud, crescendoing, hooting '*oooh-oo oooh-oo Oooh-Oo Oooh-Oo–*' (6–12 times '*oooh-oo*').

Plate 47

1   **WHYTE'S BARBET** *Stactolaema whytii*   L 18 cm. From 3 by smaller, white-yellow area on head, darker wing (with two white patches per opened wing) and white-streaked underparts. Double wing-patch diagnostic. (See also 6, 7 and 8). Habitat: miombo. Voice: high, hooted, sighing, regular '*hoo-hoo-hoo–*'.

2   **WHITE-EARED BARBET** *Stactolaema leucotis*   L 17 cm. Note prominent, white ear streak and belly. Habitat: mainly in large forest trees. Voice: very high, shrieking '*peepeepeepikpikpikpikpkper*', rather irregular in pitch.

3   **ANCHIETA'S BARBET** *Stactolaema anchietae*   L 17 cm. Note yellow face and single, white wing patch. Habitat: open woodland, riverine belts.

4   **GREEN** (or Woodward's) **BARBET** *Stactolaema olivacea*   L 17 cm. Races *woodwardi* (**a**) and *belcheri* (**b**) shown. Habitat: canopy of forests, dense woodland. Voice: high, wooden, unhurried, slightly accelerated '*tjip tjip tjip tjip tjip tjip-tjip-tjip tjip tjip*'. U

5   **SPOT-FLANKED BARBET** *Tricholaema lacrymosa*   L 13 cm. From 15, 16 and several tinkerbirds (Plate 48) by pale eye (♂), lack of red on forehead, unspotted upperparts (only edges of flight feathers are yellow), boldly spotted flanks. Habitat: woodland, bushveld, forest patches. R

6   **HAIRY-BREASTED BARBET** *Tricholaema hirsuta*   L 15 cm. Note diagnostic, yellow-spotted crown. Habitat: forests and nearby areas. Voice: mid-high, regular, fast, rapid or slow '*hoothoothoothoot–*'.

7   **GREY-THROATED BARBET** *Gymnobucco bonapartei*   L 18 cm. Pale bristle in nostril diagnostic. Note black bill, grey head. Habitat: forest glades. Voice: very high, rapid, sharp chatters and trills. R

8   **NAKED-FACED BARBET** *Gymnobucco calvus*   L 16 cm. Note pale bill, white chin, blackish, naked face. Breeds in colonies. Habitat: forests. Voice: mid-high, hesitating, bouncing, accelerated '*hoot-hoot-hootootoot*'. R

9   **DOUBLE-TOOTHED BARBET** *Lybius bidentatus*   L 25 cm. Eye colour varies between dark brown (shown) and yellow. Habitat: forest edges, riverine belts, cultivation, more or less wooded, natural and cultivated grasslands. Voice: mid-high, tinkerbird-like, sustained '*pook-pook-pook–*'.

10   **BLACK-COLLARED BARBET** *Lybius torquatus*   L 20 cm. Nominate (**a**) and race *zombae* (**b**) shown. From 12 by yellowish underparts. Habitat: woodland, grass- and farmland with scattered trees. Voice: mid-high '*tjauw-tjauw-tjauw–*', high, loud, bouncing '*-Beedidder-*', often given in duet.

11   **BLACK-BACKED BARBET** *Lybius minor*   L 15 cm. Nominate (**a**) and race *macclounii* (**b**) shown. Note pale bill, pinkish belly. Habitat: woodland, bush- and scrubveld, farmland with trees and hedges. U

12   **BROWN-BREASTED BARBET** *Lybius melanopterus*   L 15 cm. Note black thighs and pale bill. Habitat: forest edges, cultivation with trees. U

13   **CHAPLIN'S BARBET** *Lybius chaplini*   L 15 cm. Note white thighs and black bill. From 14 by red forehead and white edge of mantle. Habitat: cultivated and natural areas with a few trees, open woodland. E (Zambia)

14   **WHITE-HEADED BARBET** *Lybius leucocephalus*   L 15 cm. Habitat: dry, open wood- and bushland, gardens, cultivation, often near water. Voice: high, loud, sharp, chattering shrieks, '*peek-peek-peek-peek-*', or tinkling, chattered '*pipipipipeh*'. R

15   (Acacia) **PIED BARBET** *Tricholaema leucomelas*   L 15 cm. Note striking, black bars starting at bill and red forehead. From tinkerbirds (Plate 48) by larger size and black throat. Habitat: dry thornveld, bushveld, often along (dry) streams. Voice: high, hooting, rapid '*uhuhuhuhuhuh*' with mid-high, mewing '*nèhnèhnèhnèhnèh*' in duet.

16   **MIOMBO PIED BARBET** *Tricholaema frontata*   L 15 cm. From 48.16 and 48.17 by spotted underparts. Habitat: miombo, grassland with some trees, other more or less open woodland.

17   **YELLOW-BILLED BARBET** *Trachyphonus purpuratus*   L 25 cm. Often perches quietly in unbarbet-like, upright stance. Habitat: dense forest undergrowth, often at edges and glades, near streams. Voice: mid-high or very high, monotonous '*hoot hoot -*' (2 seconds between each '*hoot*').

18   **CRESTED BARBET** *Trachyphonus vaillantii*   L 23 cm. Habitat: dry, open wood- and bushland, riverine belts, even in suburbs. Voice: very high, coppery, long trill, '*prrrrrrruh*', and similar, slightly hoarse, fluting '*wuutwutwutwutwutwut*'.

Plate 47

Plate 48

Note: all honeyguides have a characteristic short, thick bill with a pale, flesh-coloured base of the lower mandible and a rather small head. Some have moustachial stripes and streaks on lower flanks. Most use a favourite call site. Honeybirds have a thin bill and look and behave rather like warblers or flycatchers. All have white in the tail, hidden when perched but conspicuous in flight.

1   **GREATER HONEYGUIDE** *Indicator indicator*   L 20 cm. Note pale cheek and pink bill of ♂, yellow underparts of imm, yellow upperwing coverts and white-streaked rumps of ♂ and ♀ in flight. Habitat: well-wooded areas. Voice: very high '*wéet-thrrrge*', endlessly repeated. U

2   **SCALY-THROATED HONEYGUIDE** *Indicator variegatus*   L 19 cm. Note spots and streaks on forehead, throat and breast. Habitat: forest, woodland, wooded grassland. Voice: very high, rather short, drawn-up trill, '*rrrrrruh*', at 1 minute intervals. U

3   **LYRE-TAILED HONEYGUIDE** *Melichneutes robustus*   L 20 cm. Habitat: forest. Voice: soft, shrill '*feeFeefeefeeFeeFeefee-*'. Also produces a mechanical 'song' with vibrations of its tail, sounding as a loud sequence of bleating '*mehèh-mehèh-*' as the bird flies around over the forest canopy. R

4   **PALLID** (or Eastern) **HONEYGUIDE** *Indicator meliphilus*   L 10 cm. Note plain upperparts (extremely golden individual shown), white loral spot, absence of moustachial stripe, faint streaks on flanks. Habitat: miombo, thornveld. Voice: calls from favourite tree. U

5   **LEAST HONEYGUIDE** *Indicator exilis*   L 11 cm. Note dark-centred, golden feathers of upperparts, moustachial stripe and streaks on flanks. Habitat: forest. Voice: extreme high, sharp '*weew-weew-weew-*' (each '*weew*' slightly lashed-down). U

6   **LESSER HONEYGUIDE** *Indicator minor*   L 15 cm. Note dark, narrow moustachial stripe, sharply demarcated, grey cheek, tail pattern. Habitat: forest edges, wood- and scrubland, cultivation, grassland with scattered trees. Voice: very high, level, staccato '*weew-weew-weew-*'.

7   **GREEN-BACKED** (or Slender-billed) **HONEYBIRD** *Prodotiscus zambesiae*   L 9 cm. From 8 by paler belly and white eye ring. May have dusky tips to white tail feathers. Habitat: forest,woodland. U

8   **CASSIN'S HONEYBIRD** *Prodotiscus insignis*   L 9 cm. See 7. Habitat: forests and surrounding areas. U

9   **WAHLBERG'S** (or Sharp-billed) **HONEYBIRD** *Prodotiscus regulus*   L 13 cm. Note dusky colouring and blackish, inverted 'T' pattern on tail. Habitat: woodland, plantations, cultivation. Voice: dry, insect-like trill, '*shriiiiii*' (7 seconds). U

10   **AFRICAN BROADBILL** *Smithornis capensis*   L 14 cm. Hawks insects from perch or gleans them from underside of leaves. Habitat: forest and dense woodland. Voice: low '*prrruEh*'. U

11   **SPECKLED TINKERBIRD** *Pogoniulus scolopaceus*   L 10 cm. Note pale eye and chequered colouring. Habitat: forest edges and glades.

12   **GREEN TINKERBIRD** *Pogoniulus simplex*   L 8 cm. From 13 by streaked forehead, green (not dusky) cheek, absence of moustache. Habitat: dense forest; sometimes in woodland. Voice: high, slow-trilled '*prrruh prrruh prrruh*'. U

13   **MOUSTACHED GREEN TINKERBIRD** *Pogoniulus leucomystax*   L 9 cm. From 12 by white moustache, plain forehead, dusky cheek. Habitat: forested slopes. Voice: high, loud, sharp, speedy '*widuduwi-wididiwi-widuwi-*', sometimes uttered as rattles.

14   **WESTERN GREEN TINKERBIRD** *Pogoniulus coryphaeus*   L 9 cm. Note long, yellow streak from crown to tail and green throat. Habitat: forest and wooded areas. U

15   **YELLOW-** (or Golden-) **RUMPED TINKERBIRD** *Pogoniulus bilineatus*   L 10 cm. Habitat: forest, woodland, suburbs. Voice: regular, slow or hurried, wooden '*pook-pook-pook—*' (a '*pook*' in every 3–7 is often left out) or mid-high, hooting, trilled '*prrru-prrrru-prrr—*'.

16   **RED-FRONTED TINKERBIRD** *Pogoniulus pusillus*   L 9 cm. From 17 by deeper (all-) yellow wing coverts. Habitat: forest edges, woodland, gardens. In moister areas than 17. Voice: extremely high, irregular, rapid '*bikbikbikbik-*' (10–15 seconds) and mid-high, monotonous '*buk-buk-buk—*'

17   **YELLOW-FRONTED TINKERBIRD** *Pogoniulus chrysoconus*   L 9 cm. From 16 by faint (not bright) yellow wings. Yellow-fronted **(a)** form distinctive; orange-fronted **(b)** form difficult to distinguish from 16. Habitat: woodland, more or less wooded, cultivated areas. Voice: high, regular, uninterrupted '*puk-puk-puk—*', sustained for very long periods.

▶

Plate 48

Indicatoridae 84

Eurylaimidae 84

Acanthisittidae Philepittidae Menuridae
Atrichornithidae 50

capitonidae 84

Plate 48 (continued)

18   **AFRICAN PITTA** *Pitta angolensis*   L 23 cm. Secretive and difficult to spot on the dark forest floor. Behaviour rather thrush-like. Habitat: forest, plantations. Voice: strange '*puWée*' ('*pu-*' as frog-like undertone to very high, fluting '-*Wée*'). U

Plate 49

1   **GREEN-BACKED** (or Little Spotted) **WOODPECKER** *Campethera cailliautii*   L 16 cm. Note plain tail, short bill, diagnostic lack of moustachial stripe. Race *loveridgei* (**a**) has regularly barred upperparts and spotted underparts, race *permista* (**b**) has plain upperparts and barred underparts. Habitat: forest edge, woodland, thornland. Voice: very high, questioning '*weeh*'.

2   **BROWN-EARED WOODPECKER** *Campethera caroli*   L 19 cm. Note dark colouring and diagnostic, brown ear coverts. Habitat: forest, riverine belts, plantations. Voice: high, drawn- and puffed-out, rising then lowered '*piuuúauih*'.

3   **GOLDEN-TAILED WOODPECKER** *Campethera abingoni*   L 20 cm. From 5 by boldly streaked face and almost black throat and upperbreast; from 6 by paler, brighter colouring above and streaking (not scalloping) below. Habitat: forest, woodland, often near streams. Voice: mid-high, bleating '*puWEE*' ('*pu-*' as undertone) or nasal, rapidly lowered '*wéeegh*'.

4   **BUFF-SPOTTED WOODPECKER** *Campethera nivosa*   L 15 cm. Note small size, short bill, absence of moustachial stripe, unmarked upperparts. Habitat: dense forests. Voice: high, slightly plaintive, slightly descending '*pièèèèh pièèèèh*' or very low '*kretsh kretsh*'.

5   **BENNETT'S WOODPECKER** *Campethera bennettii*   L 19 cm. Nominate (**a**) shows clean cheek and chin (♂), buffish brown in ♀. Race *scriptoricauda* (**b**) has streaked ear coverts and spotted chin (♂), while ♀ shows a diagnostic, black, white-spotted moustache; **b** also has shorter wing and paler base to lower mandible. Habitat: open woodland and scrub. Voice: mid-high, excited, cackled '*rrrrrrrutiwéetiwéetiwéeti–*' ('*rrrr-*' running up).

6   **KNYSNA WOODPECKER** *Campethera notata*   L 20 cm. Note extensive dark scalloping below (extending to neck sides), dark, finely spotted upperparts, densely streaked and spotted face: ♀ shows brown moustache. Habitat: forest, wooded scrubland, gardens. Voice: very high '*siiiii*'. E (South Africa)

7   **OLIVE WOODPECKER** *Dendropicos griseocephalus*   L 17 cm. From 9 by unmarked colouring and olive (not grey) underparts. Habitat: dense forest. Voice: high, plaintive, pushed-out '*wWeewit wWeewit wWeewit*'.

8   **ELLIOT'S WOODPECKER** *Dendropicos elliotii*   L 16 cm. Note buff face sides, plain, green upperparts, streaked underparts. Habitat: dense forest. R

9   **GREY WOODPECKER** *Dendropicos goertae*   L 19 cm. Note pale grey head and underparts and barred wings and tail. Habitat: open forests, more or less natural and cultivated areas, gardens. Voice: very high, angry, sharp, chattered '*títítitrítrítritritri*'.

10   **CARDINAL WOODPECKER** *Dendropicos fuscescens*   L 14 cm. Note very small size and erectile crest. Nominate (**a**) is densely barred above; race *lafresnayi* (**b**) has almost plain mantle, more obscure moustache and barring below. Habitat: forest, other wooded and bushed habitats. Voice: extreme high, rapid, sharp, twittered '*tuteetee tletuteetutee*' or dry, high, thrush-like '*shreeshreeshree-*'.

11   **BEARDED WOODPECKER** *Dendropicos namaquus*   L 25 cm. Note large size and brownish-green, completely barred (except head) appearance. The ♂ is more scalloped above than ♀. Habitat: dry woodland, bushveld, with some large trees. Voice: high, loud, rapid, slightly descending '*kluklukluklukluklukluklu*'.

12   **YELLOW-CRESTED WOODPECKER** *Dendropicos xantholophus*   L 23 cm. The ♂ is only woodpecker with yellow crone. Wing barring mainly visible in flight. Habitat: forest and surrounding areas. Voice: very high, shrill, excited, chattered trills like '*tierrrr-tierr-tutututututwi*'.

13   **STIERLING'S WOODPECKER** *Dendropicos stierlingi*   L 16 cm. Note small, dark appearance and plain upperparts. Habitat: miombo. U

14   **AFRICAN PICULET** *Sasia africana*   L 8 cm. Only as long as a finger. The ♂ from ♀ by rufous forehead. Very active, difficult to follow. Often in mixed bird parties. Uses its feet only, not its tail, for support. Climbs trunks, twigs, grass stems. Habitat: undergrowth at forest edges. Voice: extreme high, barely audible '*srrrrrrreeh*'. R

▶

Plate 49

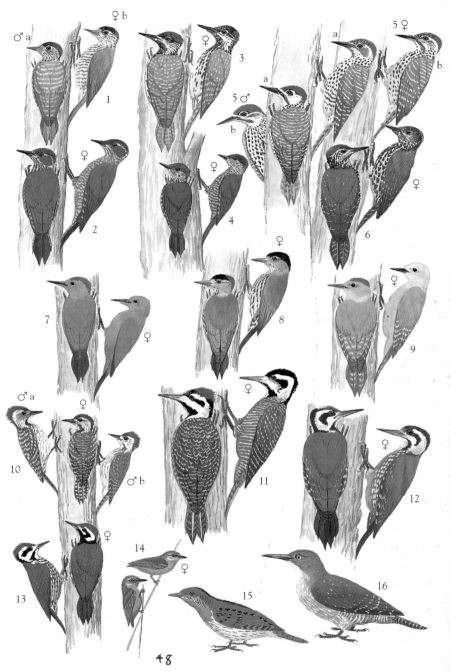

48

Plate 49 (continued)

15 **RUFOUS-BREASTED** (or Red-throated) **WRYNECK** *Jynx ruficollis*   L 19 cm. Perches crosswise. Forages more on ground than on tree stems and branches. Habitat: open, more or less wooded, natural and cultivated areas. Voice: high, bleating '*pjuuuut - pjuuut - pjuuut*'.

16 **GROUND WOODPECKER** *Geocolaptes olivaceus*   L 25 cm. Note pale eye and pink breast. Lives exclusively on the ground. Habitat: open, rock-strewn, hilly and mountainous areas.

Plate 50

1 **LONG-BILLED LARK** *Certhilauda curvirostris*   L 19 cm. Not all races depicted; *bradshawi* (**a**), *benguelensis* (**b**), nominate (**c**) and *semitorquata* (**d**) shown (note differences in bill shape, tinge and streaking). From 6 by brown (not contrasting rusty-red) rump. Habitat: grass- and scrubland with stony outcrops and ridges. Voice: when displaying rises steeply to about 20 m, calls high, sharp, resounding '*pjűer pjűer -*' and descends with folded wings.

2 **KAROO LARK** *Certhilauda albescens*   L 17 cm. Not all races depicted; *cavei* (**a**) and nominate (**b**) shown. Extensive streaking of underparts diagnostic. Note dark tail and white eyebrow. From 3 by more slender bill and (where in same area) by more streaking on upperparts. From 7 by darker, less sandy-rufous colouring. Habitat: stony, open shrubland and dunes. Voice: sings from bush top or in flight, rapid, twittering '*pitpitpittuwer*' or rattling, high '*putputputputr*'.

3 **RED LARK** *Certhilauda burra*   L 19 cm. Colour forms **a** and **b** shown. Note heavy bill, dark wings and tail, rather plain upperparts, restricted range. Hovers shortly before settling. Habitat: red sand dunes sparsely covered with grass, shrublands. Voice: from bush top or in flight, high, very fast, canary-like, twittered '*trrrrrtrui*'. U E (South Africa)

4 **SPIKE-HEELED LARK** *Chersomanes albofasciata*   L 15 cm. Not all races depicted; nominate (**a**) and *kalahari* (**b**) shown. Note short tail with white corners, thin bill, erect stance. Habitat: grass- and shrublands, gravel plains with sparse grass cover. Voice: sings in short phrases just after take-off, plover-like, sharp, very fast '*wuutwuutwuut*'.

5 **GRAY'S LARK** *Ammomanes grayi*   L 14 cm. Two forms (**a** and **b**) shown. Note very pale colouring, sometimes appearing white in the field. From 58.2 by pale bill, pale legs, different tail and rump pattern. Habitat: gravel-covered deserts with rocky outcrops. Voice: sings only before dawn, extreme high '*ee-ee-wee-ee-*'.

6 **SHORT-CLAWED LARK** *Certhilauda chuana*   L 19 cm. From 1 by rust-red rump and 'capped' appearance (due to long, white eyebrow). Habitat: dry thornveld and scrubland. Voice: extreme high to very high, drawn-out, whistled '*feeeeuh-weetweetweeuuuuh*'. U

7 **DUNE LARK** *Certhilauda erythrochlamys*   L 17 cm. Note pale appearance and black in tail. From 2 and 3 by paler colouring, finer breast streaking, different range. Habitat: scrubby places in Namib desert. Voice: sings in flight or from perch, variations on very high '*pitpitpittur-pitpittur*'. U E (Namibia)

Note: 2, 3 and 7 form a complex of very similar looking lark species, which are endemic to the desert and semi-desert of SW Africa. They are best identified by range, bill form and extent of streaking on underparts. Recent detailed studies suggest that these larks are better divided not into three, but into four species, retaining 2, 3 and 7 but adding a new species (now a subspecies of 7) named: **BARLOW'S LARK** *Certhilauda barlowi* L 18 cm (not illustrated). From 3 by smaller bill and different range, from 4 by darker, more brown colouring and different range, and from 2 (with which it shares only a small part of its range) by less extensive streaking below, (not extending over flanks and belly) and by different voice. See map 50.7 B. Habitat: scrubland and other sparsely covered areas. Voice: as 2, but with longer, sustained phrases, preceded by 2–5 (not 1–2) introductory notes. U

8 **LARGE-** (or Thick-) **BILLED LARK** *Galerida magnirostris*   L 18 cm. Note heavy bill with pale base of lower mandible. May show a crest. Heavily marked above and below, without rufous in wings or tail. Habitat: dry montane grassland, shrubland, cultivated fields. Voice: sings in flight or from perch, short, pleasant, high little phrases like '*wip-wipwurreeh*'.

9 **DUSKY LARK** *Pinarocorys nigricans*   L 18 cm. Note dark, almost black appearance with striking face pattern. From 60.5 by shorter bill and pale-edged wing feathers. Flicks wings frequently when foraging on the ground. Habitat: open, grassy thornveld, woodland. Voice: in flight, high, rasping '*sreeeeh-sreeeh-sreeeh*'. US

▶

Plate 50

Plate 50 (continued)

10   **BIMACULATED LARK** *Melanocorypha bimaculata*   L 18 cm. Black patches on breast sides diagnostic. Single individual found once in Namibia (1930) far from its natural range (Egypt, Sudan, Eritrea), presumed to be an escaped cage bird. Habitat: dry, open areas and cropped fields. Voice: very high, partly shrill, partly mellow, hurried twitter with many sudden stops. (?)

Plate 51

1   **FLAPPET LARK** *Mirafra rufocinnamomea*   L 14 cm. Not all races depicted; *mababiensis* (a) and *pintoi* (b) shown. Range extends from Johannesburg north-eastwards, away from many other larks (small area of overlap with similar 2). Note buff (not white) outer tail feathers and red in wing. Habitat: woodland, wooded grass plains. Voice: dry, short burst of wing flaps (not unlike distant motorbike exhaust) during high aerial cruise, sometimes with very high, short '*witweetríeweeh*'.

2   **CLAPPER LARK** *Mirafra apiata*   L 15 cm. Not all races depicted; *deserti* (a), *hewitti* (b) and nominate (c) shown. From 1 by redder tinge, pale, almost white outer tail feathers. Habitat: boulder-strewn, sloping grassland, dry shrublands, Kalahari scrub. Voice: flaps at the summit of an upward display flight before descending, while giving a loud whistle, '*fuuiiii titjitjirrrr*'.

3   **MONOTONOUS LARK** *Mirafra passerina*   L 14 cm. From 4 and 5 by absence of white eyebrow, from 5 by red wings and white outer tail feathers, from 12 by red range and mainly different range. Habitat: stony patches in dry bushveld and woodland. Voice: sings from top of bush (or in short display flight) puffing out its throat, very high, fluted, short '*uppertjeetjuuk*' (up to 10 times).

4   **MELODIOUS LARK** *Mirafra cheniana*   L 12 cm. From 3 by sharper eyebrow, more buffy underparts, different habitat. Habitat: grassland, cultivated fields. Voice: sings for long periods from high perch or in fluttering display flight in a continuous flow of short, repeated phrases, canary-like trills, fluted interludes, perfect imitations of other birds.

5   **SABOTA LARK** *Mirafra sabota*   L 14 cm. Bill shape variable; may be thinner or heavier than shown . Note prominent, long, white eyebrow, lack of red in wings, dark malar stripe and bold streaking on upperbreast. Habitat: bushveld, open woodland, especially on rocky slopes. Voice: normally sings from perch, occasionally in hovering, fluttering flight, unhurried, melodious twitters interspersed with extreme high '*seee*' notes.

6   **FAWN-COLOURED LARK** *Mirafra africanoides*   L 14 cm. Note white underparts, light breast streaking, white line above and below eye (both starting at bill). Upperparts often darker and more heavily streaked than shown. Habitat: more or less shrubby areas. Voice: very high, happy, lowered, accelerated '*fítji fit fi-fitjiweeweejegh*'.

7   **RUFOUS-NAPED LARK** *Mirafra africana*   L 17 cm. Not all races depicted; *transvaalensis* (a) and *pallida* (b) shown. From 8 by buff, not white, outer tail feathers. Crest and rufous wings diagnostic. Habitat: open and bushed, partly bare or overgrazed grass and pasture land. Voice: extreme high, short, sharp, yet sweet whistle '*tée-tjuih*' or '*tiú-uweek*', given from boulder or bush top.

8   **ANGOLA LARK** *Mirafra angolensis*   L 17 cm. From 7 by darker plumage, white outer tail feathers, smaller, red wing patch, barred tertials. Occupies a restricted, broken-up range. Habitat: montane grassland, moist valleys. U

9   **BOTHA'S LARK** *Spizocorys fringillaris*   L 12 cm. From 11 by less conical bill, white outer tail feathers, white chin, lower breast and belly. Habitat: upland, short grasslands. Voice: in low flight, very high '*sireee sireeeh*'. U E (South Africa)

10   **RUDD'S LARK** *Heteromirafra ruddi*   L 14 cm. Note buffy crown stripe, short tail, erect stance. From 50.4 by shorter, conical bill and different tail pattern. Habitat: montane grassland. Voice: cruises at 30 m in alternating flapping and gliding display flight, giving short whistles like high '*witurwéeh*'. U E (South Africa)

11   **PINK-BILLED LARK** *Spizocorys conirostris*   L 13 cm. General tinge varies from very pale to rather dark; intermediate form shown. From 9 by more conical bill, from 13 by absence of crest, from 9 and 13 by buff outer tail feathers. Habitat: montane grasslands. Voice: very high, short, more or less connected twitters, like sharp '*sreee-sreee*', given from ground or in flight.

12   **SCLATER'S LARK** *Spizocorys sclateri*   L 14 cm. Tinge variable. Note large head with distinctive 'tear-drops', broad, white tail edges, absence of crest. Habitat: dry, stony, sparsely grassed and shrubbed areas. Voice: a sequence of more or less connected, fluted, melodious or harsh notes, some with bee-eater- or reed warbler-like quality. U

▶

Plate 51

Plate 51 (continued)

13 STARK'S LARK *Eremalauda starki*   L 14 cm. Note very pale colouring and peaked or crested crown. From 50.5 by marking of upperparts. Habitat: dry grassland. Voice: sings on ground or in high display flight, hardly varied '*wee-sree-sree-sruh-wee-sree-tjuutjuw-wee–*'.

14 RED-CAPPED LARK *Calandrella cinerea*   L 15 cm. Note red crest (not always erect) and shoulder patch. Habitat: dry, bare, more or less grassed and scrubbed areas. Voice: very high, unstructured, connected, short twitters including '*sweeeh*' and sharp, descending '*tweeeeeh-*'.

Note: the sparrow-larks are depicted on Plate 76 for reasons of layout of the book.

Plate 52

1 WHITE-THROATED BLUE SWALLOW *Hirundo nigrita*   L 15 cm. Note white tail windows. Habitat: along forest streams, rivers.

2 MOSQUE SWALLOW *Hirundo senegalensis*   L 17 (+7) cm. From 3 by white chin, cheeks and upperbreast and white underwing coverts. Habitat: forest edge, open woodland with baobab. Voice: mid- and very high, nasal, mewing '*twit*' and '*treeek*' or '*truuuih*'.

3 RED-BREASTED SWALLOW *Hirundo semirufa*   L 16 (+8) cm. From 7 by red rump, longer tail streamers. Habitat: open and bushed habitats with some scattered trees, often near water. Voice: mid-high, explosive, rather sharp '*tit titriUOOH*'. brS

4 LESSER STRIPED SWALLOW *Hirundo abyssinica*   L 13 (+4) cm. Red cap extends further down than in 5. Striped throat and chin look uniform dark if seen from a distance. Habitat: open forests, woodland, dry, bushed grass- and farmland, areas near cliffs and buildings (needed for nesting), often near water. Voice: high, often reed warbler-like '*wit weet witwit-*'.

5 GREATER STRIPED SWALLOW *Hirundo cucullata*   L 14 (+5) cm. Note pale, chestnut cheek and throat, which is barely or not striped . Habitat: open grassland. Avoids woodland and forest. Voice: mid-high, unhurried '*trrit-trrit-treet-treet*'. brS(W)

6 BARN (or European) SWALLOW *Hirundo rustica*   L 16 (+5) cm. From 9 by unbroken breast band, longer tail streamers, paler underparts. Habitat: can be seen anywhere except in true forest. Voice: mid-high, happy, nasal twitters combined with inhaled trills. S.

7 BLACK-AND-RUFOUS SWALLOW *Hirundo nigrorufa*   L 15 cm. See 3. Appears black in the field. Note absence of rufous rump. Habitat: grass plains, open woodland, marsh edges. U

8 WIRE-TAILED SWALLOW *Hirundo smithii*   L 13 (+10) cm. Note very thin tail streamers (difficult to see in flight), pure white underparts, interrupted black ring between belly and undertail coverts, red cap. Habitat: forest edge, grassland, settlement, often near rivers and lakes. Voice: very high '*twitwit srièèh*' in short phrases.

9 ANGOLA SWALLOW *Hirundo angolensis*   L 15 cm. Similar to 6 which see. Note dusky underwing coverts. Habitat: open and bushed habitats, river edges, lakes, swamps, forest, settlement. S

10 RED-RUMPED SWALLOW *Hirundo daurica*   L 14 (+4) cm. Note rufous neck, isolating black cap from mantle, and diagnostic, black undertail coverts. Habitat: rocky hillsides. Voice: mid-high, nasal '*weet-weet*'. RS

11 WHITE-THROATED SWALLOW *Hirundo albigularis*   L 16 cm. Note white throat, black breast band, chestnut forehead. Habitat: open grass plains, inundations, dams, rivers, settlement. Voice: extreme high, soft '*sreeeeeeh sreeeeeeeh*' in flight.

12 PEARL-BREASTED SWALLOW *Hirundo dimidiata*   L 14 cm. From 53.13 by lack of rufous rump, less strong gloss on upperparts. Habitat: more or less wooded and bushed habitats, often near swamps and settlement. Voice: mid-high, nasal '*sreet*', '*sreet-sreet*' or '*sriauw-sriauw*'.

13 RED-THROATED CLIFF SWALLOW *Hirundo rufigula*   L 13 cm. From 14 by white spots in tail, darker, plain, rufous rump, blue-black crown and neck, clean throat, less obvious breast band. Ranges do not or hardly overlap except in North Zambia and maybe in Cabinda. Habitat: as 14.

14 SOUTH AFRICAN CLIFF SWALLOW *Hirundo spilodera*   L 14 cm. Similar to 13 which see. Absence of tail spots diagnostic. Habitat: grasslands not too far from buildings, bridges or buildings. Voice: very high '*srée-titirrrrrr*'. brS(W)

Plate 52

Plate 53

1   **ROCK MARTIN** *Hirundo fuligula*   L 13 cm. From 6b by paler underparts (contrasting more with upperparts), white spots in tail (difficult to see unless spread tail is seen against dark background e.g. tree or cliff). Occurs singly or in small colonies. Habitat: near cliffs, houses, bridges. Voice: very high, shrill '*sreeh*' and '*tusjirr*'.

2   **GREY-RUMPED SWALLOW** *Pseudhirundo griseopyga*   L 12 (+2) cm. Note grey rump, weak, blue gloss, dark, brown head, absence of white in tail. Habitat: sheltered areas with some grass, often near water. Voice: mid-high, shrieking '*shree free wih shree*'.

3   **BANDED MARTIN** *Riparia cincta*   L 16 cm. From 4 by darker, more contrasting upperparts, very dark eye area, whitish underwing coverts. Narrow, white eyebrow diagnostic. Nests alone in a tunnel which it excavates in sand cliff. Habitat: open, bushed grassland near rivers, marshes, dams, ponds. Voice: mid-high, reed warbler-like, hurried twitters in phrases of any length.

4   **COMMON SAND MARTIN** *Riparia riparia*   L 13 cm. Note dark underwing and breast band and shallow forked tail. From 6 by white chin. Very gregarious, forms colonies in river banks and sand cliffs. Habitat: anywhere near water except in forests and dense settlement. Voice: mid-high, slightly rasping, hurried twitters. US

5   **MASCARENE MARTIN** *Phedina borbonica*   L 13 cm. From 7 by forked tail, larger size, uniform unstreaked underwing coverts, different range. Streaking on underparts difficult to see from some distance. Nests in small groups outside the area covered by this book, at cliffs or in buildings. Habitat: open woodland. RW

6   **BROWN-THROATED SAND MARTIN** *Riparia paludicola*   L 13 cm. Pale-bellied **(a)** and dark **(b)** forms shown. Note uniform brown face sides, absence of dark eye patch, lack of white spots in tail. Forms small colonies in tunnels excavated in sand banks and cliffs. Habitat: areas near rivers, lakes and dams. Voice: mid-high, rasping shrieks and liquid twitters.

7   **BRAZZA'S MARTIN** *Phedina brazzae*   L 11 cm. From 5 by smaller size, square tail, streaked underwing coverts. Habitat: riverine belts with sand banks. R

8   **BLUE SWALLOW** *Hirundo atrocaerulea*   L 15 (+6) cm. From 10 and 11 by very long, thin tail streamers and blue-black feathering. Habitat: open, bushed and wooded grassland near swamp or forest edges, often at high altitudes. Voice: high, reed warbler-like, rapid '*weetweetweetweetweet-*' mixed with short chirps and twitters. UbrS

9   **WHITE-HEADED SAW-WING** *Psalidoprocne albiceps*   L 14 (+4) cm. Note long, shallowly forked tail. Appears dark, dusky-brown without noticeable gloss. Flight slow, often low over vegetation. Habitat: forest glades, woodland, sparsely wooded areas.

10   **BLACK SAW-WING** *Psalidoprocne pristoptera holomelaena*   L 14 (+4) cm. Uniform dark underwing diagnostic. Flight slow and steady with much low gliding over vegetation. Also hawks from perch. Habitat: forest glades and edges, more or less open woodland, marshes, often near settlement. Voice: very high '*priuuuw sreeeuw sreeeoh*'. (brS)

11   **EASTERN SAW-WING** *Psalidoprocne pristoptera orientalis*   L 13 (+3) cm. From 10 by white underwing coverts. Habitat: as 10.

12   **SQUARE-TAILED SAW-WING** *Psalidoprocne nitens*   L 13 cm. Note absence of gloss and square tail. Habitat: forest interior and edges. R

13   **COMMON HOUSE MARTIN** *Delichon urbica*   L 14 cm. Only swallow with white rump. Normally seen in flocks (often with other swallows) over any type of country. Habitat: shows some preference for rocky cliffs or high structures; in the southern parts of the region mainly coastal. Voice: very high, sharp yet liquid '*pri-wip prrri-wrip*'. (br?)S

Plate 53

Plate 54

1 **AFRICAN GOLDEN ORIOLE** *Oriolus auratus*   L 24 cm. The ♀ from ♀2 by longer, dark eye line and yellow edges to wing coverts and flight feathers. Habitat: forest edges, riverine belts, woodland, open areas with large trees. Voice: high, melodious, fluted '*wéetweetwuh weetweetwurío*' and mewing cry (sharper than 2). UbrS(W)

2 **EUROPEAN GOLDEN ORIOLE** *Oriolus oriolus*   L 24 cm. Habitat: forest edges, woodland, open forest with large trees. Voice: normally silent in Africa. Mid-high, liquid, very melodious, rapid '*wéetwéetworío*' and descending, mewing cry. S

3 **BLACK-HEADED ORIOLE** *Oriolus larvatus*   L 24 cm. The common, black-headed oriole in the area; 5 and 6 only found in NW Angola (see maps). Habitat: woodland, riverine belts, plantations. Voice: mid-high, liquid, short, hurried '*weetowéeoh*' (with emphasis on '-*wéeoh*').

4 **GREEN-HEADED ORIOLE** *Oriolus chlorocephalus*   L 24 cm. Habitat: montane forest. Voice: mid-high, liquid, short '*witwitoWeeoh*' (first part '*witwit-*' very fast) or simple, liquid, high '-*wheet*' (preceded by barely audible '*piupiu-*'). R

5 **BLACK-WINGED ORIOLE** *Oriolus nigripennis*   L 24 cm. From 3 and 6 by green mantle and wing coverts and different tail pattern. Habitat: forest.

6 **WESTERN BLACK-HEADED ORIOLE** *Oriolus brachyrhynchus*   L 22 cm. From 3 by more grey wing coverts, green- (not yellow-) edged tertials, paler (less green) middle tail feathers. Habitat: more restricted to true forest than 3. U

7 **ARROW-MARKED BABBLER** *Turdoides jardineii*   L 24 cm. Note red-rimmed, yellow eye, arrow-marked feathering, uniform brown upperparts. Note: like all babblers, found in parties of up to 10. Habitat: any type of woodland, riverine belts, acacia bush, suburbs.

8 **BLACK-FACED BABBLER** *Turdoides melanops*   L 30 cm. Note yellow eye circled in black. Habitat: bushed and wooded areas. U

9 **BARE-CHEEKED BABBLER** *Turdoides gymnogenys*   L 24 cm. Unmistakable. Habitat: dry, rocky areas with wooded outcrops.

10 **SOUTHERN PIED BABBLER** *Turdoides bicolor*   L 25 cm. Unmistakable. Habitat: dry bushveld, more or less open woodland.

11 **HARTLAUB'S** (or White-rumped) **BABBLER** *Turdoides hartlaubii*   L 25 cm. Note red eye. Habitat: reed beds, other wet habitats and nearby woodlands.

Note: the following small birds on this plate have a robin-like jizz and live in the undergrowth and on the ground of forests where they are difficult to see. Most have a very restricted range within the region.

12 **AFRICAN HILL BABBLER** *Illadopsis abyssinica*   L 13 cm. Note sharp demarcation of dark grey head from tawny brown mantle. Occurs singly or in pairs. Habitat: montane forest and riverine belts. Voice: high, up-and-down, thrush-like, fluted '*pfípfíwufíwuwwéeh*'.

13 **DAPPLED MOUNTAIN ROBIN** *Arcanator orostruthus*   L 14 cm. Note red tail, streaked underparts, long, thin bill, overall greenish tinge. Habitat: montane forest. R

14 **SPOT-THROAT** *Modulatrix stictigula*   L 14 cm. Note speckled throat, grey eye ring, long bill, reddish tinge, slightly rufous rump. Habitat: forests at higher altitudes. R

15 **MOUNTAIN ILLADOPSIS** *Illadopsis pyrrhoptera*   L 14 cm. Note very dark colouring with whitish chin. Solitary or in small groups of up to 5. Habitat: montane forest. Voice: very high, fluted, descending, calm '*ónetwothree four*' ('*four*' is very low answer in a duet of ♂ and ♀). R

16 **BROWN ILLADOPSIS** *Illadopsis fulvescens*   L 16 cm. Note sharp division between grey cheeks and white chin and uniform underparts. Less on the ground than other illadopsises. Pairs or in small family groups. Habitat: forest. Voice: three-toned, soft, unhurried, mellow, fluted '*few-ftwtue*' in duet of ♂ and ♀. Also e.g. high '*fweeeeh*' or '*due*' with varied '*pic*' as countersong. R

17 **SCALY-BREASTED ILLADOPSIS** *Illadopsis albipectus*   L 14 cm. Note pale legs and scaly breast (some individuals without, or with reduced, scaling!). Solitary or in pairs. Habitat: forest. Voice: very high, slightly rising, sharp '*piuu-piuu-péeh*' or very high, sharp, whistled '*fjuu-fjee-fjée*'.

18 **THRUSH BABBLER** *Ptyrticus turdinus*   L 22 cm. Note spotted breast band and white underparts. Habitat: swampy woodland, riverine belts. Voice: mid-high, melodious, fluted '*wuWútju-tjitjútuditjúw*' and other mellow phrases.

Plate 54

African Golden Oriole

Green-headed Oriole

Eurasian Golden Oriole

Imm

Plate 55

1   **MOUNTAIN GREENBUL** *Andropadus tephrolaemus fusciceps*   L 18 cm. From 2 by brighter plumage and whiter eye ring, from 6 by unstriped cheeks. Habitat: montane forests. R

2   **SHELLEY'S GREENBUL** *Andropadus masukuensis*   L 17 cm. Smaller, darker and duller than 1. Clings, often woodpecker-like, to trunks. Habitat: montane forests. R

3   **SOMBRE GREENBUL** *Andropadus importunus*   L 22 cm. Nominate (a) and brighter race *hypoxanthus* (b) shown. Note creamy-white eye and unmarked face sides. Habitat: forests, coastal bush. Voice: very high, fast '*fweeh twitwitwitwiti*' or '*torritrreeweehweeh*'.

4   **LITTLE GREY GREENBUL** *Andropadus gracilis*   L 15 cm. Note narrow eye ring, whitish chin, yellowish lower belly. Forages rather high in trees. Habitat: forest. Voice: very high, up-and-down '*weetúptowúp tjut*'. R

5   **LITTLE GREENBUL** *Andropadus virens*   L 15 cm. From 4 by yellowish (not greyish) chin, greenish (not olive) mantle, absence of eye ring. Habitat: mid-strata and undergrowth of forest. Voice: hurried strophes like mid-high, warbling, up-and-down '*prrrrkprrrrkjterp-fuwit*'.

6   **STRIPE-CHEEKED GREENBUL** *Andropadus milanjensis*   L 21 cm. Presence of creamy (a) or dark (b) eye is an individual variation, independent of race or sex. Note diagnostic, white upper eyelid. Habitat: forest edges and adjacent areas. Voice: mid-high '*tjah tjah tjekkertjektjek*'.

7   **SLENDER-BILLED GREENBUL** *Andropadus gracilirostris*   L 17 cm. Note yellowish undertail coverts, pale grey underparts (only forest greenbul so). Habitat: upper-strata of montane forests. Voice: very high, descending, repeated '*tjiúuuu tjúuu*' and mid-high, drawn-up '*nieaú nieaú*'.

8   **PLAIN GREENBUL** *Andropadus curvirostris*   L 16 cm. Note well-defined, grey throat, small, short bill, pale grey eyelids. Habitat: forest understorey. Voice: mid-high, fluted '*tuwéetúdírrrr*' or '*wéetowéehoh*'. R

9   **YELLOW-WHISKERED GREENBUL** *Andropadus latirostris*   L 18 cm. Note conspicuous, yellow whiskers. Habitat: forests, forest remains, plantations, large gardens. Voice: mid-high, unstructured, up-and-down, scratching, unhurried '*tjash tjesh tjesh-tjush tresh-tjash-*'. U

10   **TERRESTRIAL BROWNBUL** *Phyllastrephus terrestris*   L 18 cm. Note conspicuous, white chin. Often in small, noisy groups. Habitat: small parties in and on the ground in dense forest undergrowth, riverine belts, dense woodland. Voice: sharp, rattling '*cratchohcratchoh wiwir*'.

11   **TINY** (or Slender) **GREENBUL** *Phyllastrephus debilis*   L 14 cm. In size and habits rather warbler-like. Note long, thin, pale bill, grey face sides, pale (but occasionally dark) eye. Habitat: coastal shrub, forest, forest remains. Voice: low, ascending, nasal, fast '*mau-mau-mau-mau-kirrik*'.

12   **YELLOW-STREAKED GREENBUL** *Phyllastrephus flavostriatus*   L 19 cm. Nominate (a) and race *alfredi* (b) shown. Note striking, long bill. Yellow streaking on underparts not apparent in the field. Not shy. Constantly raises or flicks a wing on one side. Habitat: mid- and higher strata of forests. Voice: mid-high, lazy '*terrettjúp terrettjúp tjup-tjup-tjup-tjup*' or high '*tsjírrup-tsjírrup*'.

13   **PALE OLIVE GREENBUL** *Phyllastrephus fulviventris*   L 16 cm. From 10 by more pronounced contrast between upper- and (uniform) underparts and rather striped eye area. Habitat: forest undergrowth.

14   **CABANIS'S GREENBUL** *Phyllastrephus cabanisi*   L 17 cm. Note well-defined, whitish throat and creamy white eyelids. Eye colour may be pale grey. Small groups. Habitat: highland forests.

15   **GREY-OLIVE GREENBUL** *Phyllastrephus cerviniventris*   L 16 cm. Note diagnostic, pale legs. Habitat: forest undergrowth, riverine belts. U

16   **WHITE-THROATED GREENBUL** *Phyllastrephus albigularis*   L 16 cm. Note conspicuous, white throat. From 56.9 by overall less bright colouring, more slender build. Habitat: forest edges, gardens. Voice: high, melodious, '*witwitwéetwitjuu-tjuu-tjuu*' (first part rapidly chattered). R

17   **CAPE BULBUL** *Pycnonotus capensis*   L 17 cm. Habitat: any area with bush and trees including gardens. Voice: high, sharp '*tut thréetowéet tuwéet*'. E (South Africa)

18   **AFRICAN RED-EYED BULBUL** *Pycnonotus nigricans*   L 17 cm. Habitat: as 17. Voice: high, liquid '*wuutweeroweet*' like 19.

19   **COMMON** (or Black-eyed) **BULBUL** *Pycnonotus barbatus*   L 18 cm. Habitat: as 17. Voice: high, happy, up-and-down, whistled '*I'm cóming hóme*'.

▶

Plate 55

Plate 55 (continued)

20 **BUSH BLACKCAP** *Lioptilus nigricapillus*   L 17 cm. Skulking. Note: not a bulbul but a babbler, Plate 54. Habitat: montane forest, forest patches. Voice: high, liquid, melodious '*wuutweeweet*' and variations on this (like 19 but more varied). U E (South Africa)

Plate 56

1 **FORK-TAILED DRONGO** *Dicrurus adsimilis*   L 24 cm. From 2 by larger size and deeply forked tail. Noisy. Hawks insects from an exposed position. Habitat: forest edges, dry woodland, farmland.

Note: Drongos differ from other black birds, such as 11 and 12, by absence of yellow gape and different hunting technique, from 67.9 by different tail form and more obtrusive behaviour, from 72.6 and 72.7 by different behaviour (do not skulk or sing from cover), and from all these birds by dark, red eyes.

2 **SQUARE-TAILED DRONGO** *Dicrurus ludwigii*   L 18 cm. Perches in less exposed manner than 1. Habitat: forest, riverine belts. U

3 **HONEYGUIDE GREENBUL** *Baeopogon indicator*   L 19 cm. Note diagnostic tail pattern. Habitat: forest canopy. Voice: very high, fluted '*pipiupi-pjiuww*' and high '*pjiiijuuuuiw*'. U

4 **YELLOW-BELLIED GREENBUL** *Chlorocichla flaviventris*   L 21 cm. Note olive-brown upperparts, yellow underparts, broken eye ring which is broader above eye. From 55.3b by richer yellow underparts and dark (not creamy) eye. Habitat: forests, riverine belts, coastal shrub. Voice: mid-high, mewing '*tjuk tjuk tjeeh-tjeeh tjee tutje tutjitjitjitjí -*' (some parts running-up).

5 **JOYFUL GREENBUL** *Chlorocichla laetissima*   L 20 cm. From 56.4 by even more uniform and bright green upperparts and yellow underparts. Habitat: forest. Voice: low, hoarse, rather excited, chattered '*tjúut-tjúut-tjúut-tuuterútuut*'. R

6 **YELLOW-NECKED GREENBUL** *Chlorocichla falkensteini*   L 18 cm. Note grey underparts, contrasting yellow chin (grey in 55.7), bright green upperparts. Habitat: forest edges, areas with high trees and dense undergrowth.

7 **YELLOW-THROATED LEAFLOVE** *Chlorocichla flavicollis flavigula*   L 21 cm. From 8 by pale eye, absence of eye ring, greener upperparts. Puffs out throat feathers when singing. Noisy groups. Not shy. Habitat: open forest, riverine belts, abandoned cultivation, large gardens.

8 **SIMPLE GREENBUL** *Chlorocichla simplex*   L 19 cm. Note broken eye ring and white throat. Shy skulker in foliage. Habitat: as 7. Voice: high, short, hurried chatter, '*mewmaumichétchet*'.

9 **RED-TAILED GREENBUL** *Criniger calurus*   L 17 cm. Note pure white, frequently puffed-out beard, contrasting with cheek and breast, bare, blue skin around eye, red tail. Habitat: lower level of forest, riverine belts. Voice: high, fluted, short, repeated '*tutU-tjíuh*' or '*ti-tju-tjíeh*'. R

10 **RED-TAILED BRISTLEBILL** *Bleda syndactyla*   L 21 cm. Note bright yellow underparts and bare, blue skin above eye. Very shy. Habitat: forest, riverine belts and other habitats with dense undergrowth. Voice: mid-high, hurried, mewing '*kiau-kiau-kiau*' and many other repeated, thrush-like or magpie-like whistles, changing in speed, pitch and volume, often with crescendo.

11 **BLACK CUCKOOSHRIKE** *Campephaga flava*   L 18 cm. Yellow-shouldered **(a)** and more common, black-shouldered **(b)** forms shown. Note predominantly white underparts of ♀. Gleans insects from foliage. Floppy, undulating flight. Often in mixed bird parties. Habitat: open forests, other wooded and bushed habitats. Voice: extreme high, insect-like trill, '*srrrrri*'. (brS)

12 **PETIT'S CUCKOOSHRIKE** *Campephaga petiti*   L 19 cm. From 11 by more conspicuous, orange-yellow gape. The ♀ from ♀11 by yellow underparts and less barred upperparts. Ranges of 11 and 12 hardly overlap. Habitat: tall trees at forest edges and surrounding areas. Voice: combinations of extreme high '*shreeeeh*' with much lower '*weewee*', '*deedeeder*' etc. U

13 **PURPLE-THROATED CUCKOOSHRIKE** *Campephaga quiscalina*   L 18 cm. From 11 and 12 by deep purplish glow over underparts, ♀ by absence of (or hardly any) barring. Imm as ♀ but more extensively barred below. Habitat: montane forests.

14 **GREY CUCKOOSHRIKE** *Coracina caesia*   L 21 cm. Note uniform plumage. Habitat: montane forest, well-wooded streams. Voice: extreme high '*shreeu*' and other slow twittering. U

15 **WHITE-BREASTED CUCKOOSHRIKE** *Coracina pectoralis*   L 25 cm. The ♀ from 14 by almost white underparts. Habitat: open miombo and other woodland at lower altitudes. Voice: very high '*shrée-shrée witwit*' ('*witwit*' much lower).

▶

Plate 56

Plate 56 (continued)

16 **WESTERN NICATOR** *Nicator chloris*   L 21 cm. Note large bill. Solitary and secretive. Habitat: thickets, woodland, riverine belts. Voice: high, hurried '*weet-weet-weet-weet-weet Kisch Kisch*'.

17 **WHITE-THROATED** (or Yellow-spotted) **NICATOR** *Nicator gularis*   L 21 cm. From 16 by dark brown cap. Habitat: dense forest undergrowth, scrub. Voice: mid-high, partly harsh, partly melodious '*tjurk tjurk kwik-kor kwikkerkwéet*' ('*kwéet*' lashed up very high).

18 **YELLOW-THROATED NICATOR** *Nicator vireo*   L 14 cm. From 16 and 17 by size, thinner bill, yellow throat patch. Habitat: canopy and middle strata of forest.

Plate 57

1 **ISABELLINE WHEATEAR** *Oenanthe isabellina*   L 16 cm. From ♀ 2 by tail pattern, paler, almost translucent outer wing, clean (not dusky) underwing, short eyebrow, clean, pale ear coverts. Wing coverts concolorous with mantle. Habitat: (very) dry areas without, or with scarce bush and trees. Voice: (probably silent in Africa). Rich flow of short, sweeping phrases with many imitations. RS

2 **NORTHERN** (or European) **WHEATEAR** *Oenanthe oenanthe*   L 15 cm. Note tail pattern and long, narrow primary projection. Habitat: short-grassed areas often with some bush and trees. Voice: (probably silent in Africa). Alarm call is low '*taktakphéw*' ('*phew*' very high). US

3 **PIED WHEATEAR** *Oenanthe pleschanka*   L 15 cm. Note tail pattern. N-br ♂ and ♀ from 1 and 2 by duskier plumage. Habitat: open areas from rocky hillsides to moorland. Voice: very varied repertoire of very short, hurried, extreme high to mid-high strophes, like '*fifi-fih*', '*tjap-tjéeh*' or '*sriniwisu*'. RS

4 **BUFF-STREAKED CHAT** *Saxicola bifasciata*   L 16 cm. Black wings and tail of ♂ diagnostic. The ♀ from *cercomela* chats (Plate 58) by black tail, contrasting with orange-buff rump. Habitat: rocky and stony mountain slopes. Voice: short, hurried, very high phrases preceded by compact '*clickclick*' as '*clickclickFeefiurifeefwee*'.

5 **MOUNTAIN WHEATEAR** *Oenanthe monticola*   L 18 cm. Some (**a**, **b** and **c**) of the possible colour forms shown. All ♂♂ have a white shoulder. From 7 and 59.9 by white rump and partly white tail. Habitat: rocky, short-grassed slopes. Voice: high, melodious yet rasping '*sishraw titjúruwírwír*'.

6 **CAPPED WHEATEAR** *Oenanthe pileata*   L 17 cm. Unmistakable. Habitat: semi-desert, montane moorland, open coastal shrub. Voice: unhurried sequence of high, unstructured, rasping and chattered notes.

7 **WHITE-HEADED BLACK** (or Arnot's) **CHAT** *Myrmecocichla arnotti*   L 17 cm. Nominate (**a**) and black-crowned race *harterti* (**b**, in flight) shown. Note black tail. Habitat: bare patches in miombo and other woodland. Voice: very high, canary-like, hurried twittering with some rasping notes added to recurring, very high '*-feee-*'.

8 **MOCKING CLIFF CHAT** *Myrmecocichla cinnamomeiventris*   L 21 cm. From *cossypha* robin chats (Plate 60) by black breast and rump. Habitat: sloping, well-wooded areas near cliffs, rocky outcrops, buildings. Voice: very varied, extreme high whistles, sunbird-like twitters and melodious, nightingale-like strophes.

9 **KAROO SCRUB ROBIN** *Cercotrichas coryphaeus*   L 17 cm. From 10–17 by normally uncocked tail and absence of rufous in plumage. Note plain wings. Habitat: dry, shrubbed areas. Voice: very high, simple-structured flow of slightly harsh, whistled notes, '*-fiu-fri-fri-rutrit-reeh-*'.

10 **KALAHARI SCRUB ROBIN** *Cercotrichas paena*   L 16 cm. Note absence of white in wing, buff-orange mantle and tertials, orange-rufous rump and tail. Habitat: dry thornveld with open patches. Voice: sequence of very high, warbler-like, very short phrases, each repeated 2–10 times, '*wéet wéet wéettietjittietjittietjit–*', all parts well-separated.

11 **RUFOUS SCRUB ROBIN** *Cercotrichas galactotes*   L 15 cm. From 10 by paler, more creamy-buff plumage and hardly any black in tail. Habitat: areas with trees, palms, thickets in dry semi-desert. Voice: European robin-like, high, rapid warbling in short strophes, '*trrrrti-tu-trrrwiet*'. R

12 **BROWN SCRUB ROBIN** *Cercotrichas signata*   L 18 cm. Note dull plumage lacking reddish breast band and flanks. From 14 and 15 by different range; overlaps only marginally with range of 13. Habitat: dense undergrowth. Voice: rather short, clear whistles, each one starting with very high '*feee-*' then descending.

▶

Plate 57

Plate 57 (continued)

13 **EASTERN BEARDED SCRUB ROBIN** *Cercotrichas quadrivirgata* L 17 cm. More colourful than 14 with more extensive white on underparts. Habitat: undergrowth of dry forest, woodland, bushveld, gardens. Voice: continuous flow of mid-high to very high, clear, fluted notes and short phrases with very fast, repeated parts, '*tie tjutie-tietjutie-fuwie-fuwie-fuwie-riririri-tututjie-*'.

14 **MIOMBO BEARDED SCRUB ROBIN** *Cercotrichas barbata* L 17 cm. From 13 by subdued colouring and largely different range. Habitat: miombo, thick bush and scrub. Voice: very high, sharp strophes like '*fjutuweetweettjutjieweetweet*'.

15 **FOREST SCRUB ROBIN** *Cercotrichas leucosticta* L 17 cm. From 13 and 14 by much darker plumage, brown-black tail, brownish-grey breast, restricted range in Angola. Habitat: forest interior, often near termite mounds. U

16 **WHITE-BROWED SCRUB ROBIN** *Cercotrichas leucophrys* L 15 cm. In most of its range only scrub robin with streaked breast. Habitat: dense, grassy thornbush patches in more or less wooded and bushed areas. Voice: very high, loud, fluted whistles repeated 2–3 times, e.g. '*wéeduwjet-wéeduwjet-wéeduwjet-*'.

17 **BROWN-BACKED SCRUB ROBIN** *Cercotrichas hartlaubi* L 15 cm. From 16 by darker upperparts and sharply defined wing bars. Habitat: tall grass near forest and cultivation. Voice: very high, fluted whistles e.g. '*féetjudéewee*'. R

Plate 58 (continued)

17 **THRUSH NIGHTINGALE** (or Sprosser) *Luscinia luscinia*   L 17 cm. Note large, black eye and pale eye ring. Yellowish mouth corner gives face a characteristic expression. Tail is slightly russet-brown. Habitat: thickets, woodland with leafy undergrowth. Voice: can be heard singing in Africa, especially February–March. Very rich flow of highly variable, well-separated, single or repeated, liquid notes and harsh, fluted or trilling rattles (lacking famous crescendo of extra-limital Nightingale). US

Plate 58

1   **SICKLE-WINGED CHAT** *Cercomela sinuata*   L 15 cm. From 2 and 3 by rufous-edged wing feathers and larger, black wedge on a pale, rufous (not white) tail. Habitat: bare or short-grassed slopes from virtually sea level to high in the mountains. Voice: combination of fluting and harsh notes '*tsreeetsreeetfjuuwhich-which-which*'.

2   **TRACTRAC CHAT** *Cercomela tractrac*   L 14 cm. White race *albicans* **(a)** and nominate **(b)** shown. Latter from 3 by only partly white outer tail feathers. Habitat: dry, stony plains, sand dunes with very little grass and shrub. Voice: combination of high, rolling '*préeee-*' and low, sparrow-like '*tsjawitsjaw*'.

3   **KAROO CHAT** *Cercomela schlegelii*   L 16 cm. Not all races depicted; nominate **(a)** and race *pollux* **(b)** shown. Note white outer tail feathers. Habitat: dry scrubby areas with sparse bush (Karoo). Voice: mid-high, harsh, well-separated '*cratch-cratch-crút-crut-cree-*'.

4   **FAMILIAR CHAT** *Cercomela familiaris*   L 15 cm. From 1, 2 and 3 by red in tail. Habitat: dry, rocky areas, dry river courses, cultivation. Voice: low, scratchy, unhurried notes, interspersed with high '*weet*' as '*twjaktsjahwéettsjaktsjeksjikwéettsjik-*'.

5   **MIOMBO ROCK THRUSH** *Monticola angolensis*   L 17 cm. The ♂ from 6, 7, 8 and 9 by spotted crown and mantle; ♀ by well-defined, white moustache. Habitat: miombo at higher altitudes than 6. Voice: mid-high, rather short '*fiuuuuwírwír*'.

6   **SHORT-TOED ROCK THRUSH** *Monticola brevipes*   L 18 cm. Note pale forehead of nominate ♂ (shown), reduced in n-br plumage and absent in race *pretoriae* (not shown). From 8 by almost completely different range. Habitat: rocky outcrops in natural and cultivated, open areas. Voice: high, fluting '*niwiwiphrírrweerweeg*' (ascending, then descending).

7   **CAPE ROCK THRUSH** *Monticola rupestris*   L 21 cm. Note brownish-orange upperparts of ♂ and ♀. Habitat: rocky and grassy slopes with some bush. Voice: high, loud, sweet, fluting '*weewéetwreetuwie wéetweet*'.

8   **SENTINEL ROCK THRUSH** *Monticola explorator*   L 18 cm. From 6 by different range. Habitat: open, rocky mountain sides. Voice: high, slightly sharp, up-and-down '*tjítsisíruptsitsitsírriwéerrweeh*'.

9   **MOUNTAIN ROCK THRUSH** *Monticola saxatilis*   L 18 cm. Full ♂ br plumage (as shown) rarely seen in South Africa. N-br ♂ (not shown) as ♀, but scaled feathers below with larger, white centres. Habitat: open country with look-out posts (rocks, buildings, telephone wires). Voice: probably silent in Africa. Very high, sharp, fluted, strong '*weetweetree oweetweet*'. R

10   **BOULDER CHAT** *Pinarornis plumosus*   L 24 cm. Note conspicuous, spotted wing bar and white tail corners in flight. Habitat: rocks under tree cover in hilly country. Voice: sequence of well-separated, drawn-out, very high to extreme high notes, '*tekuut-tuuut-tjeeeh-feeeeh-weeh-weeh-*'. U

11   **HERERO CHAT** *Namibornis herero*   L 17 cm. Note narrow, white eyebrow and tail pattern. Hunts from low perch, catching insects from the ground. Habitat: dry, shrubbed slopes with rocks and boulders. Voice: rather oriole-like '*twi-tedeelee-doo*' or warbler-like variations on this phrase. U

12   **COMMON** (or European) **REDSTART** *Phoenicurus phoenicurus*   L 14 cm. Note constant shivering of tail. The ♀ from 11 (which has the same tail pattern) by absence of eyebrow and dusky throat. Habitat: dry scrub- and woodland, often along streams. Voice: probably silent in Africa. Song composed of very high variations on '*see-su-swee-djidjidji*' (last part as a melodious rattle). R

13   **WHINCHAT** *Saxicola rubetra*   L 13 cm. From ♀ 14 by prominent eyebrows, white sides to tail base, rump in same colour as mantle. Habitat: open woodland and other more or less wooded, natural and cultivated areas. Voice: hurried, very high '*juu wéerowéet*'. US

14   **COMMON STONECHAT** *Saxicola torquata*   L 14 cm. Note all-black tail and white neck patches. The ♀ has only an inconspicuous eyebrow. Habitat: areas with some scattered bush and shrub, moorland, swamp edges. Voice: short, nervous rattle, '*sisititírrut-trírut*'.

15   **WHITE-STARRED ROBIN** *Pogonocichla stellata*   L 16 cm. From 16 by partly orange-yellow outer tail. White patches on head normally concealed or barely visible. Habitat: coastal and montane forest edges and clearings. Voice: very high, clear, single or repeated, short phrases often sounding like carefree, human whistling.

16   **SWYNNERTON'S ROBIN** *Swynnertonia swynnertoni*   L 14 cm. Note all-dark tail and conspicuous, white throat patch. Habitat: undergrowth of montane forest. Voice: extreme high, plaintive, monotonous, descending '*pfút-pfut-pfee*'. R

◀

Plate 58

Plate 59

1   **ANGOLA CAVE CHAT** *Xenocopsychus ansorgei*   L 19 cm. Unmistakable in its restricted range. Habitat: rocky hillsides, often with cave mouths near forest patches. R E (Angola)

2   **ORANGE-BREASTED ROCKJUMPER** *Chaetops aurantius*   L 21 cm. From 3 by paler underparts and largely different range. (Note: 2 and 3 are not thrushes but babblers, Plate 54). Habitat: rocky slopes at high altitudes. Voice: sequence of very high, frequently repeated variations on 'sreesreesreesree–'.

3   **CAPE ROCKJUMPER** *Chaetops frenatus*   L 24 cm. Habitat: rocky mountain slopes. Voice: sequence of very high, 3–6 times repeated notes, '*fiufiufiufiutiptiptuetiptiptuetiptiptue-*'. E (South Africa)

4   **EAST COAST AKALAT** *Sheppardia gunningi*   L 13 cm. Note small size, dark tail, grey eyebrow and wings. Very robin-like in behaviour. Habitat: dense, moist, forest undergrowth. Voice very high, hesitating, slightly hoarse whistle, '*rrrurHée*' or '*rurrerrurrerréeh*'. R

5   **SHARPE'S AKALAT** *Sheppardia sharpei*   L 13 cm. Small, white eyebrow and uniform upperparts diagnostic. Habitat: montane forest undergrowth and bamboo. R

6   **BOCAGE'S AKALAT** *Sheppardia bocagei*   L 14 cm. Note dark, rufous rump and tail. Habitat: montane forests. Voice: very high, fluted, loud, sharp '*fuutjifuutúWéeh*'.

7   **GABELA AKALAT** *Sheppardia gabela*   L 13 cm. Small, colourless robin with pale, brown breast band and very restricted range in Angola. Habitat: dense forest undergrowth. R E (Angola)

8   **SOOTY CHAT** *Myrmecocichla nigra*   L 16 cm. From imm 57.7 by smaller, white wing patch, shorter tail, more open habitat. Habitat: open, short grassland with termite mounds. Voice: very high, sharp, calm, thrush-like, 4 or 5-toned phrase '*tututjéetutju*'.

9   **SOUTHERN ANTEATER CHAT** *Myrmecocichla formicivora*   L 17 cm. From 8 by brown (not black) plumage and large, white primary patch. The white shoulder patch is frequently absent. Habitat: dry, open, grassy areas with termite mounds. Voice: unhurried sequence of separate, slightly rasping '*wrah*' of different pitch, between recurring, high '*-fu-fu-wéet-*'.

10   **CONGO MOOR CHAT** *Myrmecocichla tholloni*   L 17 cm. Note white rump and wing patch. Habitat: open grassland with some trees, bushes and other look-out posts.

11   **OLIVE-FLANKED ROBIN CHAT** *Cossypha anomala*   L 15 cm. Note grey eyebrow and dark, rufous tail and rump. Habitat: undergrowth of forest near glades and streams.

12   **CHOLO ALETHE** *Alethe choloensis*   L 16 cm. Note diagnostic white chin and tail corners. Habitat: dense undergrowth near forest edge. U

13   **BROWN-CHESTED ALETHE** *Alethe poliocephala*   L 15 cm. Note narrow white eyebrow and reddish-brown upperparts. Habitat: forest undergrowth and nearby areas. Voice: high, fluted, descending, slow, whistled '*fju-fju-fju-fju-fju-fju-fjufju*'. R

14   **FIRE-CRESTED ALETHE** *Alethe diademata*   L 17 cm. Note orange crown with contrasting grey face sides. Habitat: lowland forests, riverine belts, plantations. Voice: mid-high, simple, repeated, strong whistle, '*fuuu fuuu fuuu -*', falling-off at the end, or '*fju wéh*'. R

15   **WHITE-CHESTED** (or -breasted) **ALETHE** *Alethe fuelleborni*   L 17 cm. Strikingly white below. Habitat: montane forest. Voice: high, monotonous, lashing, sustained, fluted '*uWéeet uWéeet -*'.

16   **WHITE-TAILED ANT THRUSH** *Neocossyphus poensis*   L 20 cm. Note white tail corners and red bar in flight, formed by red bases of all flight feathers. Habitat: mid-strata and undergrowth of forest. Voice: e.g. very high, lashed-up '*fueeeét*' or mid-high '*wéeet-weeet-wéeet*'.

17   **RUFOUS FLYCATCHER THRUSH** *Neocossyphus fraseri*   L 20 cm. Note flycatcher-like stance with characteristic tail flicking (showing red outertail feathers). From 16, in flight, by smaller, red patch formed by red bases of primaries only, red rump, red outertail feathers. Habitat: middle and higher levels in forest. Voice: mid-high, slightly drawn-out whistle, '*uweeeet-uweetteréet*' (at the end drawn-up), and mid-high, lashing '*weeet-wréet-wréet*'.

Plate 59

Plate 60

1 (Southern) **OLIVE THRUSH** *Turdus olivaceus* L 24 cm. Underparts variable from orange (as shown) to dusky (higher altitudes). Habitat: suburbs, riverine belts, plantations, forests. Voice: high, full, up-and-down, short whistles like almost level '*weetohweetthree*'.

2 **KURRICHANE THRUSH** *Turdus libonyanus* L 22 cm. From 1 by prominent moustache and white underbelly. Habitat: suburbs, woodland, bushveld. Voice: very high, short, fluted, far-carrying whistles like '*weetoweet*' or '*weetoweethrée*'.

3 **AFRICAN THRUSH** *Turdus pelios* L 21 cm. From 1 by different range, from 2 by less prominent moustache and by voice. Shown is race *bocagei*. Race *stormsi* (Zambia and East Angola) is darker, richer orange below (including throat). Habitat: forests, woodland, gardens. Voice: very high, calm, sustained, far-carrying, fluted '-*peeweepeeweetuweetuwee*-' (each part repeated 2–3 times).

4 **ORANGE GROUND THRUSH** *Zoothera gurneyi* L 22 cm. Habitat: montane forests. Voice: high, loud, piping, repeated whistles like '*tutututírtjirr*' and other variations (lacking double-toned quality of other thrushes). U

5 **GROUNDSCRAPER THRUSH** *Turdus litsitsirupa* L 21 cm. From 50.9 by larger size and uniform coloured wings. May occasionally flick one wing to show yellow-buff panel on underwing. Habitat: suburbs, cultivation, open woodland, moorland. Voice: short, mid-high, melodious, slightly harsh whistles like '*tiktiktwéedsrohweeth*'.

6 **SPOTTED GROUND THRUSH** *Zoothera guttata* L 22 cm. From 5 by spotted wing bars. Habitat: groundstrata of humid forest and woodland. Voice: high, loud, plaintive, fluted whistles like '*tweeotweetwittirrik*'. U

7 **RED-** (or Rufous-) **TAILED PALM THRUSH** *Cichladusa ruficauda* L 17 cm. Note red eye. Habitat: palm thickets, palm plantations, gardens. Voice: unhurried sequence of fluted notes, rather different in pitch, '*fiufiuflehweedjupdjupdjupweetweet*' ('*djupdjupdjup*' almost a short rattle).

8 **COLLARED PALM THRUSH** *Cichladusa arquata* L 18 cm. From 7 by black line around throat patch and different range. Habitat: riverine palm thickets, palm savannas. Voice: unhurried sequence of fluted notes and phrases of any length, '*weet weet weetweetwuweet*'. U

9 **RED-CAPPED** (or Natal) **ROBIN CHAT** *Cossypha natalensis* L 18 cm. Habitat: suburbs, forest undergrowth, coastal bush, riverine belts. Voice: '*wéeeh rurr*' (call). Song is a flow of rather short phrases with frequently repeated, rich, fluted notes incorporating adapted imitations.

10 **CHORISTER ROBIN CHAT** *Cossypha dichroa* L 19 cm. Note absence of white on head. Habitat: mid-strata of lowland forests. Voice: mid-high, rich, mellow flow of fluted phrases, like '*tutjéewurwéeroweeh*', interwoven with perfect imitations of other bird songs.

11 (African) **WHITE-THROATED ROBIN CHAT** *Cossypha humeralis* L 17 cm. Habitat: dry bush, thornveld, riverine belts. Voice: short, well-separated, fluted whistles, '*tuweet tutweereeruweeriri*'.

12 **CAPE ROBIN CHAT** *Cossypha caffra* L 17 cm. Note interruption of orange on underparts between breast and undertail coverts. Habitat: suburbs, cultivation, open forests, scrubland. Voice: short, fluted whistles, '*tuh-twitwí-rurutwéeréerée*', immediately followed by other strophes.

13 **WHITE-BROWED** (or Heuglin's) **ROBIN CHAT** *Cossypha heuglini* L 19 cm. Note diagnostic, long, white eyebrows. Habitat: well-planted gardens, bushland, open forest. Voice: high, melodious, crescendoing '*peepipurtupéePeePErtu*—', endlessly varied with small skilful tempo changes and interwoven with imitations, mainly of other birds.

14 **GREY-WINGED ROBIN CHAT** *Cossypha polioptera* L 16 cm. From 13 by shorter eyebrow, grey crown, all-red tail; from 59.6 by white eyebrow. Habitat: forest, well-wooded streams, at middle elevations. Voice: very high, sharp whistling of varied pitch, interspersed with clicks and short tempo changes, often resembling happy, at random, human whistling. R

15 **SNOWY-CROWNED ROBIN CHAT** *Cossypha niveicapilla* L 23 cm. Note absence of black on crown. Habitat: woodland thickets. Voice: beautiful, rich, liquid, sustained whistling with perfect imitations mainly of other birds. R

16 **WHITE-HEADED ROBIN CHAT** *Cossypha heinrichi* L 23 cm. Unmistakable. Habitat: riverine belts. R

Plate 60

Plate 61

1   **AFRICAN REED** (or Marsh) **WARBLER** *Acrocephalus baeticatus*   L 12 cm. Buffish above, pale buff below. Legs brown-grey, faint eye stripe, primary projection shorter than longest tertial. Habitat: lush vegetation at or away from water. Voice: as 2 but syllables more connected. brS

2   **EURASIAN REED WARBLER** *Acrocephalus scirpaceus*   L 13 cm. Only separable from 3 by song. Long, flat forehead, primary projection as long as longest tertial, rufous tinge to rump. Habitat: reed beds. Voice: mid-high, unhurried '-treetree-karrekarre-treettreet-'. US

3   (European) **MARSH WARBLER** *Acrocephalus palustris*   L 13 cm. Note pink legs. Eye ring dominates eyebrow. From 2 by more rounded head and darker eye. Habitat: as 1. Voice: very high, rapid warbling including imitations and short, canary-like rollers, 'wéetéetotokréeweetiktik-'. S

4   **GREATER SWAMP WARBLER** *Acrocephalus rufescens*   L 17 cm. Drab-brown above, brown-grey below, long bill, short wing, ill-defined eyebrow. Habitat: papyrus. Voice: low to very high, unhurried 'tjiptjip-WHáaro-PJUPJUPJU'. U

5   **GREAT REED WARBLER** *Acrocephalus arundinaceus*   L 18 cm. Strong bill, creamy eyebrow, faint streaks on throat. Habitat: as 1. Voice: mid-high, loud, hoarse 'karre-kéetkéet-weet-'. S

6   **LESSER SWAMP** (or Cape Reed) **WARBLER** *Acrocephalus gracilirostris*   L 15 cm. Note orange gape and black legs. Short-winged, faint eyebrow. Habitat: as 1. Voice: mid-high, thrush-like medleys of 'weet-weetweet-' with loud, melodious rattles, flutes and oriole-like warbles.

7   **BASRA REED WARBLER** *Acrocephalus griseldis*   L 15 cm. Long bill, prominent eyebrow, long primary projection, long tail. Habitat: low vegetation and thickets at or away from water. US

8   **SEDGE WARBLER** *Acrocephalus schoenobaenus*   L 13 cm. Prominent eyebrow, streaked mantle. Habitat: as 1. Voice: mid-high medley of hoarse, rattling, sharp and sweet syllables repeated 2–20 times. S

9   **BROAD-TAILED WARBLER** *Schoenicola platyura*   L 16 cm. Note heavy tail. Habitat: as 1. Voice: extreme high, unstructured, weak yet piercing 'sweeh sweet sweeh sweeh sweeh -'.

10   **EURASIAN RIVER WARBLER** *Locustella fluviatilis*   L 13 cm. Note striped breast and very long, chequered undertail coverts. Habitat: keeps low to the ground in dense, tangled, weedy vegetation. Voice: very high, level, sizzled 'almost-trill' with phrases of up to 8–9 seconds. US

11   **KNYSNA WARBLER** *Bradypterus sylvaticus*   L 14 cm. From 15 by different range, from 13 by pinkish legs. Habitat: forest undergrowth. Voice: 'teet teet-teet-teetitjsrrrrrr'. U E (South Africa)

12   **VICTORIN'S WARBLER** *Bradypterus victorini*   L 16 cm. Note orange eye. Habitat: rank vegetation at higher altitudes. Voice: e.g. very high 'tutuwIEtututwIETutuWIET'. E (South Africa)

13   **BARRATT'S WARBLER** *Bradypterus barratti*   L 15 cm. Note white chin, dark legs. Habitat: vegetation at edge of or under montane forests. Voice: very high, sweeping whistles, 'fífítutrrrrrrrt'.

14   **LITTLE RUSH** (or African Sedge) **WARBLER** *Bradypterus baboecala*   L 13 cm. Note rusty rump and broad tail. Habitat: vegetation over water. Voice: descending 'trrut trut-trut-truttruttrut'.

15   **EVERGREEN-FOREST WARBLER** *Bradypterus lopezi mariae*   L 14 cm. Note worn-looking tail and pale legs. Habitat: forest interior. Voice: high, hurried, rattled, sharp 'tjutjutjutjutjut-' and crescendoing, camaroptera-like 'titJu-titJu-titJu-titJu'.

16   **CINNAMON BRACKEN WARBLER** *Bradypterus cinnamomeus*   L 15 cm. Crown darker than mantle, eyebrow well-defined. Habitat: undergrowth of montane forests, bamboo, moist thickets. Voice: very high, powerful, melodious rattles, 'fjúut-rrrrr' or 'tjuut-weetweetweet'. R

17   **BAMBOO WARBLER** *Bradypterus alfredi*   L 14 cm. Note white chin and grey breast and flanks. Habitat: undergrowth of bamboo, montane forest and surroundings. R

18   **ICTERINE WARBLER** *Hippolais icterina*   L 13 cm. Normal plumage is often less yellow with paler wing panel than shown. Note peaked crown. Habitat: open woodland, bushveld, gardens. Voice: high, sustained, unhurried, varied phrases full of sharp, powerful rattles and chuckles. S

19   **OLIVE-TREE WARBLER** *Hippolais olivetorum*   L 16 cm. Note long, sloping forehead, long bill, white edges to secondaries, long primary projection. Habitat: more or less wooded areas. Voice: mid-high, pleasant but harsh, reed warbler-like, unhurried chattering. US

20   **OLIVACEOUS WARBLER** *Hippolais pallida*   L 12 cm. From marsh and reed warblers by much paler lore. Note short wings. Habitat: as 18 but often in drier areas. Voice: high, rasping warble. (?)

▶

Plate 61

Plate 61 (continued)

21 **WHITE-WINGED WARBLER** *Bradypterus carpalis*   L 13 cm. From all other warblers on this plate by all-white or creamy wing shoulder, white tips to wing coverts, white underparts streaked brown on throat and breast. Habitat: reed beds. Voice: descending, chirping whistle concluded with some explosive wing beats. (Not illustrated, no map; recently recorded from Zambia). R

Plate 62

1 **YELLOW-THROATED WOODLAND WARBLER** *Phylloscopus ruficapilla*   L 9 cm. Extent of yellow on throat and breast variable. Habitat: montane forests, bamboo. Voice: extreme high, bouncing, hurried '*wéeturi wéeturiwéeturiwéet*' and other short strophes.

2 **BURNT-NECKED EREMOMELA** *Eremomela usticollis*   L 10 cm. Note pale eye and rufous on cheeks and ear coverts (rufous on throat often absent). Habitat: thornveld and dry woodland. Voice: extreme high, wader-like, fast '*weeweeweewee*' or very high, tit-like '*tjut-tjut-tjut–*'.

3 **GREEN-CAPPED EREMOMELA** *Eremomela scotops*   L 10 cm. Note pale, red-rimmed eye and bright, yellow breast band. Habitat: open woodland, riverine belts. Voice: high, sustained, rather staccato '*trrit-trrit-trrit–*'. U

4 **YELLOW-BELLIED EREMOMELA** *Eremomela icteropygialis*   L 9 cm. Not all races depicted; nominate **(a)** and *polioxantha* **(b)** shown. Note yellow(ish) rear part of body. From 69.4b by larger size and unspotted forehead; from 5 by well-defined eyebrow. Habitat: desert, woodland, bushveld. Voice: very high '*titiWéeh-titiWeeh*' or sharp, descending, hurried, warbled '*séesirititititu-Wee*'.

5 **KAROO EREMOMELA** *Eremomela gregalis*   L 12 cm. Note uniformly coloured tail. Habitat: Karoo and semi-desert. Voice: very high, hurried, single-noted '*ti-ti-ti-ti–*'. U

6 **BLACK-NECKED EREMOMELA** *Eremomela atricollis*   L 11 cm. Habitat: miombo, bushveld.

7 **RUFOUS-CROWNED EREMOMELA** *Eremomela badiceps*   L 10 cm. Habitat: canopy at forest edges, riverine belts. Voice: extreme high, hurried, siffled '*sisisisi–*' or very high, soft, fluted warbling.

8 **RED-CAPPED CROMBEC** *Sylvietta ruficapilla*   L 12 cm. Race *chubbi* **(a)** and nominate **(b)** shown. Note rufous ear coverts. From 2 by lack of tail and larger size. Habitat: miombo. Voice: very high, hurried, warbling '*tituwreetuwreeThrée*', ('*-Three*' characteristically 4 notes higher).

9 **LONG-BILLED CROMBEC** *Sylvietta rufescens*   L 12 cm. From 18 by white eyebrow and throat. Habitat: dry bushveld, semi-desert with some shrub. Voice: very high, short, soft yet shrill '*tuwee-thréewee-thréewee-thrée*'.

10 **WILLOW WARBLER** *Phylloscopus trochilus*   L 11 cm. Variable, normally with faint-yellow eyebrow, throat and breast. Note long primary projection. Habitat: any type of wooded and bushed habitat. Voice: rich, warbling whistle '*fififufururirururu-tweet-tweet–*'. S

11 **LAURA'S WOODLAND WARBLER** *Phylloscopus laurae*   L 10 cm. Yellow underparts interrupted by white between lower breast and undertail coverts. Habitat: forest canopy.

12 **STIERLING'S BARRED WARBLER** *Calamonastes undosus*   (Northern races) L 14 cm. Regular barring of underparts diagnostic. Habitat: bushveld. Voice: extreme high '*tweet-tweet-tweet–*'. Note: 12 and 14, both a group of races, are now lumped together to form one species, *Calamonaster undosus*. Formerly they were known as two independent species.

13 **BARRED WREN WARBLER** *Calamonastes fasciolatus*   L 14 cm. Br adult from 12 by darker breast band, n-br adult by fainter barring and buff (not white) underparts. Habitat: thornveld, dry bushland. Voice: very high, piercing '*turwiet-turwiet-turwiet*' (like a badly oiled wheel).

14 **MIOMBO WREN WARBLER** *Calamonastes undosus*.   (Southern races) L 14 cm. See note under 12. Note faint barring of rear underparts. Habitat: miombo and other woodland.

15 **GREEN-BACKED BLEATING WARBLER** *Calamonastes brachyura*   (Green-backed races) L 10 cm. Habitat: dense thickets, coastal bush, forest edges. Voice: mid-high, very dry, loud, staccato '*treetreettreet*' (3–5 times) and mid-high, mewing '*mèh mèh-mèh*'. Note: 15 and 16, both a group of races, are now lumped together to form one species, *Calamonastes brachyura*.

16 **GREY-BACKED BLEATING WARBLER** *Calamonastes brachyura*   (Grey-backed races) L 10 cm. See note under 15. Habitat: often in drier areas than 15. Voice: as 15.

17 **YELLOW-BROWED CAMAROPTERA** *Camaroptera superciliaris*   L 9 cm. From 11 by white chin and throat, longer bill, shorter tail. Habitat: undergrowth at forest edge, riverine belts. Voice: mid-high, loud '*piauw-piauw piauw-piauw*' or '*eewèhwèh-eewèhwèh*'. R

▶

Plate 62

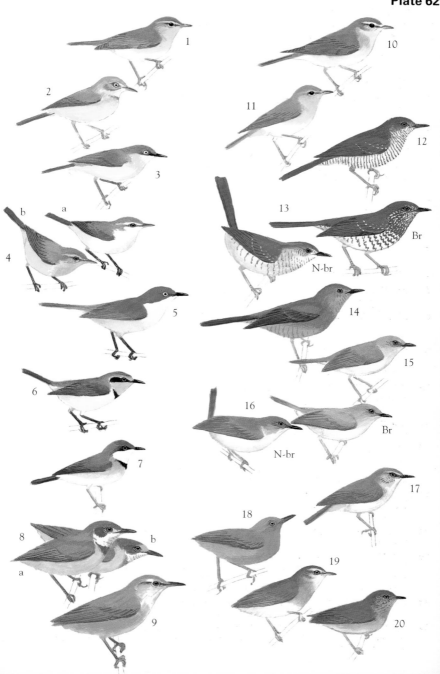

Plate 62 (continued)

18   **RED-FACED CROMBEC** *Sylvietta whytii*   L 9 cm. Eye, face sides and underparts concolorous. Habitat: forest edges, woodland. Voice: very high, soft, well-separated, cicada-like trills (each 2–3 seconds).

19   **GREEN CROMBEC** *Sylvietta virens*   L 9 cm. Note dull colouring with pale, tawny eyebrow, cheek and throat. Habitat: undergrowth of forest, riverine belts. Voice: extreme high, descending, sharp, fast twitter, 'siséesreesisiwge', often followed by softer and lower syllables.

20   **LEMON-BELLIED CROMBEC** *Sylvietta denti*   L 9 cm. Note pale, reddish throat and stripe over underparts. Habitat: canopy at forest edge, deserted cultivation. Voice: extreme high, siffled, slackened 'seeseeseeseeseesee-see-see see'. R

Plate 63

1   **BANDED PRINIA** *Prinia bairdii*   L 12 cm. Note white tips of tail feathers, tertials and wing coverts. Habitat: forest edges, often along streams. Voice: high, hurried, sharp, staccato 'witwitwit–' (sustained for up to 30 seconds). R

2   **DRAKENSBERG PRINIA** *Prinia maculosa hypoxantha*   L 14 cm. From 3 by yellower, less streaked underparts, from 11 by white tail feather tips and prominent eyebrow. Habitat: montane forest edges and bracken-covered slopes. Voice: extreme high, sharp 'sreetsreetsreet', or high 'trètrètrètrèt' and other strophes.

3   **SPOTTED PRINIA** *Prinia maculosa maculosa*   L 14 cm. Habitat: as 2. Voice: e.g. very high, rattling 'djap-djap-djap-djap' or 'titititititi'.

4   **TAWNY-FLANKED PRINIA** *Prinia subflava*   L 12 cm. Note eyebrow and rusty edges of wing and tail feathers. Habitat: bush, open areas in forest, woodland, bushveld, swamp edges. Voice: extreme high, staccato, hurried 'weet-weet-weet-weet–' or a series of rapid 'tjieptjieptjiep-' of irregular length.

5   **BLACK-CHESTED PRINIA** *Prinia flavicans*   L 14 cm. Br adult may be white below. N-br adult from 4 by uniform brownish wings; from 2, 3 and 11 by unmarked underparts. Habitat: dry areas with bush and scrub. Voice: extreme high, rapid 'weetweetweet', 'djapdjapdjap-' or rattling 'sisisisisisi-'.

6   **BRIAR WARBLER** (or Robert's Prinia) *Oreophilais robertsi*   L 14 cm. Note dark upperparts, pale eye, tawny rear underparts. Skulking. Habitat: thick herbage at edges of montane forest. Voice: very high, rapid chatter, 'chachacha–' (in chorus).

7   **WHITE-CHINNED PRINIA** *Schistolais leucopogon*   L 13 cm. Habitat: tall herbage and shrubbery in forest glades and cultivation. Voice: unsynchronized duet of extreme high, fast warbling, 'fifififi–' and very high 'weep-weep-weep-'. Also individual 'frifrifrifrifrifri'.

8   **FAIRY FLYCATCHER** *Stenostira scita*   L 11 cm. Constantly fans its tail. Habitat: woodland, thornveld, plantations, suburbs. Voice: very high, thin 'twéetowéetosrèh'.

9   **GREEN HYLIA** *Hylia prasina*   L 12 cm. Darker than 62.10 and with more pronounced eyebrow. Habitat: undergrowth and mid-strata of forest and bush.

10   **RED-WINGED WARBLER** *Heliolais erythroptera*   L 13 cm. Note long bill. Habitat: tall-grassed places in woodland. Voice: high, rapid 'fiufiufiufiu–' (or 'fitfitfit–') by ♂ with toneless twitter 'trtrtr–' of ♀ in duet. U

11   **NAMAQUA WARBLER** (or Prinia) *Phragmacia substriata*   L 13 cm. From 2 and 3 by lack of eyebrow, absence of white tail tips, white throat and breast. Habitat: vegetation along streams in the Karoo. Voice: very high, sharp, ascending then descending, bouncing trill, 'tjitritrítrrrrrgh'.

12   **RUFOUS-EARED WARBLER** *Malcorus pectoralis*   L 15 cm. Forages mainly on the ground, is even reluctant to fly. Habitat: dry, sparsely covered areas. Voice: high or extreme high, sharp, hurried 'sreetsreetsreet–' with sudden stops and interruptions by lower 'piu' (at a sustained speed).

13   **CINNAMON-BREASTED WARBLER** *Euryptila subcinnamomea*   L 13 cm. Darkest warbler, often with cocked tail. Habitat: rocky hillsides. Voice: very high, hurried 'weetweetweetweet' or drawn up 'uWeeét-uWeeét'. U

▶

Plate 63

Plate 63 (continued)

14 **AFRICAN YELLOW WARBLER** *Chloropeta natalensis*   L 14 cm. From 15 by darker cap, from 61.18 and 62.10 by brighter underparts and longer-tailed, upright profile. Habitat: skulks rather in dense under-growth. Voice: very high, melodious, staccato trills and rollers connected by low, dry '*tektek tek*'.

15 **MOUNTAIN YELLOW WARBLER** *Chloropeta similis*   L 13 cm. Crown and mantle uniform green. Habitat: more mountainous than 14 but habitats overlap. Voice: high, crescendoing '*tjuutjuuTjuuTjuuTJuuTJuu–*' and other high, fluted strophes with inbuilt tremolos and differences in pitch. U

16 **PAPYRUS YELLOW WARBLER** *Chloropeta gracilirostris*   L 13 cm. Eyebrow ill-defined. Orange tinge on flanks. Habitat: papyrus, reeds. R

17 (African) **MOUSTACHED GRASS WARBLER** *Melocichla mentalis*   L 19 cm. Skulking. Habitat: tall herbage along streams in wooded landscapes. Voice: very high, unhurried, basically staccato phrases with sudden accelerations, '*tjup tjup priweetweetweet tjup tjuwèh*'. U

18 **ROCKRUNNER** *Achaetops pycnopygius*   L 25 cm. Habitat: keeps to the ground on and between rocks and grass in hilly country. Voice: mid-high, melodious, bulbul-like, descending warble and other pleasant phrases. E (Namibia)

19 **CAPE GRASS WARBLER** (or Grassbird) *Sphenoeacus afer*   L 19 cm. Rather skulking. Habitat: areas with long grass and scrub from coast to mountain slopes. Voice: very high, hurried, running-up twitter '*sirisitisiti-----suúhwée*'.

Plate 64 (continued)

16   **CHATTERING CISTICOLA** *Cisticola anonymus*   L 14 cm. Plain plumage, black bill, rusty forehead; tail steeply graduated with faint pattern above. Habitat: grassy places with some bush near forest, plantations, cultivation. Voice: mid-high, rather harsh '*tsjitsjiPwwwrrrrrr*' or with reversed emphasis, '*Tsjitsjiwirrrrr*'. R

17   **BUBBLING CISTICOLA** *Cisticola bulliens*   L 13 cm. Pale plumage, long bill, faint streaking above. Habitat: coastal and inland areas with tall grass and some bush.

18   **LEVAILLANT'S CISTICOLA** *Cisticola tinniens*   L 13 cm. Grey wing coverts, red edges to tail feathers, black-streaked rump. Habitat: highlands. Voice: rather compressed '*jujuTHríll.*'

19   **CROAKING CISTICOLA** *Cisticola natalensis*   L 16 cm (♂), 14 cm (♀). Short tail, buff (not rufous) crown. Habitat: rank-grassed areas in bushveld and woodland. Voice: e.g. mid-high, sustained, hurried '*wreeeeep-wreeeep-wreeeep-*' or '*frjuuwhéep*' ('*-wheep*' lashed up high).

20   **STOUT CISTICOLA** *Cisticola robustus*   L 16 cm (♂), 13 cm (♀). Chestnut collar, black-striped crown. Habitat: montane bushveld and woodland with moist places. Voice: high, dry, rapid, rattled '*tit-tit-thrrree*'.

Plate 64

1   **NEDDICKY** *Cisticola fulvicapillus*   L 11 cm. Nominate **(a)** and race *hallae* **(b)** shown. Not illustrated race *angusticaudus* **(c**, inseparable from **b** except by range, see map 64.1) is often treated as a separate species. Note small, plain-backed, rather short-tailed and large-billed appearance. Crown uniform with mantle. Habitat: low down in grass and scrub of woodland. Voice: very high '*fiuu-fiuu-fiu*'.

2   **SHORT-WINGED CISTICOLA** *Cisticola brachypterus*   L 10 cm. Faint mantle streaking, short tail, no rufous. Habitat: tall grass in woodland. Voice: combinations of very high, thin, rather staccato '*tiutiutiu*', '*fwrreefwreehfwreeh*', '*tittittui*' etc.

3   **ROCK-LOVING** (or Lazy) **CISTICOLA** *Cisticola aberrans*   L 13 cm. Prominent eye stripe, buffy underparts, long, thin, unmarked tail (often held cocked). Habitat: (almost) bare, rocky areas. Voice: mid-high or high, nasal '*teehteehteeh-*' of any length with other small flutes and rolls.

4   **GREY-BACKED CISTICOLA** *Cisticola subruficapillus*   L 12 cm. Not all races depicted; nominate **(a)** and race *windhoekiensis* **(b)** shown. Underparts dull buff, crown rusty brown with or without streaks. Habitat: scrub. Voice: low, rattling '*srrreeh srrreeeh*' and high, plover-like '*puwéeh-puwéeh*'.

5   **WAILING CISTICOLA** *Cisticola lais*   L 14 cm. Wing panel, crown and tail coloured with same buff. (Buffy breast may be faintly streaked). Habitat: montane, rocky grassland. Voice: '*prrrrrrrpéeppéeppéeppéeh*' (first part as trilling rattle, rest as very high, canary-like piping).

6   **TINKLING CISTICOLA** *Cisticola rufilatus*   L 14 cm. Prominent eye stripe, thin, black bill, long, rufous tail, crown brighter than 13. Habitat: dry bushveld. Voice: dry '*tjuktjuksreeeeeh*' followed by high, hurried '*pweeepweeepweeepwee*' or extreme high, rattling '*srrrrrreeh*'. U

7   **RED-FACED CISTICOLA** *Cisticola erythrops*   L 13 cm. Note rufous face and plain wing. Habitat: rank undergrowth near water. Voice: e.g. extreme high, rapid, lashing '*weepweepweepweep*' or '*wéetjewwéetjewwéetjewéetje*'.

8   **SINGING CISTICOLA** *Cisticola cantans*   L 13 cm. From 7 by red wing panel and black loral spot. Habitat: undergrowth in highland areas. Voice: high, loud, strong, irregular '*twit twit Tréetwit-Treet Tree twit Triet tu Weet*'.

9   **TRILLING CISTICOLA** *Cisticola woosnami*   L 13 cm. Plain with little contrast between crown, mantle, wings and (rather short) tail. Rather heavy bill. Habitat: tall grass in woodland often on rocky hillsides. Voice: extreme high, crescendoing, fast trill, '*weeweeweeWeeWeeWEeWEeWEEWEE*'. U

10   **CHURRING CISTICOLA** *Cisticola njombe*   L 13 cm. From 5 and 13 by habitat and song. Crown most rufous part. Habitat: rough herbage near large rocks at high altitudes. Voice: high '*treet-treet-treet-treet-treet*'. R

11   **WINDING** (or Black-backed) **CISTICOLA** *Cisticola galactotes*   L 15 cm. From 12 by brighter colouring and narrower tail, from 18 by unstreaked rump and more red on wing coverts. Habitat: lowlands. High, weedy places near lakes and marshes. Voice: e.g. dry rattle (like fast winding of a clock), '*tritritri*' for 0.5 seconds.

12   **CHIRPING CISTICOLA** *Cisticola pipiens*   L 14 cm. Br plumage shown, n-br plumage less grey and with black subdued. Note wide tail. Habitat: swamps, moist herbage along streams. Voice: loud, decisive '*tit tit-Thréeee*'.

13   **RATTLING CISTICOLA** *Cisticola chiniana*   L 14 cm. Tail greyish brown, wings only faintly buff. Habitat: dry bushland with tall grass, sometimes in wetter areas. Voice: basically a fast, low, fluted rattle, '*tjaktjaktjak*', together with high '*tieutieu-tieu*', '*prrríet*' or '*tjèh tjèh tjèh tjèh*', all with sparrow-like quality.

14   **BLACK-LORED CISTICOLA** *Cisticola nigriloris*   L 14 cm. Montane areas along streams or at forest edge. Voice: duet of extreme high, undulating, piping, shrill (like a badly oiled wheel), sustained '*weetweetweet -*' of ♂ with faint '*trit trit trit-*' of ♀, and other variations.

15   **WHISTLING CISTICOLA** *Cisticola lateralis*   L 13 cm. Uniform dark, short tail, large bill, all tail feathers with dark spot near tip. Habitat: herbage in woodland and bushveld often along streams. Voice: high, jubilant '*pju-pjup-puPjuwuwihihi*' or mid-high, loud, scolding '*Pjneeh Pjneeh -*'. R

◀

Plate 64

Plate 65

1   **FAN-TAILED CISTICOLA** *Cisticola juncidis*   L 11 cm. Bright tawny rump, tail with subterminal black band. Habitat: dry, rank grass often near marshes and vleis. Voice: extreme high '*zeet zeet zeet -*', coinciding with dips in high, cruising display flight.

2   **DESERT CISTICOLA** *Cisticola aridulus*   L 11 cm. Unstreaked rump, tail (which is very short in br plumage) with only white terminal band. Habitat: arid, grassy areas. Voice: very high '*fififififififi*' in upward flight, followed by '*seep*'s or '*ticé*'s interspersed with short series of wing claps.

3   **CLOUD CISTICOLA** *Cisticola textrix*   L 11 cm. Not all races depicted; tawny-crowned race *major* (a) and nominate (b) shown. Habitat: grasslands. Voice: in flight, very high '*fiuweetweetweettjiptjiptjip-*' ('*tjiptjip-*' part as dry, toneless almost-rattles of any length).

4   **WING-SNAPPING** (or Ayres's) **CISTICOLA** *Cisticola ayresii*   L 9 cm. From 3 by shorter legs and more streaked crown. Habitat: montane, short grassland, occasionally near coast. Voice: very high '*swéet tree tree tree*' and rapid burst of wingclaps, '*clapclapclap-*', alternating in irregular manner.

5   **PALE-CROWNED CISTICOLA** *Cisticola cinnamomeus*   L 10 cm. All tail feathers white-tipped; dark loral spot. Br ♂ shown, n-br ♂ and ♀ have streaked crown. Habitat: montane grass- and moorland. Voice: extreme high, lowered '*sreesisisisi sisi*' in upward flight, followed by extreme high '*swee-swee-swee-tree-tree–*' in up-and-down display flight.

6   **DAMBO CISTICOLA** *Cisticola dambo*   L 12 cm. Blackish plumage especially crown, dark, white-tipped tail feathers. Habitat: floodplains.

7   **BLACK-TAILED CISTICOLA** *Cisticola melanurus*   L 11 cm. Note black, pale-tipped tail. Habitat: miombo. R

8   **BLACK-HEADED APALIS** *Apalis melanocephala*   L 15 cm. Note that eye may also be red-brown (not yellow as shown). Habitat: forest riverine belts, coastal bush. Voice: very high '*sweesweeswee–*' of ♂ often together with mid-high '*shra-shra-shra–*' of ♀ in unsynchronized duet.

9   **YELLOW-BREASTED APALIS** *Apalis flavida*   L 11 cm. Form **a** with, **b** without, black breast spot, latter with green crown. Habitat: wood-, bush- and scrubland. Voice: high, dry '*tju-tju-tju–*', '*terrúterrúterrú-*' or sustained, rapid '*tjuuptjuuptjuup-*'.

10 **BLACK-THROATED APALIS** *Apalis jacksoni*   L 12 cm. Habitat: montane forest edges. Voice: duets, '*tuuttuut-tuuttuut-tuuttet*', often not quite synchronized.

11 **RUDD'S APALIS** *Apalis ruddi*   L 13 cm. From 12 by green (not grey) tail without white edges, narrow, white eyebrow and black eye. Habitat: coastal woodland and scrub with adjoining lowland areas.

12 **BAR-THROATED APALIS** *Apalis thoracica*   L 11 cm. Many races exist, *spelonkensis* (a) and *arnoldi* (b) shown. All have black breast band, yellow eye and white outer tail feathers. Habitat: woodland . Voice: mid-high, loud '*wrutwrutwrut–*' of ♂ ; pauses filled in by ♀ with extreme high '*srrr*'.

13 **WHITE-WINGED APALIS** *Apalis chariessa*   L 12 cm. Habitat: forest, riverine belts. U

14 **CHAPIN'S APALIS** *Apalis chapini*   L 12 cm. From all apalis warblers by brown-rufous throat. Habitat: canopy of montane forest.

15 **BROWN-HEADED APALIS** *Apalis alticola*   L 12 cm. Nominate (a) and race *grandis* (b) shown, differing in tail pattern. Note: *grandis* is often treated as a race of another extra-limital species (Grey Apalis, *Apalis cinerea*). Habitat: forest and forest remains.

16 **MOREAU'S TAILORBIRD** *Artisornis moreaui*   L 11 cm. From 21 by longer bill, less orange face sides, greyer upperparts. Habitat: canopy of montane forests. R

17 **MASKED APALIS** *Apalis binotata*   L 10 cm. From 10 by all-green wings and (short) tail. Habitat: riverine belts. Voice: very high, rapid '*fiufiufiu-*' or high, fast '*krrrk krrrk kéelerkéeler*'.

18 **CHIRINDA APALIS** *Apalis chirindensis*   L 13 cm. From similar, all-grey ♀ 19 by different range. Habitat: forest. Voice: very high, loud, sharp, lashing '*tsjeeptsjeeptsjeeptsjeep*'. R

19 **GOSLING'S APALIS** *Apalis goslingi*   L 11 cm. Note short tail. Habitat: along forest streams. Voice: high, sharp, rapid, tinkling '*tingctingctingc-*' (6 times). R

20 **BUFF-THROATED APALIS** *Apalis rufogularis*   L 11 cm. The ♂ from 15b by paler eye and uniform brown upperparts, ♀ by buff-orange tinge from chin down (sexes of 15b are alike). Habitat: forests. Voice: high, rapid, rattling '*wrreetwrreetwrreet–*' (each '*wrreet*' lashed up).

▶

Plate 65

Plate 65 (continued)

21   **AFRICAN TAILORBIRD** *Artisornis metopias*   L 10 cm. See 16. Habitat: understorey of montane forests. R

Plate 66

1   **KRETSCHMER'S LONGBILL** *Macrosphenus kretschmeri*   L 14 cm. From most greenbuls (Plates 55 and 56) by small size and long bill. Note grey (not pinkish) legs. Habitat: forest undergrowth. Voice: high '*ti*' directly followed by compressed '*tiderriewdip*'. R

2   **GREY LONGBILL** *Macrosphenus concolor*   L 13 cm. Paler and fluffier than 1. Underparts only slightly paler than upperparts. Legs brownish flesh. Habitat: dense forest undergrowth. Voice: very high, hurried, crescendoing twitter, descending or with repeated phrases like '-*wéetturuweet*-'. R

3   **PULITZER'S LONGBILL** *Macrosphenus pulitzeri*   L 13 cm. From 4 by pink legs, less bright colouring and buffish (not white) chin and throat. Habitat: dry forest. R E (Angola)

4   **YELLOW LONGBILL** *Macrosphenus flavicans*   L 13 cm. Note white chin, throat and upperbreast and grey legs. Habitat: dense forest undergrowth. Voice: rapidly descending, slow, fluted '*fjuu fjuu fjuu fjuu fjuu fjuu-fjuu*' (starting very high). R

5   **RED-BELLIED PARADISE FLYCATCHER** *Terpsiphone rufiventer*   L 18 (+3) cm. Note bright, rufous underparts. Habitat: forest interior.

6   **AFRICAN PARADISE FLYCATCHER** *Terpsiphone viridis*   L 18 (+8) cm. Note white undertail coverts. Habitat: forest, wood- and bushland, gardens.

7   **RUFOUS-VENTED PARADISE FLYCATCHER** *Terpsiphone rufocinerea*   L 18 (+5) cm. From 6 by rufous undertail coverts, smaller crest and less conspicuous eye wattle. Habitat: forests.

8   **BATES'S PARADISE FLYCATCHER** *Terpsiphone batesi*   L 18 (+2) cm. From 7 by rounded head without crest. Habitat: forests. U

9   **BLUE-MANTLED CRESTED FLYCATCHER** *Trochocercus cyanomelas*   L 14 cm. (Note: like all small flycatchers on this plate, very active, constantly cocking and fanning its tail). Habitat: dense, lower storeys of forests. Voice: very varied medley of well-separated, instrumental phrases, like high, nasal '*weetwit-weetwit*', low, rapid, liquid '*weetweetweetweet*' or fluted trill, '*wrrrrrh*' etc.

10   **BLUE-HEADED CRESTED FLYCATCHER** *Trochocercus nitens*   L 13 cm. From 13 by all-black tail and sharp demarcation between black breast and pale belly. Habitat: forest undergrowth. U

11   **AFRICAN BLUE FLYCATCHER** *Elminia longicauda*   L 14 cm. From 12 by bluer colouring and lack of white in tail. Habitat: lower storeys of forest, moist woodland, bushveld, gardens. U

12   **WHITE-TAILED BLUE FLYCATCHER** *Elminia albicauda*   L 14 cm. Note tail pattern and streaked face. Habitat: montane, open forest, riverine belts. U

13   **WHITE-TAILED CRESTED FLYCATCHER** *Elminia albonotata*   L 13 cm. Note tail pattern. Habitat: montane forests and forest remains. Voice: very high, hesitating, wagtail-like '*tweet treet treetoweet*' with high, fluted '*weet tsio-weet*'.

14   **LIVINGSTONE'S FLYCATCHER** *Erythrocercus livingstonei*   L 10 cm. Very small. Habitat: open woodland, riverine belts, coastal bush. Voice: combination of hurried, short, low twitters and very high, fluted, warbling '*tititriWéetoWéetoWéet*'.

15   **COMMON WHITETHROAT** *Sylvia communis*   L 14 cm. Note pale eye (dark in 1stW), white outer tail feathers, rufous (♂) or sandy (♀) wing edges. Habitat: scrubland, undergrowth of woodland and bushveld. Voice: modest, hurried song, higher, sharper and faster than 17. S

16   **BLACKCAP** *Sylvia atricapilla*   L 14 cm. Habitat: forest, bamboo, bush, suburbs. Voice: high, rich, scratchy, unhurried warbling starting with some squeaky notes. US

17   **BARRED WARBLER** *Sylvia nisoria*   L 16 cm. The ♀ as 1stW (shown) but with pale eye; 1stW nondescript, but with diagnostic, white tail corners and slightly paler edges to wing coverts and tertials. Habitat: low scrub and undergrowth of woodland. RS

18   **GARDEN WARBLER** *Sylvia borin*   L 14 cm. Note stubby bill and faint, grey neck sides. Habitat: forest edges, wood- and bushland, cultivation, suburbs. Voice: very long, rapid sequence of jumbling, mellow, sharp and harsh notes. S

19   **LAYARD'S WARBLER** (or Titbabbler) *Parisoma layardi*   L 15 cm. From 20 by white undertail coverts. Habitat: thornveld, scrubland. Voice: short phrases with many fluted rattles.

▶

Plate 66

Plate 66 (continued)

20 **CHESTNUT-VENTED WARBLER** (or Titbabbler) *Parisoma subcaeruleum*   L 15 cm. Habitat: dense thickets. Voice: well-separated, very high, clear phrases, often with bouncing, fluted notes.

21 **BROWN PARISOMA** *Parisoma lugens*   L 13 cm. Note fine spotting on chin and throat and white tail edges. Habitat: thornveld. U

Plate 67

1 **AFRICAN DUSKY FLYCATCHER** *Muscicapa adusta*   L 12 cm. Note yellow-gaped bill, dusky plumage above, warm-brown colouring of breast, malar stripe which is more prominent than moustachial stripe. Hunts from low perch. Habitat: highland, also in coastal regions. Forest edges, riverine belts, dense woodland, suburbs. Voice: call is extreme high '*sieeèh*'.

2 **ASHY** (or Blue-grey) **FLYCATCHER** *Muscicapa caerulescens*   L 14 cm. Note strong bill with paler lower mandible, uniform upperparts (including tail), white eye ring. Hawks from mid-stratum perch. Habitat: woodland, riverine belts, coastal bush. Voice: high '*peepeepeepu-peewgh*' sometimes changing to twittering song.

3 **SPOTTED FLYCATCHER** *Muscicapa striata*   L 14 cm. Note faint streaking on forehead and slightly peaked crown. Hunts from low perch. Habitat: woodland, bushveld, gardens. Voice: extreme high '*tsjeeh-tjgh*' or thin '*tjièh*'. S

4 **CASSIN'S FLYCATCHER** *Muscicapa cassini*   L 13 cm. From 10 by white chin and lower belly, from 2 by uniform face sides. Habitat: hawks from perch over forest streams.

5 **SWAMP FLYCATCHER** *Muscicapa aquatica*   L 13 cm. Note white chin, dark brown upperparts, small, white streaks under eye. Habitat: only at lake shores and in swamps.

6 **DUSKY BLUE FLYCATCHER** *Muscicapa comitata*   L 12 cm. Note dark colouring, thin eyebrow, conspicuous, white throat, pale brown undertail coverts. Habitat: forest edges. R

7 **SOOTY FLYCATCHER** *Muscicapa infuscata*   L 12 cm. Very dark with mottled underparts. Hunts from high, exposed position. Habitat: forest edges and nearby areas. U

8 **COLLARED FLYCATCHER** *Ficedula albicollis*   L 13 cm. Imm from ♀ by uniform (not partly grey) upperparts and pale brown second wing bar. Habitat: miombo, other woodland. US

9 **SOUTHERN BLACK FLYCATCHER** *Melaenornis pammelaina*   L 20 cm. Glossy black with only slightly forked tail (see also 56.1 and 56.2). Habitat: wooded and bushed, natural and cultivated areas. Voice: high, loud, melodious, fluted '*feeh-tjuutjuu*' ('*feeh-*' extreme high).

10 **GREY-THROATED TIT FLYCATCHER** *Myioparus griseigularis*   L 11 cm. Note uniform grey colouring below. Not a 'percher', but in behaviour very much like a warbler, active, moving through the foliage gleaning insects while constantly wagging its tail. Habitat: forest and nearby areas. Voice: very high, 2-toned, fluted '*preee-prrrruuurr*'.

11 **GREY** (or Fan-tailed) **FLYCATCHER** *Myioparus plumbeus*   L 14 cm. From 10 by paler underparts and constant fanning (not only wagging like 10) of tail. Active insect-hunter. Habitat: forest edges, woodland, riverine belts. Very high '*srrieeèh*' (last part descending). U

12 **BOEHM'S FLYCATCHER** *Muscicapa boehmi*   L 12 cm. Note very upright stance and triangular spots below. Unobtrusive percher. Habitat: miombo.

13 **FRASER'S FOREST FLYCATCHER** *Fraseria ocreata*   L 14 cm. Found in groups of up to 20. Habitat: forest interiors.

14 **FISCAL FLYCATCHER** *Melaenornis silens*   L 19 cm. From 73.16 by absence of white edge to mantle, smaller bill and different tail pattern. Habitat: open country with some trees, suburbs. Voice: extreme high siffling together with very high, thin flutes, '*sreesreetuwgewgh*'.

15 **CHAT FLYCATCHER** *Melaenornis infuscatus*   L 20 cm. Underparts not white like 18 and 19 and no dark loral stripe. Perches upright on top (!) of bush (not on low perch like 18 and 19). Often seen with partly spread wings. Habitat: dry scrub- and bushland. Voice: frog- or reed warbler-like, unstructured, twittering '*treet-treet-twitwitwit-*' larded with some fluted notes.

16 **ANGOLA SLATY FLYCATCHER** *Melaenornis brunneus*   L 15 cm. Restricted range in Angola. Habitat: montane forest and woodland patches. U E (Angola)

17 **WHITE-EYED SLATY FLYCATCHER** *Melaenornis fischeri*   L 16 cm. Shows pronounced, white eye ring. Habitat: montane forest edges, woodland, gardens.

▶

Plate 67

Plate 67 (continued)

18 **PALE** (Pallid or Mouse-coloured) **FLYCATCHER** *Melaenornis pallidus* L 16 cm. From 15 by distinct lore and less bright edges to wing feathers. Perches on low branch. Habitat: woodland, bushveld.

19 **MARICO FLYCATCHER** *Melaenornis mariquensis* L 18 cm. Conspicuous white below. Note narrow eye ring and brown loral area which is uniform with forehead and ear coverts. Habitat: thornveld. Voice: short, hoarse, rapid *'retjehtjeh'* and *'freeh'*, sometimes multiplied to unstructured song with well-spaced parts.

Plate 68

1 **YELLOW-BELLIED** (or -breasted) **HYLIOTA** *Hyliota flavigaster* L 12 cm. From 2 by buff (not white) rear underparts, short, white edges to tertials, stronger overall gloss. Habitat: miombo. Voice: unstructured sequence of well-separated, very high, scratchy notes, *'treetreet twitreetreet wietwiet wit wit treetreet'*.

2 **SOUTHERN** (or Mashona) **HYLIOTA** *Hyliota australis* L 11 cm. See 1. Habitat: woodland. Voice: very high, short, slightly scratchy phrases: *'tutreetutreetweetwéetreet'*.

3 **PRIRIT BATIS** *Batis pririt* L 12 cm. No other batis species in most of its range. The ♂ from 6 by spots high on flanks, white eyebrow extending just beyond eye, different call, ♀ by different colour pattern below. Habitat: thornveld. Voice: high, slowly descending *'djuu-djuu–'* (28 times for a duration of 18 seconds).

4 **CAPE BATIS** *Batis capensis* L 12 cm. Not all races depicted; nominate **(a)** and race *dimorpha* **(b)** shown. The ♀ from ♂ 5 by well-defined, white throat band and lack of eyebrow. Note buff-orange wing bars of **a** (only ♂ batis so within its range) and extensive white on coverts of ♂ **b**. Habitat: forest, woodland, gardens. Voice: mid-high, level, fluted, 3-syllabled *'wuutwuutwuut'*.

5 **WOODWARD'S BATIS** *Batis fratrum* L 12 cm. Note absence of breast band in ♂ and pale rufous underparts. ♀ from ♀4 by lack of white throat band. Habitat: forest, riverine belts, coastal bush. Voice: hesitating, slightly hoarse *'ffuuuu'*, sometimes in duet with ♀ answering *'-woh'* (4 tones lower).

6 **CHINSPOT BATIS** *Batis molitor* L 12 cm. The ♂ (with white eyebrow extending well beyond the eye) from 7 by broad breast band. Note striking, rufous breast and throat patch of ♀. Habitat: woodland. Voice: very high, penetrating, sharp, slow, descending *'it's so sad'*.

7 **EAST COAST** (or Mozambique) **BATIS** *Batis soror* L 11 cm. Note narrow breast band of ♂. The ♀ (with partly rufous eyebrow) from ♀ 6 by paler, rufous breast and throat patch. Habitat: woodland. Voice: sustained, staccato, tooting *'tioh-tioh-tioh-'* (*'ti-'* much higher but almost simultaneous with *'-oh'*).

8 **MARGARET'S BATIS** *Batis margaritae* L 12 cm. Note very dark upperparts without white in neck of ♂ and black breast band with rufous wing bar of ♀. Habitat: mid-strata of dry, dense forest and forest patches.

9 **FOREST BATIS** *Batis mixta* L 12 cm. Only red-eyed ♂ batis (except some individuals of 5, which has different range). Note predominantly brown upperparts of ♀. Habitat: forest. R

10 **ANGOLA BATIS** *Batis minulla* L 9 cm. From 11 (in same range) by absence of long, white eyebrow, white spots on rump, broader breast band. Habitat: woodland.

11 **BLACK-HEADED BATIS** *Batis minor* L 10 cm. Note long, white eyebrows, which are more or less connected on neck. Habitat: bushy grassland. U

12 **BLACK-AND-WHITE** (or Vanga) **FLYCATCHER** *Bias musicus* L 15 cm. Habitat: open forest and woodland. Voice: sequence of mid-high to very high, short to very short phrases, *'tjútjipjútjip-weet-weet-tjiptjuweet'*. U

13 **SHRIKE FLYCATCHER** *Megabyas flammulatus* L 17 cm. Habitat: forest edges, riverine belts. Voice: very high, running-up, hurried *'wgeduwéet-wgeduwéet'*. U

14 **CHESTNUT WATTLE-EYE** *Dyaphorophyia castanea* L 10 cm. Habitat: forest undergrowth.

15 **YELLOW-BELLIED WATTLE-EYE** *Dyaphorophyia concreta* L 9 cm. The ♂ may have black breast spot. Habitat: forest. Voice: high, fluted *'whit-whit tjuu-tjuu whíp'* (descending to lashing-upward *'whíp'*).

▶

Plate 68

Plate 68 (continued)

16   **BLACK-NECKED WATTLE-EYE** *Dyaphorophyia blissetti chalybea*   L 9 cm. The ♂ more glossy than ♀. Habitat: forest understorey. R

17   **BLACK-THROATED WATTLE-EYE** (Flycatcher) *Platysteira peltata*   L 13 cm. From 18 by different wing pattern. Habitat: more or less wooded and bushed areas including gardens. Voice: high, sharp, lashing, tit-like ' *tsja-tsja-weetoweetoweeto-*'.

18   **BROWN-THROATED WATTLE-EYE** *Platysteira cyanea*   L 13 cm. Habitat: forest edges, woodland, bushveld. Voice: very high, simple melody of sharp, well-separated notes, '*fee-fee-fee-wee-wee-fee*'. R

19   **WHITE-FRONTED WATTLE-EYE** *Platysteira albifrons*   L 11 cm. Habitat: thickets, riverine belts.

Plate 69

1   **CAPE SUGARBIRD** *Promerops cafer*   L 37 cm (♂), 24 cm (♀). From 2 by prominent malar stripe, streaked chest and longer tail. Habitat: fynbos. Voice: hoarse chatter. E (South Africa)

2   **GURNEY'S SUGARBIRD** *Promerops gurneyi*   L 25 cm (♂), 23 cm (♀). Habitat: as 1 but different range. Voice: rather unstructured chattering, less hoarse than 1.

3   **SPOTTED CREEPER** *Salpornis spilonotus*   L 15 cm. Climbs tree trunks without support of tail. Habitat: miombo. Voice: extreme high, narrow, piercing '*seeeeseeeeseeeeseeee*'.

4   **CAPE PENDULINE TIT** *Anthoscopus minutus*   L 9 cm. Nominate **(a)** and race *damarensis* **(b)** shown. From 5 by spotted forehead and grey crown. Habitat: thornveld. Voice: very high '*puwee-puwee*' and extreme high '*shee-swee-swee*'.

5   **GREY PENDULINE TIT** *Anthoscopus caroli*   L 8 cm. Nominate **(a)** and race *ansorgei* **(b)** shown. From 4 by more extensive white from chin to lower breast. Habitat: open forest, woodland. Voice: extreme high '*wit wit wit witterdewitterdewitterdewit*'.

6   **TITHYLIA** *Pholidornis rushiae*   L 8 cm. Note tiny size and yellow rear part of body. Habitat: forest canopy. R

7   **MIOMBO** (or Northern) **GREY TIT** *Parus griseiventris*   L 15 cm. From 8 by blue-grey mantle, small, white neck spot, more white in wing, from 8 and 11 by grey cheeks, which are concolorous with sides of breast. Habitat: miombo.

8   **SOUTHERN GREY TIT** *Parus afer*   L 14 cm. From 7 by white tips to tail feathers, from 7 and 11 by pale, tawny underparts. Habitat: rocky areas with scrub and small thorn trees.

9   **CINNAMON-BREASTED TIT** *Parus pallidiventris*   L 14 cm. From adult 10b by dark eye. Similar to imm 10b but ranges of 9 and 10 overlap only marginally. Habitat: miombo.

10   **RUFOUS-BELLIED TIT** *Parus rufiventris*   L 14 cm. Nominate **(a)** and race *masukiensis* **(b)** shown. Immatures have dark eye! (Note: 9 and 10 are know to hybridise in the narrow area of overlap). Habitat: miombo and other woodland.

11   **ASHY TIT** *Parus cinerascens*   L 15 cm. Flanks concolorous with mantle, isolated, narrow, white cheek. Habitat: thornveld, riverine belts, Kalahari scrub.

12   **WHITE-WINGED BLACK TIT** *Parus leucomelas*   L 15 cm. From 13 by black undertail coverts and only 1–3 visible black centres in greater wing coverts. Habitat: open woodland.

13   **CARP'S TIT** *Parus carpi*   L 15 cm. From 12 by grey undertail coverts, white tip to all tail feathers, 5–6 visible black centres in greater coverts. Habitat: thornveld, scrubland.

14   **SOUTHERN BLACK TIT** *Parus niger*   L 15 cm. Nominate **(a)** and ♀ of race *ravidus* **(b)** shown; ♂ of latter as **a** but with slightly more white in wing. From 12 and 13 by more than 6 visible black centres in greater coverts, white-tipped undertail coverts and broadly white-edged tail feathers. Habitat: more or less wooded areas including plantations and suburbs.

15   **DUSKY TIT** *Parus funereus*   L 14 cm. Note conspicuous, red eye. Habitat: forest, riverine belts, plantations. Voice: loud, lowered, sometimes hoarse '*viouuuh*' or questioning '*vreeeeh?*'. R

16   **SCARLET-TUFTED MALACHITE SUNBIRD** *Nectarinia johnstoni*   L 16 (+12) cm. Reflecting (not shining as 17) green with black undertail coverts, the ♀ dusky with faintly, finely barred throat. N-br ♂ as ♀ but retaining reflecting wing coverts and rump feathers, black flight feathers and elongated middle tail feathers. Habitat: montane and alpine areas. R

▶

Plate 69

Plate 69 (continued)

Note: many sunbirds (like 16 and 17 but also some on Plates 70 and 71) have tufts at the sides of their breast, which are normally concealed and hence not shown on the plates. They can be erected, especially in courtship display.

17   **YELLOW-TUFTED MALACHITE SUNBIRD** *Nectarinia famosa*   L 15 (+9) cm. The ♀ from most other ♀♀ by rather yellow-greenish underparts with rather well-defined moustachial stripe. N-br plumage similar pattern to n-br 16. Habitat: more or less open, wooded and scrubbed areas, gardens. Voice: very high, unstructured, slow tinkling, built around high '*tink-tink*'.

18   **BRONZE SUNBIRD** *Nectarinia kilimensis*   L 15 (+7) cm. Very dark with bronze and green reflections. The ♀ has diffuse streaks below. No n-br plumage and no tufts. Habitat: montane forest edges, wooded and bushed areas. Voice: very high, excited, rapid, sustained twittering.

19   **BOCAGE'S SUNBIRD** *Nectarinia bocagii*   L 15 (+5) cm. Overall black with little reflection. The ♀ is bright yellowish below. No n-br plumage and no tufts. Habitat: woodland. U

Plate 70 (continued)

20   **BANNERMANN'S SUNBIRD** *Nectarinia bannermanni*   L 14 cm. Note dull, blue chin and throat of ♂ and blue (not green) cap of ♀. Habitat: woodland. U

Plate 70

Note: the sunbirds on this plate do not acquire a n-br plumage. See also note under 69.16.

1 **GREY SUNBIRD** *Nectarinia veroxii* L 12 cm. May show red pectoral tufts. Habitat: undergrowth of coastal wood- and bushland, mangroves, gardens. Voice: rather staccato, warbler-like '*tweetwéetweetritri*', starting very high then gradually lowered.

2 **OLIVE SUNBIRD** *Nectarinia olivacea* L 14 cm. May show yellow tufts. From 5, 12 and 13 by olive (not green) upperparts and much longer bill. Southern birds (not shown) have orange wash on throat and breast. Habitat: forest, woodland, riverine belts, gardens. Voice: as 1 but sharper.

3 **REICHENBACH'S SUNBIRD** *Nectarinia reichenbachii* L 11 cm. From 4 by blue-black crown and nape and different range. Tail graduated with pale tips. May show yellow tufts. Habitat: forest edges, cultivation, gardens. R

4 **PLAIN-BACKED** (or Blue-throated) **SUNBIRD** *Antreptes reichenowi* L 10 cm. The ♀ from ♀♀ 5, 12 and 13 by different range. No tufts. Habitat: forest canopy. Voice: very high, lowered, willow warbler-like song, '*téetéetéet-tweetweetwee-tuweetuweetuwee-errrrr*'. U

5 **FRASER'S SUNBIRD** *Anthreptes fraseri* L 11 cm. The ♂ from all other ♂ and ♀ sunbirds by (often concealed) scarlet tufts. Habitat: forest canopy. U

6 **YELLOW-CHINNED SUNBIRD** *Anthreptes rectirostris* L 9 cm. From 7 by whitish chin and belly. Habitat: forest canopy.

7 **COLLARED SUNBIRD** *Anthreptes collaris* L 10 cm. Note short bill. Habitat: forest, riverine belts, coastal bush, suburbs. Voice: very high '*tujutijutijutiju-*' and other siffles and twitters.

8 **RED-AND-BLUE SUNBIRD** *Anthreptes anchietae* L 10 cm. Habitat: miombo.

9 **VIOLET-BACKED SUNBIRD** *Anthreptes longuemarei* L 13 cm. From ♂ 10 by more reddish-purple colouring above, some bluish reflections on rump and whiter flanks. Note white eyebrow of ♀. Habitat: miombo and other woodland. Voice: high, unstructured, reed warbler-like twittering.

10 **ULUGURU VIOLET-BACKED SUNBIRD** *Anthreptes neglectus* L 13 cm. Note dusky flanks of ♂. The ♀ as ♂ but with white chin. Habitat: coastal forest. R

11 **VIOLET-TAILED SUNBIRD** *Anthreptes aurantium* L 11 cm. Note green wings. Habitat: wooded and overgrown streams.

12 **BATES'S SUNBIRD** *Nectarinia batesi* L 11 cm. From 13 by narrow bill and darker underparts. No tufts. Habitat: open forest, cultivation. U

13 **LITTLE GREEN SUNBIRD** *Nectarinia seimundi* L 9 cm. From 7 by lack of tufts, from 12 by paler underparts, from other green sunbirds by different range. Habitat: open forest. U

14 **SCARLET-CHESTED SUNBIRD** *Nectarinia senegalensis* L 14 cm. The ♀ is heavily marked below, from ♀ by sharply demarcated cheek. Habitat: woodland, bushveld, suburbs. Voice: mid-high, slow '*tuut twit-tuut twuut*'.

15 **AMETHYST** (or Black) **SUNBIRD** *Nectarinia amethystina* L 14 cm. Nominate shown; race *kirkii* from Zimbabwe and East Zambia (not shown) lacks purple rump. Looks all-black in the field with, occasionally, a small, reflecting spot. From ♂ 16 by green-reflecting forehead and crown; ♀ from ♀ 17 by distinct eyebrow. Habitat: forest edges, woodland, mangroves, suburbs. Voice: mid-high, sustained, rather slow '*tuut puwietpuwiet tututut fuwie–*'.

16 **CARMELITE SUNBIRD** *Nectarinia fuliginosa* L 13 cm. Looks all-black in the field. Rump non-reflecting. The ♀ from ♀ 15 by absence of visible eyebrow. (Other races outside the region have ♀♀ with very pale, almost white upperparts). Habitat: open, wooded country, cultivation, gardens.

17 **GREEN-THROATED SUNBIRD** *Nectarinia rubescens* L 13 cm. Note dense streaking on ♀ underparts which dominates pale background. Habitat: open forest.

18 **BLUE-THROATED BROWN SUNBIRD** *Nectarinia cyanolaema* L 14 cm. The ♂ may show yellow tufts. The ♀ shows diagnostic, white lines above and below eye. Habitat: forest canopy.

19 **GREEN-HEADED SUNBIRD** *Nectarinia verticalis* L 14 cm. The ♂ from ♂ 20 by more brilliant reflections, especially on throat and chin, ♀ by green, not blue, cap. Habitat: forest, bamboo, bushveld, gardens, cultivation.

◀

Plate 70

Plate 71

Note: see under 69.16.

1   **ORANGE-BREASTED SUNBIRD** *Nectarinia violacea*   L 12 (+2) cm. The ♀ from ♀♀ 5 and 6 by orange wash on underparts. Habitat: coastal hillsides. Voice: high, soft, fast, up-and-down, chattered song phrase. E (South Africa)

2   **COPPERY SUNBIRD** *Nectarinia cuprea*   L 11 cm. Note black tail of ♀. Habitat: forest edges, open woodland, bushveld, cultivation, gardens. Voice: song is combination of its sparrow-like call '*dutdutdutdut-*' and slow, high, nasal twittering.

3   **YELLOW-BELLIED SUNBIRD** *Nectarinia venusta*   L 10 cm. The ♂ from 70.7 by darker, more purplish reflections and longer bill. The ♀ has blue-black tail, whitish throat and upperbreast and lacks eyebrow. Habitat: forest edges, riverine belts, bushveld, gardens. Voice: very high, descending, very fast, warbler-like chatter and very high, level, fast twittering.

Note: ♂♂ 3, 4 and 7 have n-br plumages resembling their ♀♀, but retain reflecting wing coverts and rump feathers and black flight feathers.

4   **WHITE-BELLIED SUNBIRD** *Nectarinia talatala*   L 11 cm. The ♂ from 11 (which has restricted range) by lack of purplish-maroon breast band and longer, more curved bill, the ♀ by whiter throat and chest. Habitat: woodland, bushveld, gardens. Voice: combination of very high '*uweét-uweét*', a fast, wren-like trill and other short twitters.

5   **GREATER DOUBLE-COLLARED SUNBIRD** *Nectarinia afra*   L 12 cm. The ♂ from ♂ 6 by longer bill and broader, red breast band, ♀ by bill size; from 7, 8, 9 and 10 by different range. Habitat: forest edges, bush, gardens. Voice: high to very high, pleasant, warbler-like twittering.

6   **SOUTHERN** (or Lesser) **DOUBLE-COLLARED SUNBIRD** *Nectarinia chalybea*   L 10 cm. Habitat: forest edges, coastal scrub, gardens. Voice: extreme high, fast siffling, interrupted by very high, staccato '*zikzik zikzik*'.

7   **MIOMBO DOUBLE-COLLARED SUNBIRD** *Nectarinia manoensis*   L 10 cm. The ♂ from 9 by olive rump, narrower, red breast band and paler, whitish belly, ♀ by cleaner underparts. From 8 by different range. See 3. Habitat: montane forest, miombo. Voice: very high, siffled chattering (lower-pitched than 6).

8   **OLIVE-BELLIED SUNBIRD** *Nectarinia chloropygia*   L 10 cm. Note blue rump and dusky underparts of ♂. The ♀ has streaked underparts and distinct eyebrow. Habitat: forest edges, moist bushland, cultivation.

9   **EASTERN DOUBLE-COLLARED SUNBIRD** *Nectarinia mediocris*   L 10 cm. Note green rump, orange (not red) breast band and yellow underparts of ♂. The ♀ shows a rather dusky throat. Bill rather decurved. Habitat: forest edges, bamboo, gardens.

10   **SUPERB SUNBIRD** *Nectarinia superba*   L 14 cm. Note long bill and orange and yellow tinges on underparts of ♀. Habitat: forest canopy.

11   **OUSTALET'S WHITE-BELLIED SUNBIRD** *Nectarinia oustaleti*   L 10 cm. From 4 by less blue plumage; ♀ shows indistinct, dusky throat streaks. Habitat: miombo. U

12   **DUSKY SUNBIRD** *Nectarinia fusca*   L 10 cm. The ♀ (as ♂) predominantly white below. Note: n-br ♂♂ are dusky brown above with a broad, black stripe from chin to belly, leaving the throat and breast sides white. Habitat: very dry, open areas with scrub and rocks. Voice: song is a combination of mid-high trills, canary-like warbles and reed warbler-like rattles.

13   **SHELLEY'S SUNBIRD** *Nectarinia shelleyi*   L 12 cm. Note red (not maroon) breast band. From 16 by longer bill and different range, ♀ by streaked (not plain) underparts. Habitat: miombo, wood- and bushland, gardens. Voice: high, rapid, unstructured twittering around high, slightly thrush-like rattle, '*tutututututut*'.

14   **MARICO SUNBIRD** *Nectarinia mariquensis*   L 14 cm. From 15 by long, decurved bill and less brilliant colouring, from 17 by green forehead and chin and different range. Habitat: miombo, dry thornveld. Voice: high to very high, very fast warbling.

15   **PURPLE-BANDED SUNBIRD** *Nectarinia bifasciata*   L 11 cm. Note maroon (not red) breast band and rather short bill. Habitat: dense riverine belts, forest, coastal scrub, mangroves. Voice: very high '*tit-tit-trrriritrrr*'.

▶

Plate 71

Plate 71 (continued)

16 **NEERGAARD'S SUNBIRD** *Nectarinia neergaardi*   L 10 cm. Note red breast band and uniform brown-black underparts of ♂ and plain, greenish underparts of ♀. Habitat: coastal woodland. Voice: extreme high siffling, '*si-si-si-si-susususususu*' ('*susu*–' as a fast rattle).

17 **ORANGE-TUFTED SUNBIRD** *Nectarinia bouvieri*   L 10 cm. Note purple forehead and brown chin of ♂. The ♀ is densely streaked below. Habitat: open woodland.

18 **YELLOW WHITE-EYE** *Zosterops senegalensis*   L 10 cm. From 19 by brighter, more uniform colouring above and below. Habitat: forest, riverine belts, woodland, suburbs. Voice: '*sieegh siegh*' as contact call (sharper than 19), high '*pipiwee-piriwee-*' as song (more mellow than 19).

19 **CAPE WHITE-EYE** *Zosterops pallidus*   L 11 cm. Several interbreeding races, some of the resulting colour forms (**a, b** and **c**) shown. Habitat: all types of wooded and bushed habitats, including gardens. Voice: high '*sreeeh weeeh pipeeeeh*' (contact call), high '*sreee wéekweek sree wéekweek*' (song).

Plate 72 (continued)

19   **BROWN-HEADED** (or Three-streaked) **TCHAGRA** *Tchagra australis*   L 18 cm. From 20 by mainly buff eyebrow, bordered below and above (!) by black line and by row of dusky, triangular spots along edge of mantle. Normally forages on the ground. Habitat: open bush with dense thickets. Voice: e.g. loud, resounding, descending, chaffinch-like '*weeweetree-tree-tree tree*'.

20   **SOUTHERN TCHAGRA** *Tchagra tchagra*   L 20 cm. Mainly white eyebrow not, or very narrowly, bordered with black above. Habitat: dense, coastal thornbush, riverine scrub, other thick cover. Voice: very loud, sustained, staccato flutes e.g. '*piu-piu-piu-piu–*'.

21   **BLACK-CROWNED TCHAGRA** *Tchagra senegala*   L 20 cm. Note black crown and grey underparts. Habitat: dry, bushed and wooded areas with dense, weedy and thorny cover. Voice: mid-high, loud, unhurried, human-like whistles (♂), interrupted by cackling laughter of ♀.

Plate 72

1 **GREY-GREEN BUSH SHRIKE** *Malaconotus bocagei* L 16 cm. Note white loral spot and heavy bill. Habitat: undergrowth of forest, deserted cultivation.

2 **PERRIN'S BUSH SHRIKE** *Malaconotus viridis* L 18 cm. From 12 by different coloured underparts. The ♀ (not shown) from ♂ by narrower, black breast band and green tail. Habitat: dense forest undergrowth near streams. Voice: duet sounding as low, fluid, fast '*pupupuWée*'. U

3 **SOUTHERN BOUBOU** *Laniarius ferrugineus* L 22 cm. From 4 and 5 by orange-rufous underparts (and mainly different range). Skulks. Habitat: low down in dry bush, forest undergrowth. Voice: varied duets with low, hollow, pure whistles from ♂ answered by short, melodious flutes from ♀ e.g. '*weep-weep-weep-fiufiufiu*'.

4 **TROPICAL BOUBOU** *Laniarius aethiopicus* L 24 cm. From 5 by pale, pinkish wash on underparts and different habitat. Habitat: forest edges, riverine belts, thickets, gardens. Voice: varied duets e.g. raucous introduction of ♂ answered by piping flutes from ♀, '*graagraagraa-wutwut*'.

5 **SWAMP BOUBOU** *Laniarius bicolor* L 24 cm. Pure white below. Habitat: papyrus, reed beds, riverine thickets. Voice: magpie-like rattle, '*tjetjetjetjit*', immediately answered by pressed-out, hollow '*fiuu*'.

6 **FUELLEBORN'S BLACK BOUBOU** *Laniarius fuelleborni* L 19 cm. Deep slate-black. From 7 by different range. Habitat: forest undergrowth, bamboo. Voice: duet of high, fluid '*shit-whit trrrril*' (♂), directly answered by high, lashing '*ppWHéet*' (♀).

7 **SOOTY BOUBOU** *Laniarius leucorhynchus* L 21 cm. Deep, pure black. Often fluffs up its rump feathers. Habitat: forest undergrowth. R

8 **LUEHDER'S BUSH SHRIKE** *Laniarius luhderi* L 19 cm. Unmistakable. Habitat: dense undergrowth at forest edges, often near streams.

9 **MONTEIRO'S BUSH SHRIKE** *Malaconotus monteiri* L 22 cm. From 10 by white encircling eye, larger bill and pale blue (not yellow) eyes. Habitat: dense foliage of woodland.

10 **GREY-HEADED BUSH SHRIKE** *Malaconotus blanchoti* L 23 cm. Habitat: riverine belts in woodland. Voice: mid-high, fluted '*fweeee fweeee fweeee*' (each '*fweeee*' slightly crescendoing).

11 **CRIMSON-BREASTED BUSH SHRIKE** *Laniarius atrococcineus* L 23 cm. Normal **(a)** and rare, yellow **(b)** forms shown. Habitat: dry thornveld. Voice: duets e.g. '*sree*' – '*djap-djap*'.

12 **FOUR-COLOURED** (or Gorgeous) **BUSH SHRIKE** *Malaconotus quadricolor* L 18 cm. From 2 with different range by lack of rufous on forehead and rear underparts. Habitat: forest undergrowth, thickets. Voice: e.g. low, melodious, fluted '*ooh-ooh youwéh*' ('*youwéh*' is answer in duet of ♂ and ♀).

13 **BOKMAKIERIE** *Malaconotus zeylonus* L 23 cm. Does not skulk as much as other bush shrikes. Habitat: grassland and rocky areas with some scrub and bush. Often in gardens. Voice: duets, e.g. high, rapid, liquid '*wikwikwikwikwik*' (♂), answered by very high, hurried '*treetreetree*' (♀).

14 **MANY-COLOURED BUSH SHRIKE** *Malaconotus multicolor multicolor* L 18 cm. Note: 14 and 15 are races of one species, *Malaconotus multicolor*, each with yellow (14a), apricot (15) and orange (14b) colour forms. Habitat: canopy and mid-strata of forests.

15 **BLACK-FRONTED BUSH SHRIKE** *Malaconotus multicolor nigrifrons* L 18 cm. See 14. Habitat: as 14. Voice: duets, e.g. low, mellow '*prooh*' (♂), directly followed by lashed-up '*twèèèt*', together '*prooh twèèèt*'.

16 **ORANGE-BREASTED BUSH SHRIKE** *Malaconotus sulfureopectus* L 17 cm. Habitat: dense canopy and mid-strata at forest edges, dense parts of wooded and bushed areas. Voice: fluted '*fututtutèèh*', varied in pitch and speed.

17 **OLIVE BUSH SHRIKE** *Malaconotus olivaceus* L 18 cm. Habitat: from coastal forests to montane shrub. Voice: very variable e.g. melodious, rapid, fluted '*pipip púupúupúurp*'.

18 **MARSH TCHAGRA** *Tchagra minuta* L 17 cm. Note black cap of ♂, broken by eyebrow in ♀. From black-crowned 21 by buff, not grey, underparts. Habitat: tall grass and herbage near streams and in swamps. Voice: e.g. high, very loud, rapid '*weetweetweet*'.

◀

Plate 72

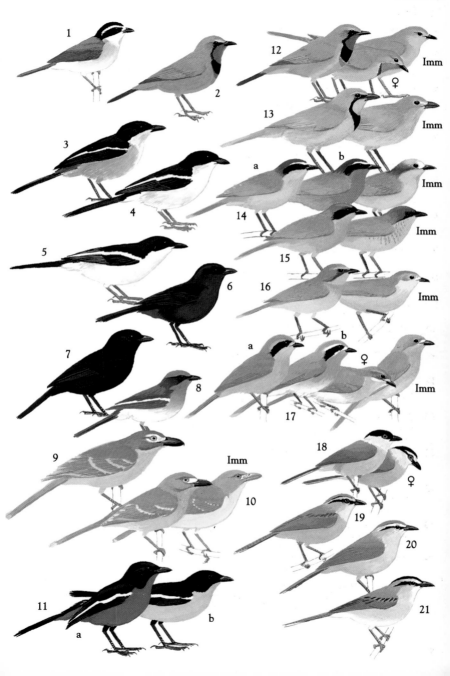

Plate 73

1   **BLACK-SHOULDERED PUFFBACK** *Dryoscopus senegalensis*   L 16 cm. 1, 2 and 3 may display (in flight and perched) as shown (2a). Habitat: open forest. R

2   **SOUTHERN PUFFBACK** *Dryoscopus cubla*   L 16 cm. From 4c by larger size, red eye and all-black mantle. Habitat: forest, riverine belts, woodland. Voice: e.g. loud, lashing whistles, like rapid '*wéet-tee-wéet-tge-wéet-tge-*' ('*tee*' low and almost toneless).

3   **PINK-FOOTED PUFFBACK** *Dryoscopus angolensis*   L 15 cm. Unmistakable. Note colour of legs. Habitat: forest.

4   **BRUBRU** *Nilaus afer*   L 13 cm. Races *brubru* (a), *nigrotemporalis* (b) and *affinis* (c) shown, differentiated by presence or otherwise of eyebrow and rufous on flanks. *Affinis* (c) from 2 by black eye and white patch through middle of mantle. Habitat: miombo, thornveld. Voice: very high, inquiring, short trill, '*prrrrriii*'.

5   **WHITE-TAILED SHRIKE** *Lanioturdus torquatus*   L 15 cm. In parties of 2–20 on the ground. Habitat: woodland, thornveld. Voice: high, loud, fluted '*feee feeee tjaw tjaw-tjaw*'.

6   **MAGPIE** (or Long-tailed) **SHRIKE** *Urolestes melanoleucus*   L 25 (+20) cm. In parties of 3–10. Habitat: open, wooded grassland, thornveld.

7   **WHITE HELMET SHRIKE** *Prionops plumatus*   L 21 cm. Parties of up to 20. Habitat: miombo, bushland, thornveld.

8   **CHESTNUT-FRONTED HELMET SHRIKE** *Prionops scopifrons*   L 17 cm. Chestnut forehead diagnostic. In groups of 3–30, occasionally mixed with species 9. Habitat: canopy of forest and woodland. U

9   **RETZ'S RED-BILLED HELMET SHRIKE** *Prionops retzii*   L 20 cm. From 10 by smaller crest and larger size. In parties of up to 20. Habitat: woodland, riverine belts.

10   **GABELA HELMET SHRIKE** *Prionops gabela*   L 19 cm. See 9. Habitat: open forest, woodland. R E (Angola)

11   **BLACK-COLLARED BULBUL SHRIKE** *Neolestes torquatus*   L 16 cm. In groups feeding on fruits. (Formerly considered to be a bulbul, Plate 55). Habitat: wooded country. Voice: high, hurried, nasal, mewing '*wéetuweetreetreetuweet treetreet*'.

12   **SOUTHERN WHITE-CROWNED SHRIKE** *Eurocephalus anguitimens*   L 20 cm. Loose groups of 2–12, hunting small prey from top of bush or perch. Note conspicuous, white crown. Habitat: wooded country. Voice: high, mewing '*peewpeew peepeew-pupieuw*'.

13   **RED-BACKED SHRIKE** *Lanius collurio*   L 17 cm. Red mantle without white edge diagnostic. The ♀ from 15 by different tail colour and scaled underparts. Habitat: open, lightly wooded and bushed areas. S

14   **SOUZA'S SHRIKE** *Lanius souzae*   L 18 cm. Note black mask and broad, white edge of dull-brown mantle. Habitat: miombo and other woodland.

15   **ISABELLINE** (or Red-tailed) **SHRIKE** *Lanius isabellinus*   L 17 cm. Adult (not shown) from 1stW (as shown) by black mask. All-red tail in all plumages diagnostic. Habitat: dry, open shrubland, bushveld, woodland, farmland. R

16   **FISCAL SHRIKE** *Lanius collaris*   L 22 cm. Not all races depicted; nominate (a) and white-eyebrowed race *subcoronatus* (b) shown. Imm from 14 by brown, not black, marking, barring below and white tail edges. Habitat: any type of country with perches from which to catch small prey and insects.

17   **MACKINNON'S SHRIKE** *Lanius mackinnoni*   L 20 cm. From 18 by white eyebrow and scapulars. Habitat: more or less bushed, natural and cultivated areas. S(W)

18   **LESSER GREY SHRIKE** *Lanius minor*   L 21 cm. Note white wing bar in flight. Adult has black forehead. Habitat: more or less bushed, natural and cultivated areas. S(W)

19   **WOODCHAT SHRIKE** *Lanius senator*   L 18 cm. Only shrike with contrasting, rusty-rufous crown and neck. One unconfirmed record from Angola. Habitat: bushed areas. (?)

Plate 73

Plate 74

1   **EUROPEAN STARLING** *Sturnus vulgaris*   L 20 cm. Introduced in South Africa. Habitat: man-made habitats like farmyards, playing fields, orchards.

2   **PIED STARLING** *Spreo bicolor*   L 25 cm. Note striking, pale eye and white undertail coverts. Habitat: grasslands, farmyards, dry riverbeds, roadsides.

3   **WATTLED STARLING** *Creatophora cinerea*   L 21 cm. Striking, white rump in flight. Highly nomadic in very large flocks. Habitat: open wood- and bushland.

4   **COMMON** (or Indian) **MYNA** *Acridotheres tristis*   L 22 cm. Note large, white wing patch in flight. Habitat: towns and cities. (Introduced from Asia).

5   **WHITE-WINGED STARLING** *Neocichla gutturalis*   L 20 cm. Rather like a helmet shrike (Plate 73) in flight and behaviour. In parties of up to 10. Habitat: miombo. U

6   **PALE-WINGED STARLING** *Onychognathus nabouroup*   L 25 cm. Habitat: cliffs and rocky slopes in dry areas. Voice: high, warbling babbles in phrases of any length, 'sree-wuwuweh freefrufuruririweh'.

7   **RED-WINGED STARLING** *Onychognathus morio*   L 30 cm. From 8, 9 and 10 by lack of green gloss on head, from 8 by longer tail, heavier bill and all-black eye. Range only slightly overlapping with 8 and 9, not with red-eyed 10. Habitat: roosts in large, social flocks in rocks and buildings. Voice: high, melodious, short whistle, 'piupiupioweeh' or 'wutuuitwée'.

8   **WALLER'S RED-WINGED STARLING** *Onychognathus walleri*   L 23 cm. Red on primaries in folded wing does not extend beyond tertials. The ♀ from 7 by less extensive grey on head. Habitat: forest. Voice: very high, whistled 'fiu-fiu-fjée-fjée'.

9   **SLENDER-BILLED CHESTNUT-WINGED STARLING** *Onychognathus tenuirostris*   L 30 cm. Note long, thin bill and strong, blotched barring above and below of ♀. Habitat: montane forest, moorland, cultivation. Voice: mid-high, mewing, rapid 'pju pjée-pjéeepjih'. U

10   **FOREST CHESTNUT-WINGED STARLING** *Onychognathus fulgidus*   L 30 cm. From other red-winged starlings by red eye (except 8) and different range. Habitat: forest. U

11   **VIOLET-BACKED** (or Plum-coloured) **STARLING** *Cinnyricinclus leucogaster*   L 18 cm. Note yellow gape of ♀. Habitat: attracted to fruiting trees at forest edges, woodland, gardens. brS

12   **NARROW-TAILED STARLING** *Poeoptera lugubris*   L 18 cm. Sparrow-sized. Purplish-blue gloss different from that of 6–10; only ♀ has partly chestnut primaries. Habitat: forest.

13   **GREATER BLUE-EARED STARLING** *Lamprotornis chalybaeus*   L 22 cm. From 14 by dark grey (not rufous) immatures. From 15 by blue (not bluish-green) belly, larger wing spots and more slender, brighter appearance. Habitat: woodland, bushveld, suburbs. Voice: very high, mewing, reed warbler-like 'mewúmewe prrrrtju tjup puti-tútjeh'.

14   **LESSER BLUE-EARED STARLING** *Lamprotornis chloropterus*   L 19 cm. Note short ear coverts (see also 13). Imm is rufous below. Gregarious in loose groups, like all glossy starlings. Habitat: as 13. Voice: high, mewing, throaty, rather staccato 'reh piu tu tju pri tju tui'.

15   **CAPE GLOSSY STARLING** *Lamprotornis nitens*   L 22 cm. Black ear-coverts not well-defined. Habitat: as 13. Voice: high, mewing yet fluting 'mehjúwee mehmehjúwee tjupuruhé'.

16   **BLACK-BELLIED GLOSSY STARLING** *Lamprotornis corruscus*   L 21 cm. Note dark appearance and absence of black wing spots. Habitat: forest edges, woodland, riverine belts, suburbs. Voice: very high, melodious, scratchy, rapid 'rutituutweet weetweettjuweet -'.

17   **SHARP-TAILED GLOSSY STARLING** *Lamprotornis acuticaudus*   L 23 cm. From 13, 14, 15 and 16 by red (♂) or orange (♀) eye, pale underwing and pointed tail. Habitat: dry woodland. Voice: high, lashing 'sreepsreep tjisreep mewi-sreep'.

18   **SOUTHERN LONG-TAILED STARLING** *Lamprotornis mevesii*   L 30 cm. From 19 by longer tail, dark-looking appearance, less reflections, especially on wings. Habitat: mopane woodland, riverine belts. Voice: mid-high, mewing 'sreetireet reereeh-'.

19   **BURCHELL'S STARLING** *Lamprotornis australis*   L 30 cm. Note large-winged appearance. Habitat: woodland, thornveld. Voice: low, throaty 'ririruak rirituah ririria ria tjouwtjouw'.

20   **SPLENDID GLOSSY STARLING** *Lamprotornis splendidus*   L 30 cm. Arboreal species with diagnostic, coppery patch on neck sides and black bar across secondaries. Habitat: forest, cultivation, gardens. Voice: low, miauling 'kiauw-kjéw'. (brS)

Plate 74

1 Br N-br
Common Starling

2
African Pied Starling

3 ♂ Br ♂ N-br
Wattled Starling ♀

4
Common Myna

5

6
Pale-winged Starling

7
Red-winged Starling ♀

8 ♀
Slender-billed Starling ♀

9

10 ♀

11 ♀
Violet-backed Starling

12 ♂ ♀ ♀ 12

13
Greater Blue-eared Glossy-Starling Imm

14
Lesser Blue-eared Glossy-Starling Imm

15
Red-shouldered Glossy-Starling

16

17

18

19
Burchell's Glossy-Starling

20
Splendid Glossy-Starling

Plate 75

1   **RED-THROATED PIPIT** *Anthus cervinus*   L 15 cm. Horizontal stance. From all other pipits by heavy streaking above and below. Often one mantle stripe seems paler than others. Habitat: lake and sea shores, moorland, wet grass. Voice: high, thin '*sièèh*'. RS

2   **PLAIN-BACKED PIPIT** *Anthus leucophrys*   L 17 cm. From 11 by fainter breast streaking and buff (not pale brown) outer tail feathers, from 12 by greyer, more two-toned colouring, from 13 by paler underparts and buff- (not yellowish-) edged wing feathers. Habitat: dry, hilly areas with short grass. Voice: high, unstructured '*tjee tjup trée swee tjup*'.

3   **MOUNTAIN PIPIT** *Anthus hoeschi*   L 18 cm. Lower mandible flesh-coloured and outer tail feathers buff. Habitat: montane grasslands. Voice: very high call, '*tuWee tuWee*'. U

4   **JACKSON'S PIPIT** *Anthus novaeseelandiae latistriatus*   L 16 cm. Note: this is the darkest race of 5, with streaking extending to lower flanks and pinkish lower mandible. Habitat: montane grassland, migrating to lower areas. R

5   **RICHARD'S** (or Grassveld) **PIPIT** *Anthus novaeseelandiae*   L 16 cm. See note under 4. Note erect, slender stance, yellow lower mandible, white outer tail feathers. From 6 by more distinct striping, from 7 by diffuse, buff (not white) eye stripe. Habitat: any open area. Voice: very high, liquid, rapid, level '*tjeetjeetjee*'. Song is a level, fast twittering '*tweetweehweehweehweehweeh*'.

6   **WOOD PIPIT** *Anthus similis nyassae*   L 18 cm. Note: this is the miombo race (often considered to be an independent species) of 7, which is a group of races found in more open habitats. Note well-defined, white eye stripe, general warm colouring, grey neck. Habitat: miombo. Voice: high, monotonous, well-spaced '*fee trit trit fee free fui fee*'.

7   **LONG-BILLED PIPIT** *Anthus similis*   L 18 cm. See note under 6. Note large size, long bill, rather plain plumage. More greyish above than 5 with more pronounced malar stripe. Habitat: stony, sparsely covered slopes. Voice: very high, monotonous '*tjuip trée tjiip tjiiip thrée*'.

8   **TREE PIPIT** *Anthus trivialis*   L 14 cm. As n-br 1 but less distinctly streaked on mantle and with unstreaked rump. Habitat: woodland at higher altitudes. Voice: extreme high, nasal '*tsjee*'. US

9   **STRIPED PIPIT** *Anthus lineiventris*   L 17 cm. Well-streaked, especially below. Note connection of cheek with mantle and greenish edges of wing feathers. Habitat: rocky, wooded slopes often near water. Voice: high, loud, rich song in short strophes '*twitwitwéetwit-witwitwéeh*'.

10   **YELLOW-BREASTED PIPIT** *Anthus chloris*   L 17 cm. Br adult from most longclaws, including their immatures (Plate 76), by absence of distinct breast band. From imm 76.10 by horizontal stance and isolated malar stripe. N-br from other pipits by buffy breast and more scalloped than streaked upperparts. Habitat: montane grasslands. Voice: high, liquid '*tiew tiew fui tiew*'. U

11   **LONG-LEGGED PIPIT** *Anthus pallidiventris*   L 17 cm. Note white underparts, pale brown outer tail feathers, yellow-based lower mandible. From 2 and 13 by different range, from 12 by darker upperparts and paler underparts. Habitat: open places in forest and woodland. Voice: extreme high '*pweet pweet pirriweet piuu-pweet pirreweet*'. R

12   **BUFFY PIPIT** *Anthus vaalensis*   L 18 cm. Note very erect stance, unstreaked upperparts and faint streaking on breast. Habitat: dry, bare or sparsely grassed areas. Voice: very high, rapid '*tríuh*' as part of an unstructured, well-spaced sequence.

Note: from the Kimberley area (RSA) within the range of 12, a new, unstreaked pipit has recently been described: **LONG-TAILED PIPIT**, *Anthus longicaudatus*. Main features are: semi-erect stance, short bill, long tail with pale margins, plain, dark upperparts. Wags its tail. (Not illustrated). UW

13   **AFRICAN ROCK PIPIT** *Anthus crenatus*   L 17 cm. Note very erect stance, dark underparts, yellowish wing edges (visible at close range). Habitat: steep, rocky slopes. Voice: high, fluted '*feeeEEpiurrrr*' (second part descending).

14   **SHORT-TAILED PIPIT** *Anthus brachyurus*   L 12 cm. Skulks in grass, reluctant to be flushed. Note thin, short tail and indistinct eyebrow; outer tail feathers greyish brown. Habitat: open woodland, grassy hillsides. Voice: call sounds like high, partly grating '*fuWeeh fuWeeh*'. U

15   **BUSH**(-veld) **PIPIT** *Anthus caffer*   L 13 cm. From 14 by less dark upperparts, white outer tail feathers, absence of malar stripe and streaking below, which is restricted to breast. Habitat: open wood- and bushland. Voice: high, rather nasal '*mèètjeh mèètjéh mèètjeh mèètjeh-*'.

16   **RED-BILLED OXPECKER** *Buphagus erythrorhynchus*   L 21 cm. Habitat: game reserves. U

▶

Plate 75

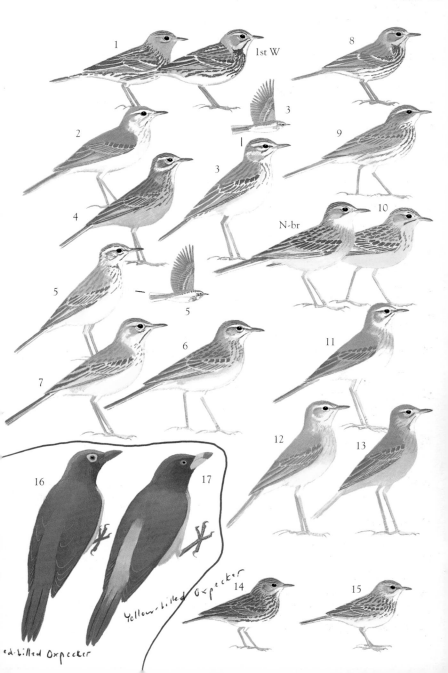

1

1st W

8

3

2

1

9

3

4

N-br

10

5

5

6

11

7

12

13

16

17

Yellow-billed Oxpecker

14

ed-billed Oxpecker

15

Plate 75 (continued)

17   **YELLOW-BILLED OXPECKER** *Buphagus africanus*   L 22 cm. Habitat: game reserves and other places with game or cattle.

Plate 76

1   **GOLDEN PIPIT** *Tmetothylacus tenellus*   L 15 cm. Feeds on the ground, but perches on bushes. Habitat: dry bushveld, scrubland. Voice: rather hoarse, warbling, hurried '*tritritréedideruh*'. RS

2   **YELLOW WAGTAIL** *Motacilla flava*   L 17 cm. Shows greenish rump in flight. Undertail coverts yellow, but this feature is not always well-developed especially not in 1stW ♀♀. Often near grazing cattle. Visiting races: *thunbergii* (a), *feldegg* (b), nominate (c), *leucocephala* (d), *flavissima* (e, most common), *lutea* (f), *beema* (g). Habitat: short grass. Voice: soft, very high, sharp '*sree-sree*'. S

3   **CAPE WAGTAIL** *Motacilla capensis*   L 19 cm. Nominate (a) and almost plain-breasted race *simplissima* (b) shown. From 4 by brownish thumb and wing bars, from imm 6 by less white in wing. Habitat: wet, open woodland, grass- and pasture land, swamp, lake edges. Voice: '*sweep tèdèdjèh*' ('*sweep*' very high, '*tèdèdjèh*' rattling and low).

4   **GREY WAGTAIL** *Motacilla cinerea*   L 18 cm. Only wagtail with yellow rump. White wing bar only visible in flight. Conspicuously long-tailed. Habitat: wooded, rocky mountain streams. Voice: very high '*twitwit weet*' ('*weet*' just within ear reach). US

5   **MOUNTAIN** (or Long-tailed) **WAGTAIL** *Motacilla clara*   L 19 cm. Without any yellow; delicately marked with black and pure grey above. Habitat: mountain streams. Voice: extreme high, descending '*sreeeegh*' or '*tréederúp*'.

6   **AFRICAN PIED WAGTAIL** *Motacilla aguimp*   L 20 cm. Habitat: edges of rivers, lakes, lagoons, golf courses, lawns. Voice: very high, liquid, very short strophes, like lashed-up '*tweeét*' or sharp, rapid '*kwikwik-tréet*'.

7   **WHITE WAGTAIL** *Motacilla alba*   L 19 cm. From other wagtails by white (br) or pale (n-br) forehead and face sides. Habitat: river banks, lake shores, large lawns, sewage ponds. Voice: extreme high, compressed '*teeWeet teeWeet*'. R

8   **ROSY-BREASTED** (or Pink-throated) **LONGCLAW** *Macronyx ameliae*   L 19 cm. The ♂ from 11 by solid, black necklace, ♀ by rosy (not buffy) underparts. Tends to skulk. Habitat: rough grass near lakes, dams, inundations, marshes. Voice: high '*weetjèh-weetjèh–*'. U

9   **CAPE** (or Orange-breasted) **LONGCLAW** *Macronyx capensis*   L 19 cm. From 10 by less-marked upperparts and deeper-coloured underparts. Habitat: short grassland. Voice: high, sharp, fluted '*piuuuw piuu-piuu-piuu weetuw-weetuw-weetuw*'.

10   **YELLOW-THROATED LONGCLAW** *Macronyx croceus*   L 20 cm. From 12 by all-white outer tail feathers. Habitat: moist, sparsely wooded grassland. Voice: very high '*mièèèèh miǫweeh*' combined with low '*chachachacha*'.

11   **GRIMWOOD'S LONGCLAW** *Macronyx grimwoodi*   L 20 cm. From 8 by larger, black centres of upperpart and wing feathers and by narrow, black streaks instead of a solid, black necklace. Habitat: open, grassy hills.

12   **FUELLEBORN'S LONGCLAW** *Macronyx fuelleborni*   L 19 cm. From 10 by partly (not all-) white outer tail feathers, absence of streaks below necklace and off-yellow underparts. Habitat: short grassland, marshes. Voice: mid-high, loud, fluted notes '*fiu feew feeuw weejeh wút fiu –*'.

Note: for the following four species (13–16) see the note under 51.14.

13   **CHESTNUT-BACKED SPARROW** (or Finch) **LARK** *Eremopterix leucotis*   L 12 cm. Note chestnut upperparts of ♂ and buff-and-chestnut wing coverts of ♀. Habitat: open, sandy or stony grasslands with some bush. Voice: (in flight) unstructured flow of very fast, compressed, partly muttered, partly clear strophes, '*wwwuchi TWWUee – –*'.

14   **GREY-BACKED SPARROW** (or Finch) **LARK** *Eremopterix verticalis*   L 13 cm. The ♀ from ♀♀ 13, 15 and 16 by pale, grey-brown, virtually unmarked mantle. Habitat: as 13. Voice: (in flight) very high, sharp, pleasant variations of '*weeweewuwwee*'.

15   **FISCHER'S SPARROW LARK** *Eremopterix leucopareia*   L 12 cm. Note rusty-tawny, black-bordered crown of ♂; ♀ from ♀ 14 by spotted mantle, from 16 by stripe over belly (difficult to see). Habitat: dry areas with some short grass.

▶

Plate 76

Plate 76 (continued)

16 BLACK-EARED SPARROW (or Finch) **LARK** *Eremopterix australis* L 13 cm. The ♀ from other ♀♀ sparrow larks by absence of black line and patch on belly. Habitat: sand and stone plains with some shrub. Voice: (in flight) high '*trutru tree tree trutru*' ('*trutru*' mellow, '*tree*' higher and sharper). U

Plate 77

1 GREY-HEADED SPARROW *Passer griseus ugandae* L 15 cm. From 2 and 3 by contrasting, white chin, yellowish, grey underparts, rusty, brown back, rather dark head. Habitat: bushed and wooded areas including cultivation and suburbs. Note: 1, as well as 2, 3, 4 and 5, has a pale-brown upper mandible and a yellowish lower mandible outside breeding season.

2 SOUTHERN GREY-HEADED SPARROW *Passer diffusus* L 16 cm. Underparts off-white, head mid-grey, mantle paler and more buff than wings. See Note under 1. Habitat: as 1.

3 SWAHILI SPARROW *Passer suahelicus* L 16 cm. Head, mantle and underparts concolorous grey. See Note under 1. Habitat: as 1.

4 RUFOUS (or Great) SPARROW *Passer motitensis* L 15 cm. The ♂ and ♀ more brightly coloured than 5. Note striking rufous rump in flight. Bib reduced in n-br plumage (not shown). See Note under 1. Habitat: dry areas away from settlement.

5 HOUSE SPARROW *Passer domesticus indicus* L 15 cm. See Note under 1. Habitat: confined to human settlement. (Introduced from Asia).

6 CAPE SPARROW *Passer melanurus* L 15 cm. The ♀ from 1, 2 and 3 by white eyebrow. Habitat: rural areas, villages, towns.

7 CHAFFINCH *Fringilla coelebs* L 16 cm. Note conspicuous wing bars. Habitat: suburbs, plantations. (Introduced). Voice: pleasant, short, melodious chatter, gradually lowered between start and finish, '*tsitsiweewirrewirrewée-wir*'. R

8 YELLOW-THROATED PETRONIA *Petronia superciliaris* L 15 cm. Long, conspicuous, white eyebrow diagnostic. Yellow throat patch normally concealed. Habitat: woodland, thornveld, riverine belts. Voice: high, fast '*tsjeetsjeetsjee*'.

9 WHITE-BROWED SPARROW WEAVER *Plocepasser mahali* L 17 cm. Striking, white rump in flight. Builds untidy, communal nests in thorn trees. Feeds on the ground. Habitat: thornveld. Voice: mid-high, enjoyable, nasal chattering, '*tjiautjitjauwtjauwitititi*'.

10 CHESTNUT-MANTLED SPARROW WEAVER *Plocepasser rufoscapulatus* L 18 cm. Note whitish crown. Habits as 9. Habitat: miombo.

11 RED-BILLED BUFFALO WEAVER *Bubalornis niger* L 23 cm. Breeds in large, untidy group nests, several in a large tree. Habitat: dry, wooded areas. Voice: mid-high, fast chatter, slightly falling-off, '*chachacha–*'.

12 THICK-BILLED WEAVER *Amblyospiza albifrons* L 18 cm. Pairs or loose colonies in tall reeds and elephant grass. Habitat: marshes, swamps, wet places in forest and woodland.

13 SOCIABLE WEAVER *Philetarius socius* L 14 cm. Breeds in large, communal nests (50 pairs or more) which are used for many years. (See 22.9). Habitat: woodland, thornveld. Voice: high, excited, collective chattering near nest.

14 ORIOLE FINCH *Linurgus olivaceus* L 13 cm. From all other small, yellow birds by dark-orange bill. Habitat: undergrowth at montane forest edges. U

15 CABANIS'S BUNTING *Emberiza cabanisi* L 16 cm. From 19 by absence of white stripe directly under eye and more grey than rufous upperparts. Habitat: miombo, other wood- and bushland. Voice: extreme high, tit-like, fast '*fijúutfijuutfijuutfijuutuderJeettuderJeet-*'. U

16 CINNAMON-BREASTED ROCK BUNTING *Emberiza tahapisi* L 15 cm. Conspicuous, orange wing panel in flight. Habitat: dry, wooded and bushed areas with rocky slopes. Often at road sides. Voice: very high, short '*tuderfiuWéet*' ('*-fiu-*' as a sort of much higher overtone).

17 LARK-LIKE BUNTING *Emberiza impetuani* L 13 cm. From most larks by longer tail, smaller bill and more horizontal stance. Note typical bunting form of bill with lower mandible seemingly larger than upper mandible. Habitat: dry, rocky areas with little scrub cover. Voice: mid-high, chaffinch-like '*ttjuderWéeetWéet*'.

▶

Plate 77

Plate 77 (continued)

18   **CAPE BUNTING** *Emberiza capensis*   L 15 cm. Note extensively rusty-red wings. Habitat: dry, rocky, mountainous and hilly areas, coastal scrub, miombo, suburbs. Voice: mid-high, hesitating '*wit wit wit weeh wit*' or '*weederwit-weederwit*'.

19   **GOLDEN-BREASTED BUNTING** *Emberiza flaviventris*   L 15 cm. White streak below eye diagnostic. Habitat: woodland, thornveld, plantations, gardens. Voice: very high, siffled '*tuéehtuéehtuéeh*'.

Plate 78

Note: The alternative South African name for species 1–9 is 'widow'.

1   **LONG-TAILED WHYDAH** *Euplectes progne*   L 57 cm (♂), 18 cm (♀). Note large size and plain colouring of ♀; n-br ♂ retains colourful wing-colouring. Habitat: damp, open grassland.

2   **MOUNTAIN MARSH WHYDAH** *Euplectes psammocromius*   L 32 cm (♂), 15 cm (♀). Note yellow traces in ♀ wing shoulder; n-br ♂ as ♀ but with wing of br plumage. Habitat: montane grassland. R

3   **RED-COLLARED WHYDAH** *Euplectes ardens*   L 27 cm (♂), 12 cm (♀). The ♀ is nondescript, n-br ♂ with blackish wings and more or less elongated tail. Habitat: marshy open grassland with some shrub.

4   **YELLOW-MANTLED WHYDAH** *Euplectes macrourus*   L 20 cm (♂), 13 cm (♀). Note yellow shoulders of ♀ and n-br ♂. Habitat: moist, open grassland at mid-high altitudes.

5   **WHITE-WINGED WHYDAH** *Euplectes albonotatus*   L 16 cm (♂), 12 cm (♀). The ♀ has some rufous in wing bend and more or less shows a white wing flash in flight. Habitat: bushed areas with tall grass.

6   **MARSH WHYDAH** *Euplectes hartlaubi*   L 20 cm (♂), 15 cm (♀). The ♂ is longer-tailed than 7; ♀ nondescript. Habitat: marshes, swamp edges, moist grassland.

7   **RED-SHOULDERED WHYDAH** *Euplectes axillaris*   L 17 cm (♂), 13 cm (♀). The ♀ shows some rufous on wing shoulder. Habitat: swamp edges, long-grassed places, sugar cane.

8   **YELLOW-CROWNED** (or Golden) **BISHOP** *Euplectes afer*   L 12 cm. Nondescript ♀ is only faintly striped below; n-br ♂ more heavily streaked above. Habitat: swamps, moist grassland.

9   **YELLOW**(-rumped) **BISHOP** *Euplectes capensis*   L 14 cm (♂), 12 cm (♀). Note rather heavy streaking below and (in flight) yellowish rump of ♀. Habitat: montane, tall grassland with some bush, forest edges.

10   **BLACK BISHOP** *Euplectes gierowii*   L 12 cm. The ♀ shows dark-mottled moustachial area and buff-coloured breast. N-br ♂ is rather dark with blackish wing. Habitat: bushed, tall grassland, sugar cane. U

11   **GOLDEN-BACKED BISHOP** *Euplectes aureus*   L 14 cm. From 9 by more extensive yellow upperparts. Habitat: reed beds, tall grass. U

12   **ZANZIBAR RED BISHOP** *Euplectes nigroventris*   L 10 cm. Note black breast of br ♂. The ♀ from ♀♀ 13 and 14 by darker ear coverts. Habitat: open and bushed grassland.

13   **RED BISHOP** *Euplectes orix*   L 12 cm. The ♂ from 14 by black forehead and red undertail coverts, ♀ by rich, tawny breast band. Habitat: reed beds, elephant grass, sugar cane.

14   **BLACK-WINGED RED** (or Fire-crowned) **BISHOP** *Euplectes hordeaceus*   L 14 cm. The ♀ from ♀ 13 by rich, tawny face sides and breast band. N-br ♂ has much darker wing than ♂ 13. Habitat: as 13. brS

15   **RED-BILLED QUELEA** *Quelea quelea*   L 12 cm. Colour forms **a** and **b** shown; form **b** also exists with pale tawny colour around black mask. Red bill diagnostic in both sexes and all colour forms. Very gregarious (flocks of well over 10,000 may occur). Habitat: dry, bushed areas. brS

16   **CARDINAL QUELEA** *Quelea cardinalis*   L 10 cm. The ♂ from 17 by gradual transition of red from head to rest of body, ♀ by yellowish chin. Gregarious (but less so than 15). Habitat: grass- and farmland. brS

▶

Plate 78

♂ N-br

1

♀

5 ♂ N-br

5

♀

2

6 ♂ N-br

♀

6

♀

3

3 ♂ N-br

7

♀

♀

8 ♂ N-br

8

♀

4

9 ♂ N-br

9

♀

♂ N-br

10 ♂ N-br

10

♀

18

a

15

b

♀

11

♀

19

♀

16

13 ♂ N-br

12

♀

♀

13

♀

20

♀

17

♀

14

14 ♂ N-br

Plate 78 (continued)

17 **RED-HEADED QUELEA** *Quelea erythrops*   L 11 cm. Note sharp demarcation of ♂ red mask, black spots on chin and throat and, in ♀, dark mark near base of bill, yellow eyebrow and white (not yellow) chin. Small flocks. Habitat: marsh shrubbery and moist grassland. brS

18 **BLUE-BILLED MALIMBE** *Malimbus nitens*   L 16 cm. Note pale bill. Habitat: moist forest, often along streams. R

19 **RED-HEADED MALIMBE** *Malimbus rubricollis*   L 17 cm. Unmistakable. In pairs. Habitat: forest, woodland, dense bushveld.

20 **CRESTED MALIMBE** *Malimbus malimbicus*   L 16 cm. Unmistakable. Habitat: forest and thickets.

Plate 79

1 **LARGE GOLDEN WEAVER** *Ploceus xanthops*   L 16 cm. Note large size, creamy eye, uniform colouring. Not colonial. Habitat: reeds, moist, bushed areas. Sometimes in suburbs.

2 **EASTERN GOLDEN** (or Yellow) **WEAVER** *Ploceus subaureus*   L 13 cm. The ♂ is uniform golden yellow, ♀ greenish above with faint streaks, both with orange eyes. N-br ♂ as ♀ but with light, rufous wash on chin. Colonial. Habitat: reed beds, thornveld, open woodland, riverine belts.

3 **SPECTACLED WEAVER** *Ploceus ocularis*   L 14 cm. The ♀ from ♂ 10 by lack of black in wing. Skulking. Not colonial. Habitat: dense vegetation at forest edge, riverine belts, suburbs. Voice: very high, lowered, fast, wader-like '*fweefweefweefweefwee*'.

4 **SOUTHERN BROWN-THROATED WEAVER** *Ploceus xanthopterus*   L 14 cm. The ♂ from ♂ 9 by brown eye and plain mantle, ♀ from all other ♀♀ by lack of pale eyebrow. N-br ♂ as ♀. Colonial. Habitat: reed beds, riverine belts, swamp edges. U

5 **SLENDER-BILLED WEAVER** *Ploceus pelzelni*   L 12 cm. Note small size. The ♀ has uniform yellow face sides and black bill. Small colonies. Habitat: marshes, swamps, damp woodland.

6 **AFRICAN** (or Southern) **MASKED WEAVER** *Ploceus velatus*   L 12 cm. From 7 and 8 by narrow black on forehead, red eye, faintly streaked mantle; ♀ from other ♀♀ by yellowish throat, buffish breast, whitish underparts. N-br ♂ as ♀. Small to large colonies. Habitat: more or less wooded areas, often away from water, suburbs.

7 **LESSER MASKED WEAVER** *Ploceus intermedius*   L 12 cm. Note yellow eye; this feature shared with ♀, which is more yellow than other ♀♀ weavers. N-br ♂ as ♀. Pairs, large colonies, often together with 16. Habitat: nests in trees over water or in reed beds. Open thornveld, woodland.

8 **LAKE LUFIRA WEAVER** *Ploceus reichardi*   L 14 cm. The ♂ from 6 by more extensive, rufous colouring and brown eye, ♀ by fainter streaking above. Habitat: swampy areas. R

9 **CAPE WEAVER** *Ploceus capensis*   L 15 cm. Note large size, pale eye and strong, rufous wash on head. N-br ♂ as ♀ but with pale eye. The ♀ from other ♀♀ weavers by size and heavy bill. Small colonies of up to 10 pairs. Habitat: trees and reed beds in woodland, swamps.

10 **ORANGE WEAVER** *Ploceus aurantius*   L 14 cm. Note golden-yellow colouring, fine bill, black lore of ♂. The ♀ has pale eye and slender bill. Colonial. Habitat: forest edges, swamps, reed beds. R

11 **OLIVE-HEADED WEAVER** *Ploceus olivaceiceps*   L 14 cm. The ♂ from 12 by red, not yellow, eye and different range. N-br ♂ as ♀. Not colonial. Habitat: miombo. U

12 **BOCAGE'S WEAVER** *Ploceus temporalis*   L 13 cm. Note pale eye, olive-green cheeks and narrow, rufous bib. N-br ♂ as ♀. Small colonies. Habitat: riverine belts, reed beds, tall grass; mid-high altitudes.

13 **YELLOW-BACKED WEAVER** *Ploceus melanocephalus*   L 14 cm. Note yellow neck and plain mantle. N-br ♂ as ♀. Colonial. Habitat: riverine belts, lake edges, swamps. R

14 **BERTRAM'S WEAVER** *Ploceus bertrandi*   L 15 cm. Note brown crown of ♂ and plain mantles of ♂ and ♀. Habitat: montane areas. Forest edges, woodland, cultivation, often along streams.

15 **BAGLAFECHT WEAVER** *Ploceus baglafecht*   L 14 cm. Only black-cheeked weaver with yellow chin and throat. Habitat: montane forest edges.

16 **VILLAGE** (or Spotted-backed) **WEAVER** *Ploceus cucullatus*   L 15 cm. Not all races depicted; races *spilonotus* (**a**) and *nigriceps* (**b**) shown. Note large size and lack of rufous colouring. Imm (not shown) and some br ♂♂ with brown eye: n-br ♂ as ♀ with red eye. Colonial. Habitat: woodland, thornveld, riverine belts, farmland, suburbs.   ▶

Plate 79

Plate 79 (continued)

17 **BLACK-CHINNED WEAVER** *Ploceus nigrimentum*   L 15 cm. From most other ♂♂ weavers (except 19 and 20) by black mantle. Habitat: woodland. U

18 **BROWN-CAPPED WEAVER** *Ploceus insignis*   L 13 cm. Note yellow, black-edged mantle of ♂ and ♀. Not colonial. Habitat: forest at higher altitudes. R

19 **BLACK-NECKED WEAVER** *Ploceus nigricollis*   L 14 cm. Note extensively black upperparts of ♂ and ♀ and black, narrow bib of ♂. Not colonial. Habitat: forest, moist woodland, riverine belts.

20 **DARK-BACKED** (or Forest) **WEAVER** *Ploceus bicolor*   L 13 cm. Nominate (a) and race *stictifrons* (b) shown. Both races have finely speckled chins. Not colonial. Habitat: forest, moist woodland. Voice: lashing '*weep*' followed by delightful, toy trumpet-like '*pwée pwee pu̲-weep-*'.

Plate 80

1 **RED-HEADED WEAVER** *Anaplectes rubriceps*   L 14 cm. N-br ♂ as ♀. In breeding season small groups of one ♂ with several ♀♀. Nomadic outside breeding season. Habitat: woodland, thornveld.

2 **BAR-WINGED WEAVER** *Ploceus angolensis*   L 12 cm. Not colonial. Often in mixed bird parties. Habitat: woodland. U

3 **CHESTNUT WEAVER** *Ploceus rubiginosus*   L 14 cm. Note brownish (not greenish as most other ♀♀ weavers) plumage of ♀. Colonial breeder. Habitat: dry woodland, bushland. brS

4 **COMPACT WEAVER** *Ploceus superciliosus*   L 12 cm. Note solid-brown upperparts. Pairs or small groups. Habitat: forest, swamps, woodland, bushveld, cultivation.

5 **VIEILLOT'S BLACK WEAVER** *Ploceus nigerrimus*   L 14 cm. Unmistakable. Habitat: forest edges, woodland.

6 **YELLOW-MANTLED WEAVER** *Ploceus tricolor*   L 14 cm. Unmistakable. Habitat: forest canopy. U

7 **CUT-THROAT FINCH** *Amadina fasciata*   L 12 cm. Note zig-zag barring of underparts (♂ and ♀). Often forages on the ground. Pairs or flocks. Habitat: dry woodland, bushveld, cultivation, near waterholes.

8 **RED-HEADED FINCH** *Amadina erythrocephala*   L 14 cm. The ♀ from ♀ 7 by plain upperparts, regular, rather scalloped barring of underparts, brownish (not grey) bill. Forages on the ground. Small flocks. Habitat: as 7.

9 **BROWN TWINSPOT** *Clytospiza monteiri*   L 13 cm. Note red (♂) or white (♀) chin. Habitat: in and under tall grass and shrubbery in forest glades, moist bushland. U

10 **PINK-THROATED TWINSPOT** *Hypargos margaritatus*   L 13 cm. From 11 by dull, pink (not crimson) face and rump and brown (not grey) crown, ♀ by grey (not pink) breast. Habitat: tall-grassed areas, forest edges, woodland, bushveld.

11 **RED-THROATED** (or Peter's) **TWINSPOT** *Hypargos niveoguttatus*   L 13 cm. As 10, which see. Habitat: as 10. Voice: extreme high, descending to mid-high, '*fififififitjehtjgh-sreeeh*' (last part extreme high again).

12 **GREEN TWINSPOT** *Mandingoa nitidula*   L 10 cm. Note tiny size. Often on the ground. Habitat: undergrowth of forest edges, moist thickets. Voice: extreme high, cicada-like trill, '*trrrrr*'.

13 **DUSKY TWINSPOT** *Euschistospiza cinereovinacea*   L 12 cm. Habitat: tall-grassed glades of montane forests.

14 **SCALY-FEATHERED FINCH** *Sporopipes squamifrons*   L 13 cm. Tiny, delicately marked. Small groups. (Compare also with 77.13). Habitat: dry thornveld, near settlement.

15 **PARASITIC WEAVER** (or Cuckoo Finch) *Anomalospiza imberbis*   L 12 cm. From other weavers and canaries by short, conical bill and combination of clean, yellow head and green, streaked upperparts. N-br ♂ less bright. Br ♀ (not shown) with streaked breast sides and flanks. Pairs or small flocks. Brood parasite, using cisticolas as host. Habitat: moist, open and bushed, natural and cultivated areas (or in all habitats where cisticolas live). Voice: high, soft chattering without the siffling inhaling and nasal quality of true weavers. UbrS(W)

▶

Plate 80

Plate 80 (continued)

16 RED-FACED CRIMSONWING *Cryptospiza reichenovii*   L 12 cm. Crimson scapulars diagnostic. Habitat: undergrowth of montane forest, often near streams. Voice: extreme high, siffled 'srrreeeeh'. U

17 LESSER (or Nyassa) SEEDCRACKER *Pyrenestes minor*   L 13 cm. From ♀ 18 by size and relatively smaller bill. Habitat: dense undergrowth at forest edges, often near water. U

18 BLACK-BELLIED SEEDCRACKER *Pyrenestes ostrinus*   L 15 cm. The ♂ from ♂ 19 by uniform dark grey bill and more red in tail. Habitat: tall grass and shrubbery at forest edge, gardens.

19 RED-HEADED BLUEBILL *Spermophaga ruficapilla*   L 15 cm. Note bright, blue-and-red bill and all-black tail. Habitat: tall grass and shrubbery, normally away from settlement. U

Plate 81

1 BRONZE MANNIKIN *Lonchura cucullata*   L 9 cm. Imm from imm 2 by buff-brown breast (and upperparts) and dark-grey bill. Habitat: long grass in woodland, bushveld, cultivation, marshes, suburbs.

2 RED-BACKED MANNIKIN *Lonchura bicolor*   L 9 cm. Note dark upperparts of imm with pale-grey bill. Habitat: forest edges, woodland, bushveld, grassland, cultivation, suburbs.

3 MAGPIE (or Pied) MANNIKIN *Lonchura fringilloides*   L 11 cm. Imm from imm 2 by larger size and darker bill. Habitat: forest edges, moist, shrubby woodland, gardens. U

4 VIOLET-EARED WAXBILL *Uraeginthus granatinus*   L 14 cm. Unmistakable. Habitat: woodland, thornveld. Voice: high, slightly lark-like phrases mixed with soft, hoarse rattles.

5 BLUE WAXBILL *Uraeginthus angolensis*   L 12 cm. The ♂ from ♀ (and from ♀ 6) by deep blue colouring which extends to lower flanks. The ♀ not safely separable from ♀ 6 but ♂ and ♀ of both species are normally always seen in pairs, making confusion unlikely. Habitat: thickets in woodland, bushveld.

6 RED-CHEEKED CORDON-BLEU *Uraeginthus bengalus*   L 13 cm. See 5. Habitat: woodland, bushveld, often near settlement.

7 QUAIL FINCH *Ortygospiza atricollis*   L 10 cm. Skulking; does not perch, but lives exclusively on the ground. Habitat: wet grassland, occasionally in drier areas. Voice: high 'ti-tjeeterik-tjeeterik–' when flushed.

8 BLACK-CHINNED QUAIL FINCH *Ortygospiza gabonensis*   L 9 cm. See 7. Habitat: moist grassland. Voice: very high, soft 'tiktiktik tjek tiktik-' when flushed.

9 LOCUST FINCH *Ortygospiza locustella*   L 9 cm. See 7. Habitat: wet grassland, swamps, open woodland. U

10 MELBA FINCH *Pytilia melba*   L 12 cm. From 11 by all-green wings and barred underparts. Forages near or on the ground. Habitat: dry woodland, thornveld, thickets, grassland, cultivation. Voice: quiet, unstructured sequence of well-separated notes, 'fjuw prri sreeh juut-tjuw-tjih'. Call is lowered 'fieeuw'.

11 ORANGE-WINGED (or Golden-backed) PYTILIA *Pytilia afra*   L 11 cm. Note deep orange in wings. Habitat: forest, miombo and other woodland, thornbush. Voice: mid-high 'trip trip trip' or extreme high 'tseep tseep tseep -'. U

12 BLUE-BILLED FIREFINCH *Lagonosticta rubricata*   L 11 cm. Shown are nominate (**a**, South African race which is not [!] blue-billed) and race *haematocephala* (**b**, with brown [not grey] crown). Habitat: forest edges, woodland, bushveld, thornbush. Voice: extreme high (or very high), shrill, warbling or silvery-rattling trills.

13 PALE-BILLED FIREFINCH *Lagonosticta landanae*   L 11 cm. The ♂ from 12 by red forehead and crown, ♂ and ♀ from 12 and 14 by partly pink upper mandible, from 15 and 16 by black lower belly and tail. Habitat: dry, grassy areas, thornveld.

14 JAMESON'S FIREFINCH *Lagonosticta rhodopareia*   L 11 cm. From 12b by fewer (and smaller) white spots, paler, pink-washed upperparts, indistinct eye ring. Habitat: tall grass and shrubbery in bushveld and woodland. Voice: mid-high, warbled, loud (or soft), rapid (or very fast) trills.

▶

Plate 81

Plate 81 (continued)

15   RED-BILLED FIREFINCH *Lagonosticta senegala*   L 10 cm. The ♂ from other firefinches by pink legs, pale, brown flanks and lower belly and, in ♀, the pink spot in front of eye. Habitat: open thornveld, cultivation, suburbs. May enter houses. Voice: unstructured song of slightly hoarse notes and trills around basic '*-tit-wéet-*'.

16   BROWN FIREFINCH *Lagonosticta nitidula*   L 10 cm. From all other firefinches by brown (not pink) rump. Habitat: thick vegetation near water.

17   GREY-CROWNED BLACKFINCH *Nigrita canicapilla*   L 13 cm. The ♂ from 18 by white wing spots and black forehead. Habitat: montane forest edges and clearings.

18   PALE-FRONTED BLACKFINCH *Nigrita luteifrons*   L 10 cm. The ♂ from ♀ by yellowish crown, red eye, black underparts. Habitat: open forest. U

19   CHESTNUT-BREASTED BLACKFINCH *Nigrita bicolor*   L 10 cm. Very dark. Skulking. Note very fine, warbler-like bill of this and next species. Habitat: forest edges and clearings.

20   WHITE-BREASTED BLACKFINCH *Nigrita fusconota*   L 10 cm. *Sylvia* warbler-like but much smaller. Habitat: forest edges and clearings, riverine belts.

Plate 82 (continued)

18 CINDERELLA WAXBILL *Estrilda thomensis* L 11 cm. Note pink bill base and partly red (not all-black) tail feathers. Habitat: dry miombo, bushveld, thorn scrub, riverine belts.

19 SWEE WAXBILL *Estrilda melanotis* L 9 cm. Note that ♀ is placed in front of ♂ for easy comparison with 20 and 21. The ♀ (with whitish chin) from ♂ and ♀ 20 by pale, buff (not yellow) underparts, from 21 by black upper mandible and black legs. Habitat: mainly in tall grass at edges of montane forest, wooded streams.

20 EAST AFRICAN SWEE WAXBILL *Estrilda quartinia* L 9 cm. Note that there is only marginal overlapping with range of similar (♀) 19 and no overlappping with 21. Habitat: as 19.

21 FAWN-BREASTED WAXBILL *Estrilda paludicola* L 12 cm. Longer-tailed than 19 and 20 with red upper and lower mandible. Habitat: wet grassland, swamps, forest edges, cultivation.

Plate 82

Note: the long-tailed (1–4) widows and black (5–9) indigobirds are brood parasites. Each species depends on a specific host whose calls and song it introduces in its own repertoire, a feature which could be helpful for identifying the very similar looking indigobirds.

1 **PIN-TAILED WIDOW** *Vidua macroura* L 30 cm (♂), 12 cm (♀). The ♀ as ♀♀ 3 and 4 but smaller. N-br ♂ as ♀. Parasitises 13. Habitat: forest edges, open wood- and scrubland, suburbs.

2 **SHAFT-TAILED WIDOW** *Vidua regia* L 32 cm (♂), 12 cm (♀). The ♀ from ♀♀ 5–9 by redder bill and more buff, overall colouring. N-br ♂ as ♀. Parasitises 81.4. Habitat: dry areas with thornbush and more or less grass cover.

3 **LONG-TAILED PARADISE WIDOW** *Vidua paradisaea* L 36 cm (♂), 15 cm (♀). The ♂ from 4 by longer, tapered tail, ♀ by blacker markings on head and upperparts. N-br ♂ as ♀ but often with some scattered, black feathers on head or mantle. Parasitises 81.10. Habitat: bushland, thornveld.

4 **BROAD-TAILED PARADISE WIDOW** *Vidua obtusa* L 30 cm (♂), 15 cm (♀). See 3. N-br ♂ as ♀. Parasitises 81.11. Habitat: as 3.

Note: the ♀♀ of 5–9 are inseparable in the field, except for white-billed ♀ 9. N-br ♂♂ as ♀♀.

5 **DUSKY** (or Black) **INDIGOBIRD** *Vidua funerea* L 11 cm. The ♂ not separable from 7a or (uncommon!) 9 other than by call. Parasitises 81.12. Habitat: forest edges, thornveld, riverine belts, suburbs.

6 **PURPLE INDIGOBIRD** *Vidua purpurascens* L 12 cm. Probably only indigobird in the region with white bill and legs (but see 8). Parasitises 81.14. Habitat: thornveld.

7 **VILLAGE** (or Steel-blue) **INDIGOBIRD** *Vidua chalybeata* L 11 cm. Southern, white-billed (**a**) form inseparable from 5; northern (**b**) form is only indigobird with pink bill. Parasitises 81.15. Habitat: woodland, thornveld, cultivation.

8 **BAR-BREASTED** (or Violet) **INDIGOBIRD** *Vidua wilsoni incognita* L 12 cm. As this species parasitises the Bar-breasted Firefinch, *Lagonosticta rufopicta*, which does not occur in the region, the occurrence of this indigobird is doubtful in Southern Africa. However, records of an indigobird imitating the Bar-breasted Firefinch continue to come from Zambia and Zimbabwe. ?

9 **PETER'S TWINSPOT INDIGOBIRD** *Vidua codringtoni* L 12 cm. Only ♂ indigobird with no white in wing. The ♀ from other ♀♀ by white bill. Parasitises 80.11. Habitat: open woodland, thornveld. U

10 **BLACK-FACED** (or -cheeked) **WAXBILL** *Estrilda erythronotus* L 13 cm. Unmistakable. Feeds on the ground. Habitat: thornveld.

11 **BLACK-HEADED WAXBILL** *Estrilda atricapilla* L 10 cm. Unmistakable. Habitat: montane forest, bamboo. R

12 **CRIMSON-RUMPED WAXBILL** *Estrilda rhodopyga* L 10 cm. Note bi-coloured bill and red rump. Habitat: tall grass and shrubbery in woodland, bushveld. R

13 **COMMON WAXBILL** *Estrilda astrild* L 11 cm. The ♂ from ♀ by more black on underparts. Imm (not shown) has blackish bill, but differs from 12 by absence of red on rump and in wings. Flocks of up to 30. Habitat: tall grass and shrubbery in woodland, bushveld, often near water or settlement. Voice: mid-high, soft, nasal song, '*tjututuweeteesj*'.

14 **ORANGE-CHEEKED WAXBILL** *Estrilda melpoda* L 10 cm. From all red-rumped waxbills by orange face sides. Habitat: forest edges, open woodland, swamps, cultivation, gardens.

15 **FLOWERPECKER WEAVER FINCH** *Parmoptila woodhousei* L 9 cm. Warbler-like in appearance and behaviour. Very secretive. Feeds on ants. Habitat: ground and understorey at forest edge. U

16 **ZEBRA** (or Orange-breasted) **WAXBILL** *Amandava subflava* L 9 cm. Unmistakable. Habitat: wet, tall grassland, reed beds, herbage at forest edge.

17 **BLACK-TAILED GREY WAXBILL** *Estrilda perreini* L 11 cm. From 18 by grey (not pink) bill, black undertail coverts, different range. Habitat: dense undergrowth at forest edge, woodland with thick, tangled grass. U

◄

Plate 82

Plate 83

1   **YELLOW CANARY** *Serinus flaviventris*   L 13 cm. Not all races depicted; yellow-rumped, bright nominate (**a**) and green-rumped race *damarensis* (**b**) shown. From 2 by yellow forehead and whitish edges to tertials. Habitat: from montane bush to coastal scrub. Voice: high, hurried flow of warbled flutes and trills around basic '*-wru-*' sound.

2   **BRIMSTONE** (or Bully) **CANARY** *Serinus sulphuratus*   L 15 cm. Races *shelleyi* (**a**) and nominate (**b**) shown. Note large bill and green rump. Habitat: open woodland, bushveld, forest edges. Voice: very high, short, warbled medleys of up-and-down flutes, trills and rolls.

3   **YELLOW-FRONTED** (or -eyed) **CANARY** *Serinus mozambicus*   L 12 cm. Note sharply demarcated eyebrow and cheek, small, pointed bill, yellow rump. Habitat: open forest, woodland, bushveld, suburbs. Voice: very high, hurried, fluted variations on a short strophe, '*prtpreepirrepieeh-wéeh*'.

4   **FOREST CANARY** *Serinus scotops*   L 13 cm. Note bright yellow eyebrow and chin and heavy streaking on lower underparts. Habitat: canopy of forests and nearby areas. Voice: extreme high, hurried siffling with some hoarse, slightly lower inclusions.

5   **BLACK-FACED CANARY** *Serinus capistratus*   L 12 cm. The ♀ from ♀ 6 by stubbier bill, less streaked underparts and just overlapping range. Habitat: forest edges and clearings, swamps. U

6   **AFRICAN CITRIL** *Serinus citrinelloides*   L 12 cm. Note lack of well-defined eyebrow. Bill is sharp-pointed. Habitat: forest edges, bamboo, woodland, lake sides, cultivation, gardens.

7   **CAPE CANARY** *Serinus canicollis*   L 13 cm. Grey nape diagnostic. Habitat: from montane grassland to coastal scrub, gardens. Voice: very high, very rapid, sustained, fluted warbling with basic '*-fiu-*' sound.

8   **DRAKENSBERG SISKIN** *Serinus symonsi*   L 13 cm. From 9 by more greenish head, streaked mantle and all-black tail and wings. Habitat: montane, grassy areas. Voice: continuous flow of hurried sifflings, flutes and rolls with inclusions of very high '*wut*' and short rattles '*djikdjikdjikdjik*'.

9   **CAPE SISKIN** *Serinus totta*   L 13 cm. Note white tail tip and trailing edge to wing. Range separated from 8. Habitat: montane forest edges, pine plantations. Also at lower altitudes. Voice: high, rather hesitating flow of flutes, trills and chatters with basic '*-tiuh-*' sound. E (South Africa)

10   **LEMON-BREASTED CANARY** *Serinus citrinipectus*   L 11 cm. Light parts in complicated face pattern may be white (as shown) or yellow. Often in flocks with 3. Habitat: dry, wood- and scrubland, grassy areas with palms, cultivation. Voice: high, rather short, hurried strophes with basic '*-sri-*' sound.

11   **STREAKY SEEDEATER** *Serinus striolatus*   L 15 cm. Often shows a greenish panel in closed wing. Habitat: montane forest edges. R

12   **BLACK-THROATED CANARY** *Serinus atrogularis*   L 11 cm. Blackish throat patch very variable, sometimes absent. Note conspicuous, yellow rump in flight. Habitat: woodland, thornveld, farmland. Voice: very high, mumbled, continuous flow of warbles, flutes, trills and rolls.

13   **WHITE-THROATED CANARY** *Serinus albogularis*   L 14 cm. Not all races depicted; green-rumped nominate (**a**) and yellow-rumped, paler race *crocopygius* (**b**, in flight) shown. From 12 by larger bill and white chin, from 14, 15, 16 and 17 by green or yellow rump. Habitat: Karoo scrub, dry grassland, coastal dunes. Voice: very high, fast series of fluted rolls and warbles with returning ' *puwee-*' sound.

14   **THICK-BILLED SEEDEATER** *Serinus burtoni*   L 15 cm. Note grey rump and yellow edges to tail and wing feathers. Habitat: undergrowth of montane forest, bamboo. R

15   **PROTEA CANARY** *Serinus leucopterus*   L 16 cm. Note absence of yellow colouring, indistinct eyebrow, variable, white throat patch. Habitat: montane, protea scrub. Voice: differs from all other canaries by nasal quality (like Bleating Warbler 62.15) and rattling repetitions, '*-tritritweetweetweet-*'. E (South Africa)

16   **STREAKY-HEADED SEEDEATER** *Serinus gularis*   L 15 cm. Adult from 17 by unmarked underparts. Imm (not shown) from 17 by warmer-brown, more heavily streaked plumage and less prominent eyebrow. Habitat: miombo, bushveld, cultivation, gardens. Voice: sequence of high, short, up-and-down rattles, flutes and trills.

17   **STRIPE-BREASTED SEEDEATER** *Serinus reichardi*   L 15 cm. From 16 by different range. Often treated as race of 16. Habitat: as 16.

▶

Plate 83

Plate 83 (continued)

18   **BLACK-EARED SEEDEATER** *Serinus mennelli*   L 13 cm. The ♀ (not shown) from ♂ by dark brown (not black) face sides. Habitat: miombo and other types of woodland. Voice: basically a sustained flow of three short phrases, together sounding as '-*wuhwuh-féeh-tjèh-*'.

19   **BLACK-HEADED CANARY** *Serinus alario*   L 13 cm. Nominate **(a)** and race *leucolaima* **(b)** shown; there is much interbreeding between these races, with resulting intermediate plumages. The ♂♂ show a long **(a)** or short **(b)** inverted 'V' mark on breast. Note rufous in wings of ♀♀. Habitat: dry, montane areas, Karoo scrub, bushveld, cultivation, gardens. Voice: mid-high, fast, mellow warbling.

Plate 84 (continued)

35   PIED FLYCATCHER *Ficedula hypoleuca*   L 13 cm.

36   WHITE-BROWED FOREST FLYCATCHER *Fraseria cinerascens*   L 14 cm.

37   PALE-BREASTED ILLADOPSIS *Illadopsis rufipennis*   L 14 cm.

38   PURPLE-HEADED GLOSSY STARLING *Lamprotornis purpureiceps*   L 20 cm.

39   BROWN SUNBIRD *Anthreptes gabonicus*   L 10 cm.

40   SPLENDID SUNBIRD *Nectarinia coccinigaster*   L 14 cm.

41   JOHANNA'S SUNBIRD *Nectarinia johannae*   L 14 cm.

42   NORTHERN PUFFBACK *Dryoscopus gambensis*   L 20 cm.

43   SABINE'S PUFFBACK *Dryoscopus sabini*   L 15 cm.

44   LOANGA SLENDER-BILLED WEAVER *Ploceus subpersonatus*   L 13 cm.

45   BLUEBILL *Spermophaga haematina*   L 15 cm.

Plate 84

Note: Cabinda is a political part of Angola situated as an exclave at the Atlantic coast between the two Congo states. Due to its forested character it shares with surrounding areas 45 species of bird which do not occur in the rest of Angola or other parts of the region. For the sake of completeness these species are depicted (not to scale!) on Plate 84.

1   **NKULENGU RAIL** *Himantornis haematopus*   L 45 cm.

2   **SENEGAL THICK-KNEE** *Burhinus senegalensis*   L 40 cm.

3   **GREY PRATINCOLE** *Glareola cinerea*   L 19 cm.

4   **BLUE-HEADED WOOD DOVE** *Turtur brehmeri*   L 25 cm.

5   **CHESTNUT-FLANKED SPARROWHAWK** *Accipiter castanilius*   L 30 cm (♂), 35 cm (♀).

6   **LONG-TAILED HAWK** *Urotriorchis macrourus*   L 60 cm.

7   **FOREST FRANCOLIN** *Francolinus lathami* (♂)   L 20 cm.

8   **BLACK GUINEAFOWL** *Agelastes niger*   L 40 cm.

9   **PLUMED GUINEAFOWL** *Guttera plumifera*   L 45 cm.

10   **VERREAUX'S TURACO** *Tauraco macrorhynchus*   L 40 cm.

11   **FRASER'S EAGLE OWL** *Bubo poensis*   L 50 cm.

12   **AKUN EAGLE OWL** *Bubo leucostictus*   L 50 cm.

13   **BOUVIER'S FISHING OWL** *Scotopelia bouvieri*   L 55 cm.

14   **SABINE'S SPINETAIL** *Rhaphidura sabini*   L 12 cm.

15   **CASSIN'S SPINETAIL** *Neafrapus cassini*   L 15 cm.

16   **BLACK DWARF HORNBILL** *Tockus hartlaubi*   L 35 cm.

17   **RED-BILLED DWARF HORNBILL** *Tockus camurus*   L 35 cm.

18   **BROWN-CHEEKED** (or White-thighed) **HORNBILL** *Ceratogymma cylindricus*   L 70 cm.

19   **YELLOW-THROATED TINKERBIRD** *Pogoniulus subsulphureus*   L 10 cm.

20   **RED-RUMPED TINKERBIRD** *Pogoniulus atroflavus*   L 13 cm.

21   **YELLOW-SPOTTED BARBET** *Buccanodon duchaillui*   L 15 cm.

22   **BLACK-HEADED BEE-EATER** *Merops breweri*   L 25 (+8) cm.

23   **ROSY BEE-EATER** *Merops malimbicus*   L 24 (+4) cm.

24   **RUFOUS-SIDED BROADBILL** *Smithornis rufolateralis*   L 12 cm.

25   **SPOTTED HONEYGUIDE** *Indicator maculatus*   L 20 cm.

26   **GOLDEN GREENBUL** *Calyptocichla serina*   L 15 cm.

27   **SPOTTED GREENBUL** *Ixonotus guttatus*   L 15 cm.

28   **SWAMP PALM BULBUL** *Thescelocichla leucopleura*   L 20 cm.

29   **ICTERINE GREENBUL** *Phyllastrephus icterinus*   L 15 cm.

30   **GREEN-TAILED BRISTLEBILL** *Bleda eximia*   L 20 cm.

31   **BEARDED GREENBUL** *Criniger chloronotus*   L 20 cm.

32   **BLUE CUCKOOSHRIKE** *Coracina azurea*   L 20 cm.

33   **NORTHERN RED-BILLED HELMET SHRIKE** *Prionops caniceps*   L 20 cm.

34   **CHESTNUT-CAPPED FLYCATCHER** *Erythrocercus mccallii*   L 10 cm.

◀

Plate 84

DISTRIBUTION MAPS

The first and most important step when trying to identify an unknown species is by comparing it with the plates. Confirmation of an identification is possible when the bird is seen in its habitat as described in the captions opposite the plates.

The information about range and status provided in the distribution maps for all species described and illustrated in the book can support or weaken your identification.

Look for instance at map 69.19, which gives the range of Bocage's Sunbird; according to the distribution map it is highly unlikely, if not impossible, to see it in Malawi, so that the long-tailed sunbird you have seen there is the Bronze Sunbird (69.18) or one of the two Malachite Sunbirds (69.16 and 69.17).

The English bird names are given below the maps: each map is further referenced to its species by the plate number and species number (e.g. species number 4 on plate 20 is 20.4).

The shaded areas on the maps give a rough impression of the known range of the species. In a number of cases the areas of races within the range of a species are indicated by letters (a, b, c), which are also mentioned in the plate captions.

The status is indicated by the intensity of the shading, an asterix or a thin cross.

STATUS	CHANCE OF SEEING SPECIES	MAPS	INDICATION IN THE TEXT
Common	60–100%	Dark shading	
Frequent	10–60%	Mid-grey shading	
Uncommon	Very small	Pale grey shading	U
Rare or vagrant	Negligible	Small cross	R
Uncertain	?	?	(?)

An asterix in a map indicates the place of a small population of a species cut off from its main range by the border of our area (e.g. see map 30.8) or points to a small isolated population of a species (e.g. see map 8.4).

If no other information within the framework of a map is given the particular species is a breeding resident in the indicated area. If there is a code in the bottom right corner, the species is at least partly a migrant (see migration key).

MIGRATION KEY					
S	Summer visitor only	W	Winter visitor only	SW	All-year visitor
S(W)	Summer visitor mainly, some stay in winter	W(S)	Winter visitor mainly, some stay in summer		
(S)	Breeding resident mainly with some n-br visitors	(W)	Resident mainly with some winter visitors	(SW)	Mainly resident, partly all-year visitor
brS	Breeding summer visitor				

brS(W)	Breeding summer visitor, some stay winter	brW(S)	Breeding winter visitor, some stay in summer
(br)S	Partly breeding, partly non-breeding summer- visitor		
(brS)	Breeding resident mainly with some breeding visitors		

A ? after a symbol in combinations indicates a possible breeder or visitor.

An interrupted line on the map indicates a breeding visitor north or south of this line.

Non-breeding, summer visitors, S and S(W), are mainly migrants who escape the winter in their European (or Asian) breeding range.

Non-breeding, winter visitors are mainly wanderers who flee from the harsh winter conditions in Antarctica.

Breeding, summer visitors are mainly intra-African migrants who come to benefit from the food supplies (insects, fruits, seeds) in summering Southern Africa.

There are often a few stragglers who can be seen in summer, winter or at any moment of the year ('all-year' visitors) when most individuals of the species are to be found outside the region (indicated e.g. by S(W) or (S)).

EXAMPLE

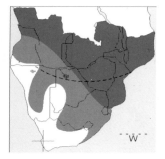

This is the distribution map of the Yellow-billed Stork, number 7 on plate 10, which is frequent in the north-east part of its range, uncommon in the south-west part and rare near Kaapstad. South of the interrupted line it is only known as an uncommon, non-breeding visitor in the winter period, north of it as a frequent, breeding resident.

Note: in this case the winter visitors in South Africa seem to be mainly 1stW immatures, (identified by a less rosy-tinged plumage than the adults) who tend to wander afield after the breeding period.

(See also: Introduction, under Occurrence).

10.7   YELLOW-BILLED STORK

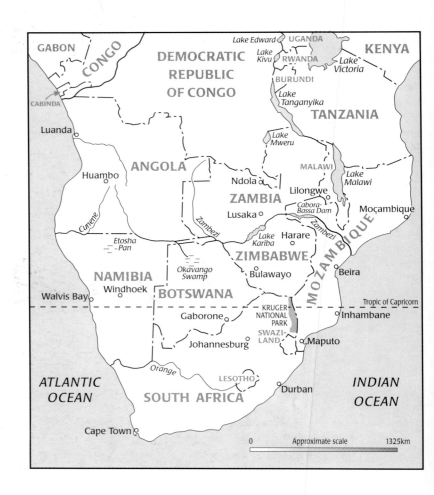

SOUTHERN AFRICA

Maps for species numbers 1.1 to 2.9

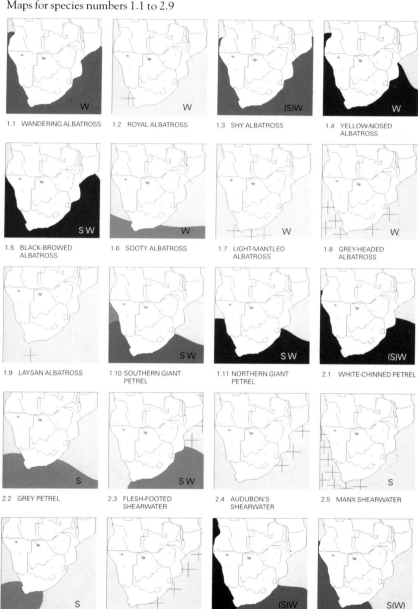

1.1 WANDERING ALBATROSS

1.2 ROYAL ALBATROSS

1.3 SHY ALBATROSS

1.4 YELLOW-NOSED ALBATROSS

1.5 BLACK-BROWED ALBATROSS

1.6 SOOTY ALBATROSS

1.7 LIGHT-MANTLED ALBATROSS

1.8 GREY-HEADED ALBATROSS

1.9 LAYSAN ALBATROSS

1.10 SOUTHERN GIANT PETREL

1.11 NORTHERN GIANT PETREL

2.1 WHITE-CHINNED PETREL

2.2 GREY PETREL

2.3 FLESH-FOOTED SHEARWATER

2.4 AUDUBON'S SHEARWATER

2.5 MANX SHEARWATER

2.6 LITTLE SHEARWATER

2.7 WEDGE-TAILED SHEARWATER

2.8 SOOTY SHEARWATER

2.9 GREAT SHEARWATER

Maps for species numbers 2.10 to 4.7

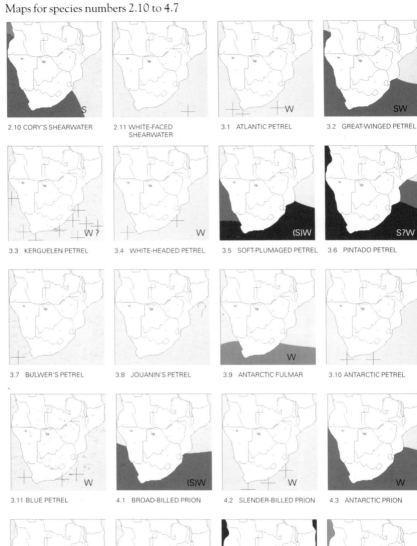

2.10 CORY'S SHEARWATER

2.11 WHITE-FACED SHEARWATER

3.1 ATLANTIC PETREL

3.2 GREAT-WINGED PETREL

3.3 KERGUELEN PETREL

3.4 WHITE-HEADED PETREL

3.5 SOFT-PLUMAGED PETREL

3.6 PINTADO PETREL

3.7 BULWER'S PETREL

3.8 JOUANIN'S PETREL

3.9 ANTARCTIC FULMAR

3.10 ANTARCTIC PETREL

3.11 BLUE PETREL

4.1 BROAD-BILLED PRION

4.2 SLENDER-BILLED PRION

4.3 ANTARCTIC PRION

4.4 FAIRY PRION

4.5 EUROPEAN STORM PETREL

4.6 WILSON'S STORM PETREL

4.7 LEACH'S STORM PETREL

206

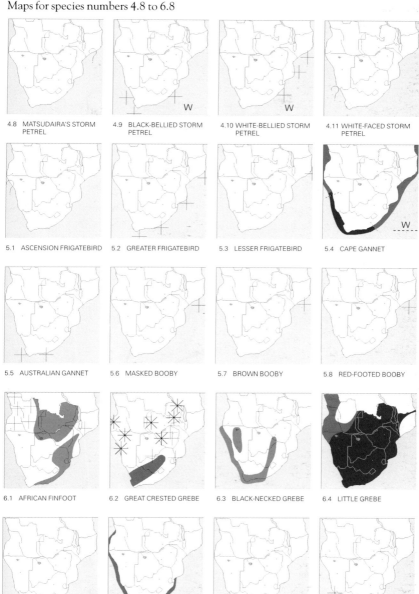

4.8 MATSUDAIRA'S STORM PETREL

4.9 BLACK-BELLIED STORM PETREL

4.10 WHITE-BELLIED STORM PETREL

4.11 WHITE-FACED STORM PETREL

5.1 ASCENSION FRIGATEBIRD

5.2 GREATER FRIGATEBIRD

5.3 LESSER FRIGATEBIRD

5.4 CAPE GANNET

5.5 AUSTRALIAN GANNET

5.6 MASKED BOOBY

5.7 BROWN BOOBY

5.8 RED-FOOTED BOOBY

6.1 AFRICAN FINFOOT

6.2 GREAT CRESTED GREBE

6.3 BLACK-NECKED GREBE

6.4 LITTLE GREBE

6.5 GREATER SHEATHBILL

6.6 JACKASS PENGUIN

6.7 KING PENGUIN

6.8 ROCKHOPPER PENGUIN

Maps for species numbers 6.9 to 8.9

6.9 MACARONI PENGUIN

6.10 GENTOO PENGUIN

7.1 RED-TAILED TROPICBIRD

7.2 RED-BILLED TROPICBIRD

7.3 WHITE-TAILED TROPICBIRD

7.4 CAPE CORMORANT

7.5 BANK CORMORANT

7.6 GREAT CORMORANT

7.7 CROWNED CORMORANT

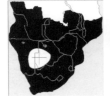

7.8 LONG-TAILED CORMORANT

7.9 DARTER

8.1 GREATER FLAMINGO

8.2 LESSER FLAMINGO

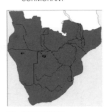

8.3 GREY HERON

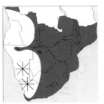

8.4 PURPLE HERON

8.5 GOLIATH HERON

8.6 BLACK-HEADED HERON

8.7 SHOEBILL

8.8 GREAT WHITE PELICAN

8.9 PINK-BACKED PELICAN

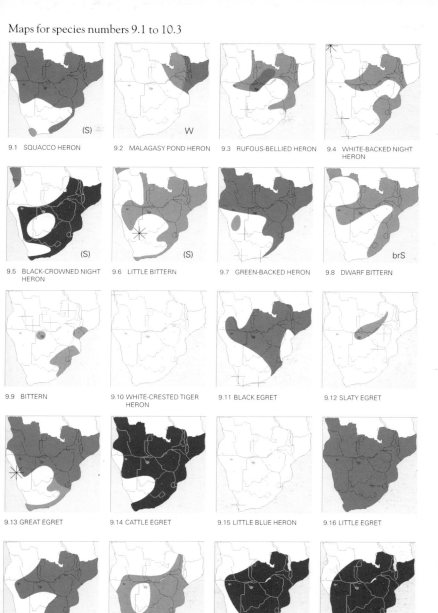

9.1 SQUACCO HERON (S)

9.2 MALAGASY POND HERON W

9.3 RUFOUS-BELLIED HERON

9.4 WHITE-BACKED NIGHT HERON

9.5 BLACK-CROWNED NIGHT HERON (S)

9.6 LITTLE BITTERN (S)

9.7 GREEN-BACKED HERON

9.8 DWARF BITTERN brS

9.9 BITTERN

9.10 WHITE-CRESTED TIGER HERON

9.11 BLACK EGRET

9.12 SLATY EGRET

9.13 GREAT EGRET

9.14 CATTLE EGRET

9.15 LITTLE BLUE HERON

9.16 LITTLE EGRET

9.17 YELLOW-BILLED EGRET

10.1 BLACK STORK

10.2 ABDIM'S STORK S

10.3 WHITE STORK (br)S

209

Maps for species numbers 10.4 to 11.8

10.4 MARABOU STORK

10.5 WOOLLY-NECKED STORK

10.6 AFRICAN OPEN-BILL STORK

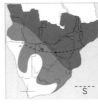

10.7 YELLOW-BILLED STORK

10.8 SADDLE-BILLED STORK

10.9 AFRICAN SPOONBILL

10.10 BALD IBIS

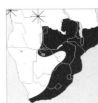

10.11 HADADA

10.12 SPOT-BREASTED IBIS

10.13 GLOSSY IBIS

10.14 SACRED IBIS

10.15 HAMERKOP

11.1 SPUR-WINGED GOOSE

11.2 EGYPTIAN GOOSE

11.3 SOUTH AFRICAN SHELDUCK

11.4 KNOB-BILLED SHELDUCK

11.5 WHITE-BACKED DUCK

11.6 AFRICAN PYGMY GOOSE

11.7 SOUTHERN POCHARD

11.8 MACCOA DUCK

Maps for species numbers 11.9 to 13.6

11.9 HARTLAUB'S DUCK

11.10 TUFTED DUCK

12.1 WHITE-FACED
WHISTLING DUCK

12.2 FULVOUS WHISTLING
DUCK

12.3 YELLOW-BILLED DUCK

12.4 AFRICAN BLACK DUCK

12.5 MALLARD

12.6 CAPE SHOVELER

12.7 NORTHERN SHOVELER

12.8 GARGANEY

12.9 CAPE TEAL

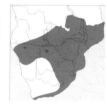

12.10 HOTTENTOT TEAL

12.11 RED-BILLED TEAL

12.12 NORTHERN PINTAIL

13.1 PALE CHANTING
GOSHAWK

13.2 DARK CHANTING
GOSHAWK

13.3 GABAR GOSHAWK

13.4 SHIKRA

13.5 AFRICAN GOSHAWK

13.6 AFRICAN LITTLE
SPARROWHAWK

211

13.7 OVAMBO
SPARROWHAWK

13.8 BLACK SPARROWHAWK

13.9 RUFOUS-CHESTED
SPARROWHAWK

13.10 RED-THIGHED
SPARROWHAWK

14.1 AFRICAN MARSH
HARRIER

14.2 NORTHERN HARRIER

14.3 BLACK HARRIER

14.4 MONTAGU'S HARRIER

14.5 PALLID HARRIER

14.6 BLACK-SHOULDERED
KITE

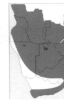

14.7 GYMNOGENE

14.8 YELLOW-BILLED KITE

14.9 BLACK KITE

15.1 AFRICAN CUCKOO HAWK

15.2 LIZARD BUZZARD

15.3 HONEY BUZZARD

15.4 AUGUR BUZZARD

15.5 STEPPE BUZZARD

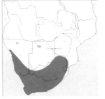

15.6 JACKALL BUZZARD

15.7 MOUNTAIN BUZZARD

Maps for species numbers 15.8 to 18.5

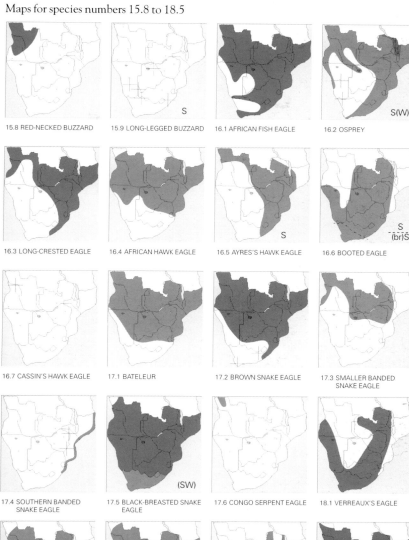

15.8 RED-NECKED BUZZARD

15.9 LONG-LEGGED BUZZARD   S

16.1 AFRICAN FISH EAGLE

16.2 OSPREY   S(W)

16.3 LONG-CRESTED EAGLE

16.4 AFRICAN HAWK EAGLE

16.5 AYRES'S HAWK EAGLE   S

16.6 BOOTED EAGLE   S (br)S

16.7 CASSIN'S HAWK EAGLE

17.1 BATELEUR

17.2 BROWN SNAKE EAGLE

17.3 SMALLER BANDED SNAKE EAGLE

17.4 SOUTHERN BANDED SNAKE EAGLE

17.5 BLACK-BREASTED SNAKE EAGLE   (SW)

17.6 CONGO SERPENT EAGLE

18.1 VERREAUX'S EAGLE

18.2 STEPPE EAGLE   S

18.3 TAWNY EAGLE

18.4 LESSER SPOTTED EAGLE   S

18.5 WAHLBERG'S EAGLE   brS

213

Maps for species numbers 19.1 to 22.2

19.1 PALM-NUT VULTURE

19.2 EGYPTIAN VULTURE

19.3 LAMMERGEIER

19.4 MARTIAL EAGLE

19.5 CROWNED EAGLE

20.1 LAPPET-FACED VULTURE

20.2 WHITE-HEADED VULTURE

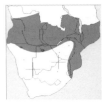

20.3 HOODED VULTURE

20.4 CAPE VULTURE

20.5 AFRICAN WHITE-BACKED VULTURE

21.1 BAT HAWK

21.2 TAITA FALCON

21.3 PEREGRINE FALCON

(S)

21.4 LANNER FALCON

21.5 RED-NECKED FALCON

21.6 ELEONORA'S FALCON

S

21.7 EUROPEAN HOBBY

S

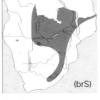

21.8 AFRICAN HOBBY

(brS)

22.1 DICKINSON'S KESTREL

22.2 GREY KESTREL

214

Maps for species numbers 22.3 to 23.13

22.3 SOOTY FALCON

22.4 EASTERN RED-FOOTED FALCON

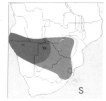

22.5 RED-FOOTED FALCON

22.6 GREATER KESTREL

22.7 LESSER KESTREL

22.8 COMMON KESTREL

22.9 PYGMY FALCON

23.1 RED-NECKED FRANCOLIN

23.2 SWAINSON'S FRANCOLIN

23.3 RED-BILLED FRANCOLIN

23.4 NATAL FRANCOLIN

23.5 CAPE FRANCOLIN

23.6 ORANGE RIVER FRANCOLIN

23.7 REDWING FRANCOLIN

23.8 GREYWING FRANCOLIN

23.9 SHELLEY'S FRANCOLIN

23.10 FINSCH'S FRANCOLIN

23.11 CRESTED FRANCOLIN

23.12 WHITE-THROATED FRANCOLIN

23.13 HARTLAUB'S FRANCOLIN

215

Maps for species numbers 23.14 to 24.14

23.14 COQUI FRANCOLIN

23.15 HILDEBRANDT'S FRANCOLIN

23.16 GREY-STRIPED FRANCOLIN

23.17 SCALY FRANCOLIN

23.18 SWIERSTRA'S FRANCOLIN

23.19 CHUKAR

24.1 AFRICAN WATER RAIL

24.2 BLACK CRAKE

24.3 ALLEN'S GALLINULE

24.4 PURPLE GALLINULE

24.5 PURPLE SWAMPHEN

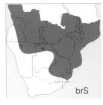

24.6 LESSER MOORHEN

24.7 COMMON MOORHEN

24.8 RED-KNOBBED COOT

24.9 STRIPED CRAKE

24.10 SPOTTED CRAKE

24.11 BAILLON'S CRAKE

24.12 LITTLE CRAKE

24.13 AFRICAN CRAKE

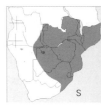

24.14 CORNCRAKE

216

24.15 CRESTED GUINEAFOWL

24.16 HELMETED GUINEAFOWL

25.1 AFRICAN BLUE QUAIL

25.2 HARLEQUIN QUAIL

25.3 COMMON QUAIL

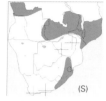

25.4 BLACK-RUMPED BUTTON-QUAIL

25.5 LITTLE BUTTON-QUAIL

25.6 CHESTNUT-HEADED FLUFFTAIL

25.7 BOEHM'S FLUFFTAIL

25.8 RED-CHESTED FLUFFTAIL

25.9 STRIPED FLUFFTAIL

25.10 WHITE-SPOTTED FLUFFTAIL

25.11 BUFF-SPOTTED FLUFFTAIL

25.12 WHITE-WINGED FLUFFTAIL

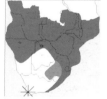

25.13 AFRICAN JACANA

25.14 LESSER JACANA

26.1 WATTLED CRANE

26.2 BLUE CRANE

26.3 GREY CROWNED CRANE

26.4 SECRETARY BIRD

217

Maps for species numbers 26.5 to 27.9

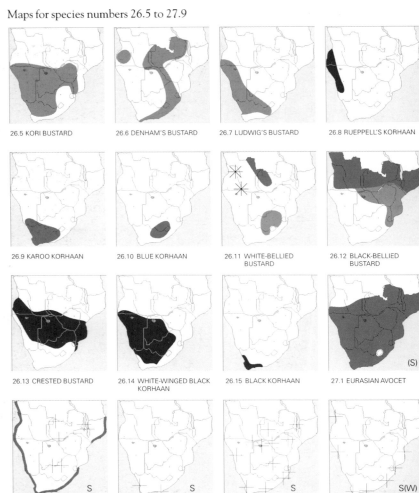

26.5 KORI BUSTARD

26.6 DENHAM'S BUSTARD

26.7 LUDWIG'S BUSTARD

26.8 RUEPPELL'S KORHAAN

26.9 KAROO KORHAAN

26.10 BLUE KORHAAN

26.11 WHITE-BELLIED BUSTARD

26.12 BLACK-BELLIED BUSTARD

26.13 CRESTED BUSTARD

26.14 WHITE-WINGED BLACK KORHAAN

26.15 BLACK KORHAAN

27.1 EURASIAN AVOCET

27.2 BAR-TAILED GODWIT

27.3 HUDSONIAN GODWIT

27.4 BLACK-TAILED GODWIT

27.5 EURASIAN OYSTERCATCHER

27.6 AFRICAN BLACK OYSTERCATCHER

27.7 COMMON STILT

27.8 EGYPTIAN-PLOVER

27.9 CRAB PLOVER

218

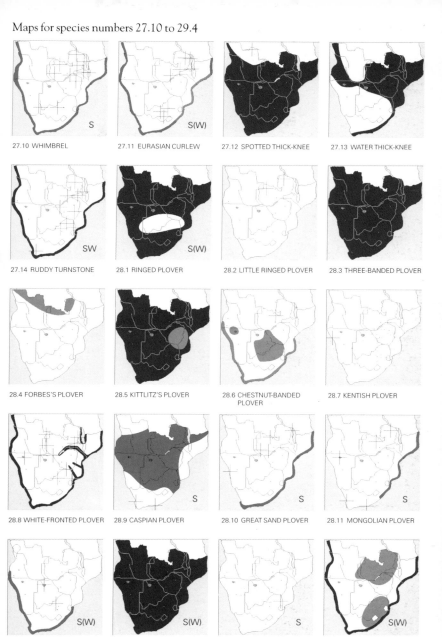

27.10 WHIMBREL

27.11 EURASIAN CURLEW

27.12 SPOTTED THICK-KNEE

27.13 WATER THICK-KNEE

27.14 RUDDY TURNSTONE

28.1 RINGED PLOVER

28.2 LITTLE RINGED PLOVER

28.3 THREE-BANDED PLOVER

28.4 FORBES'S PLOVER

28.5 KITTLITZ'S PLOVER

28.6 CHESTNUT-BANDED PLOVER

28.7 KENTISH PLOVER

28.8 WHITE-FRONTED PLOVER

28.9 CASPIAN PLOVER

28.10 GREAT SAND PLOVER

28.11 MONGOLIAN PLOVER

29.1 RED KNOT

29.2 CURLEW SANDPIPER

29.3 DUNLIN

29.4 SANDERLING

219

Maps for species numbers 29.5 to 30.12

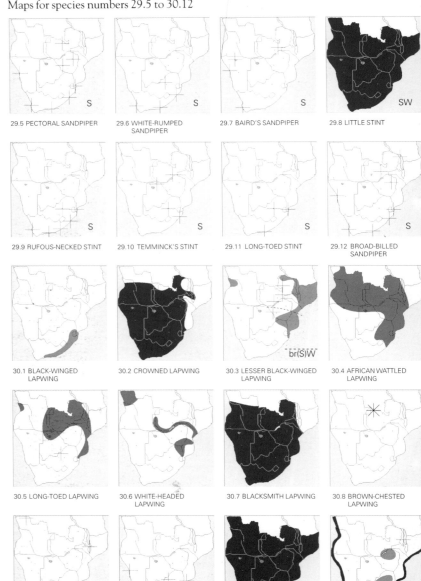

29.5 PECTORAL SANDPIPER

29.6 WHITE-RUMPED SANDPIPER

29.7 BAIRD'S SANDPIPER

29.8 LITTLE STINT

29.9 RUFOUS-NECKED STINT

29.10 TEMMINCK'S STINT

29.11 LONG-TOED STINT

29.12 BROAD-BILLED SANDPIPER

30.1 BLACK-WINGED LAPWING

30.2 CROWNED LAPWING

30.3 LESSER BLACK-WINGED LAPWING

30.4 AFRICAN WATTLED LAPWING

30.5 LONG-TOED LAPWING

30.6 WHITE-HEADED LAPWING

30.7 BLACKSMITH LAPWING

30.8 BROWN-CHESTED LAPWING

30.9 SPUR-WINGED LAPWING

30.10 BUFF-BREASTED SANDPIPER

30.11 RUFF/ REEVE

30.12 GREY PLOVER

Maps for species numbers 30.13 to 32.2

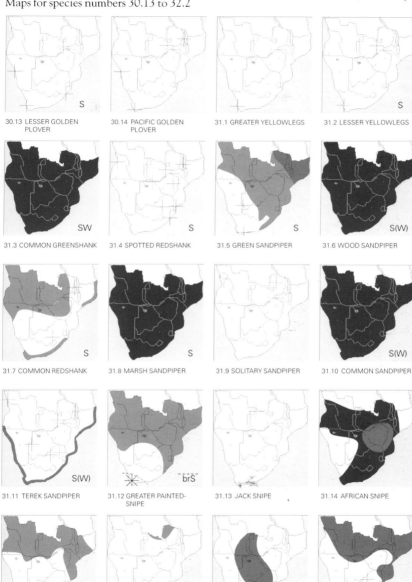

30.13 LESSER GOLDEN PLOVER   S

30.14 PACIFIC GOLDEN PLOVER

31.1 GREATER YELLOWLEGS

31.2 LESSER YELLOWLEGS   S

31.3 COMMON GREENSHANK   SW

31.4 SPOTTED REDSHANK   S

31.5 GREEN SANDPIPER   S

31.6 WOOD SANDPIPER   S(W)

31.7 COMMON REDSHANK   S

31.8 MARSH SANDPIPER   S

31.9 SOLITARY SANDPIPER

31.10 COMMON SANDPIPER   S(W)

31.11 TEREK SANDPIPER   S(W)

31.12 GREATER PAINTED-SNIPE   brS

31.13 JACK SNIPE

31.14 AFRICAN SNIPE

31.15 GREAT SNIPE   S(W)

31.16 COMMON SNIPE   S

32.1 BLACK-WINGED PRATINCOLE   S

32.2 COLLARED PRATINCOLE   brW SW

221

32.3 ROCK PRATINCOLE

32.4 MADAGASCAR PRATINCOLE

32.5 TEMMINCK'S COURSER

32.6 BURCHELL'S COURSER

32.7 DOUBLE-BANDED COURSER

32.8 THREE-BANDED COURSER

32.9 BRONZE-WINGED COURSER

32.10 WILSON'S PHALAROPE

32.11 RED-NECKED PHALAROPE

32.12 GREY PHALAROPE

33.1 SOUTH POLAR SKUA

33.2 BROWN SKUA

33.3 POMARINE SKUA

33.4 ARCTIC SKUA

33.5 LONG-TAILED SKUA

33.6 KELP GULL

33.7 LESSER BLACK-BACKED GULL

33.8 HERRING GULL

34.1 SABINE'S GULL

34.2 BLACK-LEGGED KITTIWAKE

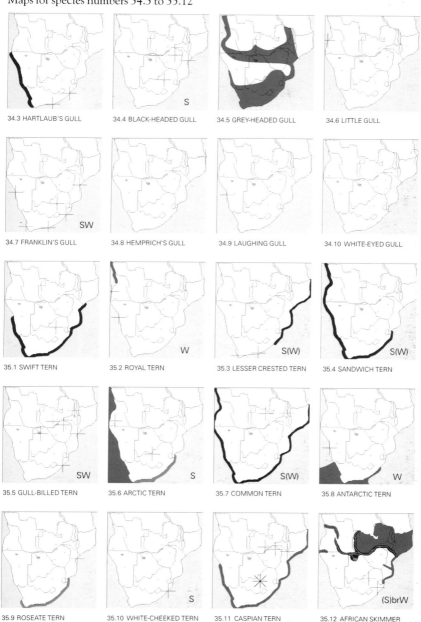

34.3 HARTLAUB'S GULL

34.4 BLACK-HEADED GULL

34.5 GREY-HEADED GULL

34.6 LITTLE GULL

34.7 FRANKLIN'S GULL

34.8 HEMPRICH'S GULL

34.9 LAUGHING GULL

34.10 WHITE-EYED GULL

35.1 SWIFT TERN

35.2 ROYAL TERN

35.3 LESSER CRESTED TERN

35.4 SANDWICH TERN

35.5 GULL-BILLED TERN

35.6 ARCTIC TERN

35.7 COMMON TERN

35.8 ANTARCTIC TERN

35.9 ROSEATE TERN

35.10 WHITE-CHEEKED TERN

35.11 CASPIAN TERN

35.12 AFRICAN SKIMMER

Maps for species numbers 36.1 to 37.9

36.1 LITTLE TERN

36.2 DAMARA TERN

36.3 BLACK-NAPED TERN

36.4 BRIDLED TERN

36.5 SOOTY TERN

36.6 BROWN NODDY

36.7 LESSER NODDY

36.8 BLACK NODDY

36.9 BLACK TERN

36.10 WHITE-WINGED TERN

36.11 WHISKERED TERN

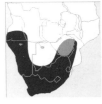

37.1 SPECKLED PIGEON

37.2 OLIVE PIGEON

37.3 ROCK DOVE

37.4 EASTERN BRONZE-
NAPED PIGEON

37.5 AFEP PIGEON

37.6 AFRICAN GREEN PIGEON

37.7 LEMON DOVE

37.8 NAMAQUA DOVE

37.9 AFRICAN MOURNING
DOVE

Maps for species numbers 37.10 to 38.12

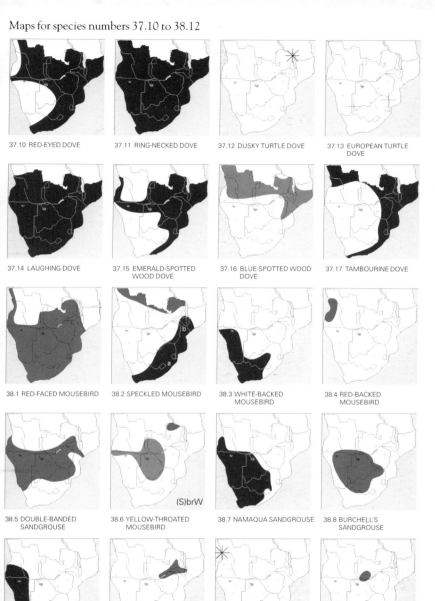

37.10 RED-EYED DOVE

37.11 RING-NECKED DOVE

37.12 DUSKY TURTLE DOVE

37.13 EUROPEAN TURTLE DOVE

37.14 LAUGHING DOVE

37.15 EMERALD-SPOTTED WOOD DOVE

37.16 BLUE-SPOTTED WOOD DOVE

37.17 TAMBOURINE DOVE

38.1 RED-FACED MOUSEBIRD

38.2 SPECKLED MOUSEBIRD

38.3 WHITE-BACKED MOUSEBIRD

38.4 RED-BACKED MOUSEBIRD

38.5 DOUBLE-BANDED SANDGROUSE

38.6 YELLOW-THROATED MOUSEBIRD

38.7 NAMAQUA SANDGROUSE

38.8 BURCHELL'S SANDGROUSE

38.9 ROSY-FACED LOVEBIRD

38.10 LILIAN'S LOVEBIRD

38.11 RED-HEADED LOVEBIRD

38.12 BLACK-CHEEKED LOVEBIRD

225

Maps for species numbers 38.13 to 39.12

38.13 BROWN-NECKED PARROT

38.14 MEYER'S PARROT

38.15 BROWN-HEADED PARROT

38.16 RUEPPELL'S PARROT

38.17 RED-FRONTED PARROT

38.18 ROSE-RINGED PARAKEET

38.19 GREY PARROT

38.20 HOOPOE

39.1 GREEN TURACO

39.2 RED-CRESTED TURACO

39.3 PURPLE-CRESTED TURACO

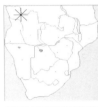

39.4 BLACK-BILLED TURACO

39.5 GREY GO-AWAY BIRD

39.6 BARE-FACED GO-AWAY BIRD

39.7 GREAT BLUE TURACO

39.8 ROSS'S TURACO

39.9 RUFOUS-CROWNED ROLLER

39.10 LILAC-BREASTED ROLLER

39.11 RACKET-TAILED ROLLER

39.12 EUROPEAN ROLLER

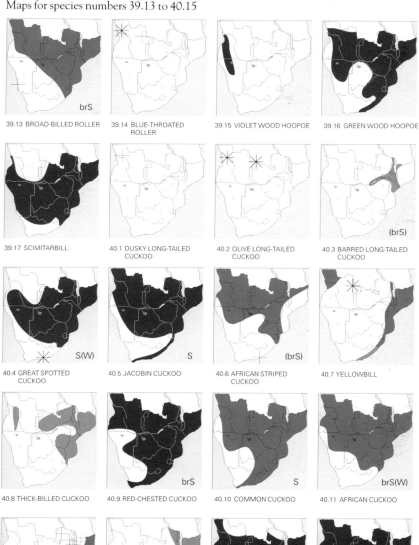

39.13 BROAD-BILLED ROLLER

39.14 BLUE-THROATED ROLLER

39.15 VIOLET WOOD HOOPOE

39.16 GREEN WOOD HOOPOE

39.17 SCIMITARBILL

40.1 DUSKY LONG-TAILED CUCKOO

40.2 OLIVE LONG-TAILED CUCKOO

40.3 BARRED LONG-TAILED CUCKOO

40.4 GREAT SPOTTED CUCKOO

40.5 JACOBIN CUCKOO

40.6 AFRICAN STRIPED CUCKOO

40.7 YELLOWBILL

40.8 THICK-BILLED CUCKOO

40.9 RED-CHESTED CUCKOO

40.10 COMMON CUCKOO

40.11 AFRICAN CUCKOO

40.12 ASIAN LESSER CUCKOO

40.13 MADAGASCAR LESSER CUCKOO

40.14 BLACK CUCKOO

40.15 DIEDERIK CUCKOO

227

Maps for species numbers 40.16 to 42.8

40.16 KLAAS'S CUCKOO

40.17 AFRICAN EMERALD CUCKOO

41.1 FIERY-NECKED NIGHTJAR

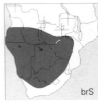

41.2 RUFOUS-CHEEKED NIGHTJAR

41.3 FRECKLED NIGHTJAR

41.4 SQUARE-TAILED NIGHTJAR

41.5 SWAMP NIGHTJAR

41.6 MOUNTAIN NIGHTJAR

41.7 SLENDER-TAILED NIGHTJAR

41.8 LONG-TAILED NIGHTJAR

41.9 EUROPEAN NIGHTJAR

41.10 PENNANT-WINGED NIGHTJAR

42.1 AFRICAN WOOD OWL

42.2 PEARL-SPOTTED OWLET

42.3 AFRICAN BARRED OWLET

42.4 WHITE-FACED SCOPS OWL

42.5 AFRICAN SCOPS OWL

42.6 PEL'S FISHING OWL

42.7 VERREAUX'S EAGLE OWL

42.8 CAPE EAGLE OWL

228

Maps for species numbers 42.9 to 43.9

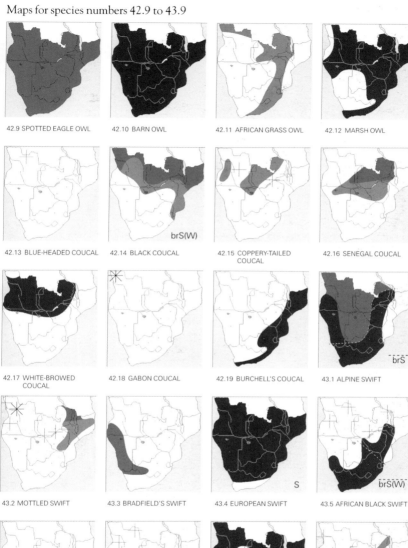

42.9 SPOTTED EAGLE OWL

42.10 BARN OWL

42.11 AFRICAN GRASS OWL

42.12 MARSH OWL

42.13 BLUE-HEADED COUCAL

42.14 BLACK COUCAL   brS(W)

42.15 COPPERY-TAILED COUCAL

42.16 SENEGAL COUCAL

42.17 WHITE-BROWED COUCAL

42.18 GABON COUCAL

42.19 BURCHELL'S COUCAL

43.1 ALPINE SWIFT   brS

43.2 MOTTLED SWIFT

43.3 BRADFIELD'S SWIFT

43.4 EUROPEAN SWIFT   S

43.5 AFRICAN BLACK SWIFT   brS(W)

43.6 PALLID SWIFT   S

43.7 FERNANDO PO SWIFT

43.8 LITTLE SWIFT

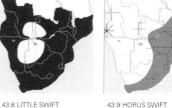

43.9 HORUS SWIFT   brS

229

Maps for species numbers 43.10 to 44.14

43.10 WHITE-RUMPED SWIFT

43.11 SCARCE SWIFT

43.12 AFRICAN PALM SWIFT

43.13 BAT-LIKE SPINETAIL

43.14 MOTTLED SPINETAIL

43.15 BLACK SPINETAIL

44.1 BLUE-BREASTED BEE-EATER

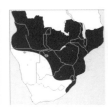

44.2 LITTLE BEE-EATER

44.3 WHITE-FRONTED BEE-EATER

44.4 BLACK BEE-EATER

44.5 EUROPEAN BEE-EATER

44.6 BLUE-CHEEKED BEE-EATER

44.7 MADAGASCAR BEE-EATER

44.8 WHITE-THROATED BEE-EATER

44.9 CARMINE BEE-EATER

44.10 SWALLOW-TAILED BEE-EATER

44.11 BOEHM'S BEE-EATER

44.12 AFRICAN GREY HORNBILL

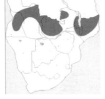

44.13 PALE-BILLED HORNBILL

44.14 MONTEIRO'S HORNBILL

Maps for species numbers 44.15 to 46.4

44.15 AFRICAN PIED HORNBILL

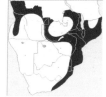

44.16 CROWNED HORNBILL

44.17 BRADFIELD'S HORNBILL

44.18 SOUTHERN YELLOW-BILLED HORNBILL

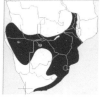

44.19 RED-BILLED HORNBILL

45.1 PIED CROW

45.2 WHITE-NECKED RAVEN

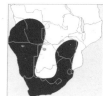

45.3 BLACK CROW

45.4 HOUSE CROW

45.5 WHITE-CRESTED HORNBILL

45.6 BLACK-CASQUED WATTLED HORNBILL

45.7 SOUTHERN GROUND HORNBILL

45.8 TRUMPETER HORNBILL

45.9 SILVERY-CHEEKED HORNBILL

45.10 BLACK-AND-WHITE-CASQUED HORNBILL

45.11 PIPING HORNBILL

46.1 PIED KINGFISHER

46.2 AFRICAN GIANT KINGFISHER

46.3 MALACHITE KINGFISHER

46.4 HALF-COLLARED KINGFISHER

231

Maps for species numbers 46.5 to 47.7

46.5 SHINING-BLUE
KINGFISHER

46.6 WHITE-BELLIED
KINGFISHER

46.7 AFRICAN DWARF
KINGFISHER

46.8 AFRICAN PYGMY
KINGFISHER

46.9 WOODLAND KINGFISHER

46.10 MANGROVE
KINGFISHER

46.11 STRIPED KINGFISHER

46.12 CHOCOLATE-BACKED
KINGFISHER

46.13 GREY-HEADED
KINGFISHER

46.14 BLUE-BREASTED
KINGFISHER

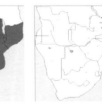

46.15 BROWN-HOODED
KINGFISHER

46.16 BAR-TAILED TROGON

46.17 NARINA'S TROGON

47.1 WHYTE'S BARBET

47.2 WHITE-EARED BARBET

47.3 ANCHIETA'S BARBET

47.4 GREEN BARBET

47.5 SPOT-FLANKED BARBET

47.6 HAIRY-BREASTED
BARBET

47.7 GREY-THROATED BARBET

232

Maps for species numbers 47.8 to 48.9

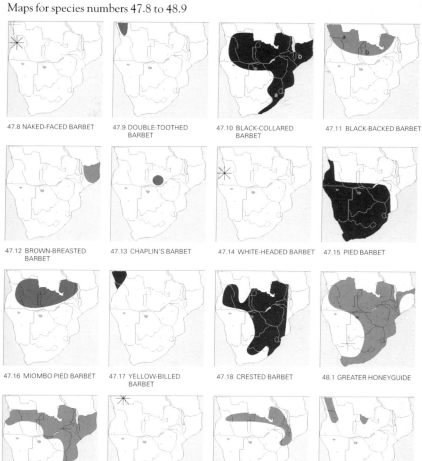

47.8 NAKED-FACED BARBET

47.9 DOUBLE-TOOTHED BARBET

47.10 BLACK-COLLARED BARBET

47.11 BLACK-BACKED BARBET

47.12 BROWN-BREASTED BARBET

47.13 CHAPLIN'S BARBET

47.14 WHITE-HEADED BARBET

47.15 PIED BARBET

47.16 MIOMBO PIED BARBET

47.17 YELLOW-BILLED BARBET

47.18 CRESTED BARBET

48.1 GREATER HONEYGUIDE

48.2 SCALY-THROATED HONEYGUIDE

48.3 LYRE-TAILED HONEYGUIDE

48.4 PALLID HONEYGUIDE

48.5 LEAST HONEYGUIDE

48.6 LESSER HONEYGUIDE

48.7 GREEN-BACKED HONEYBIRD

48.8 CASSIN'S HONEYBIRD

48.9 WAHLBERG'S HONEYBIRD

233

48.10 AFRICAN BROADBILL

48.11 SPECKLED TINKERBIRD

48.12 GREEN TINKERBIRD

48.13 MOUSTACHED GREEN TINKERBIRD

48.14 WESTERN GREEN TINKERBIRD

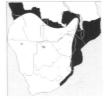

48.15 YELLOW-RUMPED TINKERBIRD

48.16 RED-FRONTED TINKERBIRD

48.17 YELLOW-FRONTED TINKERBIRD

48.18 AFRICAN PITTA

49.1 GREEN-BACKED WOODPECKER

49.2 BROWN-EARED WOODPECKER

49.3 GOLDEN-TAILED WOODPECKER

49.4 BUFF-SPOTTED WOODPECKER

49.5 BENNETT'S WOODPECKER

49.6 KNYSNA WOODPECKER

49.7 OLIVE WOODPECKER

49.8 ELLIOT'S WOODPECKER

49.9 GREY WOODPECKER

49.10 CARDINAL WOODPECKER

49.11 BEARDED WOODPECKER

234

Maps for species numbers 49.12 to 51.5

49.12 YELLOW-CRESTED WOODPECKER

49.13 STIERLING'S WOODPECKER

49.14 AFRICAN PICULET

49.15 RUFOUS-BREASTED WRYNECK

49.16 GROUND WOODPECKER

50.1 LONG-BILLED LARK

50.2 KAROO LARK

50.3 RED LARK

50.4 SPIKE-HEELED LARK

50.5 GRAY'S LARK

50.6 SHORT-CLAWED LARK

50.7A DUNE LARK
50.7B BARLOW'S LARK

50.8 LARGE-BILLED LARK

50.9 DUSKY LARK

50.10 BIMACULATED LARK

51.1 FLAPPET LARK

51.2 CLAPPER LARK

51.3 MONOTONOUS LARK

51.4 MELODIOUS LARK

51.5 SABOTA LARK

Maps for species numbers 51.6 to 52.11

51.6 FAWN-COLOURED LARK

51.7 RUFOUS-NAPED LARK

51.8 ANGOLA LARK

51.9 BOTHA'S LARK

51.10 RUDD'S LARK

51.11 PINK-BILLED LARK

51.12 SCLATER'S LARK

51.13 STARK'S LARK

51.14 RED-CAPPED LARK

52.1 WHITE-THROATED BLUE SWALLOW

52.2 MOSQUE SWALLOW

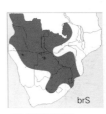

52.3 RED-BREASTED SWALLOW

52.4 LESSER STRIPED SWALLOW

52.5 GREATER STRIPED SWALLOW

52.6 BARN SWALLOW

52.7 BLACK-AND-RUFOUS SWALLOW

52.8 WIRE-TAILED SWALLOW

52.9 ANGOLA SWALLOW

52.10 RED-RUMPED SWALLOW

52.11 WHITE-THROATED SWALLOW

236

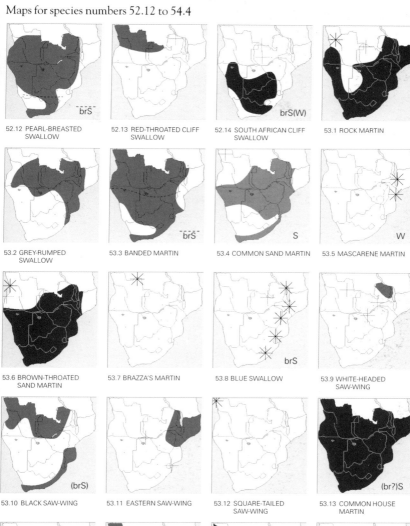

52.12 PEARL-BREASTED SWALLOW

52.13 RED-THROATED CLIFF SWALLOW

52.14 SOUTH AFRICAN CLIFF SWALLOW

53.1 ROCK MARTIN

53.2 GREY-RUMPED SWALLOW

53.3 BANDED MARTIN

53.4 COMMON SAND MARTIN

53.5 MASCARENE MARTIN

53.6 BROWN-THROATED SAND MARTIN

53.7 BRAZZA'S MARTIN

53.8 BLUE SWALLOW

53.9 WHITE-HEADED SAW-WING

53.10 BLACK SAW-WING

53.11 EASTERN SAW-WING

53.12 SQUARE-TAILED SAW-WING

53.13 COMMON HOUSE MARTIN

54.1 AFRICAN GOLDEN ORIOLE

54.2 EUROPEAN GOLDEN ORIOLE

54.3 BLACK-HEADED ORIOLE

54.4 GREEN-HEADED ORIOLE

Maps for species numbers 54.5 to 55.6

54.5 BLACK-HEADED ORIOLE

54.6 WESTERN BLACK-HEADED ORIOLE

54.7 ARROW-MARKED ORIOLE

54.8 BLACK-FACED BABBLER

54.9 BARE-CHEEKED BABBLER

54.10 SOUTHERN PIED BABBLER

54.11 HARTLAUB'S BABBLER

54.12 AFRICAN HILL BABBLER

54.13 DAPPLED MOUNTAIN BABBLER

54.14 SPOT-THROAT

54.15 MOUNTAIN ILLADOPSIS

54.16 BROWN ILLADOPSIS

54.17 SCALY-BREASTED ILLADOPSIS

54.18 THRUSH BABBLER

55.1 MOUNTAIN GREENBUL

55.2 SHELLEY'S GREENBUL

55.3 SOMBRE GREENBUL

55.4 LITTLE GREY GREENBUL

55.5 LITTLE GREENBUL

55.6 STRIPE-CHEEKED GREENBUL

238

Maps for species numbers 55.7 to 56.6

55.7 SLENDER-BILLED GREENBUL

55.8 PLAIN GREENBUL

55.9 YELLOW-WHISKERED GREENBUL

55.10 TERRESTRIAL BROWNBUL

55.11 TINY GREENBUL

55.12 YELLOW-STREAKED GREENBUL

55.13 PALE OLIVE GREENBUL

55.14 CABANIS'S GREENBUL

55.15 GREY-OLIVE GREENBUL

55.16 WHITE-THROATED GREENBUL

55.17 CAPE BULBUL

55.18 AFRICAN RED-EYED BULBUL

55.19 COMMON BULBUL

55.20 BUSH BLACKCAP

56.1 FORK-TAILED DRONGO

56.2 SQUARE-TAILED DRONGO

56.3 HONEYGUIDE GREENBUL

56.4 YELLOW-BELLIED GREENBUL

56.5 JOYFUL GREENBUL

56.6 YELLOW-NECKED GREENBUL

239

Maps for species numbers 56.7 to 57.8

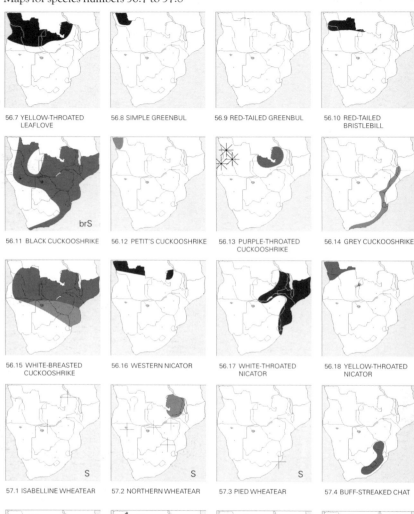

56.7 YELLOW-THROATED LEAFLOVE

56.8 SIMPLE GREENBUL

56.9 RED-TAILED GREENBUL

56.10 RED-TAILED BRISTLEBILL

56.11 BLACK CUCKOOSHRIKE

56.12 PETIT'S CUCKOOSHRIKE

56.13 PURPLE-THROATED CUCKOOSHRIKE

56.14 GREY CUCKOOSHRIKE

56.15 WHITE-BREASTED CUCKOOSHRIKE

56.16 WESTERN NICATOR

56.17 WHITE-THROATED NICATOR

56.18 YELLOW-THROATED NICATOR

57.1 ISABELLINE WHEATEAR

57.2 NORTHERN WHEATEAR

57.3 PIED WHEATEAR

57.4 BUFF-STREAKED CHAT

57.5 MOUNTAIN WHEATEAR

57.6 CAPPED WHEATEAR

57.7 WHITE-HEADED BLACK CHAT

57.8 MOCKING CLIFF CHAT

57.9 KAROO SCRUB ROBIN

57.10 KALAHARI SCRUB ROBIN

57.11 RUFOUS SCRUB ROBIN

57.12 BROWN SCRUB ROBIN

57.13 EASTERN BEARDED SCRUB ROBIN

57.14 MIOMBO BEARDED SCRUB ROBIN

57.15 FOREST SCRUB ROBIN

57.16 WHITE-BROWED SCRUB ROBIN

57.17 BROWN-BACKED SCRUB ROBIN

58.1 SICKLE-WINGED CHAT

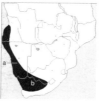

58.2 TRACTRAC CHAT

58.3 KAROO CHAT

58.4 FAMILIAR CHAT

58.5 MIOMBO ROCK THRUSH

58.6 SHORT-TOED ROCK THRUSH

58.7 CAPE ROCK THRUSH

58.8 SENTINEL ROCK THRUSH

58.9 MOUNTAIN ROCK THRUSH

58.10 BOULDER CHAT

58.11 HERERO CHAT

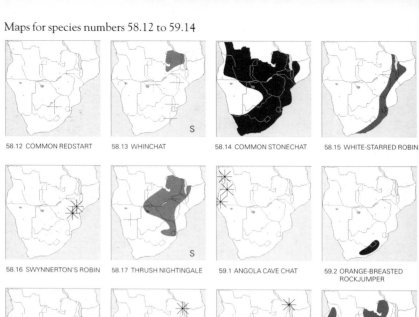

58.12 COMMON REDSTART

58.13 WHINCHAT

58.14 COMMON STONECHAT

58.15 WHITE-STARRED ROBIN

58.16 SWYNNERTON'S ROBIN

58.17 THRUSH NIGHTINGALE

59.1 ANGOLA CAVE CHAT

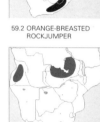

59.2 ORANGE-BREASTED ROCKJUMPER

59.3 CAPE ROCKJUMPER

59.4 EAST COAST AKALAT

59.5 SHARPE'S AKALAT

59.6 BOCAGE'S AKALAT

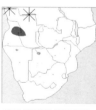

59.7 GABELA AKALAT

59.8 SOOTY CHAT

59.9 SOUTHERN ANTEATER CHAT

59.10 CONGO MOOR CHAT

59.11 OLIVE-FLANKED ROBIN CHAT

59.12 CHOLO ALETHE

59.13 BROWN-CHESTED ALETHE

59.14 FIRE-CRESTED ALETHE

Maps for species numbers 59.15 to 61.1

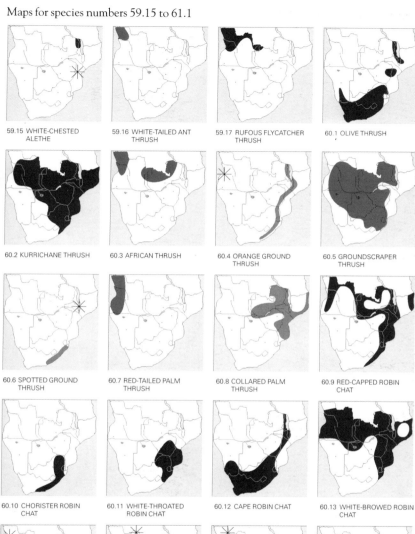

59.15 WHITE-CHESTED ALETHE

59.16 WHITE-TAILED ANT THRUSH

59.17 RUFOUS FLYCATCHER THRUSH

60.1 OLIVE THRUSH

60.2 KURRICHANE THRUSH

60.3 AFRICAN THRUSH

60.4 ORANGE GROUND THRUSH

60.5 GROUNDSCRAPER THRUSH

60.6 SPOTTED GROUND THRUSH

60.7 RED-TAILED PALM THRUSH

60.8 COLLARED PALM THRUSH

60.9 RED-CAPPED ROBIN CHAT

60.10 CHORISTER ROBIN CHAT

60.11 WHITE-THROATED ROBIN CHAT

60.12 CAPE ROBIN CHAT

60.13 WHITE-BROWED ROBIN CHAT

60.14 GREY-WINGED ROBIN CHAT

60.15 SNOWY-CROWNED ROBIN CHAT

60.16 WHITE-HEADED ROBIN CHAT

61.1 AFRICAN REED WARBLER

243

61.2 EURASIAN REED WARBLER

61.3 MARSH WARBLER

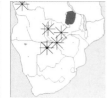

61.4 GREATER SWAMP WARBLER

61.5 GREAT REED WARBLER

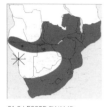

61.6 LESSER SWAMP WARBLER

61.7 BASRA REED WARBLER

61.8 SEDGE WARBLER

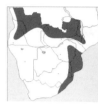

61.9 BROAD-TAILED WARBLER

61.10 EURASIAN RIVER WARBLER

61.11 KNYSNA WARBLER

61.12 VICTORIN'S WARBLER

61.13 BARRATT'S WARBLER

61.14 LITTLE RUSH WARBLER

61.15 EVERGREEN-FOREST WARBLER

61.16 CINNAMON BRACKEN WARBLER

61.17 BAMBOO WARBLER

61.18 ICTERINE WARBLER

61.19 OLIVE-TREE WARBLER

61.20 OLIVACEOUS WARBLER

62.1 YELLOW-THROATED WOODLAND WARBLER

Maps for species numbers 62.2 to 63.1

62.2 BURNT-NECKED EREMOMELA

62.3 GREEN-CAPPED EREMOMELA

62.4 YELLOW-BELLIED EREMOMELA

62.5 KAROO EREMOMELA

62.6 BLACK-NECKED EREMOMELA

62.7 RUFOUS-CROWNED EREMOMELA

62.8 RED-CAPPED CROMBEC

62.9 LONG-BILLED CROMBEC

62.10 WILLOW WARBLER

62.11 LAURA'S WOODLAND WARBLER

62.12 STIERLING'S BARRED WARBLER

62.13 BARRED WREN WARBLER

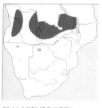

62.14 MIOMBO WREN WARBLER

62.15 GREEN-BACKED BLEATING WARBLER

62.16 GREY-BACKED BLEATING WARBLER

62.17 YELLOW-BROWED CAMAROPTERA

62.18 RED-FACED CROMBEC

62.19 GREEN CROMBEC

62.20 LEMON-BELLIED CROMBEC

63.1 BANDED PRINIA

245

Maps for species numbers 63.2 to 64.2

63.2 DRAKENSBERG PRINIA

63.3 SPOTTED PRINIA

63.4 TAWNY-FLANKED PRINIA

63.5 BLACK-CHESTED PRINIA

63.6 BRIAR WARBLER

63.7 WHITE-CHINNED PRINIA

63.8 FAIRY FLYCATCHER

63.9 GREEN HYLIA

63.10 RED-WINGED WARBLER

63.11 NAMAQUA WARBLER

63.12 RUFOUS-EARED WARBLER

63.13 CINNAMON-BREASTED WARBLER

63.14 AFRICAN YELLOW WARBLER

63.15 MOUNTAIN YELLOW WARBLER

63.16 PAPYRUS YELLOW WARBLER

63.17 MOUSTACHED GRASS WARBLER

63.18 ROCKRUNNER

63.19 CAPE GRASS WARBLER

64.1 NEDDICKY

64.2 SHORT-WINGED CISTICOLA

246

Maps for species numbers 64.3 to 65.2

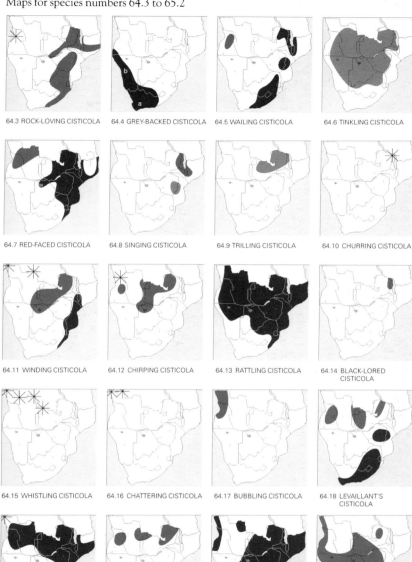

64.3 ROCK-LOVING CISTICOLA

64.4 GREY-BACKED CISTICOLA

64.5 WAILING CISTICOLA

64.6 TINKLING CISTICOLA

64.7 RED-FACED CISTICOLA

64.8 SINGING CISTICOLA

64.9 TRILLING CISTICOLA

64.10 CHURRING CISTICOLA

64.11 WINDING CISTICOLA

64.12 CHIRPING CISTICOLA

64.13 RATTLING CISTICOLA

64.14 BLACK-LORED CISTICOLA

64.15 WHISTLING CISTICOLA

64.16 CHATTERING CISTICOLA

64.17 BUBBLING CISTICOLA

64.18 LEVAILLANT'S CISTICOLA

64.19 CROAKING CISTICOLA

64.20 STOUT CISTICOLA

65.1 FAN-TAILED CISTICOLA

65.2 DESERT CISTICOLA

247

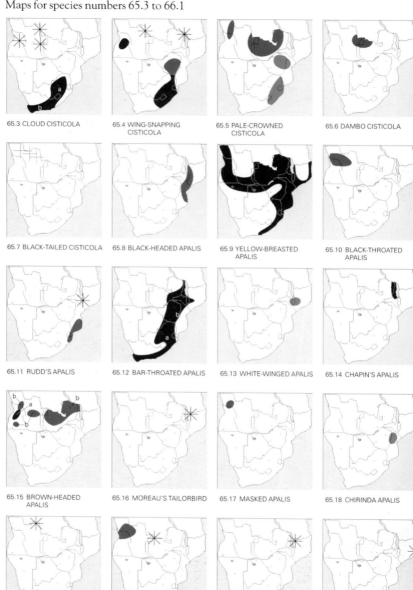

65.3 CLOUD CISTICOLA

65.4 WING-SNAPPING CISTICOLA

65.5 PALE-CROWNED CISTICOLA

65.6 DAMBO CISTICOLA

65.7 BLACK-TAILED CISTICOLA

65.8 BLACK-HEADED APALIS

65.9 YELLOW-BREASTED APALIS

65.10 BLACK-THROATED APALIS

65.11 RUDD'S APALIS

65.12 BAR-THROATED APALIS

65.13 WHITE-WINGED APALIS

65.14 CHAPIN'S APALIS

65.15 BROWN-HEADED APALIS

65.16 MOREAU'S TAILORBIRD

65.17 MASKED APALIS

65.18 CHIRINDA APALIS

65.19 GOSLING'S APALIS

65.20 BUFF-THROATED APALIS

65.21 AFRICAN TAILORBIRD

66.1 KRETSCHMER'S LONGBILL

Maps for species numbers 66.2 to 66.21

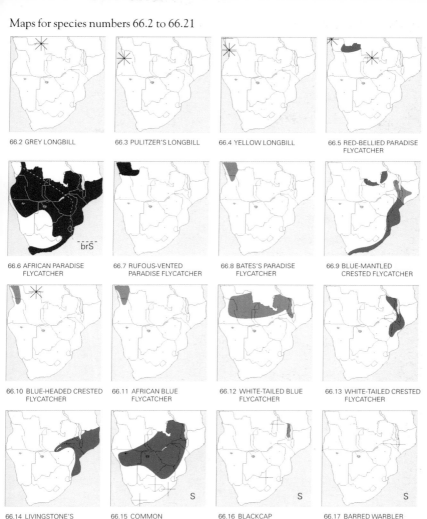

66.2 GREY LONGBILL

66.3 PULITZER'S LONGBILL

66.4 YELLOW LONGBILL

66.5 RED-BELLIED PARADISE FLYCATCHER

66.6 AFRICAN PARADISE FLYCATCHER

66.7 RUFOUS-VENTED PARADISE FLYCATCHER

66.8 BATES'S PARADISE FLYCATCHER

66.9 BLUE-MANTLED CRESTED FLYCATCHER

66.10 BLUE-HEADED CRESTED FLYCATCHER

66.11 AFRICAN BLUE FLYCATCHER

66.12 WHITE-TAILED BLUE FLYCATCHER

66.13 WHITE-TAILED CRESTED FLYCATCHER

66.14 LIVINGSTONE'S FLYCATCHER

66.15 COMMON WHITETHROAT

66.16 BLACKCAP

66.17 BARRED WARBLER

66.18 GARDEN WARBLER

66.19 LAYARD'S WARBLER

66.20 CHESTNUT-VENTED WARBLER

66.21 BROWN PARISOMA

249

Maps for species numbers 67.1 to 68.1

67.1 AFRICAN DUSKY
FLYCATCHER

67.2 ASHY FLYCATCHER

67.3 SPOTTED FLYCATCHER

67.4 CASSIN'S FLYCATCHER

67.5 SWAMP FLYCATCHER

67.6 DUSKY BLUE
FLYCATCHER

67.7 SOOTY FLYCATCHER

67.8 COLLARED FLYCATCHER

67.9 SOUTHERN BLACK
FLYCATCHER

67.10 GREY-THROATED TIT
FLYCATCHER

67.11 GREY TIT FLYCATCHER

67.12 BOEHM'S FLYCATCHER

67.13 FRASER'S FOREST
FLYCATCHER

67.14 FISCAL FLYCATCHER

67.15 CHAT FLYCATCHER

67.16 ANGOLA SLATY
FLYCATCHER

67.17 WHITE-EYED SLATY
FLYCATCHER

67.18 PALE FLYCATCHER

67.19 MARICO FLYCATCHER

68.1 YELLOW-BELLIED
HYLIOTA

250

Maps for species numbers 68.2 to 69.2

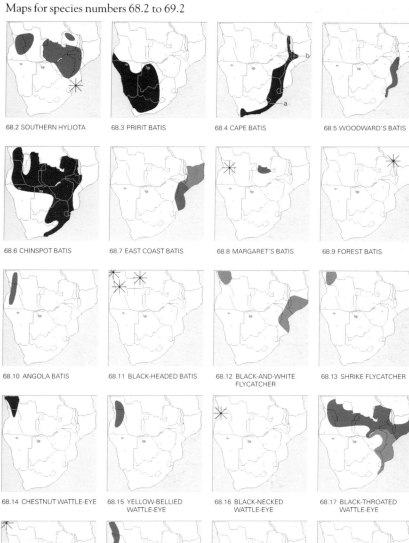

68.2 SOUTHERN HYLIOTA

68.3 PRIRIT BATIS

68.4 CAPE BATIS

68.5 WOODWARD'S BATIS

68.6 CHINSPOT BATIS

68.7 EAST COAST BATIS

68.8 MARGARET'S BATIS

68.9 FOREST BATIS

68.10 ANGOLA BATIS

68.11 BLACK-HEADED BATIS

68.12 BLACK-AND-WHITE FLYCATCHER

68.13 SHRIKE FLYCATCHER

68.14 CHESTNUT WATTLE-EYE

68.15 YELLOW-BELLIED WATTLE-EYE

68.16 BLACK-NECKED WATTLE-EYE

68.17 BLACK-THROATED WATTLE-EYE

68.18 BROWN-THROATED WATTLE-EYE

68.19 WHITE-FRONTED WATTLE-EYE

69.1 CAPE SUGARBIRD

69.2 GURNEY'S SUGARBIRD

Maps for species numbers 69.3 to 70.3

69.3 SPOTTED CREEPER

69.4 CAPE PENDULINE TIT

69.5 GREY PENDULINE TIT

69.6 TITHYLIA

69.7 MIOMBO GREY TIT

69.8 SOUTHERN GREY TIT

69.9 CINNAMON-BREASTED TIT

69.10 RUFOUS-BELLIED TIT

69.11 ASHY TIT

69.12 WHITE-WINGED BLACK TIT

69.13 CARP'S TIT

69.14 SOUTHERN BLACK TIT

69.15 DUSKY TIT

69.16 SCARLET-TUFTED MALACHITE SUNBIRD

69.17 YELLOW-TUFTED MALACHITE SUNBIRD

69.18 BRONZE SUNBIRD

69.19 BOCAGE'S SUNBIRD

70.1 GREY SUNBIRD

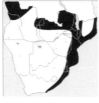

70.2 OLIVE SUNBIRD

70.3 REICHENBACH'S SUNBIRD

Maps for species numbers 70.4 to 71.3

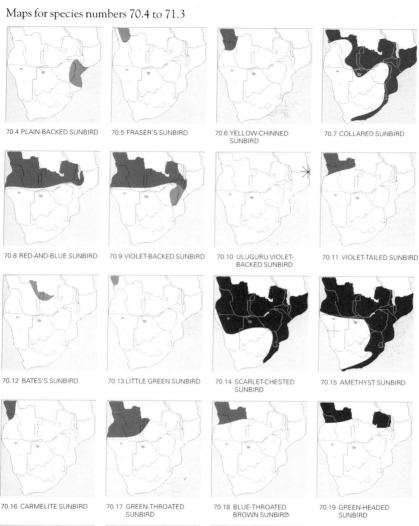

70.4 PLAIN-BACKED SUNBIRD

70.5 FRASER'S SUNBIRD

70.6 YELLOW-CHINNED SUNBIRD

70.7 COLLARED SUNBIRD

70.8 RED-AND-BLUE SUNBIRD

70.9 VIOLET-BACKED SUNBIRD

70.10 ULUGURU VIOLET-BACKED SUNBIRD

70.11 VIOLET-TAILED SUNBIRD

70.12 BATES'S SUNBIRD

70.13 LITTLE GREEN SUNBIRD

70.14 SCARLET-CHESTED SUNBIRD

70.15 AMETHYST SUNBIRD

70.16 CARMELITE SUNBIRD

70.17 GREEN-THROATED SUNBIRD

70.18 BLUE-THROATED BROWN SUNBIRD

70.19 GREEN-HEADED SUNBIRD

70.20 BANNERMANN'S SUNBIRD

71.1 ORANGE-BREASTED SUNBIRD

71.2 COPPERY SUNBIRD

71.3 YELLOW-BELLIED SUNBIRD

Maps for species numbers 71.4 to 72.4

71.4 WHITE-BELLIED SUNBIRD

71.5 GREATER DOUBLE-COLLARED SUNBIRD

71.6 SOUTHERN DOUBLE-COLLARED SUNBIRD

71.7 MIOMBO DOUBLE-COLLARED SUNBIRD

71.8 OLIVE-BELLIED SUNBIRD

71.9 EASTERN DOUBLE-COLLARED SUNBIRD

71.10 SUPERB SUNBIRD

71.11 OUSTALET'S WHITE-BELLIED SUNBIRD

71.12 DUSKY SUNBIRD

71.13 SHELLEY'S SUNBIRD

71.14 MARICO SUNBIRD

71.15 PURPLE-BANDED SUNBIRD

71.16 NEERGAARD'S SUNBIRD

71.17 ORANGE-TUFTED SUNBIRD

71.18 YELLOW WHITE-EYE

71.19 CAPE WHITE-EYE

72.1 GREY-GREEN BUSH SHRIKE

72.2 PERRIN'S BUSH SHRIKE

72.3 SOUTHERN BOUBOU

72.4 TROPICAL BOUBOU

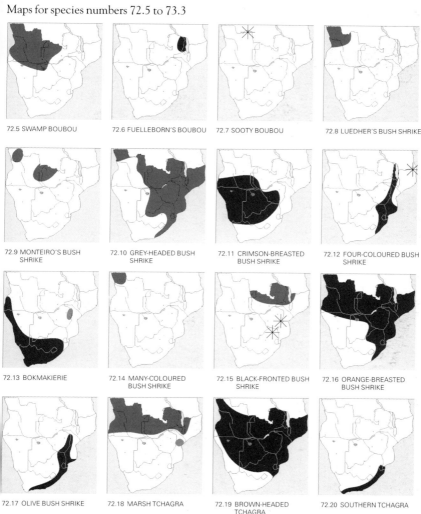

72.5 SWAMP BOUBOU

72.6 FUELLEBORN'S BOUBOU

72.7 SOOTY BOUBOU

72.8 LUEDHER'S BUSH SHRIKE

72.9 MONTEIRO'S BUSH SHRIKE

72.10 GREY-HEADED BUSH SHRIKE

72.11 CRIMSON-BREASTED BUSH SHRIKE

72.12 FOUR-COLOURED BUSH SHRIKE

72.13 BOKMAKIERIE

72.14 MANY-COLOURED BUSH SHRIKE

72.15 BLACK-FRONTED BUSH SHRIKE

72.16 ORANGE-BREASTED BUSH SHRIKE

72.17 OLIVE BUSH SHRIKE

72.18 MARSH TCHAGRA

72.19 BROWN-HEADED TCHAGRA

72.20 SOUTHERN TCHAGRA

72.21 BLACK-CROWNED TCHAGRA

73.1 BLACK-SHOULDERED PUFFBACK

73.2 SOUTHERN PUFFBACK

73.3 PINK-FOOTED PUFFBACK

Maps for species numbers 73.4 to 74.4

73.4 BRUBRU

73.5 WHITE-TAILED SHRIKE

73.6 MAGPIE SHRIKE

73.7 WHITE HELMET SHRIKE

73.8 CHESTNUT-FRONTED HELMUT SHRIKE

73.9 RETZ'S RED-BILLED HELMET SHRIKE

73.10 GABELA HELMET SHRIKE

73.11 BLACK-COLLARED BULBUL SHRIKE

73.12 SOUTHERN WHITE-CROWNED SHRIKE

73.13 RED-BACKED SHRIKE

73.14 SOUZA'S SHRIKE

73.15 ISABELLINE SHRIKE

73.16 FISCAL SHRIKE

73.17 MACKINNON'S SHRIKE

73.18 LESSER GREY SHRIKE

73.19 WOODCHAT SHRIKE

74.1 EUROPEAN STARLING

74.2 PIED STARLING

74.3 WATTLED STARLING

74.4 COMMON MYNA

Maps for species numbers 74.5 to 75.4

74.5 WHITE-WINGED STARLING

74.6 PALE-WINGED STARLING

74.7 RED-WINGED STARLING

74.8 WALLER'S RED-WINGED STARLING

74.9 SLENDER-BILLED CHESTNUT-WINGED STARLING

74.10 FOREST CHESTNUT-WINGED STARLING

74.11 VIOLET-BACKED STARLING

brS

74.12 NARROW-TAILED STARLING

74.13 GREATER BLUE-EARED STARLING

74.14 LESSER BLUE-EARED STARLING

74.15 CAPE GLOSSY STARLING

74.16 BLACK-BELLIED GLOSSY STARLING

74.17 SHARP-TAILED STARLING

74.18 SOUTHERN LONG-TAILED STARLING

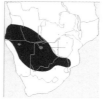

74.19 BURCHELL'S STARLING

(brS)

74.20 SPLENDID GLOSSY STARLING

S

75.1 RED-THROATED PIPIT

75.2 PLAIN-BACKED PIPIT

brS

75.3 MOUNTAIN PIPIT

75.4 JACKSON'S PIPIT

257

Maps for species numbers 75.5 to 76.7

75.5 GRASSVELD PIPIT

75.6 WOOD PIPIT

75.7 LONG-BILLED PIPIT

75.8 TREE PIPIT

75.9 STRIPED PIPIT

75.10 YELLOW-BREASTED PIPIT

75.11 LONG-LEGGED PIPIT

75.12 BUFFY PIPIT

75.13 AFRICAN ROCK PIPIT

75.14 SHORT-TAILED PIPIT

75.15 BUSH PIPIT

75.16 RED-BILLED OXPECKER

75.17 YELLOW-BILLED OXPECKER

76.1 GOLDEN PIPIT

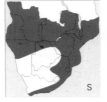

76.2 YELLOW WAGTAIL

76.3 CAPE WAGTAIL

76.4 GREY WAGTAIL

76.5 MOUNTAIN WAGTAIL

76.6 AFRICAN PIED WAGTAIL

76.7 WHITE WAGTAIL

Maps for species numbers 76.8 to 77.11

76.8 ROSY-BREASTED LONGCLAW

76.9 CAPE LONGCLAW

76.10 YELLOW-THROATED LONGCLAW

76.11 GRIMWOOD'S LONGCLAW

76.12 FUELLEBORN'S LONGCLAW

76.13 CHESTNUT-BACKED SPARROW LARK

76.14 GREY-BACKED SPARROW LARK

76.15 FISCHER'S SPARROW LARK

76.16 BLACK-EARED SPARROW LARK

77.1 GREY-HEADED SPARROW

77.2 SOUTHERN GREY-HEADED SPARROW

77.3 SWAHILI SPARROW

77.4 RUFOUS SPARROW

77.5 HOUSE SPARROW

77.6 CAPE SPARROW

77.7 CHAFFINCH

77.8 YELLOW-THROATED PETRONIA

77.9 WHITE-BROWED SPARROW WEAVER

77.10 CHESTNUT-MANTLED SPARROW WEAVER

77.11 RED-BILLED BUFFALO WEAVER

77.12 THICK-BILLED WEAVER

77.13 SOCIABLE WEAVER

77.14 ORIOLE FINCH

77.15 CABANIS'S BUNTING

77.16 CINNAMON-BREASTED ROCK BUNTING

77.17 LARK-LIKE BUNTING

77.18 CAPE BUNTING

77.19 GOLDEN-BREASTED BUNTING

78.1 LONG-TAILED WHYDAH

78.2 MOUNTAIN MARSH WHYDAH

78.3 RED-COLLARED WHYDAH

78.4 YELLOW-MANTLED WHYDAH

78.5 WHITE-WINGED WHYDAH

78.6 MARSH WHYDAH

78.7 RED-SHOULDERED WHYDAH

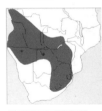

78.8 YELLOW-CROWNED BISHOP

78.9 YELLOW BISHOP

78.10 BLACK BISHOP

78.11 GOLDEN-BACKED BISHOP

78.12 ZANZIBAR RED BISHOP

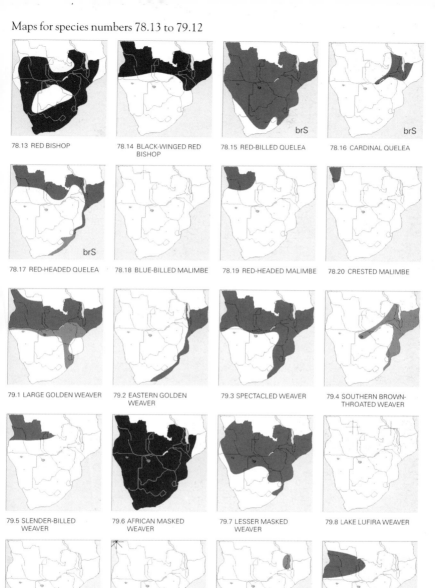

78.13 RED BISHOP

78.14 BLACK-WINGED RED BISHOP

78.15 RED-BILLED QUELEA

78.16 CARDINAL QUELEA

78.17 RED-HEADED QUELEA

78.18 BLUE-BILLED MALIMBE

78.19 RED-HEADED MALIMBE

78.20 CRESTED MALIMBE

79.1 LARGE GOLDEN WEAVER

79.2 EASTERN GOLDEN WEAVER

79.3 SPECTACLED WEAVER

79.4 SOUTHERN BROWN-THROATED WEAVER

79.5 SLENDER-BILLED WEAVER

79.6 AFRICAN MASKED WEAVER

79.7 LESSER MASKED WEAVER

79.8 LAKE LUFIRA WEAVER

79.9 CAPE WEAVER

79.10 ORANGE WEAVER

79.11 OLIVE-HEADED WEAVER

79.12 BOCAGE'S WEAVER

Maps for species numbers 79.13 to 80.12

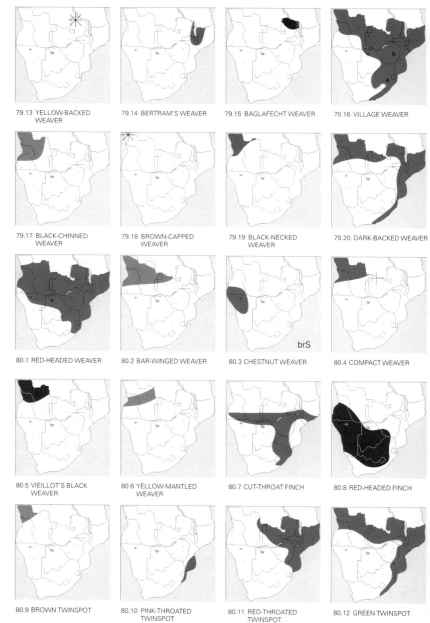

79.13 YELLOW-BACKED WEAVER

79.14 BERTRAM'S WEAVER

79.15 BAGLAFECHT WEAVER

79.16 VILLAGE WEAVER

79.17 BLACK-CHINNED WEAVER

79.18 BROWN-CAPPED WEAVER

79.19 BLACK-NECKED WEAVER

79.20 DARK-BACKED WEAVER

80.1 RED-HEADED WEAVER

80.2 BAR-WINGED WEAVER

80.3 CHESTNUT WEAVER

80.4 COMPACT WEAVER

80.5 VIEILLOT'S BLACK WEAVER

80.6 YELLOW-MANTLED WEAVER

80.7 CUT-THROAT FINCH

80.8 RED-HEADED FINCH

80.9 BROWN TWINSPOT

80.10 PINK-THROATED TWINSPOT

80.11 RED-THROATED TWINSPOT

80.12 GREEN TWINSPOT

Maps for species numbers 80.13 to 81.13

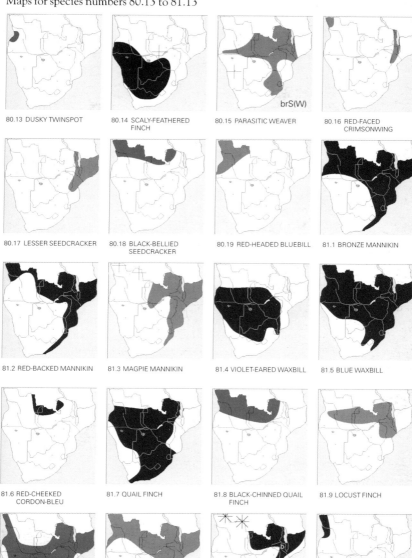

80.13 DUSKY TWINSPOT

80.14 SCALY-FEATHERED FINCH

80.15 PARASITIC WEAVER

brS(W)

80.16 RED-FACED CRIMSONWING

80.17 LESSER SEEDCRACKER

80.18 BLACK-BELLIED SEEDCRACKER

80.19 RED-HEADED BLUEBILL

81.1 BRONZE MANNIKIN

81.2 RED-BACKED MANNIKIN

81.3 MAGPIE MANNIKIN

81.4 VIOLET-EARED WAXBILL

81.5 BLUE WAXBILL

81.6 RED-CHEEKED CORDON-BLEU

81.7 QUAIL FINCH

81.8 BLACK-CHINNED QUAIL FINCH

81.9 LOCUST FINCH

81.10 MELBA FINCH

81.11 ORANGE-WINGED FINCH

81.12 BLUE-BILLED FIREFINCH

81.13 PALE-BILLED FIREFINCH

263

Maps for species numbers 81.14 to 82.13

81.14 JAMESON'S FIREFINCH

81.15 RED-BILLED FIREFINCH

81.16 BROWN FIREFINCH

81.17 GREY-CROWNED BLACKFINCH

81.18 PALE-FRONTED BLACKFINCH

81.19 CHESTNUT-BREASTED BLACKFINCH

81.20 WHITE-BREASTED BLACKFINCH

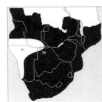

82.1 PIN-TAILED WIDOW

82.2 SHAFT-TAILED WIDOW

82.3 LONG-TAILED PARADISE WIDOW

82.4 BROAD-TAILED PARADISE WIDOW

82.5 DUSKY INDIGOBIRD

82.6 PURPLE INDIGOBIRD

82.7 VILLAGE INDIGOBIRD

82.8 BAR-BREASTED INDIGOBIRD

82.9 PETER'S TWINSPOT INDIGOBIRD

82.10 BLACK-FACED WAXBILL

82.11 BLACK-HEADED WAXBILL

82.12 CRIMSON-RUMPED WAXBILL

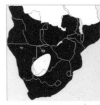

82.13 COMMON WAXBILL

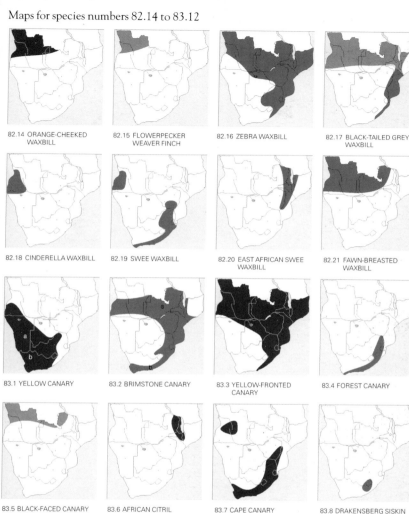

82.14 ORANGE-CHEEKED WAXBILL

82.15 FLOWERPECKER WEAVER FINCH

82.16 ZEBRA WAXBILL

82.17 BLACK-TAILED GREY WAXBILL

82.18 CINDERELLA WAXBILL

82.19 SWEE WAXBILL

82.20 EAST AFRICAN SWEE WAXBILL

82.21 FAWN-BREASTED WAXBILL

83.1 YELLOW CANARY

83.2 BRIMSTONE CANARY

83.3 YELLOW-FRONTED CANARY

83.4 FOREST CANARY

83.5 BLACK-FACED CANARY

83.6 AFRICAN CITRIL

83.7 CAPE CANARY

83.8 DRAKENSBERG SISKIN

83.9 CAPE SISKIN

83.10 LEMON-BREASTED CANARY

83.11 STREAKY SEEDEATER

83.12 BLACK-THROATED CANARY

Maps for species numbers 83.13 to 84

83.13 WHITE-THROATED
CANARY

83.14 THICK-BILLED
SEEDEATER

83.15 PROTEA CANARY

83.16 STREAKY-HEADED
SEEDEATER

83.17 STRIPE-BREASTED
SEEDEATER

83.18 BLACK-EARED
SEEDEATER

83.19 BLACK-HEADED
CANARY

84   ALL SPECIES ON PLATE 84

APPENDIX

The following appendix gives the Portuguese and Afrikaans names (where available) for every bird species mentioned in the plates. The Portuguese name is given in the middle column, and the Afrikaans name in the right-hand column. As in the main text the alternative English names, as used in other Southern African field guides, appear in brackets in lower-case type. Many birds that have not previously had an official name in Portuguese appear here for the first time in that language.

Plate 1

1	WANDERING ALBATROSS	Albatroz-viageiro	Grootmalmok
2	ROYAL ALBATROSS	Albatroz-real	Koningmalmok
3	SHY ALBATROSS	Albatroz-de-barrete-branco	Bloubekmalmok
4	YELLOW-NOSED ALBATROSS	Albatroz-de-bico-amarelo	Geelneusmalmok
5	BLACK-BROWED ALBATROSS	Albatroz-olheirudo	Swartrugmalmok
6	SOOTY ALBATROSS	Albatroz-sombrio	Bruinmalmok
7	LIGHT-MANTLED SOOTY ALBATROSS	Albatroz-de-dorso-cinzento	Swartkopmalmok
8	GREY-HEADED ALBATROSS	Albatroz-de-cabeça-cinzenta	Gryskopmalmok
9	LAYSAN ALBATROSS	Albatroz de Laysan	Laysanse Malmok
10	SOUTHERN GIANT PETREL	Fulmar-antárctico	Reusenellie
11	NORTHERN GIANT PETREL	Fulmar-subantárctico	Grootnellie
12	BULLER'S ALBATROSS	Albatroz de Buller	

Plate 2

1	WHITE-CHINNED PETREL	Painho-de-queixo-branco	Bassiaan
2	GREY PETREL	Painho-cinzento	Pediunker
3	FLESH-FOOTED SHEARWATER	Pardela-de-patas-rosadas	Bruinpylstormvoël
4	AUDUBON'S SHEARWATER	Pardela de Audubon	Swartkroonpylstormvoël
5	MANX SHEARWATER	Pardela-sombria	Swartbekpylstormvoël
6	LITTLE SHEARWATER	Pardela-pequena	Kleinpylstormvoël
7	WEDGE-TAILED SHEARWATER	Pardela do Pacífico	Keilstertpylstormvoël
8	SOOTY SHEARWATER	Pardela-preta	Malbaatjie
9	GREAT SHEARWATER	Pardela-grande	Grootpylstormvoël
10	CORY'S SHEARWATER	Cagarra	Geelbekpylstormvoël
11	WHITE-FACED SHEARWATER	Cagarra-de-faces-brancas	

Plate 3

1	ATLANTIC PETREL	Freira de Schlegel	Bruinvlerkstormvoël
2	GREAT-WINGED PETREL	Freira-de-asas-grandes	Langvlerkstormvoël
3	KERGUELEN PETREL	Freira das Kerguelen	Kergeulense Stormvoël
4	WHITE-HEADED PETREL	Freira-de-cabeça-branca	Witkopstormvoël
5	SOFT-PLUMAGED PETREL	Freira-meridional	Donsveerstormvoël
6	PINTADO PETREL (or Cape Pigeon)	Pardela do Cabo	Seeduifstormvoël
7	BULWER'S PETREL	Alma-negra	Bulwerse Stormvoël
8	JOUANIN'S PETREL	Alma-negra-arábica	Jouaninse Stormvoël
9	ANTARCTIC FULMAR	Fulmar-meridional	Silwerstormvoël
10	ANTARCTIC PETREL	Pardela-antárctica	Antarktiese Stormvoël
11	BLUE PETREL	Pardela-azul	Bloustormvoël

Plate 4

1	BROAD-BILLED PRION	Pato-petrel-de-bico-grosso	Breëbekwalvisvoël
2	SLENDER-BILLED PRION	Pato-petrel-de-bico-fino	Dunbekwalvisvoël
3	ANTARCTIC (or Dove) PRION	Pato-petrel-antárctico	Antarktiese Walvisvoël
4	FAIRY PRION	Pato-petrel-de-bico-longo	Swartstertwalvisvoël
5	BRITISH (or European) STORM PETREL	Painho-de-cauda-quadrada	Swartpootstormswael
6	WILSON'S STORM PETREL	Painho-casquilho	Geelpootstormswael
7	LEACH'S STORM PETREL	Painho-de-cauda-forcada	Swaelstertstormswael
8	MATSUDAIRA'S STORM PETREL	Painho de Matsudaira	Matsuidairase Stormvoël
9	BLACK-BELLIED STORM PETREL	Painho-de-ventre-preto	Swartstreepstormswael
10	WHITE-BELLIED STORM PETREL	Painho-de-ventre-branco	Witpensstormswael
11	WHITE-FACED STORM PETREL	Painho-de-faces-brancas	Witgesigstormswael

Plate 5

1	ASCENCION FRIGATEBIRD	Fragata de Ascensão	Ascensionse Fregatvoël
2	GREATER FRIGATEBIRD	Fragata-grande	Fregatvoël
3	LESSER FRIGATEBIRD	Fragata-pequena	Klein Fregatvoël
4	CAPE GANNET	Alcatraz do Cabo	Witmalgas
5	AUSTRALIAN GANNET	Alcatraz-australiano	Australiese Malgas
6	MASKED BOOBY	Alcatraz-mascarado	Brilmalgas
7	BROWN BOOBY	Alcatraz-pardo	Bruinmalgas
8	RED-FOOTED BOOBY	Alcatraz-de-patas-vermelhas	Rooipootmalgas

Plate 6

1	AFRICAN FINFOOT	Pés-de-barbatana	Watertrapper
2	GREAT CRESTED GREBE	Mergulhão-de-crista	Kuifkopdobbertjie
3	BLACK-NECKED GREBE	Mergulhão-de-pescoço-preto	Swartnekdobbertjie
4	LITTLE GREBE (or Dabchick)	Mergulhão-pequeno	Kleindobbertjie
5	GREATER SHEATHBILL	Bico-de-bainha-de-faces-brancas	Grootkokerbek
6	JACKASS PENGUIN	Pinguim do Cabo	Brilpikkewyn
7	KING PENGUIN	Pinguim-real	Koningspikkewyn
8	ROCKHOPPER PENGUIN	Pinguim-das-rochas	Geelkuifpikkewyn
9	MACARONI PENGUIN	Pinguim-de-tufos-dourados	Macaronipikkewyn
10	GENTOO PENGUIN	Pinguim-papua	

Plate 7

1	RED-TAILED TROPICBIRD	Rabo-de-palha-de-cauda-vermelha	Rooipylstert
2	RED-BILLED TROPICBIRD	Rabo-de-palha-de-bico-vermelho	Rooibekpylstert
3	WHITE-TAILED TROPICBIRD	Rabo-de-palha-de-bico-amarelo	Witpylstert
4	CAPE CORMORANT	Corvo-marinho do Cabo	Trekduiker
5	BANK CORMORANT	Corvo-marinho-dos-bancos	Bankduiker
6	GREAT (or White-breasted) CORMORANT	Corvo-marinho-de-faces-brancas	Witborsduiker

7	CROWNED CORMORANT	Corvo-marinho-coroado	Kuifkopduiker
8	LONG-TAILED (or Reed) CORMORANT	Corvo-marinho-africano	Rietduiker
9	DARTER	Mergulhão-serpente	Slanghalsvoël

Plate 8

1	GREATER FLAMINGO	Flamingo-comum	Grootflamink
2	LESSER FLAMINGO	Flamingo-pequeno	Kleinflamink
3	GREY HERON	Garça-real	Bloureier
4	PURPLE HERON	Garça-vermelha	Rooireier
5	GOLIATH HERON	Garça-gigante	Reusereier
6	BLACK-HEADED HERON	Garça-de-cabeça-preta	Swartkopreier
7	SHOEBILL	Bico-de-sapato	Skoenbekooievaar
8	GREAT (or Eastern) WHITE PELICAN	Pelicano-branco	Witpelikaan
9	PINK-BACKED PELICAN	Pelicano-rosado	Kleinpelikaan

Plate 9

1	SQUACCO HERON	Papa-ratos-comum	Ralreier
2	MALAGASY POND HERON	Papa-ratos-branco	Malgassiese Ralreier
3	RUFOUS-BELLIED HERON	Garça-de-barriga-vermelha	Rooipensreier
4	WHITE-BACKED NIGHT HERON	Garça-de-dorso-branco	Witrugnagreier
5	BLACK-CROWNED NIGHT HERON	Garça-nocturna	Gewone Nagreier
6	LITTLE BITTERN	Garçote-comum	Woudapie
7	GREEN-BACKED HERON	Papa-ratos-africano	Groenrugreier
8	DWARF BITTERN	Garçote-anão	Dwergrietreier
9	BITTERN	Abetouro-comum	Grootrietreier
10	WHITE-CRESTED TIGER HERON	Garça-tigre-africana	
11	BLACK EGRET	Garça-negra	Swartreier
12	SLATY EGRET	Garça-de-garganta-vermelha	Rooikeelreier
13	GREAT (White) EGRET	Garça-branca-grande	Grootwitreier
14	CATTLE EGRET	Garça-boieira	Veereier
15	LITTLE BLUE HERON	Garça-azul	
16	LITTLE EGRET	Garça-branca-pequena	Kleinwitreier
17	YELLOW-BILLED EGRET	Garça-de-bico-amarelo	Geelbekwitreier

Plate 10

1	BLACK STORK	Cegonha-preta	Grootswartooievaar
2	ABDIM'S STORK	Cegonha de Abdim	Kleinswartooievaar/ Blouwangooievaar
3	WHITE STORK	Cegonha-branca	Witooievaar
4	MARABOU STORK	Marabu	Maraboe Ooievaar
5	WOOLLY-NECKED STORK	Cegonha-de-pescoço-lanudo	Wolnekooievaar
6	AFRICAN OPEN-BILLED STORK	Cegonha-de-bico-aberto	Oopbekooievaar
7	YELLOW-BILLED STORK	Cegonha-de-bico-amarelo	Nimmersat
8	SADDLE-BILLED STORK	Jabirú-africano	Saalbekooievaar
9	AFRICAN SPOONBILL	Colhereiro-africano	Lepelaar

10	(Southern) BALD IBIS	Ibis-calvo	Kalkoenibis
11	HADADA	Ibis Hadada	Hadeda
12	SPOT-BREASTED IBIS	Ibis-malhado	
13	GLOSSY IBIS	Ibis-preto	Glansibis
14	SACRED IBIS	Ibis-sagrado	Skoorsteenveër
15	HAMERKOP	Pássaro-martelo	Hamerkop

Plate 11

1	SPUR-WINGED GOOSE	Ganso-esporado	Wildemakou
2	EGYPTIAN GOOSE	Ganso do Egipto	Kolgans
3	SOUTH-AFRICAN SHELDUCK	Tadorna-africana	Kopereend
4	KNOB-BILLED DUCK	Pato-de-crista	Knobbeleend
5	WHITE-BACKED DUCK	Pato-de-dorso-branco	Witrugeend
6	AFRICAN PYGMY GOOSE	Ganso-anão-africano	Dwerggans
7	SOUTHERN POCHARD	Zarro-africano	Bruineend
8	MACCOA DUCK	Pato-de-rabo-alçado-africano	Bloubekeend
9	HARTLAUB'S DUCK	Pato de Hartlaub	Hartlaubse Eend
10	TUFTED DUCK	Zarro-negrinha	
11	RINGED TEAL	Pato-de-colar	

Plate 12

1	WHITE-FACED WHISTLING DUCK	Pato-assobiador-de-faces-brancas	Nonnetjie-eend
2	FULVOUS WHISTLING DUCK	Pato-assobiador-de-peito-amarelo	Fluiteend
3	YELLOW-BILLED DUCK	Pato-de-bico-amarelo	Geelbekeend
4	AFRICAN BLACK DUCK	Pato-preto-africano	Swarteend
5	MALLARD	Pato-real	Mallard
6	CAPE SHOVELER	Pato-trombeteiro do Cabo	Kaapse Slopeend
7	NORTHERN (or European) SHOVELER	Pato-trombeteiro-europeu	Europese Slopeend
8	GARGANEY	Marreco	Somereend
9	CAPE TEAL	Marrequinho do Cabo	Teeleend
10	HOTTENTOT TEAL	Marrequinho-hotentote	Gevlekte Eend
11	RED-BILLED TEAL	Marrequinho-de-bico-vermelho	Rooibekeend
12	NORTHERN PINTAIL	Arrabio	Pylsterteend

Plate 13

1	PALE CHANTING GOSHAWK	Açor-cantor-pálido	Bleeksingvalk
2	DARK CHANTING GOSHAWK	Açor-cantor-escuro	Donkersingvalk
3	GABAR GOSHAWK	Gavião-gabar	Kleinsingvalk
4	SHIKRA (or Little Banded Goshawk)	Gavião-shikra	Gebande Sperwer
5	AFRICAN GOSHAWK	Açor-africano	Afrikaanse Sperwer
6	AFRICAN LITTLE SPARROWHAWK	Gavião-pequeno	Kleinsperwer
7	OVAMBO SPARROWHAWK	Gavião de Ovambo	Ovambosperwer
8	BLACK SPARROWHAWK	Açor-preto	Swartsperwer
9	RUFOUS-CHESTED (or Red-breasted) SPARROWHAWK	Gavião-de-peito-vermelho	Rooiborssperwer
10	RED-THIGHED SPARROWHAWK	Gavião de Hartlaub	

Plate 14

1	AFRICAN MARSH HARRIER	Tartaranhão-dos-pauis-africano	Afrikaanse Vleivalk
2	NORTHERN (or European) MARSH HARRIER	Tartaranhão-ruivo-dos-pauis	Europese Vleivalk
3	BLACK HARRIER	Tartaranhão-preto	Swartvleivalk
4	MONTAGU'S HARRIER	Tartaranhão-caçador	Blouvleivalk
5	PALLID HARRIER	Tartaranhão-pálido	Vaalvleivalk
6	BLACK-SHOULDERED KITE	Peneireiro-cinzento	Blouvalk
7	GYMNOGENE	Serpentário-pequeno	Kaalwangvalk
8	YELLOW-BILLED KITE	Milhafre-preto-africano	Geelbekwou
9	BLACK KITE	Milhafre-preto	Swartwou

Plate 15

1	AFRICAN CUCKOO HAWK	Falcão-cuco	Koekoekvalk
2	LIZARD BUZZARD	Mioto-papa-lagartos	Akkedisvalk
3	HONEY BUZZARD	Bútio-vespeiro	Wespedief
4	AUGUR BUZZARD	Bútio-augur	Witborsjakkalsvoël
5	STEPPE BUZZARD	Bútio-das-estepes	Bruinjakkalsvoël
6	JACKALL BUZZARD	Bútio-augur-meridional	Rooiborsjakkalsvoël
7	MOUNTAIN BUZZARD	Bútio-da-montanha	Bergjakkalsvoël
8	RED-NECKED BUZZARD	Bútio-africano	Rooinekjakkalsvoël
9	LONG-LEGGED BUZZARD	Bútio-mouro	Langbeenjakkalsvoël

Plate 16

1	AFRICAN FISH EAGLE	Águia-pesqueira-africana	Visarend
2	OSPREY	Águia-pesqueira	Visvalk
3	LONG-CRESTED EAGLE	Águia-de-poupa	Langkuifarend
4	AFRICAN HAWK EAGLE	Águia-açor-africana	Grootjagarend
5	AYRES'S HAWK EAGLE	Águia de Ayres	Kleinjagarend
6	BOOTED EAGLE	Águia-calçada	Dwergarend
7	CASSIN'S HAWK EAGLE	Águia de Cassin	

Plate 17

1	BATELEUR	Águia-bailarina	Berghaan
2	BROWN SNAKE EAGLE	Águia-cobreira-escura	Bruinslangarend
3	SMALLER (or Western) BANDED SNAKE EAGLE	Águia-cobreira-de-cauda-branca	Enkelbandslangarend
4	SOUTHERN BANDED SNAKE EAGLE	Águia-cobreira-barrada	Dubbelbandslangarend
5	BLACK-BREASTED SNAKE EAGLE	Águia-cobreira-de-peito-escuro	Swartborsslangarend
6	CONGO SERPENT EAGLE	Águia-cobreira-congolesa	

Plate 18

1	VERREAUX'S EAGLE	Águia de Verreaux	Witkruisarend
2	STEPPE EAGLE	Águia-das-estepes	Steppe-arend
3	TAWNY EAGLE	Águia-das-savanas	Roofarend
4	LESSER SPOTTED EAGLE	Águia-pomarina	Gevlekte Arend
5	WAHLBERG'S EAGLE	Águia de Wahlberg	Bruinarend
6	GREATER SPOTTED EAGLE	Águia-gritadeira	Groot Gevlekte Arend

Plate 19

1	PALM-NUT VULTURE	Abutre-das-palmeiras	Witaasvoël
2	EGYPTIAN VULTURE	Abutre do Egipto	Egiptiese Aasvoël
3	LAMMERGEIER (or Bearded Vulture)	Quebra-ossos	Lammergeier
4	MARTIAL EAGLE	Águia-marcial	Breëkoparend
5	CROWNED EAGLE	Águia-coroada	Kroonarend

Plate 20

1	LAPPET-FACED VULTURE	Abutre-real	Swartaasvoël
2	WHITE-HEADED VULTURE	Abutre-de-cabeça-branca	Witkopaasvoël
3	HOODED VULTURE	Abutre-de-capuz	Monnikaasvoël
4	CAPE VULTURE	Grifo do Cabo	Kransaasvoël
5	AFRICAN WHITE-BACKED VULTURE	Grifo-de-dorso-branco	Witrugaasvoël

Plate 21

1	BAT HAWK	Falcão-morcegueiro	Vlermuisvalk
2	TAITA FALCON	Falcão de Taita	Teitavalk
3	PEREGRINE FALCON	Falcão-peregrino	Swerfvalk
4	LANNER FALCON	Alfaneque	Edelvalk
5	RED-NECKED FALCON	Falcão-de-nuca-vermelha	Rooinekvalk
6	ELEONORA'S FALCON	Falcão-da-rainha	Eleonoravalk
7	(European) HOBBY	Ógea-europeu	Europese Boomvalk
8	AFRICAN HOBBY	Ógea-africano	Afrikaanse Boomvalk

Plate 22

1	DICKINSON'S KESTREL	Falcão de Dickinson	Dickonsonse Valk
2	GREY KESTREL	Falcão-cinzento	Donkergrysvalk
3	SOOTY FALCON	Falcão-sombrio	Roetvalk
4	EASTERN RED-FOOTED FALCON	Falcão de Amur	Oostelike Rooipootvalk
5	(Western) RED-FOOTED FALCON	Falcão-de-pés-vermelhos	Westelike Rooipootvalk
6	GREATER KESTREL	Peneireiro-de-olho-branco	Grootrooivalk
7	LESSER KESTREL	Peneireiro-das-torres	Kleinrooivalk
8	COMMON (or Rock) KESTREL	Peneireiro-vulgar	Kransvalk
9	PYGMY FALCON	Falcão-pigmeu	Dwergvalk

Plate 23

1	RED-NECKED FRANCOLIN	Francolim-de-garganta-vermelha	Rooikeelfisant
2	SWAINSON'S FRANCOLIN	Francolim de Swainson	Bosveldfisant
3	RED-BILLED FRANCOLIN	Francolim-de-bico-vermelho	Rooibekfisant
4	NATAL FRANCOLIN	Francolim de Natal	Natalse Fisant
5	CAPE FRANCOLIN	Francolim do Cabo	Kaapse Fisant
6	ORANGE RIVER FRANCOLIN	Francolim de Orange	Kalaharipatrys
7	REDWING FRANCOLIN	Francolim-de-asas-vermelhas	Rooivlerkpatrys
8	GREYWING FRANCOLIN	Francolim-de-asas-cinzentas	Bergpatrys
9	SHELLEY'S FRANCOLIN	Francolim de Shelley	Laeveldpatrys
10	FINSCH'S FRANCOLIN	Francolim de Finsch	

11	CRESTED FRANCOLIN	Francolim-de-poupa	Bospatrys
12	WHITE-THROATED FRANCOLIN	Francolim-de-garganta-branca	
13	HARTLAUB'S FRANCOLIN	Francolim de Hartlaub	Klipfisant
14	COQUI FRANCOLIN	Francolim-coqui	Swempie
15	HILDEBRANDT'S FRANCOLIN	Francolim de Hildebrandt	
16	GREY-STRIPED FRANCOLIN	Francolim-de-estrias-cinzentas	
17	SCALY FRANCOLIN	Francolim-escamado	
18	SWIERSTRA'S FRANCOLIN	Francolim de Swierstra	
19	CHUKAR	Perdiz-chucar	Asiatiese Patrys

Plate 24

1	AFRICAN WATER RAIL	Frango-de-água-azul	Grootriethaan
2	BLACK CRAKE	Franga-de-água-preta	Swartriethaan
3	ALLEN'S (or Lesser) GALLINULE	Caimão de Allen	Kleinkoningriethaan
4	(American) PURPLE GALLINULE	Caimão-americano	Amerikaanse Koningriethaan
5	PURPLE SWAMPHEN (or Gallinule)	Caimão-comum	Koningriethaan
6	LESSER MOORHEN	Galinha-de-água-pequena	Kleinwaterhoender
7	COMMON MOORHEN	Galinha-de-água-comum	Grootwaterhoender
8	RED-KNOBBED COOT	Galeirão-de-crista	Bleshoender
9	STRIPED CRAKE	Franga-de-água-estriada	Gestreepte Riethaan
10	SPOTTED CRAKE	Franga-de-água-grande	Gevlekte Riethaan
11	BAILLON'S CRAKE	Franga-de-água-pequena	Kleinriethaan
12	LITTLE CRAKE	Franga-de-água-bastarda	
13	AFRICAN CRAKE	Codornizão-africano	Afrikaanse Riethaan
14	CORNCRAKE	Codornizão-europeu	Kwartelkoning
15	CRESTED GUINEAFOWL	Fraca-de-crista	Kuifkoptarentaal
16	HELMETED GUINEAFOWL	Fraca da Guiné	Gewone Tarentaal

Plate 25

1	AFRICAN BLUE QUAIL	Codorniz-azul	Bloukwartel
2	HARLEQUIN QUAIL	Codorniz-arlequim	Bontkwartel
3	COMMON QUAIL	Codorniz-comum	Afrikaanse Kwartel
4	BLACK-RUMPED BUTTON-QUAIL	Toirão-hotentote	Kaapse Kwarteltjie
5	LITTLE (or Kurrichane) BUTTON-QUAIL	Toirão-comum	Bosveldkwarteltjie
6	CHESTNUT-HEADED FLUFFTAIL	Frango-de-água-de-cabeça-vermelha	Langtoonvleikuiken
7	BOEHM'S (or Streaky-breasted) FLUFFTAIL	Frango-de-água de Boehm	Streepborsvleikuiken
8	RED-CHESTED FLUFFTAIL	Frango-de-água-de-peito-vermelho	Rooiborsvleikuiken
9	STRIPED FLUFFTAIL	Frango-de-água-estriada	Gestreepte Vleikuiken
10	WHITE-SPOTTED FLUFFTAIL	Frango-de-água-mosqueada	
11	BUFF-SPOTTED FLUFFTAIL	Frango-de-água-elegante	Gevlekte Vleikuiken
12	WHITE-WINGED FLUFFTAIL	Frango-de-água-de-asa-branca	Witvlerkvleikuiken
13	AFRICAN JACANA	Jacana-africana	Grootlangtoon
14	LESSER JACANA	Jacana-pequena	Dwerglangtoon

Plate 26

1	WATTLED CRANE	Grou-carunculado	Lelkraanvoël
2	BLUE CRANE	Grou-do-paraíso	Bloukraanvoël
3	GREY (or Southern) CROWNED CRANE	Grou-coroado-austral	Mahem
4	SECRETARY BIRD	Secretário	Sekretarisvoël
5	KORI BUSTARD	Abetarda-kori	Gompou
6	DENHAM'S (or Stanley's) BUSTARD	Abetarda de Denham	Veldpou
7	LUDWIG'S BUSTARD	Abetarda de Ludwig	Ludwigse Pou
8	RUEPPELL'S KORHAAN	Sisão de Rueppell	Woestynkorhaan
9	KAROO KORHAAN	Sisão de Vigors	Vaalkorhaan
10	BLUE KORHAAN	Sisão-azulado	Bloukorhaan
11	WHITE-BELLIED BUSTARD	Sisão do Senegal	Witpenskorhaan
12	BLACK-BELLIED BUSTARD	Sisão-de-barriga-preta	Langbeenkorhaan
13	(Red-)CRESTED BUSTARD	Sisão-de-poupa-vermelha	Boskorhaan
14	WHITE-WINGED BLACK KORHAAN	Sisão-de-asa-branca	Witvlerkswartkorhaan
15	BLACK KORHAAN	Sisão-de-asa-preta	Swartkorhaan

Plate 27

1	EURASIAN AVOCET	Alfaiate	Bontelsie
2	BAR-TAILED GODWIT	Fuselo	Bandstertgriet
3	HUDSONIAN GODWIT	Fuselo-americano	Amerikaanse Griet
4	BLACK-TAILED GODWIT	Maçarico-de-bico-direito	Swartstertgriet
5	EURASIAN OYSTERCATCHER	Ostraceiro-europeu	Bonttobie
6	AFRICAN BLACK OYSTERCATCHER	Ostraceiro-preto-africano	Swarttobie
7	COMMON (or Black-winged) STILT	Perna-longa	Rooipootelsie
8	EGYPTIAN-PLOVER	Ave-crocodilo	
9	CRAB PLOVER	Caranguejeiro	Krapvreter
10	WHIMBREL	Maçarico-galego	Kleinwulp
11	EURASIAN CURLEW	Maçarico-real	Grootwulp
12	SPOTTED THICK-KNEE	Alcaravão do Cabo	Dikkop
13	WATER THICK-KNEE	Alcaravão-aquático	Waterdikkop
14	RUDDY TURNSTONE	Rola-do-mar	Steenloper

Plate 28

1	RINGED PLOVER	Borrelho-grande-de-coleira	Ringnekstrandkiewiet
2	LITTLE RINGED PLOVER	Borrelho-pequeno-de-coleira	Kleinringnekstrandkiewiet
3	THREE-BANDED PLOVER	Borrelho-de-tripla-coleira	Driebandstrandkiewiet
4	FORBES'S PLOVER	Borrelho de Forbes	
5	KITTLITZ'S PLOVER	Borrelho de Kittlitz	Geelborsstrandkiewiet
6	CHESTNUT-BANDED PLOVER	Borrelho-pálido	Rooibandstrandkiewiet
7	KENTISH PLOVER	Borrelho-de-coleira-interrompida	Alexandria Strandkiewiet
8	WHITE-FRONTED PLOVER	Borrelho-de-testa-branca	Vaalstrandkiewiet
9	CASPIAN PLOVER	Borrelho-asiático	Asiatiese Strandkiewiet
10	GREATER SAND PLOVER	Borrelho-do-deserto	Grootstrandkiewiet
11	MONGOLIAN PLOVER	Borrelho-mongol	Mongoolse Strandkiewiet

Plate 29

1	RED KNOT	Seixoeira	Knoet
2	CURLEW SANDPIPER	Pilrito-de-bico-comprido	Krombekstrandloper
3	DUNLIN	Pilrito-comum	Bontstrandloper
4	SANDERLING	Pilrito-sanderlingo	Drietoonstrandloper
5	PECTORAL SANDPIPER	Pilrito-peitoral	Geelpootstrandloper
6	WHITE-RUMPED SANDPIPER	Pilrito de Bonaparte	Witrugstrandloper
7	BAIRD'S SANDPIPER	Pilrito de Baird	Bairdse Strandloper
8	LITTLE STINT	Pilrito-pequeno	Kleinstrandloper
9	RUFOUS- (or Red-)NECKED STINT	Pilrito-de-nuca-vermelha	Rooinekstrandloper
10	TEMMINCK'S STINT	Pilrito de Temminck	Temminckse Strandloper
11	LONG-TOED STINT	Pilrito-de-dedos-compridos	Langtoonstrandloper
12	BROAD-BILLED SANDPIPER	Pilrito-de-bico-largo	Breëbekstrandloper

Plate 30

1	BLACK-WINGED LAPWING	Abibe-de-asa-preta	Grootswartvlerkkiewiet
2	CROWNED LAPWING	Abibe-coroado	Kroonkiewiet
3	LESSER BLACK-WINGED LAPWING	Abibe-lúgubre	Kleinswartvlerkkiewiet
4	AFRICAN WATTLED LAPWING	Abibe do Senegal	Lelkiewiet
5	LONG-TOED LAPWING	Abibe-de-faces-brancas	Witvlerkkiewiet
6	WHITE-HEADED (or -crowned) LAPWING	Abibe-de-coroa-branca	Witkopkiewiet
7	BLACKSMITH LAPWING	Abibe-armado	Bontkiewiet
8	BROWN-CHESTED LAPWING	Abibe-de-peito-ruivo	
9	SPUR-WINGED LAPWING	Abibe-esporado	
10	BUFF-BREASTED SANDPIPER	Pilrito-canela	Taanborsstrandloper
11	RUFF (♂), REEVE (♀)	Combatente	Kemphaan
12	GREY PLOVER	Tarambola-cinzenta	Grysstrandkiewiet
13	AMERICAN (or Lesser) GOLDEN PLOVER	Tarambola-dourada-americana	Amerikaanse Gouestrandkiewiet
14	PACIFIC GOLDEN PLOVER	Tarambola-dourada-siberiana	Stille Oseaan Gouestrandkiewiet

Plate 31

1	GREATER YELLOWLEGS	Perna-amarela-grande	Grootgeelpootruiter
2	LESSER YELLOWLEGS	Perna-amarela-pequeno	Kleingeelpootruiter
3	COMMON GREENSHANK	Perna-verde-comum	Groenpootruiter
4	SPOTTED REDSHANK	Perna-vermelha-escuro	Gevlekte Rooipootruiter
5	GREEN SANDPIPER	Pássaro-bique-bique	Witgatruiter
6	WOOD SANDPIPER	Maçarico-bastardo	Bosruiter
7	COMMON REDSHANK	Perna-vermelha-comum	Rooipootruiter
8	MARSH SANDPIPER	Perna-verde-fino	Moerasruiter
9	SOLITARY SANDPIPER	Maçarico-solitário	
10	COMMON SANDPIPER	Maçarico-das-rochas	Gewone Ruiter
11	TEREK SANDPIPER	Maçarico-sovela	Terekruiter
12	GREATER PAINTED-SNIPE	Narceja-pintada	Goudsnip
13	JACK SNIPE	Narceja-galega	
14	AFRICAN SNIPE	Narceja-africana	Afrikaanse Snip
15	GREAT SNIPE	Narceja-real	Dubbelsnip
16	COMMON SNIPE	Narceja-comum	

Plate 32

1	BLACK-WINGED PRATINCOLE	Perdiz-do-mar-de-asa-preta	Swartvlerksprinkaanvoël
2	COLLARED (or Red-winged) PRATINCOLE	Perdiz-do-mar-europeia	Rooivlerksprinkaanvoël
3	ROCK PRATINCOLE	Perdiz-do-mar-escura	Withalssprinkaanvoël
4	MADAGASCAR PRATINCOLE	Perdiz-do-mar-malgaxe	
5	TEMMINCK'S COURSER	Corredor de Temminck	Trekdrawwertjie
6	BURCHELL'S COURSER	Corredor de Burchell	Bloukopdrawwertjie
7	DOUBLE-BANDED COURSER	Corredor-de-duas-coleiras	Dubbelbanddrawwertjie
8	THREE-BANDED COURSER	Corredor-de-três-coleiras	Driebanddrawwertjie
9	BRONZE-WINGED COURSER	Corredor-de-patas-vermelhas	Bronsvlerkdrawwertjie
10	WILSON'S PHALAROPE	Falaropo de Wilson	Bontfraiingpoot
11	RED-NECKED PHALAROPE	Falaropo-de-bico-fino	Rooihalsfraiingpoot
12	GREY PHALAROPE	Falaropo-de-bico-grosso	Grysfraiingpoot

Plate 33

1	SOUTH POLAR SKUA	Moleiro-antárctico	Suidpoolroofmeeu
2	BROWN (or Subantarctic) SKUA	Moleiro-subantárctico	Bruinroofmeeu
3	POMARINE SKUA	Moleiro-pomarino	Knopstertroofmeeu
4	ARCTIC SKUA	Moleiro-parasita	Arktiese Roofmeeu
5	LONG-TAILED SKUA	Moleiro-de-cauda-comprida	Langstertroofmeeu
6	KELP GULL	Gaivota-dominicana	Swartrugmeeu
7	LESSER BLACK-BACKED GULL	Gaivota-de-asa-escura	Klein Swartrugmeeu
8	HERRING GULL	Gaivota-argêntea	Haringmeeu

Plate 34

1	SABINE'S GULL	Gaivota de Sabine	Mikstertmeeu
2	BLACK-LEGGED KITTIWAKE	Gaivota-tridáctila	Swartpootbrandervoël
3	HARTLAUB'S GULL	Gaivota de Hartlaub	Hartlaubse Meeu
4	BLACK-HEADED GULL	Guincho-comum	Swartkopmeeu
5	GREY-HEADED GULL	Gaivota-de-cabeça-cinzenta	Gryskopmeeu
6	LITTLE GULL	Gaivota-pequena	
7	FRANKLIN'S GULL	Gaivota de Franklin	Franklinse Meeu
8	HEMPRICH'S GULL	Gaivota-sombria	Hemprichse Meeu
9	LAUGHING GULL	Gaivota-risonha	
10	WHITE-EYED GULL	Gaivota-de-olho-branco	

Plate 35

1	SWIFT TERN	Gaivina-de-bico-amarelo	Geelbeksterretjie
2	ROYAL TERN	Gaivina-real	Koningsterretjie
3	LESSER CRESTED TERN	Gaivina-de-bico-laranja	Kuifkopsterretjie
4	SANDWICH TERN	Garajau-comum	Grootsterretjie
5	GULL-BILLED TERN	Gaivina-de-bico-preto	Oostelike Sterretjie
6	ARCTIC TERN	Gaivina-árctica	Arktiese Sterretjie
7	COMMON TERN	Gaivina-comum	Gewone Sterretjie
8	ANTARCTIC TERN	Gaivina-antárctica	Grysborssterretjie
9	ROSEATE TERN	Gaivina-rósea	Rooiborssterretjie
10	WHITE-CHEEKED TERN	Gaivina-do-mar-vermelho	Witwangsterretjie
11	CASPIAN TERN	Gaivina-de-bico-vermelho	Kaspiese Sterretjie
12	AFRICAN SKIMMER	Bico-de-tesoura-africano	Waterploeër

Plate 36

1	LITTLE TERN	Gaivina-pequena	Kleinsterretjie
2	DAMARA TERN	Gaivina de Damara	Damarasterretjie
3	BLACK-NAPED TERN	Gaivina de Sumatra	Swartkroonsterretjie
4	BRIDLED TERN	Gaivina-de-dorso-castanho	Brilsterretjie
5	SOOTY TERN	Gaivina-sombria	Roetsterretjie
6	BROWN NODDY	Nodi-castanho	Grootbruinsterretjie
7	LESSER NODDY	Nodi-pequeno	Kleinbruinsterretjie
8	BLACK NODDY	Nodi-preto	
9	BLACK TERN	Gaivina-preta	Swartsterretjie
10	WHITE-WINGED BLACK TERN	Gaivina-de-asa-branca	Witvlerksterretjie
11	WHISKERED TERN	Gaivina-dos-pauis	Witbaardsterretjie

Plate 37

1	SPECKLED (or Rock) PIGEON	Pombo da Guiné	Kransduif
2	OLIVE (or Rameron) PIGEON	Pombo-de-olho-amarelo	Geelbekbosduif
3	FERAL PIGEON	Pombo-doméstico	Tuinduif
4	EASTERN BRONZE-NAPED (or Delegorgue's) PIGEON	Pombo de Delegorgue	Withalsbosduif
5	AFEP PIGEON	Pombo-congolês	
6	AFRICAN GREEN PIGEON	Pombo-verde-africano	Papegaaiduif
7	LEMON (or Cinnamon) DOVE	Pombo-de-faces-brancas	Kaneelduifie
8	NAMAQUA DOVE	Rola-rabilonga	Namakwaduifie
9	AFRICAN MOURNING DOVE	Rola-chorosa	Rooioogtortelduif
10	RED-EYED DOVE	Rola-de-olhos-vermelhos	Grootringduif
11	RING-NECKED (or Cape Turtle) DOVE	Rola do Cabo	Gewone Tortelduif
12	DUSKY TURTLE DOVE	Rola-escura	
13	EUROPEAN TURTLE DOVE	Rola-europeia	Europese Tortelduif
14	LAUGHING DOVE	Rola-das-palmeiras	Rooiborsduifie/ Lemoenduifie
15	EMERALD-(or Green-) SPOTTED WOOD DOVE	Rola-esmeraldina	Groenvlekduif
16	BLUE-SPOTTED WOOD DOVE	Rola-de-manchas-azuis	Blouvlekduif
17	TAMBOURINE DOVE	Rola-tamborina	Witborsduif

Plate 38

1	RED-FACED MOUSEBIRD	Rabo-de-junco-de-faces-vermelhas	Rooiwangmuisvoël
2	SPECKLED MOUSEBIRD	Rabo-de-junco-estriado	Gevlekte Muisvoël
3	WHITE-BACKED MOUSEBIRD	Rabo-de-junco-de-dorso-branco	Witkruismuisvoël
4	RED-BACKED MOUSEBIRD	Rabo-de-junco-de-dorso-vermelho	
5	DOUBLE-BANDED SANDGROUSE	Cortiçol-de-duas-bandas	Dubbelbandsandpatrys
6	YELLOW-THROATED SANDGROUSE	Cortiçol-de-garganta-amarela	Geelkeelsandpatrys
7	NAMAQUA SANDGROUSE	Cortiçol-namaqua	Kelkiewyn
8	BURCHELL'S SANDGROUSE	Cortiçol de Burchell	Gevlekte Sandpatrys
9	ROSY-FACED LOVEBIRD	Inseparável-de-faces-rosadas	Rooiwangparkiet

10	LILIAN'S LOVEBIRD	Inseparável do Niassa	Niassaparkiet
11	RED-HEADED LOVEBIRD	Inseparável-de-cabeça-vermelha	Rooikopparkiet
12	BLACK-CHEEKED LOVEBIRD	Inseparável-de-faces-pretas	Swartwangparkiet
13	BROWN-NECKED (or Cape) PARROT	Papagaio-de-pescoço-castanho	Grootpapegaai
14	MEYER'S PARROT	Papagaio de Meyer	Bosveldpapegaai
15	BROWN-HEADED PARROT	Papagaio-de-cabeça-castanha	Bruinkoppapegaai
16	RUEPPELL'S PARROT	Papagaio de Rueppell	Bloupenspapegaai
17	RED-FRONTED PARROT	Papagaio-de-testa-vermelha	
18	ROSE-RINGED PARAKEET	Periquito-de-colar	Ringnekpapegaai
19	GREY PARROT	Papagaio-cinzento	
20	HOOPOE	Poupa	Hoephoep

Plate 39

1	GREEN TURACO	Tauraco da Guiné	
2	RED-CRESTED TURACO	Tauraco-de-crista-vermelha	
3	PURPLE-CRESTED TURACO (or Lourie)	Tauraco-de-crista-violeta	Bloukuifloerie
4	BLACK-BILLED TURACO	Tauraco-de-bico-preto	
5	GREY GO-AWAY BIRD (or Lourie)	Tauraco-unicolor	Kwêvoël
6	BARE-FACED GO-AWAY BIRD	Tauraco-mascarado	
7	GREAT BLUE TURACO	Tauraco-gigante	
8	ROSS'S TURACO (or Lourie)	Tauraco de Ross	Rooikuifloerie
9	RUFOUS-CROWNED (or Purple) ROLLER	Rolieiro-de-coroa-vermelha	Groottroupant
10	LILAC-BREASTED ROLLER	Rolieiro-de-peito-lilás	Gewone Troupant
11	RACKET-TAILED ROLLER	Rolieiro-de-cauda-espalmada	Knopsterttroupant
12	EUROPEAN ROLLER	Rolieiro-europeu	Europese Troupant
13	BROAD-BILLED ROLLER	Rolieiro-de-bico-amarelo	Geelbektroupant
14	BLUE-THROATED ROLLER	Rolieiro-de-garganta-azul	
15	VIOLET WOOD HOOPOE	Zombeteiro de Damaralândia	Perskakelaar
16	GREEN (or Red-billed) WOOD HOOPOE	Zombeteiro-de-bico-vermelho	Gewone Kakelaar
17	(Greater) SCIMITARBILL	Bico-de-cimitarra	Swartbekkakelaar

Plate 40

1	DUSKY LONG-TAILED CUCKOO	Cuco-escuro	
2	OLIVE LONG-TAILED CUCKOO	Cuco-oliváceo	
3	BARRED LONG-TAILED CUCKOO	Cuco-da-montanha	Langstertkoekoek
4	GREAT SPOTTED CUCKOO	Cuco-rabilongo	Gevlekte Koekoek
5	JACOBIN CUCKOO	Cuco-jacobino	Bontnuwejaarsvoël
6	AFRICAN STRIPED CUCKOO	Cuco de Levaillant	Gestreepte Nuwejaarsvoël
7	YELLOWBILL (or Green Coucal)	Cucal-verde	Groenvleiloerie
8	THICK-BILLED CUCKOO	Cuco-de-bico-grosso	Dikbekkoekoek
9	RED-CHESTED CUCKOO	Cuco-de-peito-vermelho	Piet-my-vrou
10	COMMON (or European) CUCKOO	Cuco-canoro	Europese Koekoek

11	AFRICAN CUCKOO	Cuco-africano	Afrikaanse Koekoek
12	ASIAN LESSER CUCKOO	Cuco-pequeno	Kleinkoekoek
13	MADAGASCAR LESSER CUCKOO	Cuco-malgaxe	Malgassiese Koekoek
14	BLACK CUCKOO	Cuco-preto	Swartkoekoek
15	DIEDERIK CUCKOO	Cuco-didrique	Diederikkie
16	KLAAS'S CUCKOO	Cuco de Klaas	Meidjie
17	AFRICAN EMERALD CUCKOO	Cuco-esmeraldino	Mooimeisie

Plate 41

1	FIERY-NECKED NIGHTJAR	Noitibó-musical	Afrikaanse Naguil
2	RUFOUS-CHEEKED NIGHTJAR	Noitibó-de-faces-vermelhas	Rooiwangnaguil
3	FRECKLED NIGHTJAR	Noitibó-das-rochas	Donkernaguil
4	SQUARE-TAILED (or Mozambique) NIGHTJAR	Noitibó de Moçambique	Laeveldnaguil
5	SWAMP (or Natal) NIGHTJAR	Noitibó de Natal	Natalse Naguil
6	MOUNTAIN NIGHTJAR	Noitibó-montês	
7	SLENDER-TAILED NIGHTJAR	Noitibó de Reichenow	
8	LONG-TAILED NIGHTJAR	Noitibó-rabilongo	
9	EUROPEAN NIGHTJAR	Noitibó da Europa	Europese Naguil
10	PENNANT-WINGED NIGHTJAR	Noitibó-de-estandarte	Wimpelvlerknaguil

Plate 42

1	AFRICAN WOOD OWL	Coruja-da-floresta	Bosuil
2	PEARL-SPOTTED OWLET	Mocho-pigmeu-africano	Witkoluil
3	AFRICAN BARRED OWLET	Mocho-barrado	Gebande Uil
4	WHITE-FACED SCOPS OWL	Mocho-de-faces-brancas	Witwanguil
5	AFRICAN SCOPS OWL	Mocho do Senegal	Skopsuil
6	PEL'S FISHING OWL	Corujão-pesqueiro	Visuil
7	VERREAUX'S (or Giant) EAGLE OWL	Bufo de Verreaux	Reuse Ooruil
8	CAPE EAGLE OWL	Bufo do Cabo	Kaapse Ooruil
9	SPOTTED EAGLE OWL	Bufo-africano	Gevlekte Ooruil
10	BARN OWL	Coruja-das-torres	Nonnetjie-uil
11	AFRICAN GRASS OWL	Coruja-dos-campos	Grasuil
12	MARSH OWL	Coruja-dos-pauis	Vlei Uil
13	BLUE-HEADED COUCAL	Cucal-de-nuca-azul	
14	BLACK COUCAL	Cucal-preto	Swartvleiloerie
15	COPPERY-TAILED COUCAL	Cucal-cauda-de-cobre	Grootvleiloerie
16	SENEGAL COUCAL	Cucal do Senegal	Senegalvleiloerie
17	WHITE-BROWED COUCAL	Cucal-de-sobrancelhas-brancas	Witstreepvleiloerie
18	GABON COUCAL	Cucal do Gabão	
19	BURCHELL'S COUCAL	Cucal de Burchell	Gewone Vleiloerie

Plate 43

1	ALPINE SWIFT	Andorinhão-real	Witpenswindswael
2	MOTTLED SWIFT	Andorinhão-malhado	Bontwindswael
3	BRADFIELD'S SWIFT	Andorinhão de Bradfield	Muiskleurwindswael
4	EUROPEAN SWIFT	Andorinhão-preto-europeu	Europese Windswael
5	AFRICAN BLACK SWIFT	Andorinhão-preto-africano	Swartwindswael
6	PALLID SWIFT	Andorinhão-pálido	Bruinwindswael

7	FERNANDO PO SWIFT	Andorinhão de Fernando Pó	
8	LITTLE SWIFT	Andorinhão-pequeno	Kleinwindswael
9	HORUS SWIFT	Andorinhão-horus	Horuswindswael
10	WHITE-RUMPED SWIFT	Andorinhão-cafre	Witkruiswindswael
11	SCARCE SWIFT	Andorinhão de Shoa	Skaarswindswael
12	AFRICAN PALM SWIFT	Andorinhão-das-palmeiras	Palmwindswael
13	BAT-LIKE (or Böhm's) SPINETAIL	Rabo-espinhoso de Böhm	Witpensstekelstert
14	MOTTLED SPINETAIL	Rabo-espinhoso de Ussher	Gevlekte Stekelstert
15	BLACK SPINETAIL	Rabo-espinhoso de Chapin	Swartstekelstert

Plate 44

1	BLUE-BREASTED BEE-EATER	Abelharuco-de-peito-azul	Blouborsbyevreter
2	LITTLE BEE-EATER	Abelharuco-pequeno	Kleinbyevreter
3	WHITE-FRONTED BEE-EATER	Abelharuco-de-testa-branca	Rooikeelbyevreter
4	BLACK BEE-EATER	Abelharuco-preto	Swartbyevreter
5	EUROPEAN BEE-EATER	Abelharuco-europeu	Europese Byevreter
6	BLUE-CHEEKED BEE-EATER	Abelharuco-verde	Blouwangbyevreter
7	MADAGASCAR (or Olive) BEE-EATER	Abelharuco-malgaxe	Olyfbyevreter
8	WHITE-THROATED BEE-EATER	Abelharuco-de-garganta-branca	Witkeelbyevreter
9	CARMINE BEE-EATER	Abelharuco-carmim	Rooiborsbyevreter
10	SWALLOW-TAILED BEE-EATER	Abelharuco-de-cauda-forcada	Swaelstertbyevreter
11	BOEHM'S BEE-EATER	Abelharuco de Boehm	Roeskopbyevreter
12	AFRICAN GREY HORNBILL	Calau-cinzento	Grysneushoringvoël
13	PALE-BILLED HORNBILL	Calau-de-bico-pálido	Bleekbekneushoringvoël
14	MONTEIRO'S HORNBILL	Calau de Monteiro	Monteirose Neushoringvoël
15	AFRICAN PIED HORNBILL	Calau-preto	Bontneushoringvoël
16	CROWNED HORNBILL	Calau-coroado	Gekroonde Neushoringvoël
17	BRADFIELD'S HORNBILL	Calau de Bradfield	Bradfieldse Neushoringvoël
18	SOUTHERN YELLOW-BILLED HORNBILL	Calau-de-bico-amarelo	Geelbekneushoringvoël
19	RED-BILLED HORNBILL	Calau-de-bico-vermelho	Rooibekneushoringvoël

Plate 45

1	PIED CROW	Gralha-africana	Witborskraai
2	WHITE-NECKED RAVEN	Corvo-de-nuca-branca	Withalskraai
3	BLACK CROW	Gralha do Cabo	Swartkraai
4	HOUSE CROW	Gralha-das-casas	Huiskraai
5	WHITE-CRESTED HORNBILL	Calau-de-crista-branca	Witkuifboskraai
6	BLACK-CASQUED WATTLED HORNBILL	Calau-grande	
7	SOUTHERN GROUND HORNBILL	Calau-gigante	Bromvoël
8	TRUMPETER HORNBILL	Calau-trombeteiro	Gewone Boskraai
9	SILVERY-CHEEKED HORNBILL	Calau-de-faces-prateadas	Kuifkopboskraai
10	BLACK-AND-WHITE-CASQUED HORNBILL	Calau-de-faces-cinzentas	
11	PIPING HORNBILL	Calau-assobiador	

Plate 46

1	PIED KINGFISHER	Guarda-rios-malhado	Bontvisvanger
2	AFRICAN GIANT KINGFISHER	Guarda-rios-gigante	Reusevisvanger
3	MALACHITE KINGFISHER	Guarda-rios-de-poupa	Kuifkopvisvanger
4	HALF-COLLARED KINGFISHER	Guarda-rios-de-colar	Blouvisvanger
5	SHINING-BLUE KINGFISHER	Guarda-rios-resplandecente	
6	WHITE-BELLIED KINGFISHER	Guarda-rios-de-ventre-branco	Witpensvisvanger
7	AFRICAN DWARF KINGFISHER	Guarda-rios-anão	
8	AFRICAN PYGMY KINGFISHER	Guarda-rios-pigmeu	Dwergvisvanger
9	WOODLAND KINGFISHER	Guarda-rios-dos-bosques	Bosveldvisvanger
10	MANGROVE KINGFISHER	Guarda-rios-dos-mangais	Mangoliedvisvanger
11	STRIPED KINGFISHER	Guarda-rios-estriado	Gestreepte Visvanger
12	CHOCOLATE-BACKED KINGFISHER	Guarda-rios-de-dorso-castanho	Bruinrugvisvanger
13	GREY-HEADED (or -hooded) KINGFISHER	Guarda-rios-de-cabeça-cinzenta	Gryskopvisvanger
14	BLUE-BREASTED KINGFISHER	Guarda-rios-de-peito-azul	Blouborsvisvanger
15	BROWN-HOODED KINGFISHER	Guarda-rios-de-cabeça-castanha	Bruinkopvisvanger
16	BAR-TAILED TROGON	Republicano-de-cauda-barrada	
17	NARINA'S TROGON	Republicano	Bosloerie

Plate 47

1	WHYTE'S BARBET	Barbaças de Whyte	Geelbleshoutkapper
2	WHITE-EARED BARBET	Barbaças-de-orelha-branca	Witoorhoutkapper
3	ANCHIETA'S BARBET	Barbaças de Anchieta	Ancietase Houtkapper
4	GREEN (or Woodward's) BARBET	Barbaças-verde	Groenhoutkapper
5	SPOT-FLANKED BARBET	Barbaças-fúnebre	
6	HAIRY-BREASTED BARBET	Barbaças-hirsuto	
7	GREY-THROATED BARBET	Barbaças-de-garganta-cinzenta	Gryskeelhoutkapper
8	NAKED-FACED BARBET	Barbaças-calvo	
9	DOUBLE-TOOTHED BARBET	Barbaças-bidenteado	
10	BLACK-COLLARED BARBET	Barbaças-de-colar	Rooikophoutkapper
11	BLACK-BACKED BARBET	Barbaças-pequeno	Swartrughoutkapper
12	BROWN-BREASTED BARBET	Barbaças-de-peito-castanho	Bruinborshoutkapper
13	CHAPLIN'S BARBET	Barbaças de Chaplin	Chaplinse Houtkapper
14	WHITE-HEADED BARBET	Barbaças-de-cabeça-branca	Witkophoutkapper
15	(Acacia) PIED BARBET	Barbaças-das-acácias	Bonthoutkapper
16	MIOMBO PIED BARBET	Barbaças-do-miombo	
17	YELLOW-BILLED BARBET	Barbaças-de-bico-amarelo	Geelbekhoutkapper
18	CRESTED BARBET	Barbaças-de-poupa	Kuifkophoutkapper

Plate 48

1	GREATER HONEYGUIDE	Indicador-grande	Grootheuningwyser
2	SCALY-THROATED HONEYGUIDE	Indicador-de-garganta-malhada	Gevlekte Heuningwyser

3	LYRE-TAILED HONEYGUIDE	Indicador-de-cauda-lira	
4	PALLID (or Eastern) HONEYGUIDE	Indicador-oriental	Oostelike Heuningwyser
5	LEAST HONEYGUIDE	Indicador-pigmeu	
6	LESSER HONEYGUIDE	Indicador-pequeno	Kleinheuningwyser
7	GREEN-BACKED (or Slender-billed) HONEYBIRD	Indicador-cinzento	Dunbekheuningvoël
8	CASSIN'S HONEYBIRD	Indicador de Cassin	Cassinse Heuningvoël
9	WAHLBERG'S (or Sharp-billed) HONEYBIRD	Indicador de Wahlberg	Skerpbekheuningvoël
10	AFRICAN BROADBILL	Bico-largo-africano	Breëbek
11	SPECKLED TINKERBIRD	Barbadinho-malhado	
12	GREEN TINKERBIRD	Barbadinho-verde	Groentinker
13	MOUSTACHED GREEN TINKERBIRD	Barbadinho-de-bigodes	Baardgroentinker
14	WESTERN GREEN TINKERBIRD	Barbadinho-da-montanha	
15	YELLOW- (or Golden-)RUMPED TINKERBIRD	Barbadinho-de-uropígio-amarelo	Swartblestinker
16	RED-FRONTED TINKERBIRD	Barbadinho-de-testa-vermelha	Rooiblestinker
17	YELLOW-FRONTED TINKERBIRD	Barbadinho-de-testa-amarela	Geelblestinker
18	AFRICAN PITTA	Tordo-formigueiro	

Plate 49

1	GREEN-BACKED (or Little Spotted) WOODPECKER	Pica-pau-de-dorso-verde	Gevlekte Speg
2	BROWN-EARED WOODPECKER	Pica-pau-de-orelhas-castanhas	
3	GOLDEN-TAILED WOODPECKER	Pica-pau-de-cauda-dourada	Goudstertspeg
4	BUFF-SPOTTED WOODPECKER	Pica-pau-malhado	
5	BENNETT'S WOODPECKER	Pica-pau de Bennett	Bennetse Speg
6	KNYSNA WOODPECKER	Pica-pau de Knysna	Knysnaspeg
7	OLIVE WOODPECKER	Pica-pau-esverdeado	Gryskopspeg
8	ELLIOT'S WOODPECKER	Pica-pau de Elliott	Elliotse Speg
9	GREY WOODPECKER	Pica-pau-cinzento-africano	Grysspeg
10	CARDINAL WOODPECKER	Pica-pau-cardeal	Kardinalespeg
11	BEARDED WOODPECKER	Pica-pau-de-bigode	Baardspeg
12	YELLOW-CRESTED WOODPECKER	Pica-pau-de-crista-amarela	Geelkuifspeg
13	STIERLING'S WOODPECKER	Pica-pau de Stierling	Stierlingse Speg
14	AFRICAN PICULET	Pica-pau-pigmeu	
15	RUFOUS-BREASTED (or Red-throated) WRYNECK	Torcicolo-de-garganta-vermelha	Draaihals
16	GROUND WOODPECKER	Pica-pau-de-cabeça-cinzenta	Grondspeg

Plate 50

1	LONG-BILLED LARK	Cotovia-de-bico-comprido	Langbeklewerik
2	KAROO LARK	Cotovia de Karoo	Karoolewerik
3	RED LARK	Cotovia-vermelha	Rooilewerik

4	SPIKE-HEELED LARK	Cotovia-esporada	Vlaktelewerik
5	GRAY'S LARK	Cotovia de Gray	Namiblewerik
6	SHORT-CLAWED LARK	Cotovia-de-unhas-curtas	Kortkloulewerik
7	DUNE LARK	Cotovia-de-dorso-ruivo	Duinelewerik
8	LARGE- (or Thick-)BILLED LARK	Cotovia-de-bico-grosso	Dikbeklewerik
9	DUSKY LARK	Calhandra-sombria	Donkerlewerik
10	BIMACULATED LARK	Calhandra-bimaculada	

Plate 51

1	FLAPPET LARK	Cotovia-zumbidora	Laeveldklappertjie
2	CLAPPER LARK	Cotovia-batedora	Hoëveldklappertjie
3	MONOTONOUS LARK	Cotovia-monótona	Bosveldlewerik
4	MELODIOUS LARK	Cotovia-melodiosa	Spotlewerik
5	SABOTA LARK	Cotovia-sabota	Sabotalewerik
6	FAWN-COLOURED LARK	Cotovia-beige	Vaalbruinlewerik
7	RUFOUS-NAPED LARK	Cotovia-de-nuca-vermelha	Rooineklewerik
8	ANGOLA LARK	Cotovia de Angola	Angolalewerik
9	BOTHA'S LARK	Calhandrinha de Botha	Vaalrivierlewerik
10	RUDD'S LARK	Calhandrinha de Rudd	Drakensberglewerik
11	PINK-BILLED LARK	Calhandrinha-de-bico-rosado	Pienkbeklewerik
12	SCLATER'S LARK	Calhandrinha de Scatler	Namakwalandlewerik
13	STARK'S LARK	Calhandrinha de Stark	Woestynlewerik
14	RED-CAPPED LARK	Calhandrinha-de-barrete-vermelho	Rooikoplewerik

Plate 52

1	WHITE-THROATED BLUE SWALLOW	Andorinha-azul-de-garganta-branca	
2	MOSQUE SWALLOW	Andorinha do Senegal	Moskeeswael
3	RED-BREASTED SWALLOW	Andorinha-de-ventre-vermelho	Rooiborsswael
4	LESSER STRIPED SWALLOW	Andorinha-estriada	Kleinstreepswael
5	GREATER STRIPED SWALLOW	Andorinha-de-cabeça-vermelha	Grootstreepswael
6	BARN (or European) SWALLOW	Andorinha-das-chaminés	Europese Swael
7	BLACK-AND-RUFOUS SWALLOW	Andorinha-vermelha-e-preta	
8	WIRE-TAILED SWALLOW	Andorinha-de-cauda-longa	Draadstertswael
9	ANGOLA SWALLOW	Andorinha de Angola	Angolaswael
10	RED-RUMPED SWALLOW	Andorinha-dáurica	Rooikruisswael
11	WHITE-THROATED SWALLOW	Andorinha-de-garganta-branca	Witkeelswael
12	PEARL-BREASTED SWALLOW	Andorinha-de-pérolas	Pêrelborsswael
13	RED-THROATED CLIFF SWALLOW	Andorinha-de-garganta-amarela	
14	SOUTH AFRICAN CLIFF SWALLOW	Andorinha-sul-africana	Familieswael

Plate 53

1	ROCK MARTIN	Andorinha-isabel	Kransswael
2	GREY-RUMPED SWALLOW	Andorinha-de-uropígio-cinzento	Gryskruisswael

3	BANDED MARTIN	Andorinha-de-colar	Gebande Oewerswael
4	COMMON SAND MARTIN	Andorinha-das-barreiras	Europese Oewerswael
5	MASCARENE MARTIN	Andorinha das Mascarenhas	Gestreepte Kransswael
6	BROWN-THROATED SAND MARTIN	Andorinha-das-barreiras-africana	Afrikaanse Oewerswael
7	BRAZZA'S MARTIN	Andorinha de Brazza	
8	BLUE SWALLOW	Andorinha-azul	Blouswael
9	WHITE-HEADED SAW-WING	Andorinha-de-cabeça-branca	Witkopsaagvlerkswael
10	BLACK SAW-WING	Andorinha-preta	Swartsaagvlerkswael
11	EASTERN SAW-WING	Andorinha-preta-oriental	Tropiese Saagvlerkswael
12	SQUARE-TAILED SAW-WING	Andorinha-de-cauda-curta	
13	COMMON HOUSE MARTIN	Andorinha-dos-beirais	Huisswael

Plate 54

1	AFRICAN GOLDEN ORIOLE	Papa-figos-africano	Afrikaanse Wielewaal
2	EUROPEAN GOLDEN ORIOLE	Papa-figos-europeu	Europese Wielewaal
3	BLACK-HEADED ORIOLE	Papa-figos-de-cabeça-preta	Swartkopwielewaal
4	GREEN-HEADED ORIOLE	Papa-figos-de-cabeça-verde	Groenkopwielewaal
5	BLACK-WINGED ORIOLE	Papa-figos-de-asa-preta	Swartvlerkwielewaal
6	WESTERN BLACK-HEADED ORIOLE	Papa-figos-de-cabeça-preta-ocidental	Westelike Swartkopwielewaal
7	ARROW-MARKED BABBLER	Zaragateiro de Jardine	Pylvlekkatlagter
8	BLACK-FACED BABBLER	Zaragateiro-de-faces-pretas	Swartwangkatlagter
9	BARE-CHEEKED BABBLER	Zaragateiro-de-faces-nuas	Kaalwangkatlagter
10	SOUTHERN PIED BABBLER	Zaragateiro-meridional	Witkatlagter
11	HARTLAUB'S (or White-rumped) BABBLER	Zaragateiro de Hartlaub	Witkruiskatlagter
12	AFRICAN HILL BABBLER	Zaragateiro-montês	
13	DAPPLED MOUNTAIN ROBIN	Tordo-malhado	
14	SPOT-THROAT	Tordo-de-garganta-malhada	
15	MOUNTAIN ILLADOPSIS	Falso-tordo-da-montanha	
16	BROWN ILLADOPSIS	Falso-tordo-de-colar	
17	SCALY-BREASTED ILLADOPSIS	Falso-tordo-de-peito-escamoso	
18	THRUSH BABBLER	Zaragateiro-tordo	

Plate 55

1	MOUNTAIN GREENBUL	Bulbul-de-garganta-cinzenta	
2	SHELLEY'S GREENBUL	Bulbul de Masuku	
3	SOMBRE GREENBUL	Bulbul-importuno	Gewone Willie
4	LITTLE GREY GREENBUL	Bulbul-cinzento-pequeno	
5	LITTLE GREENBUL	Bulbul-pequeno	
6	STRIPE-CHEEKED GREENBUL	Bulbul-montês	Streepwangwillie
7	SLENDER-BILLED GREENBUL	Bulbul-de-bico-fino	
8	PLAIN GREENBUL	Bulbul-camaronês	
9	YELLOW-WHISKERED GREENBUL	Bulbul-de-bigodes-amarelos	
10	TERRESTRIAL BROWNBUL	Bulbul-terrestre	Boskrapper
11	TINY (or Slender) GREENBUL	Bulbul-pigmeu	Kleinboskruiper
12	YELLOW-STREAKED GREENBUL	Bulbul-de-estrias-amarelas	Geelstreepboskruiper

13	PALE OLIVE GREENBUL	Bulbul-de-ventre-vermelho	
14	CABANIS'S GREENBUL	Bulbul de Cabanis	
15	GREY-OLIVE GREENBUL	Bulbul-verde-azeitona	
16	WHITE-THROATED GREENBUL	Bulbul-de-garganta-branca	
17	CAPE BULBUL	Bulbul do Cabo	Kaapse Tiptol
18	AFRICAN RED-EYED BULBUL	Bulbul-de-olho-vermelho	Rooioogtiptol
19	COMMON (or Black-eyed) BULBUL	Bulbul-comum	Swartoogtiptol
20	BUSH BLACKCAP	Zaragateiro-de-barrete-preto	Rooibektiptol

Plate 56

1	FORK-TAILED DRONGO	Drongo-de-cauda-forcada	Mikstertbyvanger
2	SQUARE-TAILED DRONGO	Drongo-de-cauda-quadrada	Kleinbyvanger
3	HONEYGUIDE GREENBUL	Bulbul-de-cauda-branca	
4	YELLOW-BELLIED GREENBUL	Bulbul-de-ventre-amarelo	Geelborswillie
5	JOYFUL GREENBUL	Bulbul-alegre	
6	YELLOW-NECKED GREENBUL	Bulbul de Falkenstein	
7	YELLOW-THROATED LEAFLOVE	Bulbul-de-garganta-amarela	
8	SIMPLE GREENBUL	Bulbul-modesto	
9	RED-TAILED GREENBUL	Bulbul-de-cauda-vermelha	
10	RED-TAILED BRISTLEBILL	Bulbul-de-cauda-ruiva	
11	BLACK CUCKOOSHRIKE	Picanço-cuco-preto	Swartkatakoeroe
12	PETIT'S CUCKOOSHRIKE	Picanço-cuco de Petit	Petitse Katakoeroe
13	PURPLE-THROATED CUCKOOSHRIKE	Picanço-cuco-de-garganta-púrpura	Perskeelkatakoeroe
14	GREY CUCKOOSHRIKE	Picanço-cuco-cinzento	Bloukatakoeroe
15	WHITE-BREASTED CUCKOOSHRIKE	Picanço-cuco-de-peito-branco	Witborskatakoeroe
16	WESTERN NICATOR	Tuta-malhada	
17	WHITE-THROATED (or Yellow-spotted) NICATOR	Tuta-de-garganta-branca	Geelvleknikator
18	YELLOW-THROATED NICATOR	Tuta-de-garganta-amarela	

Plate 57

1	ISABELLINE WHEATEAR	Chasco-isabel	Isabellinaskaapwagter
2	NORTHERN (or European) WHEATEAR	Chasco-cinzento	Europese Skaapwagter
3	PIED WHEATEAR	Chasco-dominó	Bontskaapwagter
4	BUFF-STREAKED CHAT	Cartaxo-de-estrias-castanhas	Bergklipwagter
5	MOUNTAIN WHEATEAR	Chasco-da-montanha	Bergwagter
6	CAPPED WHEATEAR	Chasco-de-barrete	Hoëveldskaapwagter
7	WHITE-HEADED BLACK (or Arnot's) CHAT	Cartaxo de Arnot	Bontpiek
8	MOCKING CLIFF CHAT	Cartaxo-das-rochas-de-ventre-vermelho	Dassievoël
9	KAROO SCRUB ROBIN	Rouxinol do Karoo	Slangverklikker
10	KALAHARI SCRUB ROBIN	Rouxinol do Kalahari	Kalahariwipstert
11	RUFOUS SCRUB ROBIN	Rouxinol-do-mato	
12	BROWN SCRUB ROBIN	Rouxinol-castanho	Bruinwipstert
13	EASTERN BEARDED SCRUB ROBIN	Rouxinol-oriental	Baardwipstert

14	MIOMBO BEARDED SCRUB ROBIN	Rouxinol-do-miombo	Angola Wipstert
15	FOREST SCRUB ROBIN	Rouxinol-da-floresta	
16	WHITE-BROWED SCRUB ROBIN	Rouxinol-de-dorso-vermelho	Gestreepte Wipstert
17	BROWN-BACKED SCRUB ROBIN	Rouxinol-de-dorso-castanho	

Plate 58

1	SICKLE-WINGED CHAT	Cartaxo-das-rochas	Vlaktespekvreter
2	TRACTRAC CHAT	Cartaxo-pálido	Woestynspekvreter
3	KAROO CHAT	Cartaxo do Karoo	Karoospekvreter
4	FAMILIAR CHAT	Cartaxo-de-cauda-vermelha	Gewone Spekvreter
5	MIOMBO ROCK THRUSH	Melro-das-rochas-do-miombo	Angolakliplyster
6	SHORT-TOED ROCK THRUSH	Melro-das-rochas-de-dedos-curtos	Korttoonkliplyster
7	CAPE ROCK THRUSH	Melro-das-rochas do Cabo	Kaapse Kliplyster
8	SENTINEL ROCK THRUSH	Melro-das-rochas-sentinela	Langtoonkliplyster
9	MOUNTAIN ROCK THRUSH	Melro-das-rochas-europeu	Bergkliplyster
10	BOULDER CHAT	Melro-preto-das-rochas	
11	HERERO CHAT	Cartaxo de Herero	Hererospekvreter
12	COMMON (or European) REDSTART	Rabirruivo-de-testa-branca	Europese Rooistert
13	WHINCHAT	Cartaxo-nortenho	Europese Bontrokkie
14	COMMON STONECHAT	Cartaxo-comum	Gewone Bontrokkie
15	WHITE-STARRED ROBIN	Pisco-de-ventre-amarelo	Witkoljanfrederik
16	SWYNNERTON'S ROBIN	Pisco de Swynnerton	Bandkeeljanfrederik
17	THRUSH NIGHTINGALE (or Sprosser)	Rouxinol-grande	Lysternagtegaal

Plate 59

1	ANGOLA CAVE CHAT	Pisco-das-grutas	
2	ORANGE-BREASTED ROCKJUMPER	Melro-das-rochas-de-peito-laranja	Oranjeborsberglyster
3	CAPE ROCKJUMPER	Melro-das-rochas do Cabo	Kaapse Berglyster
4	EAST COAST AKALAT	Pisco de Gunning	Gunningse Janfrederik
5	SHARPE'S AKALAT	Pisco de Sharpe	Sharpese Janfrederik
6	BOCAGE'S AKALAT	Pisco de Bocage	
7	GABELA AKALAT	Pisco de Gabela	
8	SOOTY CHAT	Cartaxo-formigueiro-preto	
9	SOUTHERN ANTEATER CHAT	Cartaxo-formigueiro-meridional	Swartpiek
10	CONGO MOOR CHAT	Cartaxo-formigueiro-congolês	
11	OLIVE-FLANKED ROBIN CHAT	Pisco-de-flancos-esverdeados	
12	CHOLO ALETHE	Pisco de Cholo	
13	BROWN-CHESTED ALETHE	Pisco-de-peito-castanho	
14	FIRE-CRESTED ALETHE	Pisco-de-poupa-vermelha	
15	WHITE-CHESTED (or -breasted) ALETHE	Pisco-de-peito-branco	Witborsboslyster

16	WHITE-TAILED ANT THRUSH	Pisco-formigueiro-de-cauda-branca	
17	RUFOUS FLYCATCHER THRUSH	Pisco-formigueiro-ruivo	

Plate 60

1	(Southern) OLIVE THRUSH	Melro-oliváceo	Olyflyster
2	KURRICHANE THRUSH	Melro de Kurrichane	Rooibeklyster
3	AFRICAN THRUSH	Melro-africano	
4	ORANGE GROUND THRUSH	Tordo de Gurney	Oranjelyster
5	GROUNDSCRAPER THRUSH	Tordo de Litsitsirupa	Gevlekte Lyster
6	SPOTTED GROUND THRUSH	Tordo-malhado	Natallyster
7	RED- (or Rufous-)TAILED PALM THRUSH	Tordo-das-palmeiras-de-cauda-vermelha	Rooistertmôrelyster
8	COLLARED PALM THRUSH	Tordo-das-palmeiras-de-colar	Palmmôrelyster
9	RED-CAPPED (or Natal) ROBIN CHAT	Pisco-de-barrete-vermelho	Nataljanfrederik
10	CHORISTER ROBIN CHAT	Pisco-corista	Lawaaimakerjanfrederik
11	(African) WHITE-THROATED ROBIN CHAT	Pisco-de-garganta-branca	Witkeeljanfrederik
12	CAPE ROBIN CHAT	Pisco do Cabo	Gewone Janfrederik
13	WHITE-BROWED (or Heuglin's) ROBIN CHAT	Pisco de Heuglin	Heuglinse Janfrederik
14	GREY-WINGED ROBIN CHAT	Pisco-de-asa-cinzenta	
15	SNOWY-CROWNED ROBIN CHAT	Pisco-de-barrete-branco	
16	WHITE-HEADED ROBIN CHAT	Pisco-de-cabeça-branca	

Plate 61

1	AFRICAN REED (or Marsh) WARBLER	Rouxinol-dos-caniços-africano	Kleinrietsanger
2	EURASIAN REED WARBLER	Rouxinol-pequeno-dos-caniços	Hermanse Rietsanger
3	(European) MARSH WARBLER	Felosa-palustre	Europese Rietsanger
4	GREATER SWAMP WARBLER	Rouxinol-grande-dos-pântanos	Rooibruinrietsanger
5	GREAT REED WARBLER	Rouxinol-grande-dos-caniços	Grootrietsanger
6	LESSER SWAMP (or Cape Reed) WARBLER	Rouxinol-pequeno-dos-pântanos	Kaapse Rietsanger
7	BASRA REED WARBLER	Felosa do Iraque	Basrarietsanger
8	SEDGE WARBLER	Felosa-dos-juncos	Kaapse Vleisanger
9	BROAD-TAILED WARBLER	Felosa-de-cauda-larga	Breëstertsanger
10	EURASIAN RIVER WARBLER	Felosa-fluvial	Sprinkaansanger
11	KNYSNA WARBLER	Felosa de Knysna	Knysnaruigtesanger
12	VICTORIN'S WARBLER	Felosa de Victorin	Rooiborsruigtesanger
13	BARRATT'S WARBLER	Felosa de Barratt	Ruigtesanger
14	LITTLE RUSH (or African Sedge) WARBLER	Felosa-dos-juncos-africana	Kaapse Vleisanger
15	EVERGREEN-FOREST WARBLER	Felosa de Lopes	
16	CINNAMON BRACKEN WARBLER	Felosa-canela	
17	BAMBOO WARBLER	Felosa-dos-bambus	

18	ICTERINE WARBLER	Felosa-icterina	Spotvoël
19	OLIVE-TREE WARBLER	Felosa-das-oliveiras	Olyfboomsanger
20	OLIVACEOUS WARBLER	Felosa-pálida	
21	WHITE-WINGED WARBLER	Felosa-de-asa-branca	

Plate 62

1	YELLOW-THROATED WOODLAND WARBLER	Felosa-de-garganta-amarela	Geelkeelsanger
2	BURNT-NECKED EREMOMELA	Eremomela-de-pescoço-castanho	Bruinkeelbossanger
3	GREEN-CAPPED EREMOMELA	Eremomela-de-barrete-verde	Donkerwangbossanger
4	YELLOW-BELLIED EREMOMELA	Eremomela-de-ventre-amarelo	Geelpensbossanger
5	KAROO EREMOMELA	Eremomela de Karoo	Groenbossanger
6	BLACK-NECKED EREMOMELA	Eremomela-de-pescoço-preto	
7	RUFOUS-CROWNED EREMOMELA	Eremomela-de-barrete-castanho	
8	RED-CAPPED CROMBEC	Felosa-de-barrete-vermelho	Rooikroonstompstert
9	LONG-BILLED CROMBEC	Felosa-de-bico-comprido	Bosveldstompstert
10	WILLOW WARBLER	Felosa-musical	Hofsanger
11	LAURA'S WOODLAND WARBLER	Felosa de Laura	
12	STIERLING'S BARRED WARBLER	Felosa de Stierling	Stierlingse Sanger
13	BARRED WREN WARBLER	Felosa-barrada	
14	MIOMBO WREN WARBLER	Felosa-do-miombo	
15	GREEN-BACKED BLEATING WARBLER	Felosa-de-dorso-verde	
16	GREY-BACKED BLEATING WARBLER	Felosa-de-dorso-cinzento	
17	YELLOW-BROWED CAMAROPTERA	Felosa-de-sobrancelha-amarela	
18	RED-FACED CROMBEC	Felosa-de-faces-vermelhas	Rooiwangstompstert
19	GREEN CROMBEC	Felosa-verde	Groenstompstert
20	LEMON-BELLIED CROMBEC	Felosa-de-ventre-amarelo	

Plate 63

1	BANDED PRINIA	Prínia-barrada	
2	DRAKENSBERG PRINIA	Prínia-malhada de Drakensberg	Drakensberglangstertjie
3	SPOTTED SPRINIA	Prínia-malhada	Karoolangstertjie
4	TAWNY-FLANKED PRINIA	Prínia-de-flancos-castanhos	Bruinsylangstertjie
5	BLACK-CHESTED PRINIA	Prínia-de-peito-preto	Swartbandlangstertjie
6	BRIAR WARBLER (or Roberts's Prinia)	Prínia de Roberts	Woudlangstertjie
7	WHITE-CHINNED PRINIA	Prínia-de-garganta-branca	
8	FAIRY FLYCATCHER	Papa-moscas-de-asa-branca	Feevlieëvanger
9	GREEN HYLIA	Beija-flor-verdinho	
10	RED-WINGED WARBLER	Prínia-de-asa-vermelha	Rooivlerksanger
11	NAMAQUA WARBLER (or Prinia)	Prínia de Namaqua	Namakwalangstertjie
12	RUFOUS-EARED WARBLER	Felosa-de-faces-vermelhas	Rooioorlangstertjie
13	CINNAMON-BREASTED WARBLER	Felosa-canela	Kaneelborssanger

14	AFRICAN YELLOW WARBLER	Felosa-amarela-africana	Geelsanger
15	MOUNTAIN YELLOW WARBLER	Felosa-amarela-da-montanha	
16	PAPYRUS YELLOW WARBLER	Felosa-amarela-do-papiro	
17	(African) MOUSTACHED GRASS WARBLER	Felosa-de-bigodes	
18	ROCKRUNNER	Felosa-das-rochas	Rotsvoël
19	CAPE GRASS WARBLER (or Grassbird)	Felosa de Cabo	Grasvoël

Plate 64

1	NEDDICKY	Fuinha-de-barrete-vermelho	Neddikkie
2	SHORT-WINGED CISTICOLA	Fuinha-de-asa-curta	Kortvlerktinktinkie
3	ROCK-LOVING (or Lazy) CISTICOLA	Fuinha-preguiçosa	Luitinktinkie
4	GREY-BACKED CISTICOLA	Fuinha-de-dorso-cinzento	Grysrugtinktinkie
5	WAILING CISTICOLA	Fuinha-lastimosa	Huiltinktinkie
6	TINKLING CISTICOLA	Fuinha-cinzenta	Rooitinktinkie
7	RED-FACED CISTICOLA	Fuinha-de-faces-vermelhas	Rooiwangtinktinkie
8	SINGING CISTICOLA	Fuinha-cantora	Singende Tinktinkie
9	TRILLING CISTICOLA	Fuinha de Woosnam	
10	CHURRING CISTICOLA	Fuinha-njombe	
11	WINDING (or Black-backed) CISTICOLA	Fuinha-de-dorso-preto	Swartrugtinktinkie
12	CHIRPING CISTICOLA	Fuinha-chilreante	Piepende Tinktinkie
13	RATTLING CISTICOLA	Fuinha-chocalheira	Bosveldtinktinkie
14	BLACK-LORED CISTICOLA	Fuinha-de-faces-pretas	
15	WHISTLING CISTICOLA	Fuinha-assobiadeira	
16	CHATTERING CISTICOLA	Fuinha-tagarela	
17	BUBBLING CISTICOLA	Fuinha-sussurrante	
18	LEVAILLANT'S CISTICOLA	Fuinha de Levaillant	Vleitinktinkie
19	CROAKING CISTICOLA	Fuinha de Natal	Groottinktinkie
20	STOUT CISTICOLA	Fuinha-grande	

Plate 65

1	FAN-TAILED CISTICOLA	Fuinha-dos-juncos	Landeryklopkloppie
2	DESERT CISTICOLA	Fuinha-do-deserto	Woestynklopkloppie
3	CLOUD CISTICOLA	Fuinha-textrix	Gevlekte Klopkloppie
4	WING-SNAPPING (or Ayres's) CISTICOLA	Fuinha de Ayres	Kleinste Klopkloppie
5	PALE-CROWNED CISTICOLA	Fuinha-de-barrete-pálido	Bleekkopklopkloppie
6	DAMBO CISTICOLA	Fuinha-dambo	
7	BLACK-TAILED CISTICOLA	Fuinha-de-cauda-preta	
8	BLACK-HEADED APALIS	Apalis-de-cabeça-preta	Swartkopkleinjantjie
9	YELLOW-BREASTED APALIS	Apalis-de-peito-amarelo	Geelborskleinjantjie
10	BLACK-THROATED APALIS	Apalis-de-garganta-preta	Swartkeelkleinjantjie
11	RUDD'S APALIS	Apalis de Rudd	Ruddse Kleinjantjie
12	BAR-THROATED APALIS	Apalis-de-colar	Bandkeelkleinjantjie
13	WHITE-WINGED APALIS	Apalis-de-asa-branca	Witvlerkkleinjantjie
14	CHAPIN'S APALIS	Apalis de Chapin	
15	BROWN-HEADED APALIS	Apalis-de-cabeça-castanha	Bruinkopkleinjantjie
16	MOREAU'S TAILORBIRD	Costureiro de Moreau	

17	MASKED APALIS	Apalis-mascarado	
18	CHIRINDA APALIS	Apalis de Chirinda	Gryskleinjantjie
19	GOSLING'S APALIS	Apalis de Gosling	
20	BUFF-THROATED APALIS	Apalis-de-garganta-vermelha	
21	AFRICAN TAILORBIRD	Costureiro-africano	

Plate 66

1	KRETSCHMER'S LONGBILL	Felosa de Kretschmer	
2	GREY LONGBILL	Felosa-cinzenta	
3	PULITZER'S LONGBILL	Felosa de Pulitzer	
4	YELLOW LONGBILL	Felosa-amarela	
5	RED-BELLIED PARADISE FLYCATCHER	Papa-moscas-de-barriga-vermelha	
6	AFRICAN PARADISE FLYCATCHER	Papa-moscas-africano	Paradysvlieëvanger
7	RUFOUS-VENTED PARADISE FLYCATCHER	Papa-moscas-congolês	
8	BATES'S PARADISE FLYCATCHER	Papa-moscas de Bates	
9	BLUE-MANTLED CRESTED FLYCATCHER	Papa-moscas do Cabo	Bloukuifvlieëvanger
10	BLUE-HEADED CRESTED FLYCATCHER	Papa-moscas-de-cabeça-azul	Bloukopvlieëvanger
11	AFRICAN BLUE FLYCATCHER	Papa-moscas-azul	
12	WHITE-TAILED BLUE FLYCATCHER	Papa-moscas-de-cauda-branca	
13	WHITE-TAILED CRESTED FLYCATCHER	Papa-moscas-de-poupa	
14	LIVINGSTONE'S FLYCATCHER	Papa-moscas de Livingstone	Rooistertvlieëvanger
15	COMMON WHITETHROAT	Papa-amoras-comum	Witkeelsanger
16	BLACKCAP	Toutinegra-de-barrete-preto	Swartkroonsanger
17	BARRED WARBLER	Toutinegra-gavião	
18	GARDEN WARBLER	Felosa-das-figueiras	Tuinsanger
19	LAYARD'S WARBLER (or Titbabbler)	Felosa de Layard	Grystjeriktik
20	CHESTNUT-VENTED WARBLER (or Titbabbler)	Felosa-de-ventre-castanho	Bosveldtjeriktik
21	BROWN PARISOMA	Felosa-castanha	

Plate 67

1	AFRICAN DUSKY FLYCATCHER	Papa-moscas-castanho	Donkervlieëvanger
2	ASHY (or Blue-grey) FLYCATCHER	Papa-moscas-de-lunetas	Blougrysvlieëvanger
3	SPOTTED FLYCATCHER	Papa-moscas-cinzento	Europese Vlieëvanger
4	CASSIN'S FLYCATCHER	Papa-moscas de Cassin	
5	SWAMP FLYCATCHER	Papa-moscas-dos-pauis	
6	DUSKY BLUE FLYCATCHER	Papa-moscas-ardósia	
7	SOOTY FLYCATCHER	Papa-moscas-sombrio	
8	COLLARED FLYCATCHER	Papa-moscas-de-colar	Withalsvlieëvanger

9	SOUTHERN BLACK FLYCATCHER	Papa-moscas-sul-africano	Swartvlieëvanger
10	GREY-THROATED TIT FLYCATCHER	Papa-moscas-de-garganta-cinzenta	
11	GREY (or Fan-tailed) FLYCATCHER	Papa-moscas-chapim	Waaierstertvlieëvanger
12	BOEHM'S FLYCATCHER	Papa-moscas de Boehm	
13	FRASER'S FOREST FLYCATCHER	Papa-moscas-da-floresta	
14	FISCAL FLYCATCHER	Papa-moscas-fiscal	Fiskaalvlieëvanger
15	CHAT FLYCATCHER	Papa-moscas-cartaxo	Grootvlieëvanger
16	ANGOLA SLATY FLYCATCHER	Papa-moscas de Angola	
17	WHITE-EYED SLATY FLYCATCHER	Papa-moscas-de-olho-branco	
18	PALE(, Pallid or Mouse-coloured) FLYCATCHER	Papa-moscas-pálido	Muiskleurvlieëvanger
19	MARICO FLYCATCHER	Papa-moscas de Marico	Maricovlieëvanger

Plate 68

1	YELLOW-BELLIED (or -breasted) HYLIOTA	Papa-moscas-de-barriga-amarela	Geelborshyliota
2	SOUTHERN (or Mashona) HYLIOTA	Papa-moscas-austral	Mashonahyliota
3	PRIRIT BATIS	Papa-moscas de Vieillot	Priritbosbontrokkie
4	CAPE BATIS	Papa-moscas do Cabo	Kaapse Bosbontrokkie
5	WOODWARD'S BATIS	Papa-moscas de Woodward	Woodwardse Bosbontrokkie
6	CHINSPOT BATIS	Papa-moscas-molitor	Witliesbosbontrokkie
7	EAST COAST (or Mozambique) BATIS	Papa-moscas-oriental	Mosambiekbosbontrokkie
8	MARGARET'S BATIS	Papa-moscas de Margaret	
9	FOREST BATIS	Papa-moscas-de-cauda-curta	Woudbosbontrokkie
10	ANGOLA BATIS	Papa-moscas-angolano	Angola Bosbontrokkie
11	BLACK-HEADED BATIS	Papa-moscas-de-cabeça-preta	
12	BLACK-AND-WHITE (or Vanga) FLYCATCHER	Papa-moscas de Vanga	Witpensvlieëvanger
13	SHRIKE FLYCATCHER	Papa-moscas-picanço	
14	CHESTNUT WATTLE-EYE	Papa-moscas-de-olheiras-castanho	
15	YELLOW-BELLIED WATTLE-EYE	Papa-moscas-de-olheiras-de-barriga-amarela	
16	BLACK-NECKED WATTLE-EYE	Papa-moscas-de-olheiras-de-pescoço-preto	
17	BLACK-THROATED WATTLE-EYE (Flycatcher)	Papa-moscas-de-olheiras-de-garganta-preta	Beloogbosbontrokkie
18	BROWN-THROATED WATTLE-EYE	Papa-moscas-de-olheiras-de-garganta-castanha	
19	WHITE-FRONTED WATTLE-EYE	Papa-moscas-de-olheiras-de-testa-branca	

Plate 69

1	CAPE SUGARBIRD	Papa-açucar do Cabo	Kaapse Suikervoël
2	GURNEY'S SUGARBIRD	Papa-açucar de Gurney	Rooiborssuikervoël
3	SPOTTED CREEPER	Trepadeira-malhada	Boomkruiper
4	CAPE PENDULINE TIT	Chapim do Cabo	Kaapse Kapokvoël
5	GREY PENDULINE TIT	Chapim-de-garganta-branca	Gryskapokvoël
6	TITHYLIA	Titília	
7	MIOMBO (or Northern) GREY TIT	Chapim-do-miombo	Miombogrysmees
8	SOUTHERN GREY TIT	Chapim-cinzento-meridional	Piet-tjou-tjougrysmees
9	CINNAMON-BREASTED TIT	Chapim-de-peito-canelado	
10	RUFOUS-BELLIED TIT	Chapim-de-ventre-vermelho	Swartkopmees
11	ASHY TIT	Chapim-cinzento	Acaciagrysmees
12	WHITE-WINGED BLACK TIT	Chapim-de-asa-branca	
13	CARP'S TIT	Chapim de Carp	Ovamboswartmees
14	SOUTHERN BLACK TIT	Chapim-preto-meridional	Gewone Swartmees
15	DUSKY TIT	Chapim-sombrio	
16	SCARLET-TUFTED MALACHITE SUNBIRD	Beija-flor-de-tufos-escarlates	
17	YELLOW-TUFTED MALACHITE SUNBIRD	Beija-flor-verde	Jangroentjie
18	BRONZE SUNBIRD	Beija-flor-bronzeado	Bronssuikerbekkie
19	BOCAGE'S SUNBIRD	Beija-flor de Bocage	

Plate 70

1	GREY SUNBIRD	Beija-flor-cinzento	Gryssuikerbekkie
2	OLIVE SUNBIRD	Beija-flor-esverdado	Olyfsuikerbekkie
3	REICHENBACH'S SUNBIRD	Beija-flor de Reichenbach	
4	PLAIN-BACKED (or Blue-throated) SUNBIRD	Beija-flor-de-garganta-azul	Bloukeelsuikerbekkie
5	FRASER'S SUNBIRD	Beija-flor de Fraser	
6	YELLOW-CHINNED SUNBIRD	Beija-flor-de-queixo-amarelo	
7	COLLARED SUNBIRD	Beija-flor-de-colar	Kortbeksuikerbekkie
8	RED-AND-BLUE SUNBIRD	Beija-flor-azul-e-vermelho	
9	VIOLET-BACKED SUNBIRD	Beija-flor-de-dorso-violeta	Blousuikerbekkie
10	ULUGURU VIOLET-BACKED SUNBIRD	Beija-flor de Uluguru	
11	VIOLET-TAILED SUNBIRD	Beija-flor-de-cauda-violeta	
12	BATES'S SUNBIRD	Beija-flor de Bates	
13	LITTLE GREEN SUNBIRD	Beija-flor-verde-pequeno	
14	SCARLET-CHESTED SUNBIRD	Beija-flor-de-peito-escarlate	Rooikeelsuikerbekkie
15	AMETHYST (or Black) SUNBIRD	Beija-flor-preto	Swartsuikerbekkie
16	CARMELITE SUNBIRD	Beija-flor-carmelita	
17	GREEN-THROATED SUNBIRD	Beija-flor-de-garganta-verde	
18	BLUE-THROATED BROWN SUNBIRD	Beija-flor-castanho-de-garganta-azul	
19	GREEN-HEADED SUNBIRD	Beija-flor-de-cabeça-verde	
20	BANNERMANN'S SUNBIRD	Beija-flor de Bannermann	

Plate 71

1	ORANGE-BREASTED SUNBIRD	Beija-flor-de-peito-laranja	Oranjeborssuikerbekkie

2	COPPERY SUNBIRD	Beija-flor-cobreado	Kopersuikerbekkie
3	YELLOW-BELLIED SUNBIRD	Beija-flor-de-barriga-amarela	Geelpenssuikerbekkie
4	WHITE-BELLIED SUNBIRD	Beija-flor-de-barriga-branca	Witpenssuikerbekkie
5	GREATER DOUBLE-COLLARED SUNBIRD	Beija-flor-grande-de-colar	Grootrooiborssuikerbekkie
6	SOUTHERN (or Lesser) DOUBLE-COLLARED SUNBIRD	Beija-flor-pequeno-de-colar	Kleinrooiborssuikerbekkie
7	MIOMBO DOUBLE-COLLARED SUNBIRD	Beija-flor-do-miombo	Miombo Rooiborssuikerbekkie
8	OLIVE-BELLIED SUNBIRD	Beija-flor-de-barriga-verde	
9	EASTERN DOUBLE-COLLARED SUNBIRD	Beija-flor-oriental-de-colar	
10	SUPERB SUNBIRD	Beija-flor-soberbo	
11	OUSTALET'S WHITE-BELLIED SUNBIRD	Beija-flor de Oustalet	
12	DUSKY SUNBIRD	Beija-flor-sombrio	Namakwasuikerbekkie
13	SHELLEY'S SUNBIRD	Beija-flor de Shelley	Swartpenssuikerbekkie
14	MARICO SUNBIRD	Beija-flor de Marico	
15	PURPLE-BANDED SUNBIRD	Beija-flor-de-colar-púrpura	Purperbandsuikerbekkie
16	NEERGAARD'S SUNBIRD	Beija-flor de Neergaard	Bloukruissuikerbekkie
17	ORANGE-TUFTED SUNBIRD	Beija-flor-de-tufos-laranja	
18	YELLOW WHITE-EYE	Olho-branco-amarelo	Geelglasogie
19	CAPE WHITE-EYE	Olho-branco do Cabo	Kaapse Glasogie

Plate 72

1	GREY-GREEN BUSH SHRIKE	Picanço de Bocage	
2	PERRIN'S BUSH SHRIKE	Picanço de Perrin	
3	SOUTHERN BOUBOU	Picanço-meridional	Suidelike Waterfiskaal
4	TROPICAL BOUBOU	Picanço-tropical	Tropiese Waterfiskaal
5	SWAMP BOUBOU	Picanço-bicolor	Moeraswaterfiskaal
6	FUELLEBORN'S BLACK BOUBOU	Picanço de Fuelleborn	
7	SOOTY BOUBOU	Picanço-sombrio	
8	LUEHDER'S BUSH SHRIKE	Picanço de Luehder	
9	MONTEIRO'S BUSH SHRIKE	Picanço de Monteiro	
10	GREY-HEADED BUSH SHRIKE	Picanço-de-cabeça-cinzenta	Spookvoël
11	CRIMSON-BREASTED BUSH SHRIKE	Picanço-de-peito-vermelho	Rooiborslaksman
12	FOUR-COLOURED (or Gorgeous) BUSH SHRIKE	Picanço-quadricolor	Konkoit
13	BOKMAKIERIE	Picanço-de-colar	Bokmakierie
14	MANY-COLOURED BUSH SHRIKE	Picanço-multicolor	
15	BLACK-FRONTED BUSH SHRIKE	Picanço-de-testa-preta	Swartoogboslaksman
16	ORANGE-BREASTED BUSH SHRIKE	Picanço-de-peito-laranja	Oranjeborsboslaksman
17	OLIVE BUSH SHRIKE	Picanço-esverdeado	Olyfboslaksman
18	MARSH TCHAGRA	Picanço-dos-pauis	Vleitjagra
19	BROWN-HEADED (or Three-streaked) TCHAGRA	Picanço-de-barrete-castanho	Rooivlerktjagra

| 20 | SOUTHERN TCHAGRA | Picanço-austral | Grysborstjagra |
| 21 | BLACK-CROWNED TCHAGRA | Picanço-de-barrete-preto | Swartkroontjagra |

16	BLACK-BELLIED GLOSSY STARLING	Estorninho-de-barriga-preta	Swartpensglansspreeu
17	SHARP-TAILED GLOSSY STARLING	Estorninho-de-cauda-afilada	Spitsstertglansspreeu
18	SOUTHERN LONG-TAILED STARLING	Estorninho-rabilongo	Langstertglansspreeu
19	BURCHELL'S STARLING	Estorninho de Burchell	Grootglansspreeu
20	SPLENDID GLOSSY STARLING	Estorninho-esplêndido	

Plate 75

1	RED-THROATED PIPIT	Petinha-de-garganta-ruiva	Rooikeelkoester
2	PLAIN-BACKED PIPIT	Petinha-de-dorso-liso	Donkerkoester
3	MOUNTAIN PIPIT	Petinha-da-montanha	Bergkoester
4	JACKSON'S PIPIT	Petinha de Jackson	
5	RICHARD'S (or Grassveld) PIPIT	Petinha de Richard	Gewone Koester
6	WOOD PIPIT	Petinha do Niassa	Boskoester
7	LONG-BILLED PIPIT	Petinha-de-bico-comprido	Nicholsonse Koester
8	TREE PIPIT	Petinha-das-árvores	Boomkoester
9	STRIPED PIPIT	Petinha-estriada	Gestreepte Koester
10	YELLOW-BREASTED PIPIT	Petinha-de-peito-amarelo	Geelborskoester
11	LONG-LEGGED PIPIT	Petinha-de-ventre-pálido	
12	BUFFY PIPIT	Petinha de Vaal	Vaalkoester
13	AFRICAN ROCK PIPIT	Petinha-das-rochas	Klipkoester
14	SHORT-TAILED PIPIT	Petinha-de-cauda-curta	Kortstertkoester
15	BUSH(-veld) PIPIT	Petinha-dos-arbustos	Bosveldkoester
16	RED-BILLED OXPECKER	Pica-boi-de-bico-vermelho	Rooibekrenostervoël
17	YELLOW-BILLED OXPECKER	Pica-boi-de-bico-amarelo	Geelbekrenostervoël

Plate 76

1	GOLDEN PIPIT	Petinha-dourada	Goudkoester
2	YELLOW WAGTAIL	Alvéola-amarela	Geelkwikkie
3	CAPE WAGTAIL	Alvéola do Cabo	Gewone Kwikkie
4	GREY WAGTAIL	Alvéola-cinzenta	Gryskwikkie
5	MOUNTAIN (or Long-tailed) WAGTAIL	Alvéola-de-cauda-comprida	Bergkwikkie
6	AFRICAN PIED WAGTAIL	Alvéola-africana	Bontkwikkie
7	WHITE WAGTAIL	Alvéola-branca	Witkwikkie
8	ROSY-BREASTED (or Pink-throated) LONGCLAW	Sentinela-de-garganta-rosada	Rooskeelkalkoentjie
9	CAPE (or Orange-breasted) LONGCLAW	Sentinela do Cabo	Oranjekeelkalkoentjie
10	YELLOW-THROATED LONGCLAW	Sentinela-de-garganta-amarela	Geelkeelkalkoentjie
11	GRIMWOOD'S LONGCLAW	Sentinela de Grimwood	
12	FUELLEBORN'S LONGCLAW	Sentinela de Fuelleborn	
13	CHESTNUT-BACKED SPARROW (or Finch) LARK	Cotovia-pardal-de-dorso-castanho	Rooiruglewerik
14	GREY-BACKED SPARROW (or Finch) LARK	Cotovia-pardal-de-dorso-cinzento	Grysruglewerik
15	FISCHER'S SPARROW LARK	Cotovia-pardal de Fischer	
16	BLACK-EARED SPARROW (or Finch) LARK	Cotovia-pardal-de-cabeça-preta	Swartoorlewerik

Plate 77

1	GREY-HEADED SPARROW	Pardal-de-cabeça-cinzenta	Gryskopmossie
2	SOUTHERN GREY-HEADED SPARROW	Pardal-meridional	
3	SWAHILI SPARROW	Pardal-suahili	
4	RUFOUS (or Great) SPARROW	Pardal-grande	Grootmossie
5	HOUSE SPARROW	Pardal-comum	Huismossie
6	CAPE SPARROW	Pardal do Cabo	Gewone Mossie
7	CHAFFINCH	Tentilhão-comum	Gryskoppie
8	YELLOW-THROATED PETRONIA	Pardal-de-garganta-amarela	Geelvlekmossie
9	WHITE-BROWED SPARROW WEAVER	Tecelão-de-sobrancelha-branca	Koringvoël
10	CHESTNUT-MANTLED SPARROW WEAVER	Tecelão-de-dorso-castanho	
11	RED-BILLED BUFFALO WEAVER	Tecelão-de-bico-vermelho	Buffelwewer
12	THICK-BILLED WEAVER	Tecelão-de-bico-grosso	Dikbekwewer
13	SOCIABLE WEAVER	Tecelão-sociável	Versamelvoël
14	ORIOLE FINCH	Bico-grosso-de-cabeça-preta	
15	CABANIS'S BUNTING	Escrevedeira de Cabanis	
16	CINNAMON-BREASTED ROCK BUNTING	Escrevedeira-de-peito-canelado	
17	LARK-LIKE BUNTING	Escrevedeira-cotovia	
18	CAPE BUNTING	Escrevedeira do Cabo	
19	GOLDEN-BREASTED BUNTING	Escrevedeira-de-peito-dourado	

Plate 78

1	LONG-TAILED WHYDAH	Viúva-de-cauda-comprida	Langstertflap
2	MOUNTAIN MARSH WHYDAH	Viúva-da-montanha	
3	RED-COLLARED WHYDAH	Viúva-de-coleira-vermelha	Rooikeelflap
4	YELLOW-MANTLED WHYDAH	Viúva-de-manto-amarelo	Geelrugflap
5	WHITE-WINGED WHYDAH	Viúva-de-asa-branca	Witvlerkflap
6	MARSH WHYDAH	Viúva-dos-paúis	
7	RED-SHOULDERED WHYDAH	Viúva-de-ombro-vermelho	Kortstertflap
8	YELLOW-CROWNED (or Golden) BISHOP	Bispo-de-coroa-amarela	Goudgeelvink
9	YELLOW(-rumped) BISHOP	Viúva-de-uropígio-amarelo	
10	BLACK BISHOP	Bispo-negro	
11	GOLDEN-BACKED BISHOP	Bispo-de-dorso-amarelo	
12	ZANZIBAR RED BISHOP	Bispo-de-peito-preto	
13	RED BISHOP	Bispo-de-testa-preta	Rooivink
14	BLACK-WINGED RED (or Fire-crowned) BISHOP	Bispo-de-coroa-vermelha	Vuurkopvink
15	RED-BILLED QUELEA	Quelea-de-bico-vermelho	Rooibekkwelea
16	CARDINAL QUELEA	Quelea-cardinal	Kardinaalkwelea
17	RED-HEADED QUELEA	Quelea-de-cabeça-vermelha	Rooikopkwelea
18	BLUE-BILLED MALIMBE	Tecelão-de-bico-azul	
19	RED-HEADED MALIMBE	Tecelão-de-cabeça-vermelha	
20	CRESTED MALIMBE	Tecelão-de-poupa	

Plate 79

1	LARGE GOLDEN WEAVER	Tecelão-dourado-grande	Goudwewer
2	EASTERN GOLDEN (or Yellow) WEAVER	Tecelão-dourado-oriental	Geelwewer
3	SPECTACLED WEAVER	Tecelão-de-lunetas	Brilwewer
4	SOUTHERN BROWN-THROATED WEAVER	Tecelão-de-garganta-castanha	Bruinkeelwewer
5	SLENDER-BILLED WEAVER	Tecelão-de-bico-fino	
6	AFRICAN (or Southern) MASKED WEAVER	Tecelão-de-mascarilha	Swartkeelgeelvink
7	LESSER MASKED WEAVER	Tecelão-pequeno-de-mascarilha	Kleingeelvink
8	LAKE LUFIRA WEAVER	Tecelão de Lufira	
9	CAPE WEAVER	Tecelão do Cabo	Kaapse Wewer
10	ORANGE WEAVER	Tecelão-laranja	
11	OLIVE-HEADED WEAVER	Tecelão-de-cabeça-esverdeada	Olyfkopwewer
12	BOCAGE'S WEAVER	Tecelão de Bocage	
13	YELLOW-BACKED WEAVER	Tecelão-de-cabeça-preta	
14	BERTRAM'S WEAVER	Tecelão de Bertram	
15	BAGLAFECHT WEAVER	Tecelão de Baglafecht	
16	VILLAGE (or Spotted-backed) WEAVER	Tecelão-de-dorso-malhado	Bontrugwewer
17	BLACK-CHINNED WEAVER	Tecelão-de-queixo-preto	
18	BROWN-CAPPED WEAVER	Tecelão-de-barrete-castanho	
19	BLACK-NECKED WEAVER	Tecelão-de-pescoço-preto	
20	DARK-BACKED (or Forest) WEAVER	Tecelão-de-dorso-escuro	Bosmusikant

Plate 80

1	RED-HEADED WEAVER	Tecelão-de-cabeça-vermelha	Rooikopwewer
2	BAR-WINGED WEAVER	Tecelão de Angola	
3	CHESTNUT WEAVER	Tecelão-castanho	Bruinwewer
4	COMPACT WEAVER	Tecelão-compacto	
5	VIEILLOT'S BLACK WEAVER	Tecelão-preto	
6	YELLOW-MANTLED WEAVER	Tecelão-de-dorso-amarelo	
7	CUT-THROAT FINCH	Degolado-africano	Bandkeelvink
8	RED-HEADED FINCH	Degolado-de-cabeça-vermelha	Rooikopvink
9	BROWN TWINSPOT	Pintadinho-castanho	
10	PINK-THROATED TWINSPOT	Pintadinho-de-garganta-rosada	Rooskeelrobbin
11	RED-THROATED (or Peter's) TWINSPOT	Pintadinho-de-garganta-vermelha	Rooikeelrobbin
12	GREEN TWINSPOT	Pintadinho-verde	Groenrobbin
13	DUSKY TWINSPOT	Pintadinho-sombrio	
14	SCALY-FEATHERED FINCH	Tecelão-escamado	Baardmannetjie
15	PARASITIC WEAVER (or Cuckoo Finch)	Tecelão-parasita	Koekoekvink
16	RED-FACED CRIMSONWING	Asa-rosada-de-faces-vermelhas	Rooirugrobbin
17	LESSER (or Nyassa) SEEDCRACKER	Bico-grosso-pequeno	Rooistertrobbin

| 18 | BLACK-BELLIED SEEDCRACKER | Bico-grosso-de-barriga-preta | |
| 19 | RED-HEADED BLUEBILL | Tecelinho-de-cabeça-vermelha | |

Plate 81

1	BRONZE MANNIKIN	Bico-de-chumbo-bronzeado	Gewone Fret
2	RED-BACKED MANNIKIN	Bico-de-chumbo-de-dorso-preto	Rooirugfret
3	MAGPIE (or Pied) MANNIKIN	Bico-de-chumbo-de-dorso-castanho	Dikbekfret
4	VIOLET-EARED WAXBILL	Peito-celeste-de-faces-violetas	Koningblousysie
5	BLUE WAXBILL	Peito-celeste-de-faces-azuis	Gewone Blousysie
6	RED-CHEEKED CORDON-BLEU	Peito-celeste-de-faces-violetas	
7	QUAIL FINCH	Freirinha de Ansorge	Gewone Kwartelvinkie
8	BLACK-CHINNED QUAIL FINCH	Freirinha-de-queixo-preto	
9	LOCUST FINCH	Freirinha-gafanhoto	Rooivlerkkwartelvinkie
10	MELBA FINCH	Aurora-melba	Gewone Melba
11	ORANGE-WINGED (or Golden-backed) PYTILIA	Aurora-de-dorso-amarelo	Geelrugmelba
12	BLUE-BILLED FIREFINCH	Granadeiro-de-bico-azul	Kaapse Robbin
13	PALE-BILLED FIREFINCH	Granadeiro-de-bico-pálido	
14	JAMESON'S FIREFINCH	Granadeiro de Jameson	Jamesonse Robbin
15	RED-BILLED FIREFINCH	Granadeiro-de-bico-vermelho	Rooibekrobbin
16	BROWN FIREFINCH	Granadeiro-castanho	Bruinrobbin
17	GREY-CROWNED BLACKFINCH	Negrito-de-cabeça-cinzenta	
18	PALE-FRONTED BLACKFINCH	Negrito-de-testa-clara	
19	CHESTNUT-BREASTED BLACKFINCH	Negrito-de-peito-castanho	
20	WHITE-BREASTED BLACKFINCH	Negrito-de-peito-branco	

Plate 82

1	PIN-TAILED WIDOW	Viúva-de-cauda-fina	Koningrooibekkie
2	SHAFT-TAILED WIDOW	Viúva-de-cauda-seta	Pylstertrooibekkie
3	LONG-TAILED PARADISE WIDOW	Viúva-rabilonga	Gewone Paradysvink
4	BROAD-TAILED PARADISE WIDOW	Viúva-de-cauda-larga	Beëstertparadysvink
5	DUSKY (or Black) INDIGOBIRD	Bico-de-prata de Wilson	Gewone Blouvinkie
6	PURPLE INDIGOBIRD	Bico-de-prata-púrpura	Witpootblouvinkie
7	VILLAGE (or Steel-blue) INDIGOBIRD	Bico-de-prata do Senegal	Staalblouvinkie
8	BAR-BREASTED (or Violet) INDIGOBIRD	Bico-de-prata-de-peito-barrado	Persblouvinkie

9	PETER'S TWINSPOT INDIGOBIRD	Bico-de-prata de Codrington	
10	BLACK-FACED (or -cheeked) WAXBILL	Bico-de-lacre-de-faces-pretas	Swartwangsysie
11	BLACK-HEADED WAXBILL	Bico-de-lacre-de-cabeça-preta	Swartkopsysie
12	CRIMSON-RUMPED WAXBILL	Bico-de-lacre-de-uropígio-vermelho	
13	COMMON WAXBILL	Bico-de-lacre-comum	Rooibeksysie
14	ORANGE-CHEEKED WAXBILL	Bico-de-lacre-de-faces-laranja	
15	FLOWERPECKER WEAVER FINCH	Papa-formigas	
16	ZEBRA (or Orange-breasted) WAXBILL	Bico-de-lacre-de-peito-laranja	
17	BLACK-TAILED GREY WAXBIL	Bico-de-lacre-de-cauda-preta	Gryssysie
18	CINDERELLA WAXBILL	Bico-de-lacre-são-tomense	Swartoogsysie
19	SWEE WAXBILL	Bico-de-lacre-de-queixo-preto	Suidelike Swee
20	EAST AFRICAN SWEE WAXBILL	Bico-de-lacre-de-ventre-amarelo	Tropiese Swee
21	FAWN-BREASTED WAXBILL	Bico-de-lacre-de-cabeça-cinzenta	

Plate 83

1	YELLOW CANARY	Canário-de-ventre-amarelo	Geelkanarie
2	BRIMSTONE (or Bully) CANARY	Canário-grande	Dekbekkanarie
3	YELLOW-FRONTED (or -eyed) CANARY	Canário-de-testa-amarela	Geeloogkanarie
4	FOREST CANARY	Canário-da-floresta	Gestreepte Kanarie
5	BLACK-FACED CANARY	Canário-de-faces-pretas	
6	AFRICAN CITRIL	Canário-africano	
7	CAPE CANARY	Canário-de-nuca-cinzenta	Kaapse Kanarie
8	DRAKENSBERG SISKIN	Canário de Drakensberg	Bergpietjiekanarie
9	CAPE SISKIN	Canário do Cabo	Kaapse Pietjiekanarie
10	LEMON-BREASTED CANARY	Canário-de-peito-limão	Geelborskanarie
11	STREAKY SEEDEATER	Canário-estriado	
12	BLACK-THROATED CANARY	Canário-de-garganta-preta	Bergkanarie
13	WHITE-THROATED CANARY	Canário-de-garganta-branca	Witkeelkanarie
14	THICK-BILLED SEEDEATER	Canário-de-bico-grosso	
15	PROTEA CANARY	Canário-de-asa-branca	Witvlerkkanarie
16	STREAKY-HEADED SEEDEATER	Canário-de-cabeça-estriada	Streepkopkanarie
17	STRIPE-BREASTED SEEDEATER	Canário-de-peito-estriado	
18	BLACK-EARED SEEDEATER	Canário-de-orelha-preta	Swartoorkanarie ·
19	BLACK-HEADED CANARY	Canário-de-cabeça-preta	

Plate 84

1	NKULENGU RAIL	Frango-de-água-de-pés-vermelhos
2	SENEGAL THICK-KNEE	Alcaravão do Senegal
3	GREY PRATINCOLE	Perdiz-do-mar-cinzenta
4	BLUE-HEADED WOOD DOVE	Rola-de-cabeça-azul
5	CHESTNUT-FLANKED SPARROWHAWK	Gavião-de-flancos-vermelhos
6	LONG-TAILED HAWK	Açor-rabilongo
7	FOREST FRANCOLIN	Francolim de Latham
8	BLACK GUINEAFOWL	Pintada-preta
9	PLUMED GUINEAFOWL	Pintada-plumífera
10	VERREAUX'S TURACO	Turaco de Verreaux
11	FRASER'S EAGLE OWL	Bufo de Fraser
12	AKUN EAGLE OWL	Bufo-malhado
13	BOUVIER'S FISHING OWL	Coruja-pesqueira de Bouvier
14	SABINE'S SPINETAIL	Rabo-espinhoso de Sabine
15	CASSIN'S SPINETAIL	Rabo-espinhoso de Cassin
16	BLACK DWARF HORNBILL	Calau-pigmeu-de-bico-preto
17	RED-BILLED DWARF HORNBILL	Calau-pigmeu-de-bico-vermelho
18	BROWN-CHEEKED (or White-thighed) HORNBILL	Calau-de-faces-castanhas
19	YELLOW-THROATED TINKERBIRD	Barbadinho-de-garganta-amarela
20	RED-RUMPED TINKERBIRD	Barbadinho-de-uropígio-vermelho
21	YELLOW-SPOTTED BARBET	Barbaças-de-malhas-amarelas
22	BLACK-HEADED BEE-EATER	Abelharuco-de-cabeça-preta
23	ROSY BEE-EATER	Abelharuco-rosado
24	RUFOUS-SIDED BROADBILL	Bico-largo-de-flancos-vermelhos
25	SPOTTED HONEYGUIDE	Indicador-malhado
26	GOLDEN GREENBUL	Bulbul-dourado
27	SPOTTED GREENBUL	Bulbul-malhado
28	SWAMP PALM BULBUL	Bulbul-de-cauda-branca
29	ICTERINE GREENBUL	Bulbul-icterino
30	GREEN-TAILED BRISTLEBILL	Bulbul-de-cauda-verde
31	BEARDED GREENBUL	Bulbul-de-bigode
32	BLUE CUCKOOSHRIKE	Picanço-cuco-azul
33	NORTHERN RED-BILLED HELMET SHRIKE	Picanço-de-bico-vermelho
34	CHESTNUT-CAPPED FLYCATCHER	Papa-moscas-de-barrete-vermelho
35	PIED FLYCATCHER	Papa-moscas-preto
36	WHITE-BROWED FOREST FLYCATCHER	Papa-moscas-de-sobrancelha-branca
37	PALE-BREASTED ILLADOPSIS	Falso-tordo-de-peito-pálido
38	PURPLE-HEADED GLOSSY STARLING	Estorninho-de-cabeça-púrpura
39	BROWN SUNBIRD	Beija-flor do Gabão
40	SPLENDID SUNBIRD	Beija-flor-esplêndido

41	JOHANNA'S SUNBIRD	Beija-flor de Johanna
42	NORTHERN PUFFBACK	Picanço da Gâmbia
43	SABINE'S PUFFBACK	Picanço de Sabine
44	LOANGA SLENDER-BILLED WEAVER	Tecelão-de-bico-fino de Loanga
45	BLUEBILL	Tecelinho-de-bico-azul

BIBLIOGRAPHY AND FURTHER READING

FIELD GUIDES:

K. Newman, *Newman's Birds of Southern Africa* (Johannesburg, 1996).
K. Newman et al, *Birds of Malawi* (Johannesburg, 1992).
G.L. Maclean, *Robert's Birds of Southern Africa* (Cape Town, 1993).
J. Sinclair et al, *Illustrated Guide to the Birds of Southern Africa* (Cape Town, 1998).

PHOTOGRAPHIC GUIDES:

P.J. Ginn et al (editors), *The Complete Book of Southern African Birds* (Cape Town, 1996).
J. Sinclair, *Field Guide to the Birds of Southern Africa* (Cape Town, 1984).
J. Sinclair, & J. Davidson, *Southern African Birds: A Photographic Guide* (Cape Town, 1995).

HANDBOOKS:

Birds of Africa
L.M. Brown et al, Volume 1 Ostriches to Birds of Prey (London, 1982).
E.K. Urban et al, Volume 2 Game Birds to Pigeons (London, 1986).
C.H. Fry et al, Volume 3 Parrots to Woodpeckers (London, 1988).
S. Keith et al, Volume 4 Broadbills to Chats (London, 1992).
E.K. Urban et al, Volume 5 Thrushes to Puffback Flycatchers (London, 1997).

Handbook of the Birds of the World
J. del Hoyo et al (editors), Volume 1 Ostrich to Ducks (Barcelona, 1992).
J. del Hoyo et al (editors), Volume 2 New World Vultures to Guineafowl (Barcelona, 1994).
J. del Hoyo et al (editors), Volume 3 Hoatzin to Auks (Barcelona, 1996).
J. del Hoyo et al (editors), Volume 4 Sandgrouse to Cuckoos (Barcelona, 1996).

African Handbook of Birds, series 2
C.W. Mackworh-Praed, & C.H.B. Grant (London, vol 1, 1962, vol 2, 1963).

BIRD FAMILIES AND GROUPS:

A. Kemp et al,	*The Hornbills* (Oxford University Press, 1995).
S. Madge et al,	*Crows and Jays* (Helm/A&C Black).
P. Clement et al,	*Finches & Sparrows* (Helm/A&C Black, 1993).
J. Hancock et al,	*The Herons Handbook* (Croom Helm, 1984).
C. Hilary Fry et al,	*Kingfishers, Bee-eaters & Rollers* (Helm/A&C Black, 1992).
P. Harrison,	*Seabirds* (Croom Helm, 1985).
A. Turner et al,	*Swallows and Martins* (Helm, 1989).
S. Harrap et al,	*Tits, Nuthatches & Treecreepers* (Helm/A&C Black, 1996).
S. Madge et al,	*Wildfowl* (Helm/A&C Black, 1988).
C. Byers et al,	*Buntings and Sparrows* (Pica Press, 1995).
F. Lambert et al,	*Pittas, Bradbills and Asities* (Pica Press, 1996).
B. Taylor et al,	*Rails, Crakes and Coots* (Pica Press, 1998).
N. Lefranc et al,	*Shrikes* (Pica Press, 1997).
K.M. Olsen et al,	*Skuas and Jaegers* (Pica Press, 1997).
P. Chantler et al,	*Swifts* (Pica Press, 1995).
H. Winkler et al,	*Woodpeckers* (Pica Press, 1995).
P. Hayman et al,	*Shorebirds* (Houghton Mifflin Company, 1986).

SOUTHERN AFRICAN BIRD SOUNDS on tape or CD:

Guy Gibbon, *Southern African Bird Sounds* (6 cassettes with 888 species or 6 CDs with 900 species, 1995).

R. Stjernstedt, *Birdsong of Zambia* (3 cassettes featuring 415 species, 1995).

S. Keith, *Birds of African Rain Forests* (2 cassettes featuring 95 species).

ORNITHOLOGICAL SOCIETIES

The African Bird Club was established in 1994 to provide a worldwide focus for African ornithology, encourage an interest in bird conservation, liaise with and promote the work of existing regional societies and publish a twice-yearly colour bulletin. This Bulletin of the African Bird Club publishes articles on conservation projects, identification of difficult groups (e.g. sparrowhawks, greenbuls, indigobirds), bird inventories of certain areas, reports on recent sightings, reviews of new publications etc. Further details can be obtained from the Membership Secretary, African Bird Club, c/o Birdlife International, Wellbrook Court, Girton Road, Cambridge CB3 0NA, U.K.

Southern African Ornithological Society: P.O. Box 84394, Greenside, Johannesburg 2034, South Africa.

National and local Bird Clubs and Wildlife Societies exist at least in Botswana, Namibia, Zimbabwe, Malawi, Mozambique, Zambia and many regions in South Africa. Their addresses can be obtained from the African Bird Club or the Southern African Ornithological Society. Several of these Bird Clubs and Wildlife Societies produce journals and bulletins.

Index of scientific names

Numbers refer to the relevant plate, followed by the number of the bird on that plate.

Index of common names

Numbers refer to the relevant plate, followed by the number of the bird on that plate.

315

316